"With this impressive book, David G. Horrell highlights the urgent need to recognize the ongoing religious status of the Pauline letters. Representing almost two decades of investigation, the essays reflect not only the best of scholarship on socio-historical context, but also thought-provoking dialogue between the ancient texts and modern ethical challenges. This conversation is facilitated by one of the most knowledgeable and astute New Testament scholars working in the field today. David Horrell is deeply committed to New Testament work which engages the challenges of the contemporary world, especially issues of ecology and environmental concern. This is a learned but highly accessible book, of interest to a range of readers, including students and senior scholars alike."

Margaret Y. MacDonald
Saint Mary's University

"David Horrell is currently one of the most distinguished scholars on Pauline ethics. This collection of essays offers a summary of his exegetical work over the past decade. Horrell's reading of Paul's letters, though deeply rooted in historical analysis, addresses current ethical debates and challenges, including such issues as the ecological crises. This volume comes with my highest recommendation for anyone interested in stimulating, inspiring, and relevant Pauline scholarship."

Ruben Zimmermann
Johannes Gutenberg-University

The Making of Christian Morality

Reading Paul in Ancient and Modern Contexts

David G. Horrell

William B. Eerdmans Publishing Company
Grand Rapids, Michigan

Wm. B. Eerdmans Publishing Co.
4035 Park East Court SE, Grand Rapids, Michigan 49546
www.eerdmans.com

Published 2019
Printed in the United States of America

28 27 26 25 24 23 22 21 20 19   1 2 3 4 5 6 7 8 9 10

ISBN 978-0-8028-7607-2

Library of Congress Cataloging-in-Publication Data

Names: Horrell, David G., author.
Title: The making of Christian morality : reading Paul in ancient and modern contexts / David G. Horrell.
Description: Grand Rapids : Eerdmans Publishing Co., 2019. | Includes bibliographical references and index.
Identifiers: LCCN 2018030509 | ISBN 9780802876072 (pbk. : alk. paper)
Subjects: LCSH: Bible. Epistles of Paul—Criticism, interpretation, etc. | Ethics—Biblical teaching. | Ethics in the Bible.
Classification: LCC BS2655.E8 H665 2019 | DDC 227/.06—dc23
LC record available at https://lccn.loc.gov/2018030509

For Mum and Dad

Contents

Foreword

To read these ten outstanding essays by David Horrell is to be taken to the cutting edge of New Testament scholarship. On every front—in their historical expertise, in their exegetical sensitivity, and in their engagement with contemporary issues of pressing social concern—these essays demonstrate the very best of what it is to be a biblical scholar in the early twenty-first century.

In the first place, anyone reading these essays will receive an education in critical thinking of the highest order. At numerous points, and with gentle persistence, Horrell probes the scholarly consensus, asks telling questions, evaluates the evidence afresh, and demarcates precisely what it is (and is not) possible to conclude. Hidden assumptions are brought to the surface, awkward data are added to the picture, and simplistic or exaggerated conclusions are challenged. All of that is done with exemplary courtesy and a winsome modesty, including a self-reflective ability to keep conscious of our contemporary intellectual biases. If one ever wondered what "transferable skills" are provided by the best training in biblical studies, one need look no further than here. Horrell's internationally respected powers of reasoning and his clarity of mind and expression are everywhere here on display.

But what these essays also demonstrate is both the depth and the range of biblical scholarship in its contemporary mode. The historical essays, of the first two parts, dig deep into the ancient conditions of the churches addressed by Paul, right down to their physical locations and contexts: adept in archaeology and ancient history, Horrell shows how much it matters, for instance, if we imagine the Corinthians meeting in a sumptuous villa or in a crowded apartment over a workshop. The research here, and on other matters, is up-to-date and broad-ranging, drawing from the best in both

Anglophone and German scholarship. The historical work is inflected by "disciplined imagination" and by the subtle influence of social theory, while the exegesis is marked by nuance and exemplary attention to detail. But what particularly marks out this collection of essays is the way that it moves progressively from text-as-history to text-as-resource for contemporary moral and political reflection, ending with special focus on two issues that biblical scholars have rarely dared to address. The first is our pressing, postmodern need to honor cultural and religious particularity while also creating a frame for sufficiently common moral and political communication to save us from tearing our societies and nations apart. Horrell here juxtaposes the communitarian and liberal traditions in contemporary thought, and finds in the letters of Paul surprising resonance and suggestive resources for negotiating these crucial debates (and for an important element within them, the relation of church to "world").[1] The second is the ecological crisis, where Horrell points to theological strands within the Pauline texts that could and should invigorate Christian moral and theological contributions to this urgent problem.[2] As Horrell notes, one can trace the relevant Pauline themes, with their christological vision of the reconciliation of "all things," on a developmental trajectory from the undisputed to the "deutero-Pauline" letters. And if one were to follow this trajectory through to Irenaeus and on into the christologically inflected theologies of creation that have been developed in subsequent Christian theology, one could perhaps trace a Pauline imprint right through the history of Christian thought, which could itself help us further in thinking through the implications of his letters. What is significant here is that Horrell, without imposing modern presumptions onto the text, and without claiming that we have in Paul more than some essential chemicals with which to fertilize our thinking, is able to draw the text meaningfully into a debate whose contemporary importance is second to none.

Biblical scholars throughout the world are increasingly wondering among themselves (but not too loudly outside) about the future of their discipline, not only, that is, what shape it will take but also what uses it will serve. These essays constitute, I think, one of the best imaginable answers

1. See also David G. Horrell, *Solidarity and Difference: A Contemporary Reading of Paul's Ethics* (London: T&T Clark, 2005; 2nd ed., 2015).

2. See also David G. Horrell, *The Bible and the Environment: Towards a Critical Ecological Biblical Theology*, Biblical Challenges in the Contemporary World (London: Equinox, 2010; London: Routledge, 2014); David G. Horrell, Cherryl Hunt, and Christopher Southgate, *Greening Paul: Rereading the Apostle in an Age of Ecological Crisis* (Waco, TX: Baylor University Press, 2010).

to that question. They demonstrate biblical (here New Testament) studies as an intellectual exercise of the highest quality, equipping students with the reasoning and communicative skills that will enable them to act as critical citizens in any walk of life. They use the best historical tools to situate the texts in their ancient and original context. They draw on a range of intellectual resources—sociological, philosophical, and theological—to tease out the potential of these extraordinarily rich and hugely influential texts. And they engage, constructively and critically, with matters of pressing contemporary concern. Taught by such a masterful scholar as Horrell, those who read these essays will not only learn much about their subject matter but will surely be inspired to "go and do likewise" in their own engagement with the biblical texts.

JOHN M. G. BARCLAY

Preface

The essays collected together in this volume focus on the themes of community and ethics in Paul, moving from the concrete social circumstances in which the earliest communities gathered, through studies of Paul's ethics, to the contemporary appropriation of the Pauline writings in relation to very modern ethical challenges, particularly those concerning ecology and the environment. As such, these essays illustrate various facets of the making of Christian morality, from the ancient social contexts in which Paul's epistolary exhortations were formed, to the changing modern contexts in which his thought is engaged, appropriated, and applied. Bringing these studies together is intended not only to collect in one place a series of essays focusing on particular aspects of the interpretation of Pauline texts, but also to illustrate ways in which Pauline studies may encompass both sociohistorical analysis rooted in the ancient context and readings of Paul oriented towards contemporary issues and challenges. Indeed, showing how these differing kinds of studies may be connected as part of a coherent scholarly project is one goal of the collection as a whole.

The essays were originally written, presented, and in most cases published, between 2001 and 2016 (for details see below), and most of them are reproduced here in their originally published form, except for the correction of minor points and standardization with regard to format and citation style. One chapter is previously unpublished (as far as I am aware!), and two others are presented in a form somewhat different from that in which they were published (again, see details below). There are a few points of overlap in some cases, since the essays cluster around treatment of certain themes, and I have not sought to remove all such similarity, since to do so would detract from the integrity of each essay.

One issue that revisiting these essays raised for me is the extent to which, particularly in the older essays, I was more inclined to use the words "church," "Christian," "Christianity," and so on, than I would be now, given the increasing awareness of their potentially anachronistic implications and the shift towards alternatives ("assembly," "Christ-follower," etc.) that are intended to guard against this risk. Notwithstanding the value of this shift, I am not fully persuaded that new terminology is always the best way to avoid anachronism, though we certainly need to be reminded that the meaning and implications of particular terms change through history and social context; nor am I entirely convinced that the older terminology, old-fashioned though it may sound, is always inappropriate, though it should probably be used more sparingly than I have done in the past. To use the term "Christian" of those addressed in Paul's letters, for example, might be taken to imply anachronistic implications concerning the identity of the recipients; but on the other hand, the term—which does after all at least appear in the NT records—is perhaps not an unreasonable way to denote those for whom "being in Christ" has, according to Paul at least, become the most defining and prominent designation of their identity. Most importantly, however, it seems to me that in terms of assessing the arguments made and the analyses presented, nothing significant hangs on the particular terms used, which could be substituted for others, so I hope that readers will not unduly stumble over them—or will mentally substitute them, and see if the broader point still stands.

In preparing these essays for publication here, conforming them to a common style and compiling the bibliography, I have been greatly assisted by a number of colleagues at various times: Katy Hockey, Helen John, and Sarah Molyneaux-Hetherington. Cherryl Hunt compiled the indexes. I am very grateful to them all. I would also like to thank Bradley Arnold for research assistance with the papers now presented as chapters 3 and 7, and for helpful comments on what is now chapter 9. As will be clear from the references, chapters 9 and 10 also owe a considerable amount to collaborative research undertaken with Cherryl Hunt and Christopher Southgate, to whom I would like to renew my gratitude. I have not repeated the full acknowledgments originally made for each of the individual papers, but among many who have helpfully offered comments and support in relation to essays included here, I would like to thank Edward Adams, Barry Matlock, Peter Oakes, Gerd Theissen, Geoff Thompson, Ekaterini Tsalampouni, Mary Hoskins Walbank, Mark Wynn, and Ruben Zimmermann. I am also hugely grateful to John Barclay, for agreeing to write a foreword to this collection and for wise and incisive comments on my ideas, drafts, and papers, not only those included here. I would also like to record my gratitude to the bodies that have funded the research projects from which these essays derive: the British Academy, the UK's Arts and Humanities Research Council, and the Alexander von Humboldt Foundation. I am also very grateful to Michael Thomson at Eerdmans publishers, for his long-standing interest in my work and encouragement to publish it with Eerdmans. The original publication details for each of the essays are given in the following section of formal acknowledgments.

Finally, as I have done on previous occasions, I would like to record my profound thanks and appreciation to my immediate family: to Caroline, Emily, and Cate. They make life rich and fun, and are fully supportive of my work without taking it (or me) too seriously. My extended family, special friends, and colleagues at Exeter all help me stay afloat too. But I would like to dedicate this volume to my parents, George and Rosemary Horrell. It goes without saying that I owe them a great deal. In particular, having chosen the career that I have, I am often reminded of the lasting importance of the energy and commitment with which they valued and supported their children's education.

Exeter, December 2017

Acknowledgments

Listed below are the places of original presentation and publication. I hereby express my gratitude to the various publishers for their permission to reproduce the essays here.

Chapter 1. A paper presented at the British New Testament Conference, Liverpool, September 2005, and (as part of a longer paper) at the SNTS Third East-Western Symposium of New Testament Scholars, St. Petersburg, August 2005. The longer paper was published as "Pauline Churches or Early Christian Churches? Unity, Disagreement, and the Eucharist," in *Einheit der Kirche im Neuen Testament*, ed. Anatoly Alexeev, Christos Karakolis, Ulrich Luz, with Karl-Wilhelm Niebuhr, WUNT 218 (Tübingen: Mohr Siebeck, 2008), 185–203 (with the relevant section on 186–96). © Mohr Siebeck Tübingen. Reprinted with permission.

Chapter 2. A short paper presented to the SNTS conference in Bonn, August 2003. Published in *NTS* 50 (2004): 349–69, © Cambridge University Press. Reprinted with permission.

Chapter 3. A paper presented to the 23rd Colloquium Oecumenicum Paulinum, held at the Abbey of St Paul Outside the Walls, Rome, September 2014. Published in Daniel Marguerat, ed., *La lettre à Philémon et l'ecclésiologie paulinienne/Philemon and Pauline Ecclesiology*, Colloquium Oecumenicum Paulinum 22 (Leuven: Peeters, 2016), 51–74. Reprinted with the permission of Peeters.

Chapter 4. A paper presented to the Pauline Epistles Section at the SBL Annual Meeting in November 1999. Published in *JBL* 120 (2001): 293–311. Reprinted with permission.

Chapter 5. A chapter in Friedrich Wilhelm Horn and Ruben Zimmermann, eds., *Jenseits von Indikativ und Imperativ: Kontexte und Normen neutestamentlicher Ethik/Contexts and Norms of New Testament Ethics*, WUNT 238 (Tübingen: Mohr Siebeck, 2009), 197–212. © Mohr Siebeck Tübingen. Reprinted with permission.

Chapter 6. An extended version of a chapter in Stephen C. Barton, ed., *Idolatry: False Worship in the Bible, Early Judaism and Christianity* (London: Bloomsbury T&T Clark, 2007), 120–40. Reprinted with permission.

Chapter 7. A paper presented at the conference "Paul-Apostle. Two Thousand Years of the European Vision of the Apostle to the Nations," held in Philippi in May 2011 and hosted by the Metropolitan Bishop of Philippi, Neapolis, and Thasos. Not previously published, to my knowledge.

Chapter 8. A main paper presented at the annual conference of the Society for the Study of Theology held in Exeter in April 2004. Published in *Pacifica* 18 (2005): 33–52. Reprinted with permission of SAGE publishers.

Chapter 9. The T. W. Manson Memorial Lecture at the University of Manchester, in October 2009. Published in *JSNT* 33 (2010): 3–30. Reprinted with permission of SAGE publishers.

Chapter 10. A paper presented at the Bible and Justice Conference, University of Sheffield, in 2008. Published in Matthew J. M. Coomber, ed., *Bible and Justice: Ancient Texts, Modern Challenges* (London and New York: Routledge, 2011), 158–77. Reprinted with permission.

Abbreviations

Abbreviations for primary texts and scholarly resources follow those given in *The SBL Handbook of Style*, 2nd ed. (Atlanta: SBL Press, 2014).

AB	Anchor Bible
AGJU	Arbeiten zur Geschichte des antiken Judentums und des Urchristentums
AJA	*American Journal of Archaeology*
ANRW	*Aufstieg und Niedergang der römischen Welt*
b.	Babylonian Talmud
BDAG	Danker, Frederick W., Walter Bauer, William F. Arndt, and F. Wilbur Gingrich. *Greek-English Lexicon of the New Testament and Other Early Christian Literature*. 3rd ed. Chicago: University of Chicago Press, 2000.
BEvT	Beiträge zur evangelischen Theologie
BHT	Beiträge zur historischen Theologie
Bib	*Biblica*
BibInt	*Biblical Interpretation*
BJ	*Bonner Jahrbücher*
BJRL	*Bulletin of the John Rylands University Library of Manchester*
BNTC	Black's New Testament Commentaries
BR	*Biblical Research*
BTB	*Biblical Theology Bulletin*
BZNW	Beihefte zur Zeitschrift für die neutestamentliche Wissenschaft
ChrCent	*Christian Century*
ConBNT	Coniectanea Biblica: New Testament Series
EKKNT	Evangelisch-katholischer Kommentar zum Neuen Testament

ESV	English Standard Version
ET	English translation
ETL	*Ephemerides Theologicae Lovanienses*
EvQ	*Evangelical Quarterly*
ExpTim	*Expository Times*
GNS	Good News Studies
HNT	Handbuch zum Neuen Testament
HThKNT	Herders theologischer Kommentar zum Neuen Testament
HTR	*Harvard Theological Review*
IBC	Interpretation: A Bible Commentary for Teaching and Preaching
ICC	International Critical Commentary
JAAR	*Journal of the American Academy of Religion*
JAC	*Jahrbuch für Antike und Christentum*
JBL	*Journal of Biblical Literature*
JJS	*Journal of Jewish Studies*
JRA	*Journal of Roman Archaeology*
JRASup	Journal of Roman Archaeology Supplement Series
JRS	*Journal of Roman Studies*
JSNT	*Journal for the Study of the New Testament*
JSNTSup	Journal for the Study of the New Testament Supplement Series
JSOTSup	Journal for the Study of the Old Testament Supplement Series
JTS	*Journal of Theological Studies*
JTSA	*Journal of Theology for Southern Africa*
KEK	Kritisch-exegetischer Kommentar über das Neue Testament
LCL	Loeb Classical Library
LNTS	Library of New Testament Studies
LSJ	Liddell, Henry George, Robert Scott, Henry Stuart Jones. *A Greek-English Lexicon*. 9th ed. with revised supplement. Oxford: Clarendon, 1996.
LXX	Septuagint
m.	Mishnah
NA	Nestle-Aland, *Novum Testamentum Graece*, 26th ed. 1979; 27th ed. 1993; 28th ed. 2012. Stuttgart: Deutsche Bibelgesellschaft.
NCB	New Century Bible
NewDocs	*New Documents Illustrating Early Christianity*. Edited by Greg H. R. Horsley and Stephen Llewelyn. North Ryde, NSW: Ancient History Documentary Research Centre, Macquarie University, 1981–.

NICNT	New International Commentary on the New Testament
NIGTC	New International Greek Testament Commentary
NIV	New International Version
NovT	*Novum Testamentum*
NovTSup	Supplements to Novum Testamentum
NRSV	New Revised Standard Version
NTOA	Novum Testamentum et Orbis Antiquus
NTS	*New Testament Studies*
OBO	Orbis Biblicus et Orientalis
ÖTK	Ökumenischer Taschenbuch-Kommentar zum Neuen Testament
PKNT	Papyrologische Kommentare zum Neuen Testament
PNTC	Pillar New Testament Commentary
RAC	*Reallexikon für Antike und Christentum.* Edited by Theodor Klauser et al. Stuttgart: Hiersemann, 1966–.
RB	*Revue biblique*
RBS	Resources for Biblical Study
RGRW	Religions in the Graeco-Roman World
RNT	Regensburger Neues Testament
SBLDS	Society of Biblical Literature Dissertation Series
SBS	Stuttgarter Bibelstudien
SJT	*Scottish Journal of Theology*
SNTSMS	Society for New Testament Studies Monograph Series
SNTW	Studies of the New Testament and Its World
SP	Sacra Pagina
Str-B	Strack, H. L., and P. Billerbeck. *Kommentar zum Neuen Testament aus Talmud und Midrasch.* 6 vols. Munich: Beck, 1922–1961.
SymS	Symposium Studies
TDNT	*Theological Dictionary of the New Testament.* Edited by Gerhard Kittel and Gerhard Friedrich. Translated by Geoffrey W. Bromiley. 10 vols. Grand Rapids: Eerdmans, 1964–1976.
TDOT	*Theological Dictionary of the Old Testament.* Edited by G. Johannes Botterweck, Helmer Ringgren, and H.-J. Fabry. Translated by John T. Willis et al. 16 vols. Grand Rapids: Eerdmans, 1974–2006.
THKNT	Theologischer Handkommentar zum Neuen Testament
ThTo	*Theology Today*
TLZ	*Theologische Literaturzeitung*

TynBul	*Tyndale Bulletin*
VT	*Vetus Testamentum*
WBC	Word Biblical Commentary
WMANT	Wissenschaftliche Monographien zum Alten und Neuen Testament
WUNT	Wissenschaftliche Untersuchungen zum Neuen Testament
ZNW	*Zeitschrift für die neutestamentliche Wissenschaft und die Kunde der älteren Kirche*

Figures

Introduction

In one of his evocative poems, R. S. Thomas depicts Paul as a "mountain"—the vast and solid mass into which Jesus's teaching "congealed" and with which theologians continue to grapple.[1] Whether this mountain is seen as an obstacle or an achievement, Paul's epistolary legacy continues to attract a great deal of scholarly attention and to provoke a wide range of thought and reaction from many different perspectives; Paul is undoubtedly a major figure in ongoing discussion of Christian morality. Recent decades have seen an explosion of methodological diversity in the field of NT studies and beyond, such that the kinds of questions addressed to Paul's letters, and the contexts in which his thought is engaged, have greatly expanded. One of the particular results of this diversification is that the historical-critical paradigm is no longer an assumed norm. Even supposedly objective historical-critical research was generally practiced with theological convictions and debates woven closely into its modes of analysis and forms of expression. But many of the more recent approaches and methods bring explicit kinds of contemporary theological, ethical, or political perspectives and commitments to the fore.

Many of the directions now well established in contemporary research trace their particular modern stimulus to the 1970s. More specifically, this was the time when an interest in the social aspects of the earliest Christian movement (re)emerged, and when the study of NT texts began to be informed by perspectives from the social sciences.[2] In relation to Paul, the most influential

1. R. S. Thomas, "Covenanters," in *Later Poems: A Selection 1972–1982* (London: Macmillan, Papermac, 1984), 170–73.

2. For an overview of this development, see David G. Horrell, "Social Sciences Studying

early work was by Gerd Theissen, who, as James Dunn remarked, "almost single-handedly, brought about a minor revolution in the study of Christian beginnings."[3] Among those working along similar lines in the United States, Wayne Meeks's magisterial work, *The First Urban Christians*, drew together a wide range of research, including that of Theissen, to present a portrait of the social world of the earliest Christians who gathered in the assemblies addressed in Paul's letters.[4] It was the work of Theissen and Meeks in particular that first stimulated my own interest—and that of many others too—in the social dimensions of the communities depicted and addressed in the Pauline letters. This focus is prominent in the first section of essays presented here.

The impetus behind the emergence of social-scientific approaches to the Pauline communities was fundamentally historical, in the sense that scholars sought to shift attention away from the theological orientation of earlier exegesis towards the social realities of the communities. As Robin Scroggs put it in an early survey of the field:

> Interest in the sociology of early Christianity is no attempt to limit reductionistically the reality of Christianity to social dynamic; rather it should be seen as an effort to guard against a reductionism from the other extreme, a limitation of the reality of Christianity to an inner-spiritual, or objective-cognitive system. In short, sociology of early Christianity wants to put body and soul together again.[5]

This turn to the social, away from the theological, was, however, not infrequently driven by its own kind of theological and political convictions,

---

Formative Christian Phenomena: A Creative Movement," in *Handbook of Early Christianity: Social Science Approaches*, ed. Anthony Blasi, Jean Duhaime, and Paul-André Turcotte (Walnut Creek, CA: Alta Mira, 2002), 3–28.

3. James D. G. Dunn, review of Gerd Theissen, *The Social Setting of Pauline Christianity*, *Theology* 86 (1983): 456. Theissen's key early essays on Paul are collected in Gerd Theissen, *Studien zur Soziologie des Urchristentums*, 3rd ed., WUNT 19 (Tübingen: Mohr Siebeck, 1988); and translated in Gerd Theissen, *The Social Setting of Pauline Christianity: Essays on Corinth*, ed. and trans. John H. Schütz (Edinburgh: T&T Clark, 1982).

4. Wayne A. Meeks, *The First Urban Christians: The Social World of the Apostle Paul* (New Haven: Yale University Press, 1983). For an assessment of the legacy of this book and subsequent developments in the field, see Todd D. Still and David G. Horrell, eds., *After the First Urban Christians: The Social-Scientific Study of Pauline Christianity Twenty-Five Years Later* (London: T&T Clark, 2009).

5. Robin Scroggs, "The Sociological Interpretation of the New Testament: The Present State of Research," *NTS* 26 (1980): 165–66.

as Stephen Barton has pointed out.[6] In other words, unsurprisingly and inevitably, contemporary convictions, priorities, and ideologies continue to shape even such (socio)historical inquiries.[7] Nonetheless, it remains the case that much NT study remains primarily historical in its orientation, eschewing or treating only very briefly the contemporary implications or motivations of the study. However, among the diversity of reading perspectives developed in recent decades there are plenty that give explicit attention to bridging the gap between past and present, recognizing that the NT texts are read not only as documents of historical evidence but also as canonical texts that continue to shape and inform Christian theology and practice, and, more broadly, the contours of moral debate in Christian and post-Christian contexts. Explicitly theological interpretation, for example—energetically developed in recent years—gives priority to the texts' canonical status.[8]

More broadly, readings of NT texts may be shaped not only by contemporary theoretical perspectives—as takes place in much social-scientific exegesis—but also by a concern to contribute to contemporary theological and moral reflection. It is not difficult to see, particularly in retrospect, that much historical inquiry is shaped by the concerns and priorities of the interpreter's own context, but these concerns are often kept resolutely in the background. Yet part of the motivation for developing more hermeneutically explicit modes of engagement has been precisely to develop these kinds of connection, such that engaging with the Pauline material may be one way whereby we seek to reflect fruitfully on contemporary challenges. This concern to undertake exegesis in ways explicitly connected with modern theoretical and ethical perspectives, and to contribute to constructive theological and ethical reflection, comes to the fore in the third part of this book, with the second part serving as a bridge between the sociohistorical and contemporary perspectives.

6. Stephen C. Barton, "Early Christianity and the Sociology of the Sect," in *The Open Text: New Directions for Biblical Studies?*, ed. Francis Watson (London: SCM, 1993), 140–62. For example, commenting on Robin Scroggs's early application of the sect model to the earliest Christian movement, Barton states that "Scroggs' sociological analysis is wedded to his own theological and ideological agenda" (143).

7. See, for example, the critical analysis of the influence of changing modes of contemporary capitalism on the perspectives presented in the work of Theissen, Meeks, and others, in Steven J. Friesen, "Poverty in Pauline Studies: Beyond the So-called New Consensus," *JSNT* 26 (2004): 323–61.

8. See, e.g., Francis Watson, *Text, Church and World: Biblical Interpretation in Theological Perspective* (Edinburgh: T&T Clark, 1994); Stephen E. Fowl, *Engaging Scripture: A Model for Theological Interpretation* (Oxford: Blackwell, 1998).

The essays collected in this volume, then, traverse the terrain that encompasses both sociohistorical reconstruction and contemporary appropriation, different facets of the making of Christian morality. Together they seek to illustrate how these various concerns may be pursued. Each essay makes its own particular argument, related to a particular text or issue, but as a whole the essays follow a trajectory from sociohistorical analysis to contemporary reflection and engagement. The following sections briefly introduce each essay, and also set each essay into the context of the particular section in which it appears, as well as into the wider context of the volume as a whole.

Early Christian Assemblies in Sociohistorical Context

In the first section, the focus is on the social context of the Pauline communities, though the first essay raises the question about how cogent it is to refer to "Pauline" churches—or communities, or assemblies—as is so commonly and unquestioningly done. Building on the stimulus of Richard Bauckham's provocative and much-discussed work on the audiences of the gospels, this chapter investigates the extent to which there is evidence for ideologically and socially distinct "Pauline" communities, as opposed to various kinds of early Christian groups. Of course, Paul's letters were written to specific local settings (though even that point may be qualified somewhat) so the question is different from that addressed by Bauckham; but one may nonetheless ask whether the evidence from Paul's letters suggests that Paul writes to distinctively "Pauline" groups, or rather to assemblies of believers in Christ, "early Christian communities." The analysis in this chapter suggests the latter. While the label "Pauline community" (or similar) is almost unavoidable as shorthand, it is seriously misleading—so this chapter argues—if taken to imply that there were "Pauline" assemblies, separated from those of other ideological or theological alignment. This does not by any means constitute a suggestion that the earliest Christian movement was, after all, united or singular in character, practice, or belief. Far from it: the local groups were varied and exhibited competing allegiances. But it does suggest that the diversity of local groups cannot be rightly grasped by referring to one type as "Pauline," and others in different but comparable terms.

The next two chapters examine the concrete socioeconomic circumstances in which these early Christians met, and form a closely related pair of essays. Together they contribute to the reassessment of the socioeconomic level of the earliest Christians and the spaces in which they were therefore likely to have met that follows from the challenge to the so-called new consensus initiated by Justin Meggitt and continued by Steven Friesen and others.[9] This critique of the "new consensus"—which often emphasized the wealth and high social status of prominent individuals in the early Christian movement—insists that the Pauline assemblies should instead be located among the non-elite of the Roman Empire, who mostly lived close to subsistence level.

Chapter 2 engages with the influential reconstruction of the setting for the Corinthian eucharistic meal presented by Jerome Murphy-O'Connor, which finds a basis for the divisions Paul confronts in the architectural layout of the Roman house. There are various reasons to challenge this reconstruction, related both to the specific archaeological evidence cited and to the wider assumptions about the socioeconomic level of the hosts. This chapter develops a critique of Murphy-O'Connor's proposal and, more broadly, of the widely established consensus that the kind of house in which the first urban Christians met would have been a *domus*-type dwelling. The essay then proceeds to offer an alternative kind of scenario based on different archaeological evidence from Corinth, which depicts a rather different kind of domestic space, likely owned or rented by people of a rather lower socioeconomic level. This is an entirely imaginative scenario, since there is no suggestion—let alone any evidence—that Christians ever met in this particular place, east of Corinth's theater, but it is argued to be a kind of setting more plausibly "typical" of the kind of meeting places we might envisage.

The following chapter deals with a different example—that of Philemon—but engages with some of the ongoing arguments and debates concerning meeting places and socioeconomic level that have continued in more recent years, including some of the criticisms and responses to the essay in ch. 2, notably by Murphy-O'Connor and Daniel Schowalter. Under the influence of the "new consensus," commentators have tended to depict Philemon as a wealthy individual with multiple slaves and a large house with guest room(s). Reviewing the shifting scholarly landscape on the issues of meeting places and socioeconomic level leads to a serious questioning of this kind of depiction. Indeed, a more realistic portrait of Philemon and his "house" would suggest a less exalted or wealthy position: he is much more likely to have been an artisan (perhaps like Prisca and Aquila) who owned a few slaves at most and inhabited a much more modest dwelling.

9. Justin J. Meggitt, *Paul, Poverty, and Survival*, SNTW (Edinburgh: T&T Clark, 1998); Friesen, "Poverty."

The final essay in this section, ch. 4, shifts the focus onto the ideological construction of social relationships within the Pauline assemblies—or, as we might say in light of ch. 1, the assemblies addressed in Paul's letters and the social ethos conveyed by those letters. This is a study of the language used in the Pauline letters, and the implications this has for the shaping of social relationships within the communities; it does not pretend that there is any straightforward correlation between these epistolary and ideological constructions and the social realities in particular places. The focus is the language of kinship and household—ἀδελφός and οἶκος language—and the ways in which these change over time, taking a fairly standard view of authorship and date as a basis. The picture that emerges is one in which ἀδελφός language, which is very prominent in the undisputed Pauline letters, decreases in prominence as we move through the deutero-Pauline and Pastoral letters, while οἶκος language becomes more prominent. Beyond mere counting of words, however, it is the kinds of appeal to this language and the ways in which it is taken to shape social relationships within the assemblies that reveal a picture of shifting social ethos, encapsulated concisely in the phrase "from ἀδελφοί to οἶκος θεοῦ." This chapter begins, then, to reflect an interest in what is essentially "ethics"—not in the sense of regulation on specific ethical quandaries but in the broad sense of the shaping of social relationships in communities. This becomes the major focus in the second main section of the book.

Pauline Ethics in Historical Context

The second section moves on from considerations of concrete social contexts to focus on Pauline ethics in their ancient historical context—though with an eye also on their contemporary significance. As in the immediately preceding chapter, the interest is in the ways in which Paul approaches questions of ethics, and what this can tell us about the kind of theoretical orientation or ethical theory that they embody.

The first such essay (ch. 5) focuses on the notorious case of sexual immorality Paul reports and reacts to in 1 Cor 5. The essay begins with Rudolf Bultmann's famous antinomy of indicative and imperative, so influential in understanding Paul's ethics, and argues that this is better construed in terms of identity construction. Turning to 1 Cor 5 in particular, we find that various features of Paul's treatment of the case of what he regards as scandalous immorality are particularly interesting. One such feature is his focus on identity (the man in question has not merely committed πορνεία, he is a πόρνος) and another is his focus on the community, rather than the individual; it is their collective purity and holiness that Paul fears will be infected. But another significant feature is the extent to which both Paul's text and the wider historical evidence indicate that the ethical conviction that Paul invokes in relation to this case is widely shared at the time. This provokes us to reflect on the ways in which Paul seeks to develop a sense of distinct group identity at the same time as indicating that the ethical norms he reinforces are actually widely accepted in the society from which the Christian group seeks to distinguish itself. Put concisely, Paul seeks to cultivate a sense of distinctive group identity yet at the same time indicates a common ethics. This combination, I argue, is significant not only for our understanding of Paul but also—gesturing towards concerns that will dominate part 3 of the book—for our reflections on contemporary ethical theories and how Paul might fruitfully inform them.

The next essay (ch. 6) explores similar issues in relation to Paul's much-discussed teaching about "idol food" (1 Cor 8–10). Setting Paul's instruction in the sociohistorical context of ancient Corinth, the analysis identifies two key instructions in Paul's teaching that form parameters around much of his more extended discussion: the negative prohibition is to avoid idolatry (1 Cor 10:14); the positive exhortation is to "eat everything sold in the marketplace without making inquiries" (1 Cor 10:25). Within these parameters it is striking how far Paul's instruction focuses not on rules about which foods may or may not be eaten but rather on a christologically grounded regard for the other—an ethical norm that requires right action to be judged, within certain limits, according to its impact on others. Drawing on Fredrik Barth's work, we can see that, for Paul, (certain) bodily actions are deemed crucial for maintaining the boundary around the community's identity (as exemplified in 1 Cor 5, dealt with in the previous chapter), while food in itself does not serve this purpose. Moreover, despite the strong rhetoric of distinction marking "community" off from "world"—as we saw too in 1 Cor 5—Paul also exhibits concern for accommodation and peaceful coexistence. Once again, this combination of concerns is not irrelevant to our consideration of some of the most pressing contemporary ethical challenges.

The third essay in this section (ch. 7) examines the highly influential christological hymn in Phil 2:6–11, focusing in particular on its depiction of Christ's humility and the significance of this for Pauline ethics specifically and for the place of humility as a virtue in the Christian tradition more generally. While it has been widely recognized that social humility—lowering oneself for the sake of other people, including those beneath oneself in social status—is not seen as a virtue in Greek and Roman ethics, there have been some challenges to this conclusion. The essay addresses two such challenges in particular: first, the comparison with Lucian's *Toxaris* and the argument that an aristocrat is there depicted as showing humility out of concern for his slave, presented by Michael White and Stanley Stowers; second, the comparison with Seneca's *On Clemency* and the argument that forms of social humility are valued in Stoic ethics, presented by Runar Thorsteinsson. The first of these arguments, notwithstanding its value in locating Philippians among the conventions of Greco-Roman friendship, seems flawed in its particular claims about the demonstration of social humility. The second of these arguments succeeds, it seems to me, in showing that we should not overly stress the uniqueness of the early Christian emphasis on social humility as a virtue. However, the distinctiveness of an emphasis on this particular mode of interaction, and its elevation as a significant virtue, seems to remain an innovative characteristic of earliest Christianity, and one in which Phil 2 plays a significant part. This does not mean that the legacy of Paul's elevation of humility as a Christian virtue should be evaluated entirely positively; on the contrary, its impact is ambivalent. But it does appear that this passage makes a crucial contribution to the shaping of the Christian ethical tradition and its distinctive focus on humility.

Pauline Ethics in Modern Contexts

The second section of the book has already begun to signal ways in which studies of Pauline ethics in their ancient context are suggestive and potentially fruitful for contemporary ethics. This focus on contemporary appropriation of the Pauline legacy comes to the fore in the third and final section of the book. While the essays here continue to engage in historical and exegetical analysis, their main concern is to reflect on contemporary issues and challenges, and specifically the challenge of the environmental impact of human activity.

The first essay in this section (ch. 8) is closely connected to the previous group of essays, picking up largely the same main exegetical examples (though considering Rom 14–15 rather than 1 Cor 8–10) but setting them explicitly into the context of debates in contemporary ethical theory, specifically the liberal-communitarian debate.[10] This sets the study of Pauline

10. This essay therefore presents, *in nuce*, some of the main features of the method

ethics into the context of contemporary ethical debate. However, the main focus is not, as it often is, on particular ethical "quandaries" (e.g., in the field of sexual ethics) but rather on the broader context of social and political ethics, specifically concerning the nature of the church's relationship to the "world." Sketching the work of Jürgen Habermas and Stanley Hauerwas as representatives of highly contrasting "liberal" and "communitarian" positions, the three exegetical examples (Phil 2:5–11; 1 Cor 5; Rom 14–15) provide the basis for reflections on three possible models for Christian ethics deriving from a reading of Paul. The first such model is an ecclesial one, in which the Christian community embodies the narrative of Christ which underpins its distinct identity in the world. The second model is one in which the distinctive identity of the church is seen to coexist with the possibility of shared consensus on ethical norms, thus finding certain points of contact with the kind of "liberal" vision articulated by Habermas or, rather differently, John Rawls. The third model, following Thomas Ogletree, uses Paul's ecclesial ethic—and in particular his approach to legitimating diversity of both conviction and practice—as a potentially fruitful analogy for contemporary plural societies, even if this implies moving not only beyond but also against Paul insofar as such a model for plural societies might relativize (and thus compromise, in the eyes of some) the claims of Christ. Crucially, reading Paul does not simply provide or affirm any single model of ecclesial ethics, nor any single model of church-world relationships, but does, I want to claim, offer fruitful material for thinking about more and less adequate models for contemporary political ethics.

The last two essays in the volume develop the contemporary appropriation of Pauline ethics in particular connection with issues of ecology and environmental concern. This is undoubtedly one of the most pressing concerns in the contemporary world, yet is also a concern not directly conceivable—at least in its modern form—to Paul and other biblical writers, who clearly knew nothing of climate change on a global scale caused by the high-tech industrial processes of a massive human population. Hence it is an issue that raises hermeneutical as well as ethical issues, and provides a good case study in how to appropriate Pauline ethics fruitfully in a world vastly different from that which Paul inhabited.[11]

---

and conclusions in my *Solidarity and Difference: A Contemporary Reading of Paul's Ethics* (London: T&T Clark, 2005). A second edition was published in 2015.

11. For a more extended presentation of this engagement with Paul, see David G. Horrell, Cherryl Hunt, and Christopher Southgate, *Greening Paul: Rereading the Apostle in an Age of Ecological Crisis* (Waco, TX: Baylor University Press, 2010).

The first of these essays (ch. 9) begins by illustrating how readings of Paul are shaped by, and emerge within, particular and changing contemporary contexts. The "new perspective" on Paul is a case in point, however much its proponents claimed to be setting Paul back into his first-century context, freed at last from the distortions imposed by Luther's sixteenth-century setting. This New Perspective is a product not simply of new historical insight but also of the pressures and priorities (rightly) exerted by reflection on the iconic and horrific event of the Holocaust and by social and political changes in the post–World War 2 era. Similarly, it is argued, the environmental crisis deserves the development of another new perspective on Paul. Yet it is surprising how little such pressing concerns feature on the landscape of contemporary Pauline studies—even though that comment, illustrated with examples in the essay, is less true now than it was in 2010, when the essay was first published. The essay therefore seeks to explore and to outline the potential for an ecological reading of Paul.

Beginning with the obvious favorites of Rom 8:19–23 and Col 1:15–20, I argue that there is the potential for a more broadly based rereading of Pauline theology, oriented around the idea of God's "incorporative transformation of the whole creation in Christ." This in turn leads to questions about the reconfiguration of Pauline ethics in an ecological direction. The anthropocentric, indeed ecclesiocentric, focus of Paul's ethics is not to be denied; but the logic of Paul's own theology offers the potential to develop his ethics of "other-regard" in a broader direction, incorporating "all things" within its scope. This does not offer any easy resolution to our specific ethical challenges, but it does suggest that Paul's letters may offer something to the task of reconfiguring Christian theology and ethics in an age of ecological crisis.

The second essay on this theme (ch. 10) sets my approach within the context of the range of approaches to ecological interpretation of the Bible, and then explores one specific Pauline passage in depth as an example. The starting point is Lynn White's classic and provocative essay from 1967, which played a significant part in goading biblical scholars (among others) to respond to White's critique of the Western Christian tradition and its impact on attitudes to the environment. While some Christians see environmentalism as a threat, or at least a distraction from the true priority of evangelism in light of an imminent return of Christ, many others have defended the Bible against White's charges, insisting that it is a "green" book that fosters responsible stewardship and environmental care. A contrasting position, however, is taken by the Earth Bible Project, which resists claims that the

Bible can straightforwardly be claimed as "ecofriendly." The method employed in the Project's work employs steps of "suspicion," "identification," and "retrieval" to discern the voice of earth in the texts, and adopts a set of "ecojustice principles" as a basic stance of ethical orientation and commitment.[12] A critique of both these kinds of perspective serves as the basis for an attempt to articulate a more theologically oriented hermeneutic, drawing on the work of Ernst Conradie.

I should note here that I would now express my critique of the Earth Bible approach in somewhat more cautious terms, not least on account of the diversity of work included within the Project, and also the theological engagement of many of its contributors, including Habel himself.[13] Nonetheless, I think it remains the case that what is explicitly stated about the approach and its principles does not sufficiently articulate how—if one is seeking to do Christian theology and ethics (which is not, of course, to be assumed)—the Bible may be shown to play a formative and constructive role in the development of ethical principles, rather than being read in the light of a non-theological set of principles.[14]

After this critical evaluation of methodologies, the essay turns to the interpretation of 2 Cor 5:14–21, a passage rightly seen as a central statement of key themes in Paul's theology. It invites consideration of how far notions such as reconciliation, new creation, and being the righteousness of God can be read in an ecologically relevant way. Without denying the degree to which anthropocentrism characterizes Paul's own perspective, and without pretending that Paul intended the ecological dimensions of his theological vision, we can nonetheless read this passage, attentively but also constructively, as a fruitful contribution to a kind of Pauline ecotheology at the center of which stands God's act of cosmic reconciliation in Christ. If the theolog-

12. See the brief outline of this method in Norman C. Habel, "Introducing Ecological Hermeneutics," in *Exploring Ecological Hermeneutics*, ed. Norman C. Habel and Peter Trudinger, SymS 46 (Atlanta: Society of Biblical Literature, 2008), 3–5; for a discussion of the ecojustice principles, see The Earth Bible Team, "Guiding Ecojustice Principles," in *Readings from the Perspective of Earth*, ed. Norman C. Habel, Earth Bible 1 (Sheffield: Sheffield Academic Press, 2000), 38–53.

13. See, e.g., Norman Habel, *An Inconvenient Text: Is a Green Reading of the Bible Possible?* (Adelaide: ATF, 2009).

14. For my more recent reflections and critical evaluation on contrasting methods in the field of ecological hermeneutics, see David G. Horrell, "Ecological Hermeneutics: Reflections on Methods and Prospects for the Future," *Colloquium: The Australian and New Zealand Theological Review* 46 (2014): 139–65, with responses by Elaine Wainwright (166–69) and Steven Bouma-Prediger (170–74).

ical vision is cosmic in its scope, so too are its ethical implications—beyond social justice to ecojustice, we might say, even if this leaves unspecified and open to ongoing debate what the concrete implications of this commitment might be: Should we be vegetarian? Should we intervene to save endangered species, and how actively? To answer such questions, and many others, we need the insights of contemporary science, economics, theology, ethics, and so on. But reading Paul may also have a part to play, enriching the Christian vision and undergirding theologically an ethical commitment to the flourishing of all things. While such readings need to be acknowledged as deliberately creative and constructive readings of Paul, produced in the light of our current ecological concerns, through such a process texts such as 2 Cor 5:14–21 can make a significant contribution to notions of ecological ethics and ecojustice.

To have begun with sociohistorical questions about the concrete circumstances of the earliest Christian communities and ended up with discussions of contemporary environmental ethics may seem a considerable leap. But I hope to have shown, with the collection as a whole, that responsible and fruitful interpretation of Paul can encompass and even integrate such diverse concerns. Although Paul's letters and the earliest Christian communities can, indeed should, be studied as a particular part of ancient history, the religious status of these texts—and the religious convictions that often shape their study, for better or worse—means that attention to their contemporary influence and potential to inform contemporary thought and action is an equally important and urgent task, and crucial to the ongoing challenge of making Christian morality.

Part I

Early Christian Assemblies in Sociohistorical Context

Chapter 1

The Letters for All (Local) Christians

Were There "Pauline Churches"?

Introduction

Richard Bauckham's provocative and by now well-known essay, "For Whom Were the Gospels Written?," sets out to challenge the widely held view that the gospels were shaped by, and written for, specific and different local communities: Markan, Matthean, Lukan, and Johannine, respectively.[1] Instead, Bauckham argues, "the Gospels were written for general circulation around the churches and so envisaged a very general Christian audience."[2] Bauckham does not deny that "the community in which a Gospel was written is likely to have influenced the writing of the Gospel,"[3] though he stresses that many of the issues addressed would have been faced not only by one specific Christian community, but by many of the churches of the time.[4] Moreover, the evangelists most likely traveled, or were in other ways made aware of the translocal dimensions of the Christian movement.[5] Thus the "historical

1. Richard J. Bauckham, "For Whom Were the Gospels Written?," in *The Gospels for All Christians: Rethinking the Gospel Audiences*, ed. Richard J. Bauckham (Grand Rapids: Eerdmans, 1998), 9–48.

2. Richard J. Bauckham, "Introduction," in *Gospels for All Christians*, ed. Bauckham, 1.

3. Bauckham, "Gospels," 44.

4. Bauckham makes this point with reference to the example of expulsion from the synagogue, as addressed, at least on J. Louis Martyn's thesis, in John 9: "If John 9 addresses that situation, it addresses, not a circumstance peculiar to the Johannine community, but a circumstance that would have been common in the churches of the late first century" ("Gospels," 23). Issues regarding law observance would be another such instance.

5. Bauckham, "Gospels," 44–45.

context" of the gospels is "not the evangelist's community. It is the early Christian movement in the late first century."[6]

One of the points Bauckham makes is that the gospels have been interpreted as if they were letters, and that this is a crucial hermeneutical error. Letters, of course, *were* sent to specific communities to address their particular needs and problems.[7] Nevertheless, and without intending to signal uncritical acceptance of Bauckham's case,[8] Bauckham's arguments prompt me to raise some comparable questions about the so-called Pauline communities, which we know primarily through the Pauline letters. Just as Bauckham forcefully questions the validity of the concepts "Markan community," "Matthean community," and so on—arguing that they "should disappear from the terminology of Gospels scholarship"[9]—so we might ask how valid are the terms "Pauline community," "Pauline church," *paulinische Gemeinde*, and other equivalents, which appear in abundance in the scholarly literature.[10] Just as Bauckham suggests is the case with the concepts

6. Bauckham, "Gospels," 46.

7. Bauckham, "Gospels," 26–27.

8. Among the significant critiques of Bauckham's thesis are Philip F. Esler, "Community and Gospel in Early Christianity: A Response to Richard Bauckham's *Gospels for All Christians*," *SJT* 51 (1998): 235–48 (with response from Bauckham, 249–54); David C. Sim, "The Gospels for All Christians? A Response to Richard Bauckham," *JSNT* 84 (2001): 3–27; Wendy E. Sproston North, "John for Readers of Mark? A Response to Richard Bauckham's Proposal," *JSNT* 25 (2003): 449–68; Margaret M. Mitchell, "Patristic Counter-Evidence to the Claim That 'The Gospels Were Written for All Christians,'" *NTS* 51 (2005): 36–79. Mitchell's critique is particularly important: her examination of the patristic evidence leads her to question Bauckham's assertion that the notion of a gospel being addressed to a specific, local Christian community arises only in modern redaction criticism. On the contrary, patristic writers saw the gospels as addressed to the needs and concerns of specific audiences but also as having importance for a wider, and indefinite, Christian readership. Thus Mitchell questions the dichotomy Bauckham sets up, between either "written for a specific local community," or "written for all Christians." In what follows, however, I am not concerned with the question about whether Paul's letters were addressed to local communities—they undoubtedly were!—but with the question as to whether these communities can be meaningfully described as "Pauline." Esler ("Community," 244–47) and North ("John," passim) also raise questions specifically about Bauckham's treatment of John as intended to supplement Mark; Esler argues that John reflects an introverted sectarian ethos. Indeed, the Johannine literature might perhaps be taken to reflect the existence and outlook of (a) distinctive Christian group(s); certainly Bauckham's case needs to be assessed, to some extent, on a "case-by-case" basis.

9. Bauckham, "Introduction," 4; cf. Bauckham, "Gospels," 45.

10. The terms are so common that it would be pointless, and perhaps invidious, to single out specific examples. Indeed, it is interesting that Bauckham adopts this standard

of "Markan" or "Matthean" communities, and so on, so perhaps the term "Pauline church" has become part of our standard vocabulary without serious and critical reflection on precisely what we intend that term to mean.[11] The issue here, it should be stressed, is not whether the Pauline letters were written for specific local or for wider Christian audiences—the two alternatives that Bauckham considers in the case of the gospels and upon which Margaret Mitchell focuses in her critique[12]—but rather whether the local communities to which the letters were undoubtedly sent can in any sense be meaningfully labeled "Pauline." In other words, the issue is not one of geographical localization but of theological or ideological distinctiveness.[13]

First I should make clear that I do not intend to dispute two rather indisputable data: that Paul was the founder of a number of early Christian communities, and that he wrote letters to specific Christian communities. Insofar as the term "Pauline community" is used as implicit shorthand in relation to either of these basic facts—to denote a church that Paul founded or the view of the church depicted and promoted in the Pauline letters—it has a certain historical legitimacy. But it is the further connotations that deliberately or unconsciously expand this denotation that may prove more problematic. Indeed, even with regard to the two "facts" mentioned above, some caution may be in order.

On the first point, we may suspect Paul of a certain amount of rhetorical exaggeration when he insists on his singular role as founder of any particular church. Take the Corinthian church as an example. When Paul is seeking to defuse Corinthian factionalism and dismantle party allegiances, he insists that he (alone) "planted" (ἐγὼ ἐφύτευσα, 1 Cor 3:6), laid a foundation "like

---

language at one point in his response to Esler's critique, referring to Christian leaders "found at different times living in several different Christian communities (often both Pauline and non-Pauline)." However, he immediately proceeds to note, rightly in my view, that there is "very little to suggest exclusive orientation to a particular network of like-minded churches distinguished from others (evidence for this is not found in Paul's writings, where we should have expected to find it if anywhere)" ("Response," 251).

11. Cf. Bauckham, "Gospels," 13–17.

12. Mitchell, "Patristic Counter-Evidence."

13. The question as to what the local Christian communities can legitimately be called might in this sense indeed also be relevant in the case of the gospels. If we use the term "Markan community" do we mean "the local early Christian community in which Mark was located and for which he particularly wrote" or "the particular community that shared a distinctive set of theological presumptions, issues, practices, etc., which Mark's gospel reflects or confronts"? The unreflective use of terms such as "Markan community" can allow such distinctions to be blurred or to remain unexamined.

a skilled master builder" (1 Cor 3:10, NRSV), and, indeed, gave them birth (ἐγὼ ὑμᾶς ἐγέννησα, 1 Cor 4:15). Yet elsewhere it becomes apparent that the founding mission at Corinth was not conducted by Paul alone but by Paul, Silvanus, and Timothy (2 Cor 1:19)—also the coauthors of 1 Thessalonians (1 Thess 1:1). Moreover, there is the distinct possibility that there were Christians in Corinth prior to Paul's arrival there: Prisca and Aquila, according to Acts (18:2), had come to Corinth having been expelled from Rome by Claudius, and provided Paul's first point of contact and hospitality. Acts does not record that they were already Christians on arriving in Corinth, but neither is there any mention of their conversion there; and the fact that Paul makes their household his base suggests their Christian sympathies.[14] Such factors complicate the picture of Paul as the sole founder of known Christian communities. And, of course, there are other churches to which Paul writes or refers, such as those in Antioch or in Rome, which he certainly did not found.

On the second point, it is worth noting that Paul sometimes addresses his letters to a broad geographical area (e.g., 2 Cor 1:1), or urges that a letter be widely read (1 Thess 5:27; cf. Col 4:16),[15] or, indeed, gives an indication that his letter is addressed to all Christians everywhere (1 Cor 1:2)—so the later circulation of Pauline letters as documents of universal Christian importance only picks up a claim already expressed within the letters themselves. Furthermore, as we shall see, insofar as the historical realities are concerned, Paul's letters themselves do not even depict the churches to which he writes as "Pauline" communities, in the sense of being theologically and ideologically distinct communities, with "little contact"[16] with other competing factions. So even the idea that the term "Pauline community" might validly describe the church as depicted in Paul's letters is not entirely secure. We might perhaps want to suggest that the term "Pauline community" could be used in a sense analogous to the use of "ideal" or "implied" reader—to refer to the "ideal" or "implied" church as it is constructed and envisaged by the

14. For arguments that Prisca and Aquila were already Christians before leaving Rome, see Helga Botermann, *Das Judenedikt des Kaisers Claudius: Römischer Staat und Christiani im 1 Jahrhundert*, Hermes Einzelschriften 71 (Stuttgart: Steiner, 1996), 46–47; Peter Lampe, *From Paul to Valentinus: Christians at Rome in the First Two Centuries* (London: T&T Clark, 2003), 11–13.

15. Col 4:16 would be a particularly revealing indication of letters being intended to be shared beyond their local context, but since there are doubts about Colossians's authenticity I do not rely on this to show Paul's view of his letters.

16. This phrase is taken from Sim, "Response," 11, on which see below.

author of the letters, Paul. Such a church would, by definition, be a "Pauline" church, since it would dance to the tune of Paul's instructions and accept his authority without question. Yet the historical churches, even as Paul allows us to glimpse them in his letters, never conformed neatly to such Pauline ideals, whatever the apostle might have wished.

Although these observations, then, are important qualifications of data all-too-easily assumed at face value, it is the question about whether there were Pauline *communities* that I particularly want to address. It was Ferdinand Christian Baur, of course, who famously placed onto the agenda of NT studies the thesis that early Christianity was riven by a twofold division between Petrine, law-observant, Jewish Christianity and Pauline, non-law-observant, gentile, "universal" Christianity.[17] Although widely criticized, this basic thesis still has its contemporary proponents.[18] The particular question that concerns us here is not whether Baur was right or wrong, but whether the divisions and arguments that undoubtedly existed in some forms in the early Christian movement were embodied in distinct *communities*. David Sim, in his response to Bauckham's thesis, presumes that this was the case. Given the very strong disagreement over questions of law observance, we should speak, Sim insists, not of the Christian movement, but "of very different Christian movements."[19] Taking the Pauline epistles as evidence, Sim argues that "our sources strongly suggest that the rival Christian factions had little contact with one another."[20] Different churches were aligned with different early Christian factions and those with one theological perspective on the law would not have recognized those of a different perspective as belonging to the same movement.[21] Thus, according to Sim, each gospel writer would have written for their own community—not necessarily "a single church," but perhaps "a cluster of churches linked by geographical

17. Ferdinand Christian Baur, "Die Christuspartei in der korinthische Gemeinde, der Gegensatz des petrinischen und paulinischen Christentums in der ältesten Kirche, der Apostel Petrus in Rom," *Tübinger Zeitschrift* 4 (1831): 61–206. See also the extract from Baur, with discussion and other literature, in Edward Adams and David G. Horrell, eds., *Christianity at Corinth: The Quest for the Pauline Church* (Louisville: Westminster John Knox, 2004), 13–16, 51–59.

18. Michael D. Goulder, "ΣΟΦΙΑ in 1 Corinthians," *NTS* 37 (1991): 516–34; Goulder, *A Tale of Two Missions* (London: SCM, 1994); Goulder, *Paul and the Competing Mission in Corinth* (Peabody, MA: Hendrickson, 2001).

19. Sim, "Response," 10.

20. Sim, "Response," 11.

21. Cf. Sim, "Response," 14, 20.

proximity and a shared theological perspective"[22]—so while "Mark wrote for a Christian community that did not observe the Torah. . . . Matthew wrote for one that did."[23]

But does the evidence from the Pauline letters—the most important source for the earliest period—support Sim's conclusions? Let us briefly survey that evidence, moving through the letters in what may approximate to their chronological order, though nothing in particular hangs on this choice of order.

The Evidence of Paul's Letters

First Thessalonians, probably Paul's earliest letter, might certainly be taken as evidence that the church at Thessalonica was, at this time at least, a "Pauline" community, so long as we qualify that by insisting that it is Paul, Silvanus, and Timothy who founded the church there and now write to its members. There is no explicit indication of any anti-Pauline opposition in, or known to, the church, nor any mention of other leading Christian figures. Second Thessalonians, though probably inauthentic, does reveal that a certain version of Paul's gospel now has to be defended against alternatives; but this text, if a later and pseudonymous attempt to correct misreadings of Paulinism, may not be particularly revealing of conditions specifically in Thessalonica. Nonetheless, given the early date of 1 Thessalonians, its silence on any non-Pauline influences in the community should not be overinterpreted as indicating that the churches of Thessalonica continued to be exclusively "Pauline." Indeed, the inclusion of Silvanus in the team of those who founded this church, and that at Corinth, is in itself a significant qualification of the idea that these churches were "Pauline" as opposed to "early Christian": Silvanus/Silas first appears in Jerusalem, helping to bear a letter from there to Antioch, after which he joins Paul's missionary team (Acts 15:22–40). John Elliott goes too far in claiming Silvanus as a chief representative of a *Petrine* circle (cf. 1 Pet 5:12), but neither should he be seen as an exclusively Pauline collaborator.[24]

22. Sim, "Response," 24. This comment links, of course, geographical and ideological specificity; they should, I think, be distinguished (see above with n. 13).

23. Sim, "Response," 25.

24. See John H. Elliott, "Peter, Silvanus and Mark in I Peter and Acts: Sociological-Exegetical Perspectives on a Petrine Group in Rome," in *Wort in der Zeit: Neutestamentliche Studien. Festgabe für Karl Heinrich Rengstorf zum 75. Geburtstag*, ed. W. Haubeck and M. Bachmann (Leiden: Brill, 1980), 250; cf. John H. Elliott, *1 Peter: A New Translation with*

Galatians may or may not be early, but the information it yields does not depend on its chronological placement. The letter gives a certain window onto Christian communities in two different locations: in Antioch and in Galatia. Without needing to resolve the many complex questions about the incident at Antioch, we may make some basic observations. First, the table fellowship includes both gentile Christians and Jewish Christians, and, more specifically, includes Paul and Barnabas on the one hand, associated especially with the gentile mission, and also Peter on the other. And when "certain people from James" come to Antioch, they come to this very church, and cause the divisions Paul so bitterly laments. We do not know what happened after the incident, but up to this time at least, there is, as far as we know, an early Christian community (or communities) in Antioch, in which gentile and Jewish believers share a communal meal, and to which Paul, Barnabas, Peter, and people from James come when they visit the city. It would be possible to suggest, following the incident, and particularly following the subsequent council in Jerusalem, that henceforth distinct Jewish-Christian and gentile-Christian missions led to distinct communities (cf. Gal 2:7–9). But further evidence from Paul's letters suggests that this did not in fact happen.

The occasion for Galatians, indeed, is that the communities of Christians initially persuaded by the so-called law-free Pauline gospel have since come under the influence of "Judaizers," who regard adoption of the marks of Jewish Torah observance as crucial for membership of God's people, for gentiles as well as Jews. If these countermissionaries had been operative and influential in different and distinct communities, then Paul's anger might never have been fired: it is the fact that his gentile converts are subject to persuasion from these teachers that provokes him. There is a competition for influence in the same Christian communities. In other words, the agreement recorded in Gal 2:7–9 regarding the distinct and complementary missions of Paul (to the gentiles) and Peter (to the Jews) did not in practice lead to distinct communities or factions, with "little contact" with one another. This is shown not only by the evident influence of Jewish-Christian missionaries, including Peter himself (see below on 1 Corinthians), on Paul's gentile converts, but also by the indications that the communities to which Paul

---

Introduction and Commentary, AB 37B (New York: Doubleday, 2000), 127–30, 889–90. For criticisms, see David G. Horrell, "The Product of a Petrine Circle? A Reassessment of the Origin and Character of 1 Peter," *JSNT* 86 (2002): 29–60. Similar things may be said about (John) Mark (see Horrell, "Petrine Circle?," 48–50).

writes contained Jewish as well as gentile members, though the latter were generally in the majority.[25]

First Corinthians, again written to a community founded by Paul, along with Silvanus and Timothy, reveals a comparable picture with regard to the character of the early Christian communities, although there is no indication that circumcision and law observance were issues of controversy at Corinth. Though Paul was their founder, as he insists, there are those in the community who express allegiance to Apollos, who is evidently known to the Christians at Corinth (1 Cor 1:12; 3:4–22; 16:12; Acts 18:24–19:1), or to Peter, who may or may not have visited Corinth but who clearly also has his following there (1 Cor 1:12; 3:22; 9:5).[26] Again the point is this: there *is* no separate Petrine community down the road. In one and the same church, or group of churches—that is, among those Christians to whom *Paul* writes—the influences of Paul, Apollos, Peter, and others jostle alongside one another, with all the tensions that represents.

The various letters that comprise 2 Corinthians give similar indications. As in Galatians, so in 2 Cor 10–13 Paul is angry not least about the false apostles who have been persuading the Corinthians and turning them against him. Again it is clear that these missionaries have Jewish connections, as did Paul's opponents in Galatia (2 Cor 11:22). Certainly Paul makes the bold claim that these Corinthian converts are *his*, such that others should keep their hands off: he feels what he legitimates as a "divine" jealousy for his converts (11:2), and accuses the other missionaries of transgressing their geographical or ethnic limits in intruding upon his ecclesial space (10:13; cf. Gal 2:9; Rom 15:20). Thus it seems that Paul indeed *wants* there to be

25. E.g., at Corinth gentiles seem to have formed the majority (1 Cor 8:7; 12:2), though there were certainly Jews among the membership too: Prisca and Aquila, along with Lucius, Jason, and Sosipater (Rom 16:21), and Crispus and Sosthenes (Acts 18:2, 8, 17; 1 Cor 1:1, 14; 16:19). Cf. also 1 Cor 7:18–19, which implies a Jewish presence among the congregation, since otherwise it would have been without significance to them. At Rome the evidence also suggests a largely gentile church with a minority of Jewish Christians. See, e.g., Peter Lampe, "The Roman Christians of Romans 16," in *The Romans Debate*, revised and expanded edition, ed. Karl Paul Donfried (Edinburgh: T&T Clark, 1991), 224–25; Andrew D. Clarke, "Jew and Greek, Slave and Free, Male and Female: Paul's Theology of Ethnic, Social and Gender Inclusiveness in Romans 16," in *Rome in the Bible and the Early Church*, ed. Peter Oakes (Carlisle: Paternoster, 2002), 109–13.

26. C. K. Barrett argues that Cephas had visited Corinth: "Cephas and Corinth," in *Abraham unser Vater: Juden und Christen im Gespräch über die Bibel: Festschrift für Otto Michel zum 60. Geburtstag*, ed. Otto Betz, Martin Hengel, and Peter Schmidt (Leiden: Brill, 1963), 1–12. Reprinted in C. K. Barrett, *Essays on Paul* (London: SPCK, 1982), 28–39.

Pauline communities, and does his best to keep others out of the way, at least when driven to polemic by a dangerously successful opposition. Yet Paul's polemical insistences should not be assumed as historical realities. And the fact that these opponents are, once again, competing for influence among the very same converts Paul claims as his own, operating in the very same Christian communities, should make clear that Paul's ideal does *not* correspond to the reality of early Christian communities, in Corinth and the wider province of Achaia, as well as in Antioch and Galatia.

The church or churches of Philippi seem to have enjoyed a generally warm and close relationship with Paul (cf. Phil 1:3–11), providing him support on more than one occasion (Phil 4:15–16) and, presumably along with the Thessalonians, contributing to his collection project willingly, despite their poverty (2 Cor 8:1–5). Yet here too Paul is concerned that the promoters of the circumcision gospel may exert their influence, and gives the Philippians a stern warning to beware of them (Phil 3:2–6). Insofar as the Philippian church, like that at Thessalonica, is a largely gentile church that seems to follow Paul's lead in relation to issues of law observance, it might be described as a "Pauline" community. But it is equally important to note Paul's fear: not that his converts will be enticed away to another assembly down the road, but that, as elsewhere, Judaizing opponents will turn up in *this* community and persuade its members to alter their perspective and practices.

Romans is of course written to a church or group of churches[27] not founded by Paul and not previously visited by him (Rom 1:10–15; 15:22). Whatever flavor or flavors of Christianity characterize the Roman churches, they cannot be meaningfully called Pauline; indeed, some suspicion of Paul's gospel would seem to be evident in Rome (Rom 3:8).[28] Tensions and disagreements between Jewish and gentile Christians, or between the law-

27. It is most likely that Rom 16 indicates the existence of several house-churches in Rome; see Lampe, "Roman Christians"; Lampe, *From Paul to Valentinus*, 359–65.

28. Cf. further Raymond E. Brown, "The Roman Church near the End of the First Christian Generation (A.D. 58—Paul to the Romans)," in Raymond E. Brown and John P. Meier, *Antioch and Rome: New Testament Cradles of Catholic Christianity* (London: Chapman, 1983), 105–27. Karlmann Beyschlag suggests that in writing Romans, Paul accommodated his views "in bezug auf die theologische Voraussetzungen einer Gemeinde . . . die eine andersartige, unpaulinische Tradition bewahrte, deren Abbild uns dreißig Jahre später der römische Clemensbrief präsentiert" (*Clemens Romanus und der Frühkatholizismus: Untersuchungen zu I Clemens 1–7*, BHT 35 [Tübingen: Mohr Siebeck, 1966], 349). It is questionable, however, whether such a later source can reliably be used to construct a picture of pre-Pauline Christianity in Rome.

observant and non-law-observant of whatever background, are evident, and Paul seeks to effect their reconciliation and unity, such that their communal meals may proceed in a spirit of mutual tolerance and welcome.[29]

Conclusions

We may now draw some conclusions from this brief sketch. First, although some of the communities Paul addresses (those at Thessalonica and Philippi) might be thought of as "Pauline" churches, in the absence of any explicit indication of other influences present and in view of their general adherence to Paul's gospel, the general picture is one in which competing and conflicting perspectives relate to and are present in the same early Christian communities. There is no clear evidence of any alternative Petrine or Jacobite community, down the street from a Pauline one. Rather, these figures and their representatives turn up in the same communities and compete for influence among the same groups of converts.[30] Nor do missionaries necessarily belong clearly or exclusively to one "team," Pauline or other: Silvanus/Silas, as we have already mentioned, first appears as a letter bearer from the Jerusalem church; and Barnabas, though initially a close collaborator of Paul's, was persuaded by the arguments of James's people to side with Peter at Antioch, much to Paul's annoyance (Gal 2:13; cf. Acts 15:35–40). In other words, the "networks" that seem to have been so crucial for the growth of early Christianity, and certainly for the spread of information and literature within the movement, should not be envisaged as comprising separate and isolated networks of Pauline workers, Petrine ad-

29. Cf. further John M. G. Barclay, "'Do We Undermine the Law?' A Study of Romans 14:1–15:6," in *Paul and the Mosaic Law*, ed. James D. G. Dunn (Tübingen: Mohr Siebeck, 1996), 287–308; David G. Horrell, *Solidarity and Difference: A Contemporary Reading of Paul's Ethics* (London: T&T Clark, 2005), 182–89.

30. I do not think that the evidence of Acts contradicts this scenario, though it is difficult to be sure. In particular, Acts 19:1–7 suggests that there were "disciples" who understood baptism differently (cf. also Acts 8:14–16), and/or retained an allegiance to John the Baptist. Whether these people represent distinct "communities" of Christian believers, or of disciples of John, is unclear. It is notable, however, that even such apparently "heterodox" groups of disciples are precisely those with whom Paul makes contact (or, in Acts 8, to whom Peter and John are sent): Paul is simply described as having "found some disciples" in Ephesus (Acts 19:1). To what extent Luke's theological interests have shaped the narrative—with the Jerusalem apostles and Paul depicted as bringing "orthodoxy" and blessing to various groups of converts—is hard to determine.

herents, and so on.[31] Indeed, even where we might perhaps speak in broad terms of a Pauline community, in Thessalonica and possibly Philippi, it is important to note that there is absolutely no indication of any other Christian community in those cities. In short, there is nothing to support Sim's argument that "the rival Christian factions had little contact with one another" or that different churches were aligned with different early Christian factions.[32] The evidence we have seems to point strongly in the opposite direction. When a traveling missionary arrived in Antioch, Galatia, Corinth, or elsewhere, whether their theological allegiances were Pauline, Petrine, or whatever, they went to the same communities, joined in meals and found hospitality there. Indeed, it is precisely this that led to Paul's engaging in such combative and aggressive writing.

Bauckham, in the context of his argument that the gospels were intended for wide, rather than only local, circulation, argues that the early Christians were conscious of belonging to a worldwide movement (rather than to a Markan, Matthean, or even Pauline community).[33] A similar observation would seem to be true in relation to the local Christian communities to which Paul wrote: they did not think of themselves as "Pauline" assemblies, whatever Paul might on occasion have wished, but rather as "early Christian" churches—though this is an anachronistic and etic label. And rather than Mark, Matthew, or indeed Paul, writing to confirm the beliefs and practices of different communities that were respectively law-observant (Matthew) or non-law-observant (Mark, Paul), as Sim suggests, it seems much more likely that each of them sought to *persuade* early Christians of the validity of their approach, in the face of evident and competing alternatives.

None of this is intended to cast doubt on the idea that early Christianity was characterized by diversity and by frequent conflict, a point Bauckham also stresses. Walter Bauer long ago rightly warned us not to conceive of early Christianity as an originally unified and "orthodox" body, from which heretical groups later arose and split off; on the contrary, orthodoxy was created and imposed upon an always diverse and varied movement.[34] We

31. On the importance and practicalities of the networks of early Christian communication, see Michael B. Thompson, "The Holy Internet," in *Gospels for All Christians*, ed. Bauckham, 49–70; and specifically in relation to the production and circulation of early Christian literature, see Loveday C. Alexander, "Ancient Book Production and the Circulation of the Gospels," in *Gospels for All Christians*, ed. Bauckham, 71–105.

32. Sim, "Response," 11, 14.

33. Bauckham, "Gospels," 33.

34. Walter Bauer, *Orthodoxy and Heresy in Earliest Christianity* (London: SCM, 1972).

can and must accept, on the one hand, that the early Christian assemblies were from the start diverse, internally and in comparison with one another; early Christian missionaries proclaimed somewhat different versions of the gospel, and—at least if Paul is anything to go by—argued vehemently against those who thought differently. On the other hand, there is no evidence to support the notion that, in its earliest period, Christianity's diversity was embodied in distinct communities in which there was a shared allegiance to a particular form of Christianity, Pauline, Petrine, or whatever. Indeed, the disagreements so blatantly evident in Paul's letters only make sense on the opposite scenario: that these diversities and disagreements were evident and encompassed within local early Christian communities. Indeed, it may well have been that diversity in the earliest decades was as much connected with geographical location as with theological alignment; rather than think of distinctions between Pauline and Petrine Christianity, we should perhaps think of differences between Thessalonian Christianity and Corinthian Christianity, and so on.[35]

What our earliest evidence (in the Pauline letters) suggests, then, is that, though often characterized by disagreement, and by diversity associated with differences in cultural background, geographical location, ethnic identity, and theological persuasion, the early Christian movement found communal embodiment in early Christian communities, and not in Pauline (or Petrine) communities.

Finally, just as gospels specialists have been forced to think hard about whether to use terms such as "Markan community," and, if they do, what exactly they mean by them, so too Pauline scholars should perhaps pause to think about the validity of the term "Pauline community." If they use it, or similar equivalents, they should at least pause to consider what exactly they mean by it, and whether its use is justifiable in view of the historical evidence.

35. See further John M. G. Barclay, "Thessalonica and Corinth: Social Contrasts in Pauline Christianity," *JSNT* 47 (1992): 49–74; Edward Adams, *Constructing the World: A Study in Paul's Cosmological Language* (Edinburgh: T&T Clark, 2000).

Chapter 2

Domestic Space and Christian Meetings at Corinth

Imagining New Contexts and the Buildings East of the Theater

Jerome Murphy-O'Connor: "House-Churches and the Eucharist"

When NT scholars have tried to imagine the kind of domestic space in which the divisions at the Lord's Supper arose at Corinth (1 Cor 11:17–34) they have generally thought in terms of a Roman villa with triclinium and atrium or peristyle.[1] Jerome Murphy-O'Connor, in his well-known book *St. Paul's Corinth*, first published in 1983 and rereleased in 2002 in a third, revised, and expanded edition, draws on the archaeological evidence from Corinth and elsewhere to show what this domestic context may have been like and specifically how the physical structures shaped social interaction such that the origins of the σχίσματα Paul confronts are given a plausible explanation.[2]

In a section entitled "a typical house," Murphy-O'Connor considers first the villa at Anaploga, one of very few houses excavated at Corinth and the only one to have existed in the time of Paul (see fig. 1).[3] Here, according to Murphy-O'Connor, the triclinium, with a "magnificent mosaic floor," measures 5.5 by 7.5 meters.[4] These dimensions, Murphy-O'Connor suggests,

1. The triclinium refers to a Roman-style dining room, so named because of the three couches placed in a U shape in the room. The atrium (courtyard) was sometimes built using columns to form a surrounding colonnaded portico, when it is termed a peristyle.

2. Jerome Murphy-O'Connor, *St. Paul's Corinth: Texts and Archaeology*, 3rd rev. and exp. ed. (Collegeville, MN: Liturgical Press, 2002), 178–85.

3. Murphy-O'Connor, *St. Paul's Corinth*, 178.

4. In fact, the floor on which the mosaic was laid measures about 9.25 m from north to south by 5.14 m (at the north), 5.23 m (at the south); see Stella G. Miller, "A Mosaic Floor from a Roman Villa at Anaploga," *Hesperia* 41 (1972): 333. These are the dimensions represented on the plan in fig. 1 and reproduced by Murphy-O'Connor. The smaller dimensions

were "very typical," based on a comparison with another Roman villa from Corinth and with other houses from Pompeii, Olynthus, and Ephesus.[5] The average floor area for an atrium in these houses is 74 square meters, the average for a triclinium 37 square meters, according to Murphy-O'Connor's calculations. However, he continues: "Not all of this area was usable. The effective space in the triclinium was limited by the couches around the walls; the rooms surveyed would not have accommodated more than nine diners (the usual number . . .) who reclined as they ate."[6]

Imagining a house of such proportions to be the home of Gaius, and suggesting a plausible "base figure" of around forty to fifty persons "for the Christian community at Corinth"—a figure derived from the number of named individuals plus their likely spouses and household adherents—Murphy-O'Connor considers what might have happened when "the whole church" (1 Cor 14:23) gathered together with Gaius as host (Rom 16:23):[7]

> The mere fact that all the believers could not be accommodated in the triclinium meant that there had to be an overflow into the atrium. It became imperative for the host to divide his guests into two categories: the first class believers were invited into the triclinium while the rest stayed outside. Even a slight knowledge of human nature indicates the criterion used. The host must have been a wealthy member of the community, so he invited into the triclinium his closest friends among the believers, who would have been of the same social class and from whom he might expect the same courtesy on a future occasion. The rest could take their places in the atrium, where conditions were greatly inferior.[8]

given by Murphy-O'Connor represent the size of the room in its earlier phase, on which see further below and fig. 2.

5. Murphy-O'Connor, *St. Paul's Corinth*, 178–80. The other Roman villa from Corinth is the villa excavated by T. L. Shear (and sometimes known as the Shear villa); see T. L. Shear, *Corinth V: The Roman Villa* (Cambridge: Harvard University Press, 1930).

6. Murphy-O'Connor, *St. Paul's Corinth*, 180. Cf. further Katherine M. D. Dunbabin, "Triclinium and Stibadium," in *Dining in a Classical Context*, ed. W. J. Slater (Ann Arbor: University of Michigan Press, 1991), 121–48; she refers to "the conventional number of nine guests" but notes also developments and changes from this convention (127). Simon P. Ellis, *Roman Housing* (London: Duckworth, 2000), 148, suggests that up to seven diners could be accommodated on the three couches of a triclinium, while the semicircular stibadium, introduced by the first century CE, might take five to seven diners.

7. Murphy-O'Connor, *St. Paul's Corinth*, 182.

8. Murphy-O'Connor, *St. Paul's Corinth*, 183.

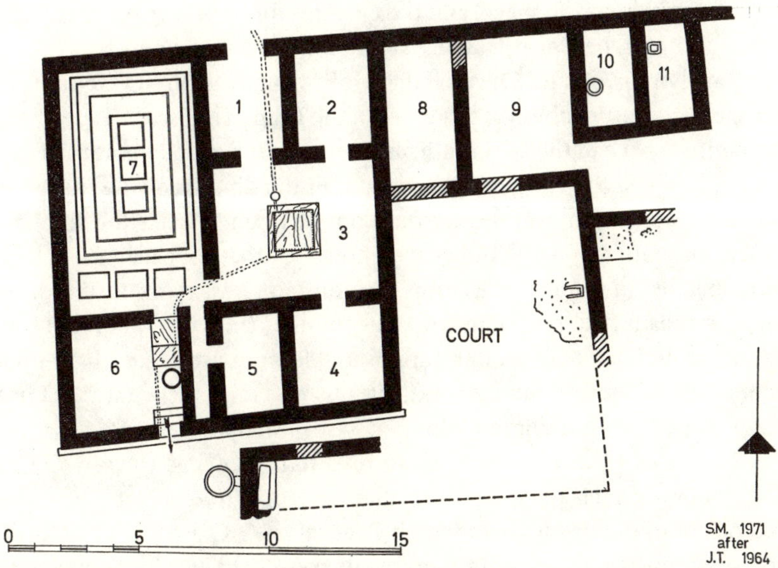

Figure 1: Plan of the Anaploga Villa. Taken from Miller, "A Mosaic Floor from a Roman Villa at Anaploga," 335, reproduced here with permission and by courtesy of the artists: S. G. Miller and J. Travlos, American School of Classical Studies at Athens, Corinth Excavations. (The same plan is presented by Murphy-O'Connor, *St. Paul's Corinth*, 179, though with the labels "triclinium" and "atrium" added to rooms 7 and 3, respectively.)

The nature of the domestic space available made such discrimination inevitable, and so constitutes "one possible source of the tensions that appear in Paul's account."[9]

Peter Lampe reiterates Murphy-O'Connor's point, particularly in relation to the situation created by the different arrival times of various members of the congregation, with the socially lower members having less control over their time and thus being more likely to arrive later. "When those of lower social position arrived only later to the Corinthian assembly, and then found no available places in the triclinium, but only in the atrium and peristyle, so in this trait too a pre-baptismal habit was reflected: socially lower clients were greeted and dismissed by the patron in the atrium."[10] Again, the

9. Murphy-O'Connor, *St. Paul's Corinth*, 184.

10. Peter Lampe, "Das korinthische Herrenmahl im Schnittpunkt hellenistisch-römischer Mahlpraxis und paulinischer Theologia Crucis (1 Kor 11, 17–34)," *ZNW* 82 (1991): 201: "Wenn die sozial niedriger Stehenden erst später zur korinthischen Versammlung eintrafen und dann nicht mehr im Triclinium, sondern nur noch in Atrium und Peristyl Platz finden, so spiegelt sich auch in diesem Zug ein vorbaptismaler Habitus: Sozial niedriger

nature of the domestic space, and the customs for its use, are seen as partial explanations of the Corinthian divisions at the Lord's Supper.

Carolyn Osiek and David Balch, following Murphy-O'Connor and Lampe, also see the physical structure of the Roman house, and specifically the limited space in the triclinium, as a cause of the problems at the Lord's Supper.[11] When the latecomers arrived, "all the dining couches in the triclinium would be in use; there would not be enough space for the whole congregation to recline."[12] They stress, however, that the existence of larger "dining halls" in some houses, plus the common peristyle courtyards and gardens, means that much larger overall numbers (into the hundreds) could be accommodated than is often supposed: "It is unwise to set a hard upper limit of 30 to 40 for the number of Christians who might celebrate the Lord's Supper in a Roman triclinium plus peristyle or in open gardens."[13]

A number of recent commentators, often following Murphy-O'Connor, adopt a similar perspective in their attempts to elucidate the nature and origin of the divisions to which Paul refers (1 Cor 11:18–22). Gordon Fee, assuming that the Corinthian meals were held "in the homes of the rich," where the host therefore also served as "the patron of the meal," reports that "archaeology has shown rather conclusively that the dining room (the triclinium) in such homes would scarcely accommodate many guests; the majority would therefore eat in the atrium . . . which would still seat only about 30 to 50 guests on the average." Fee refers in a note to the average size of triclinia as "about 36 square meters," providing space "for about 9 to 12 guests at table," assuming they reclined, and cites (only) Murphy-O'Connor in support.[14] Similar comments are made by Richard Hays and Raymond Collins.[15] Anthony Thiselton speaks in glowing

---

stehende Klienten wurden vom Patron im Atrium empfangen und abgefertigt." Cf. also 197 with n43, referring to Murphy-O'Connor.

11. Carolyn Osiek and David L. Balch, *Families in the New Testament World: Households and House Churches* (Louisville: Westminster John Knox, 1997), 200–203.

12. Osiek and Balch, *Families*, 201.

13. Osiek and Balch, *Families*, 203.

14. Gordon D. Fee, *The First Epistle to the Corinthians*, NICNT (Grand Rapids: Eerdmans, 1987), 533–34n10.

15. Richard B. Hays, *First Corinthians*, IBC (Louisville: Westminster John Knox, 1997), 196; Raymond F. Collins, *First Corinthians*, SP 7 (Collegeville, MN: Liturgical Press, 1999), 418–19. Cf. also Ben Witherington, *Conflict and Community in Corinth: A Socio-Rhetorical Commentary on 1 and 2 Corinthians* (Grand Rapids: Eerdmans, 1995), 249n24, also 191–95. Recent commentaries in German, however, make little reference to this hypothesis, focusing rather on the customs concerning eating that may also have affected the character of the meal.

terms of the new insights that have been made possible by this historical reconstruction:

> These verses [sc. 1 Cor 11:20–21] offer a classic and well-known example of how historical and archaeological research can shed a flood of light on the meaning of a biblical text which would not otherwise have been available. Initially with Theissen but then most clearly with Jerome Murphy-O'Connor's application of James Wiseman's archaeological work, a foundation has been laid which has transformed exegesis since the early 1980s.[16]

Thiselton identifies two aspects of this research, the focus on "cultural customs of distinction," as pioneered by Gerd Theissen,[17] and the focus on "issues of space within a large Roman villa," as presented by Murphy-O'Connor.[18] His own presentation of the latter aspect follows Murphy-O'Connor closely.[19]

Critical Questions

There are, however, a number of reasons to question whether this reconstruction offers a typical or even plausible domestic setting for the Corinthian Lord's Supper. First, there are questions about the Corinthian evidence, especially about Murphy-O'Connor's key example, the villa at

---

See, e.g., Wolfgang Schrage, *Der erste Brief an die Korinther (1 Kor 11,17–14,40)*, EKKNT 7.3 (Zurich: Benziger; Neukirchen-Vluyn: Neukirchener Verlag, 1999), 22–28; Andreas Lindemann, *Der erste Korintherbrief*, HNT 9.1 (Tübingen: Mohr Siebeck, 2000), 248–53. Christian Wolff, *Der erste Brief des Paulus an die Korinther*, 2nd ed., THKNT (Leipzig: Evangelische Verlagsanstalt, 2000), 261n109, notes Murphy-O'Connor's suggestion with regard to "einer räumlichen Trennung—die Wohlhabenden speisten im Triclinium, die Späterkommenden im Atrium des Hauses"—but concentrates his attention on the nature of the meal itself and the social customs that may have led to the divisions, following Theissen and others.

16. Anthony C. Thiselton, *The First Epistle to the Corinthians*, NIGTC (Grand Rapids: Eerdmans, 2000), 860.

17. Gerd Theissen, "Soziale Integration und sakramentales Handeln: Eine Analyse von 1 Cor. XI 17–34," *NovT* 16 (1974): 179–206; ET: "Social Integration and Sacramental Activity: An Analysis of 1 Cor. 11:17–34," in Gerd Theissen, *The Social Setting of Pauline Christianity: Essays on Corinth*, ed. and trans. John H. Schütz (Edinburgh: T&T Clark, 1982), 145–74.

18. Thiselton, *First Epistle*, 860.

19. Thiselton, *First Epistle*, 860–61.

Anaploga. The bedding and fill underneath the mosaic date from the third quarter of the first century, as Murphy-O'Connor notes, but this provides only an archaeological *terminus post quem* for the floor.[20] (Thiselton is simply inaccurate when he refers to "the villa dated between AD 50 and 75 at Anaploga."[21]) The mosaic itself was dated by Stella Miller to the last quarter of the first century; but more recent scholarship has inclined to a somewhat later estimate, perhaps as late as the third century CE.[22] The villa existed prior to laying of the mosaic floor, the latter being added during a second phase of construction that involved shifting a wall (fig. 2).[23] But this being so, it is, of course, much more difficult to say anything about the patterns of use for the room in Paul's time, prior to its adaptation and mosaic flooring, especially since the villa has not been fully excavated or published.[24] Indeed, while Murphy-O'Connor simply describes the room as the triclinium, Miller (to whom Murphy-O'Connor refers) notes only as a "suggestion" the idea that dining may have been its function, referring to the room as possibly the *andron*.[25] Given that this room is the largest in the villa (as far as the partial excavations reveal), it is indeed likely that it served as the main reception room; but that does not mean that it functioned as a Roman-style triclinium, nor that other rooms were not also used for dining. Furthermore, the

20. Miller, "Mosaic Floor," 332; James Wiseman, "Corinth and Rome I: 228 B.C.–A.D. 267," *ANRW* 7.1:528.

21. Thiselton, *First Epistle*, 860.

22. Miller, "Mosaic Floor," 332. G. Hellenkemper Salies, "Römische Mosaiken im Griechenland," *BJ* 186 (1986): 241–84, argues strongly for a third-century date on the basis of style: "Aus dem späten 1. oder dem frühen 2. Jahrhundert dagegen läßt sich dem Mosaik von Anaploga nichts Vergleichbares an die Seite stellen. . . . Es kann somit kein Zweifel bestehen, daß das Mosaik von Anaploga in die Gruppe der reich ornamentierten, sehr bunten Böden des 3. Jahrhunderts gehört, für deren Komposition und Ornamentik Parallelen zu hellenistischen Mosaiken charakteristisch sind" (278–79). Katherine M. D. Dunbabin, *Mosaics of the Greek and Roman World* (Cambridge: Cambridge University Press, 1999), 210n6, suggests that "a late first to early second century date" remains "more convincing," though the second-century parallels she cites come not from Greece but from Pergamon. I am grateful to Mary Hoskins Walbank for drawing my attention to this point.

23. See Miller, "Mosaic Floor," 332.

24. Wiseman, "Corinth and Rome," 528; Richard M. Rothaus, *Corinth: The First City of Greece*, RGRW 139 (Leiden: Brill, 2000), 28.

25. Miller, "Mosaic Floor," 333n8: "Mr. John Travlos, who drew the plans of the villa, suggested that Room 7 served as a dining room. Since standard-sized couches do not fit evenly end-to-end around the room, one must assume some less regular arrangement if the room is designated as the andron." The *andron* was the main reception room in the traditional Greek house (see Ellis, *Roman Housing*, 24).

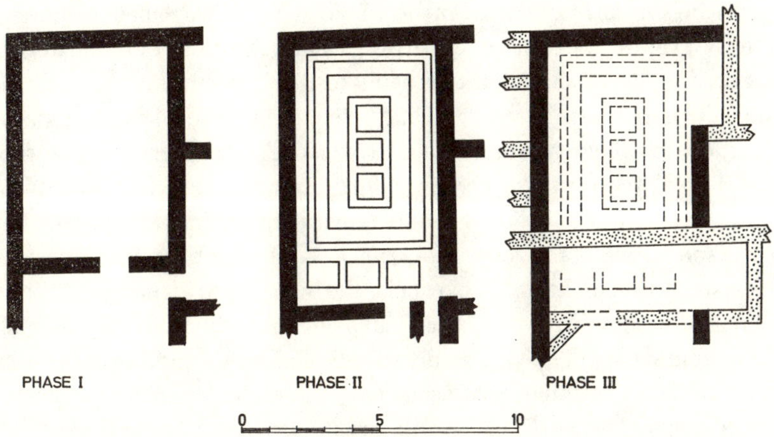

Figure 2: Anaploga Villa, plan of room 7, phases I, II, and III. From Miller, "A Mosaic Floor from a Roman Villa at Anaploga," 337, reproduced here with permission and by courtesy of the American School of Classical Studies at Athens, Corinth Excavations.

villa at Anaploga may have lain outside the city walls in Roman times and quite probably functioned as a working farmhouse belonging to a wealthy landowner.[26] Nor do any of the other houses of the Roman period (partially) excavated at Corinth yield evidence for the period of Paul's visits to the city.[27]

This cautionary note should be linked to a second point, of a more methodological kind. Penelope Allison forcefully criticizes the common approach in studies of Roman domestic space that involves deriving from the "literary sources . . . nomenclature for the individual spaces" and then applying this nomenclature to the material contexts, "creating the fallacious perception that

26. Cf. Mary E. Hoskins Walbank, "The Nature and Development of Roman Corinth from 44 BCE to the end of the Antonine Period" (PhD diss., Open University, 1986), 323; Hoskins Walbank, "The Foundation and Planning of Early Roman Corinth," *JRA* 10 (1997): 95–130; Daniel P. Tompkins, review of D. Engels, *Roman Corinth, Bryn Mawr Classical Review* 1 (1990): 30. More generally on villas as working farms, see Ellis, *Roman Housing*, 13–14.

27. Wiseman, "Corinth and Rome," 528, mentions four excavated houses of the period he surveys (228 BCE–267 CE) (followed by Murphy-O'Connor, *St. Paul's Corinth*, 178): in addition to the villa at Anaploga, the one attached to Temple E is of uncertain function, being possibly connected with the cult of that temple; the Roman/Shear villa dates from the second century; and the house located against the east wall of the South Basilica along the road to Cenchreae is still later (Wiseman estimates c. 200 CE). For discussion of a fifth- to sixth-century CE house on the Lechaion Road, see Robert L. Scranton, *Corinth XVI: Mediaeval Architecture in the Central Area of Corinth* (Princeton: ASCSA, 1957), 17–21.

such labels are an integral part of the primary data."[28] This labeling, moreover, often serves as "the point of departure for investigations of the material remains."[29] Allison is sharply critical of this tendency, noting that "it is extremely subjective to interpret the domestic behavior in these villas through room functions for which there is no material evidence."[30] In other words, we should not simply presume that a certain room must function as the triclinium, and function as depicted in literary sources, without material evidence that indicates something of the room's functions, which may have been several and diverse. Allison mentions in particular the difficulty in identifying rooms for dining, echoing and developing a point made earlier by Katherine Dunbabin. Dunbabin writes that "secure identification of rooms for dining is possible only under exceptional circumstances. . . . In the great luxury villas we can usually only guess at the range and variety of rooms used for dining."[31] The implications of this point should be clear: so far as the archaeological evidence is concerned, we cannot with any confidence presume that the mosaic room at Anaploga functioned as a triclinium, and certainly not for Paul's time.

None of this renders Murphy-O'Connor's imaginative scenario impossible, of course, but there is a further reason to question its plausibility, related to his depiction of the findings as concerning "a typical house."[32] Both of the Corinthian houses to which Murphy-O'Connor refers in ascertaining dimensions of a typical triclinium—the villa at Anaploga and the Roman (Shear) villa—are, he suggests, "sumptuous" villas, their quality indicated not least by the marvellous mosaic floors found within them.[33] Similarly, the

28. Penelope M. Allison, "Using the Material and Written Sources: Turn of the Millennium Approaches to Roman Domestic Space," *AJA* 105 (2001): 185.

29. Allison, "Material and Written Sources," 185.

30. Allison, "Material and Written Sources," 189. Cf. also J. T. Smith, *Roman Villas: A Study in Social Structure* (London: Routledge, 1997), 6, who refers to the problems of "text-hindered archaeology."

31. Katherine M. D. Dunbabin, "Convivial Space: Dining and Entertainment in the Roman Villa," *JRA* 9 (1996): 67–68. There is some contrast here with the opening comments in her study of "Triclinium and Stibadium," where she refers to "numerous securely identifiable examples" of rooms clearly intended for dining (121); the essay offers a survey of the patterns and developments. Nonetheless, the point holds that in particular cases, such as the Corinthian villa at Anaploga, we should not presume, following certain literary depictions, that a certain room, and that room only, functioned as the dining room according to set custom without relevant material evidence.

32. Murphy-O'Connor, *St. Paul's Corinth*, 178.

33. Murphy-O'Connor, *St. Paul's Corinth*, 178; cf. Wiseman, "Corinth and Rome," 528. For the Roman villa, see Shear, *Corinth V: The Roman Villa*.

houses considered from Pompeii, Olynthus, and Ephesus are all, on Murphy-O'Connor's own view, upper-class homes belonging to the wealthy.[34] They are thus unlikely to be "typical," at least insofar as typical is taken to refer to the kind of dwellings in which the majority of the population might have lived.[35] Whether it is plausible, then, to imagine the first Christians at Corinth meeting in such a house depends to a considerable extent on judgments concerning their socioeconomic status. Indeed, in order to imagine such a setting as the one in which Gaius hosted the church, Murphy-O'Connor adopts the necessary corollary: that Gaius was "a wealthy member of the Christian community."[36]

Until recently, views on the social level of the first Christians had reached a fair degree of consensus, the so-called new consensus reported by Abraham Malherbe in 1977.[37] (The description of a new consensus replacing an old one is, however, simplistic and in some respects inaccurate.[38]) This "consensus" view was that the early Christian groups, and specifically those in Corinth,[39] encompassed a greater degree of social diversity than had previously been acknowledged, with some members coming from the ranks of the well-to-do.[40] There were, nonetheless, significant differences of opin-

34. Murphy-O'Connor, *St. Paul's Corinth*, 180.

35. Ellis, for example, treats villas as aristocratic, elite housing (*Roman Housing*, 22–72, 73, 112). Cf. the comment of Beryl Rawson, "'The Roman Family' in Recent Research: State of the Question," *BibInt* 11 (2003): 124: "I envisage the great majority of the population in Rome, and perhaps other major towns and cities, living in small, cramped apartments which had little space for more than the conjugal family and a small number of slaves."

36. Murphy-O'Connor, *St. Paul's Corinth*, 182; cf. 183 (quoted above).

37. Abraham J. Malherbe, *Social Aspects of Early Christianity*, 2nd ed. (Philadelphia: Fortress, 1983), 31.

38. Cf. Gerd Theissen, "The Social Structure of Pauline Communities: Some Critical Remarks on Justin J. Meggitt, *Paul, Poverty, and Survival*," *JSNT* 84 (2001): 66: "The 'new consensus' is neither new nor is it a consensus." For further questioning of the contrasts depicted between old and new consensus see Steven J. Friesen, "Poverty in Pauline Studies: Beyond the So-Called New Consensus," *JSNT* 26 (2004): 323–61.

39. Corinth provides the most substantial early evidence, as pointed out by Georg Schöllgen, "Was wissen wir über die Sozialstruktur der Paulinischen Gemeinden?," *NTS* 34 (1988): 71–82.

40. See further David G. Horrell, *The Social Ethos of the Corinthian Correspondence: Interests and Ideology from 1 Corinthians to 1 Clement*, SNTW (Edinburgh: T&T Clark, 1996), 91–101; Bengt Holmberg, *Sociology and the New Testament: An Appraisal* (Minneapolis: Fortress, 1990), 21–70. Especially influential on this new consensus are Gerd Theissen, "Soziale Schichtung in der korinthischen Gemeinde: Ein Beitrag zur Soziologie des hellenistischen Urchristentums," *ZNW* 65 (1974): 232–72 (ET: "Social Stratification in the Corinthian Com-

ion concerning whether these higher status members of the church should be seen as elite, "ruling class" persons, "from the upper stratum,"[41] or only as relatively better-off but not elite or upper class.[42] This "new consensus" received a major challenge with the publication in 1998 of Justin Meggitt's *Paul, Poverty, and Survival*, in which Meggitt argues that the evidence used to identify named Corinthian Christians as members of the wealthy elite cannot sustain this conclusion, and that Paul and the early Christians shared the absolute poverty that was the fate of the vast majority of the population of the Roman Empire, a conclusion also supported in Steven Friesen's recent work.[43] Following the publication of Meggitt's book there has been renewed discussion, with Dale Martin and Gerd Theissen defending a new consensus position against Meggitt's critique.[44]

Space does not permit a detailed engagement with that debate here, but a few key points of particular relevance may be outlined.[45] First, in defense of the new consensus, I think that Meggitt has downplayed the extent and significance of socioeconomic diversity among the so-called non-elite and thus among the early Christians at Corinth. Meggitt's prime concern is to argue

---

munity: A Contribution to the Sociology of Early Christianity," in *Social Setting*, 69–119); and Wayne A. Meeks, *The First Urban Christians: The Social World of the Apostle Paul* (New Haven: Yale University Press, 1983), 51–73.

41. Theissen, "Soziale Schichtung," 232 ("aus der Oberschicht"); cf. Theissen, *Social Setting*, 69: "from the upper classes"; Andrew D. Clarke, *Secular and Christian Leadership in Corinth: A Socio-Historical and Exegetical Study of 1 Corinthians 1–6*, AGJU 18 (Leiden: Brill, 1993), 130 ("some members from the Corinthian social élite . . . the ruling class of the city"; cf. also 45, 59, 88); David W. J. Gill, "In Search of the Social Elite in the Corinthian Church," *TynBul* 44 (1993): 323–37.

42. E.g., Horrell, *Social Ethos*, 98; Dale B. Martin, *The Corinthian Body* (New Haven: Yale University Press, 1995), xv–xvii. Meeks, *First Urban Christians*, 73, comments, "The extreme top and bottom of the Greco-Roman social scale are missing," but the churches contain "a fair cross-section of urban society." Note Clarke's disagreement with Meeks's assessment that the extreme top of the scale is missing (*Leadership in Corinth*, 45).

43. Justin J. Meggitt, *Paul, Poverty, and Survival*, SNTW (Edinburgh: T&T Clark, 1998), 153, 179, passim; Friesen, "Poverty."

44. Dale B. Martin, "Review Essay: Justin J. Meggitt, *Paul, Poverty, and Survival*," *JSNT* 84 (2001): 51–64; Theissen, "Social Structure of Pauline Communities"; Theissen, "Social Conflicts in the Corinthian Community: Further Remarks on J. J. Meggitt, *Paul, Poverty, and Survival*," *JSNT* 25 (2003): 371–91. For further discussion, see also Bengt Holmberg, "The Methods of Historical Reconstruction in the Scholarly 'Recovery' of Corinthian Christianity," in *Christianity at Corinth: The Quest for the Pauline Church*, ed. Edward Adams and David G. Horrell (Louisville: Westminster John Knox, 2004), 255–71; Friesen, "Poverty."

45. For relevant extracts, bibliography, etc., see further Adams and Horrell, eds., *Christianity at Corinth*.

for the economic and absolute poverty of all of the members of the Pauline churches, and the vast majority of the empire's population, in a clear polemic against the new consensus view, and this leads, as Meggitt acknowledges, to a focus on this broad context rather than on the possible levels of social differentiation.[46] Bengt Holmberg may also be right to speak of a "pauperistic" tendency in Meggitt's reading of the evidence;[47] in other words, evidence that might indicate some level of higher social or economic status on the part of Paul or other early Christians is downplayed or rejected as uncertain,[48] while evidence to support the view of their absolute poverty is maximized.[49] It may be, then, that rather than reject the "new consensus" altogether, a somewhat revised, more cautious form of it may emerge as most plausible. However, it also seems to me that Meggitt has forcefully highlighted how little *firm* evidence there is to identify any of the Corinthian Christians known to us as elite, wealthy, aristocratic, or upper class.[50] Certainly, mention of someone's

46. Meggitt, *Paul*, 5: "Of course, there were significant differences between members of this group [sc. the poor] and these would have appeared important to the poor themselves. Some would have lived more precarious lives than others. . . . But in order to emphasise the reality of the economic predicament that was shared by *all* members of this group, it is important that this term is used without lengthy qualifications, wherever applicable." Sometimes, therefore, despite his polemic against the new consensus, Meggitt qualifies his criticisms of it, noting that he is focusing on economic and not social differentiation; cf. 99n118, 153–54n417.

47. Holmberg, "Methods of Historical Reconstruction," 270.

48. Cf. also Martin's criticism of Meggitt for raising "the bar for historical evidence to heights impossible for normal historiography" ("Review Essay," 62).

49. Sometimes this tendency is also evident in Meggitt's concern to show that practices commonly claimed to demonstrate elite or upper-class status need not do so. For example, arguing against Theissen's view that a reference to travel (e.g., in the case of Phoebe) indicates high status, Meggitt cites the example of "Flavius Zeuxis, a Hierapolis merchant, who sailed seventy-two times to Italy [and] did not leave a very prestigious monument behind him. . . . His personal fortune could not have been great" (Meggitt, *Paul*, 149n393). Yet this evidence at least suggests that Flavius Zeuxis was not destitute, nor consistently living at subsistence level, thus implying a greater degree of economic (as well as social) distinction within the empire's population than Meggitt seems to allow.

50. In terms of what might be firm evidence, Erastus is a key figure for the view that there were upper-class members of the Corinthian church. If the Christian Erastus of Rom 16:23 is rightly identified with the Erastus who laid the theater pavement in return for being elected *aedile* (as argued, e.g., by Theissen, *Social Setting*, 75–83; Clarke, *Leadership in Corinth*, 46–56), then we clearly have a wealthy and elite individual within the church's membership. For the Erastus inscription, see J. H. Kent, *Corinth VIII.3: The Inscriptions 1926–1950* (Princeton: ASCSA, 1966), 99–100 §232. Here too, however, Meggitt has shown that the evidence for this identification is hardly indisputable, not least due to problems in dating the inscription (Justin J. Meggitt, "The Social Status of Erastus [Rom 16:23]," *NovT*

οἶκος or οἰκία is an insufficient basis for such a conclusion.[51] And all we know about Gaius, after all, apart from his name and his baptism by Paul (1 Cor 1:14), is that he served as host not only to Paul but also to "the whole church" (Rom 16:23). Such hospitality hardly requires that he owned a villa like the one at Anaploga or that he belonged to the upper stratum of Corinthian society.[52] The crucial point in the context of the present argument is that it is at the very least uncertain whether any of the Corinthian Christians, and their "host" Gaius in particular, would likely have owned a large, sumptuous villa.[53]

Imagining New Contexts: The Buildings East of the Theater

There is, then, considerable uncertainty concerning the scenario which Murphy-O'Connor depicts. First, the archaeological evidence is much less clear than he implies, and does not allow us to be confident about the character and use of dining rooms in the villa at Anaploga nor elsewhere in Corinth at the time of Paul. Second, we can hardly be confident that such a villa is a plausible context in which to imagine the Corinthian Christians meeting. Furthermore, given that even proponents of the new consensus consider the lower classes to have comprised the majority in the congregations,[54] we

38 [1996]: 218–23). Even if the identification is judged on balance probable, there is no hint that the Corinthians ever met in Erastus's home. See also pp. 55–56, below.

51. *Pace* Gill, "In Search of the Social Elite," 336: "There is a hint that Stephanas is a member of the élite as his household is mentioned." The words οἶκος and οἰκία, largely overlapping terms by NT times (cf. 1 Cor 1:16; 16:15), are used to refer to a wide range of dwellings (houses, rooms, apartments, etc.) and household groups, so do not by any means imply a house(hold) of elite proportions (cf. LSJ, 1203–5; O. Michel, *TDNT*, 5:119–34). If Fortunatus and Achaicus are dependent members of Stephanas's household (cf. 1 Cor 16:15–18), then certainly Stephanas is a householder with a social position higher than that of his slaves or dependents. But there is no indication that this is a particularly large or wealthy household.

52. Probably the most likely scenario is that "the whole church" refers to the (occasional) gathering together of smaller household groups, which may indeed imply that Gaius had a larger space available than other members of the congregations. But it is a big jump from this inference to the supposition that he was a wealthy aristocrat who owned a large country villa.

53. Notably, while Meeks (*First Urban Christians*, 57) thinks (on the basis of rather slender evidence) that Gaius "is evidently a man of some wealth," he also considers that "we meet no landed aristocrats" among the Pauline Christians (73). That would seem to suggest that Gaius's ownership of something like the villa at Anaploga is unlikely. On villas as working farms belonging to aristocrats, see nn. 26 and 35 above.

54. Cf., e.g., Theissen, *Social Setting*, 69. Meeks, *First Urban Christians*, 73, suggests that "the 'typical' Christian . . . is a free artisan or small trader."

would do well to try and describe some of the domestic contexts in which it is realistic to imagine such groups meeting.[55] Indeed, Murphy-O'Connor provides just such a consideration in his treatment of the workshop as a setting for mission and church meetings.[56]

Unfortunately, despite the major and long-established excavations at Corinth, very little is known about the character of many of the residential areas of Roman Corinth, since excavations have been largely concentrated around the forum area, on the sanctuaries of Demeter and Kore and of Asclepius, on a small number of selected villas, and on other significant structures in and outside the city. There are also both pragmatic and ideological considerations why knowledge of poorer-quality housing is limited: in practical terms it is simply the case that the poorer the accommodation, the less enduring are the materials with which it is constructed and so the less likely is its record to remain; in ideological terms, there is an understandable tendency in archaeology to concentrate on impressive and major structures, particularly those of religio-political significance.[57] As Ramsay MacMullen observes, "no one has sought fame through the excavation of a slum."[58] The rather recent rise of interest in domestic space is, however, beginning to lead to some significant correction of this comparative neglect.[59]

Some general information may nonetheless be gleaned.[60] Corinth was laid out as a Roman city after its refounding in 44 BCE following the Roman grid-plan known as centuriation.[61] This divided the majority of the city into

55. Cf. Justin J. Meggitt, "Response to Martin and Theissen," *JSNT* 24 (2001): 93, who in querying the supposition that the Christians at Corinth must have met in a "larger-than-'average' private house" suggests: "We may need to engage our imagination a little more when we try to envisage the meetings of the early Christians."

56. Murphy-O'Connor, *St. Paul's Corinth*, 192–98. Alternative settings for Christian meetings have also been explored by Robert Jewett, "Tenement Churches and Communal Meals in the Early Church: The Implications of a Form-Critical Analysis of 2 Thessalonians 3:10," *BR* 38 (1993): 23–43.

57. Cf. Meggitt, *Paul*, 62.

58. Ramsay MacMullen, *Roman Social Relations 50 BC to AD 284* (New Haven: Yale University Press, 1974), 93, quoted by Meggitt, *Paul*, 62.

59. See, e.g., Ray Laurence and Andrew Wallace-Hadrill, eds., *Domestic Space in the Roman World: Pompeii and Beyond*, JRASup 22 (Portsmouth, RI: Journal of Roman Archaeology, 1997); Ian M. Barton, ed., *Roman Domestic Buildings* (Exeter: University of Exeter Press, 1996); Ellis, *Roman Housing*.

60. See esp. Hoskins Walbank, "Nature and Development," 294–389; more briefly, Dirk Jongkind, "Corinth in the First Century AD: The Search for Another Class," *TynBul* 52 (2001): 139–48.

61. David Gillman Romano, "Post-146 B.C. Land Use in Corinth, and Planning of the

insulae,[62] though it should be noted that there is no archaeological evidence in Corinth for the existence of *insulae* in the sense of multistoried blocks of five or more stories, such as are known from Rome, Ostia, and Herculaneum.[63] Indeed, the high-rise developments elsewhere may often be explained by particular pressures of population expansion and space restrictions that are less applicable to Corinth. Outside the city there is some evidence for poorer accommodation, such as two-room peasant houses[64] and the makeshift quarry workers' accommodation at Cenchreae.[65] Within the city, shops and workshops are an important and relevant form of domestic as well as commercial space, since they often provided accommodation for those who worked in them, along with their families, in a back room, loft, or mezzanine floor, or sometimes even in the workshop itself.[66] These, as Murphy-O'Connor notes with reference to the shop units in the North Market, close to the Forum, provided less sumptuous accommodation and the potential for meetings too, though given their size (on average around 3 x 4 meters) only relatively small numbers could be assembled (Murphy-O'Connor estimates ten to fifteen).[67]

More specific and detailed possibilities may be derived from the excavations east of the theater, which took place over successive seasons through the 1980s. Here, primarily due to their proximity to the theater, the Corinth archaeologists, under the direction of Charles K. Williams, unearthed a series of buildings running along the east side of the Roman street known by the archaeologists as East Theater Street. The buildings are referred to by numbers: 1, 3, 5, and 7 (see figs. 3–7). The history of these buildings is complex, with evidence of damage, alteration, and habitation leading Williams and Zervos to distinguish eight phases, the first of which was later subdivided.[68] Despite

---

Roman Colony of 44 B.C.," in *The Corinthia in the Roman Period*, ed. Timothy E. Gregory, JRASup 8 (Ann Arbor: Journal of Roman Archaeology, 1993), 9–30; Hoskins Walbank, "Foundation and Planning."

62. Using the term here to refer to rectangular blocks of land in the city created by the grid plan layout and not to the blocks of accommodation also known as *insulae*; cf., e.g., Romano, "Post-146 B.C. Land Use," 19–20.

63. See further M. Wheeler, *Roman Art and Architecture* (London: Thames & Hudson; New York: Praeger, 1964), 129–32; Barton, *Roman Domestic Buildings*.

64. Hoskins Walbank, "Nature and Development," 315.

65. Robert L. Scranton, "The Upper Town," in *Kenchreai: Eastern Port of Corinth*, ed. Robert L. Scranton, J. W. Shaw, and Leila Ibrahim (Leiden: Brill, 1978), 8.

66. Cf. Ellis, *Roman Housing*, 78–80.

67. Murphy-O'Connor, *St. Paul's Corinth*, 194–96.

68. Charles K. Williams and O. H. Zervos, "Corinth, 1987: South of Temple E and East of the Theater," *Hesperia* 57 (1988): 95–146.

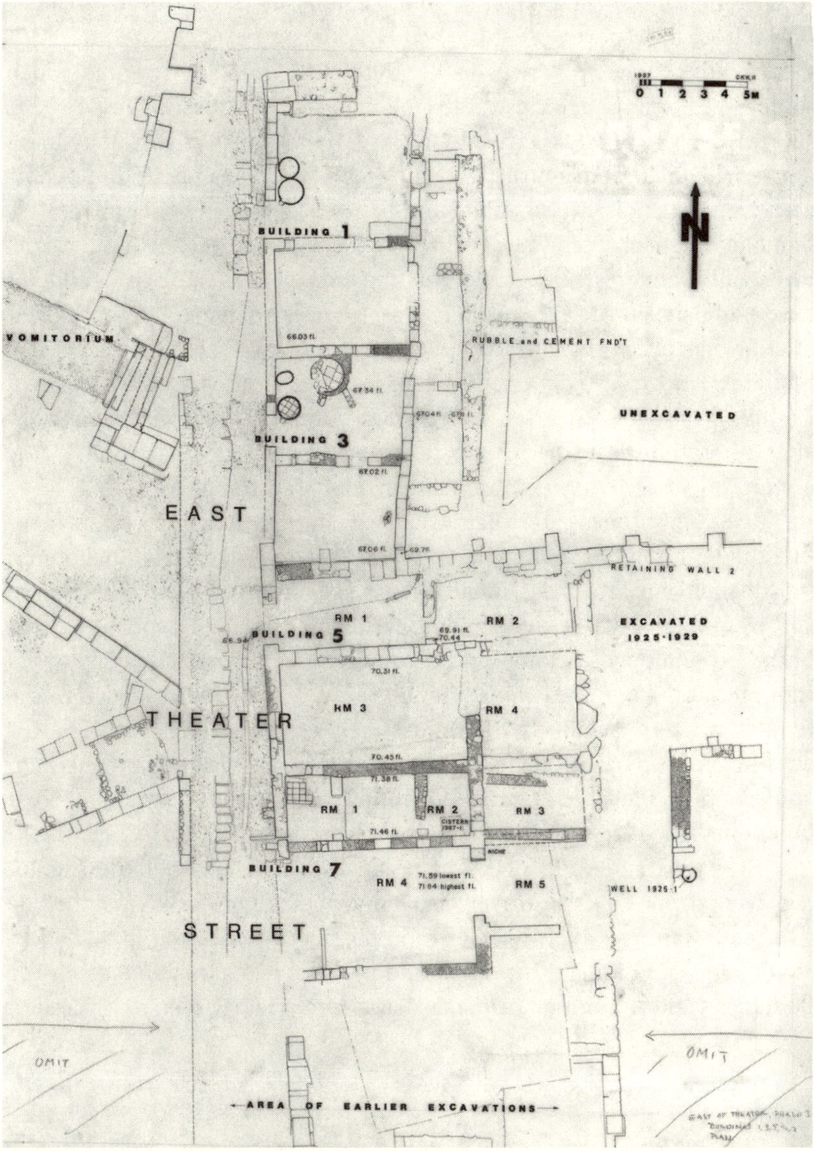

Figure 3: Plan of buildings 1, 3, 5, 7, east of the theater. From Williams and Zervos, "Corinth, 1987: South of Temple E and East of the Theater," 121, reproduced with permission and by courtesy of the artist: Charles K. Williams II, American School of Classical Studies at Athens, Corinth Excavations.

this complex history, a number of points significant for our purposes can be drawn from the reports.

Buildings 1 and 3 were probably built early in the first century, then somewhat altered and reconstructed following the earthquake in the 70s CE. Buildings 5 and 7 (7 being treated in the earlier reports as part of building 5) probably date from a little later, "probably the Flavian period," possibly earlier, though no earlier than the mid-first century CE.[69] While all of these buildings might profitably be considered, due to their earlier date and particular points of interest, I shall focus on numbers 1 and 3. These two buildings have a similar plan. The ground floor of each consists of two rooms, the northern of which in each case has a number of ovens—two in building 1, three in building 3. As well as a doorway, each has a window onto East Theater Street (building 1 also has a window facing north). Probably following alterations after the earthquake in the 70s, smaller rooms at the back of each unit, on the eastern side, were created, most likely windowless storage rooms.[70]

Because of the greater than usual size and number of ovens in these buildings, and because of the large quantities of discarded animal bones, mostly skulls and lower legs, found piled in the southwest room of building 3 and around the ovens in that building, Williams and Zervos concluded that both were equipped for some kind of commercial use. One possibility is that they were *tabernae* or *popinae*, though the lack of drinking vessels in the remains makes this unlikely. They most likely served as some kind of butchery kitchens, preparing and selling cooked meats to visitors to the theater and others resident in the neighborhood.[71] The windows onto the street functioned as counters, "to allow one to sell prepared foods to passers-by."[72]

The nature and extent of the materials that had fallen when these buildings were damaged or destroyed also led Williams and Zervos to conclude that there was most likely a second and possibly a third story in each case, "with families residing on the upper floor or floors."[73] The same applies to buildings 5 and 7.[74] These stories may have been original, then repaired after

69. Charles K. Williams and O. H. Zervos, "Corinth, 1985: East of the Theater," *Hesperia* 55 (1986): 153.

70. Williams and Zervos, "Corinth, 1985," 132; Williams and Zervos, "Corinth, 1987," 122.

71. See Williams and Zervos, "Corinth, 1985," 146–48.

72. Williams and Zervos, "Corinth, 1985," 131.

73. Williams and Zervos, "Corinth, 1985," 148; cf. 134, 139–42, 147–48. But see p. 66, below, with n. 82.

74. Charles K. Williams and O. H. Zervos, "Corinth, 1988: East of the Theater," *Hesperia* 58 (1989): 7.

Figure 4: Looking north down East Theater Street, with buildings 7, 5, 3, 1 on the righthand side of the street. Photo © David Horrell.

Figure 5: Looking south up East Theater Street, with the buildings to the left. Photo © David Horrell.

Figure 6: Building 3 viewed from the south, with the ovens clearly visible. Photo © David Horrell.

Figure 7: Building 3 from the northeast. Photo © David Horrell.

the earthquake of the 70s CE, or possibly were added at this point in time. Nothing detailed has emerged about the structure or layout of the residential accommodation that seems to have existed on the upper floors of these buildings, though based on the evidence of fallen frescoes found in 1984, "at least one upper floor of building 3 must have had rooms decorated with a quite presentable fresco programme," probably one large room and at least one other room.[75] The available floor area in each building, assuming similar dimensions to the ground floor, would have been approximately 10 x 5 meters in each case (building 1 is actually somewhat larger than building 3, but only by a meter or so).

Despite this lack of detail, the information about buildings 1 and 3 does give us some insight into one kind of domestic space in first-century Corinth, a kind of space rather different from that of the "sumptuous" villas described by Murphy-O'Connor. How might this information then help us to reflect on the possible contexts of early Christian meetings?

It is important first to stress two caveats. One is that there is of course no suggestion that Christians ever met in any of the buildings east of the theater, any more than in the villa at Anaploga. Indeed, if we discount the Erastus inscription, which in any case has no Christian content itself, there is as yet no direct archaeological evidence for Christianity in Corinth until around and after the fourth century.[76] Our knowledge is severely limited, and requires the use of disciplined imagination to apply it to early Christianity. The second caveat is that the buildings on East Theater Street are not to be thought of as "typical" of domestic accommodation in first-century

75. Williams and Zervos, "Corinth, 1985," 140. On the wall paintings in building 3, see Laura M. Gadbery, "Roman Wall-Painting at Corinth: New Evidence from East of the Theater," in *Corinthia in the Roman Period*, ed. Gregory, 47–64. Buildings 5 and 7 (more than 1 and 3) resemble the kind of apartment housing described, for example, by Ellis (*Roman Housing*, 73–78), though there is no corridor evident in the Corinth plans here.

76. For overviews of this evidence, see Scranton, *Corinth XVI*, 6–26; Rothaus, *Corinth*, 93–104; Peter Richardson, "Judaism and Christianity in Corinth after Paul: Texts and Material Evidence," in *Pauline Conversations in Context: Essays in Honor of Calvin J. Roetzel*, ed. Janice C. Anderson, Philip Sellew, and Claudia Setzer, JSNTSup 221 (Sheffield: Sheffield Academic Press, 2002), 61–65. The tomb of Bishop Eustathios, found in the (probably) sixth-century cemetery basilica (the Kodratos/Quadratus basilica, may also be a piece of somewhat earlier evidence. For a description, see G. Daux, "Chronique des fouilles et découvertes archéologiques en Grèce en 1961," *Bulletin de correspondance hellénique* 86 (1962): 695–704; more briefly, James Wiseman, *The Land of the Ancient Corinthians* (Göteborg: Åströms, 1978), 85–86 with nn. 46–48; Rothaus, *Corinth*, 97–98. I am grateful to Mary Hoskins Walbank for drawing my attention to this point.

Corinth.[77] The buildings clearly had a quite specialized purpose, next to the theater, which determines the character and use of the ground floor space. Furthermore, the considerable variety of possible types of domestic space—from country villas to peasant homes, smart town apartments to rooms behind or over a shop, not to mention the more ramshackle and temporary dwellings of the destitute—means that we should be wary of labeling any specific form as "typical."

By way of more constructive conclusions, we may begin by noting that the buildings east of the theater add some specifically Corinthian evidence to Meggitt's argument that the non-elite regularly encountered meat in "decidedly unsacral" settings.[78] Meggitt's discussion is focused on the issue of "meat consumption in Corinth," disputing Theissen's reconstruction of the background to 1 Cor 8–10,[79] but most of his evidence is drawn from Roman sources generally, or relates to Rome itself rather than Corinth. The evidence from buildings 1 and 3 hardly enables us to say how regularly the non-elite of Corinth purchased cooked meat, but given that the theater could seat very large numbers—Wiseman estimates a capacity of "about 14,000 persons"[80]—we can certainly say that the clientele of East Theater Street were not only the well-to-do or the social elite.

The discoveries of East Theater Street also enable us, using our "disciplined imagination," to go some way towards picturing one kind of domestic space in which Christians could have met, the kind of space that might well have been occupied by small traders and business folk, not too different in social level, perhaps, from artisans like Prisca and Aquila, and Paul himself. Such people were not from the lowest social strata; they may have owned one or two slaves and may have had the ability to afford some "luxuries," as the wall paintings in building 3 indicate—so this alternative scenario does not by any means presume that such a domestic setting implies a host who is poor in the sense of living at or around subsistence level.[81] Just as the

77. Cf. also Jongkind, "Corinth in the First Century AD."

78. Justin J. Meggitt, "Meat Consumption and Social Conflict in Corinth," *JTS* 45 (1994): 138. The location of these buildings directly opposite an exit (*vomitorium*) from the theater suggests that they were well placed to capture a large market of potential customers (see fig. 3).

79. Theissen, *Social Setting*, 121–43.

80. Wiseman, "Corinth and Rome," 487.

81. Cf. Jongkind, "Corinth in the First Century AD," 147. On the wall paintings see Gadbery, "Roman Wall-Painting at Corinth." A. J. Brothers comments, for example, that apartments in *insulae* were by no means always for the poor, and that the poorer residents tended to be on the upper floors where accommodation was of lower (and less enduring)

artisans Prisca and Aquila hosted meetings of the ἐκκλησία in their home, presumably in the room(s) above or behind their workshop,[82] so too the butchers of East Theater Street (or whoever occupied the upper floor[s]) could have hosted meetings in the upstairs room(s).[83] In a fairly large upper room, or rooms, equipped perhaps with some tables and benches, it would by no means be impossible to cram in fifty or so people, though this would probably be pretty crowded.[84] Knowing virtually nothing about the shape or size of the rooms makes it impossible to posit an architectural explanation for the σχίσματα that arose in the Christian meetings at Corinth, in contrast to Murphy-O'Connor's attractively neat hypothesis based on the nine available places in the triclinium. But just as Allison warns against unwarranted assumptions and oversimplifications that create the impression that we are more well-informed than we are about Roman domestic life,[85] so too, as Meggitt has recently argued, NT scholars may need to learn to infer less from certain sources, to abandon detailed yet ultimately implausible reconstructions, and to acknowledge how little we know about so many aspects of ancient life, particularly for the non-elite.[86] There are, as we have seen, a good many reasons to doubt the validity of Murphy-O'Connor's Corinthian reconstructions, given the extent of the available evidence.

Picturing the first Christians in Corinth meeting in an upper-story room in East Theater Street is, of course, entirely imaginative, though no more so (and probably a good deal less so) than imagining them meeting in the villa at Anaploga. Though vague and unspecific, and yielding no particular insight

quality ("Urban Housing," in *Roman Domestic Buildings*, ed. Ian M. Barton [Exeter: University of Exeter Press, 1996], 54).

82. Cf. Murphy-O'Connor, *St. Paul's Corinth*, 192–98; 1 Cor 16:19; cf. Acts 18:2–3; Rom 16:3.

83. Given the possibilities for multiple occupation of buildings, and for inhabitants of different social levels to occupy different accommodation units within a building, we should not simply presume that those who conducted their business on the ground floor were the (sole) occupants of the whole building, though this seems likely in the case of buildings 1 and 3, given the lack of external staircases, corridors, etc. I am grateful to Michael White for drawing these possibilities to my attention.

84. Osiek and Balch reckon "one half-square meter per person and an equal half square meter for furniture" etc. (*Families*, 201), referring to work by Jay Dozier on the numbers that could dine in various rooms and gardens (201–2). The roughly 50 sq m that we have to reckon with in this instance could thus accommodate fifty diners, on their figures.

85. Allison, "Material and Written Sources," 188.

86. Justin J. Meggitt, "Sources: Use, Abuse, Neglect. The Importance of Ancient Popular Culture," in *Christianity at Corinth: The Quest for the Pauline Church*, ed. Edward Adams and David G. Horrell (Louisville: Westminster John Knox, 2004), 241–53.

into how the divisions at the Lord's Supper were related to the domestic space in which the Christians met, the East Theater Street scenario does at least fit rather well with an unusually precise piece of information given to us by Luke.[87] Describing what was perhaps a rather crowded meeting in Troas (maybe even a meeting of "the whole church" there?), in an upper-story room (ὑπερῷον), with people sitting on the window ledges, Luke ensures the eternal fame of Eutychus by recording the soporific effect of Paul's lengthy discourse upon him: "Overcome by sleep, he fell to the ground three floors below [ἀπὸ τοῦ τριστέγου] and was picked up dead" (Acts 20:9).[88]

Conclusions

There are, as we have seen, good reasons to doubt the plausibility of the imaginative reconstruction of the Corinthian Lord's Supper presented by Murphy-O'Connor; the extent to which this scenario has been presumed and reinforced in recent commentaries makes a critical reassessment all the more important. Certainly, NT studies should pay more attention to the varieties of domestic space in the urban setting of Corinth and other cities of the Roman Empire, and consider these as possible settings for early Christian meetings. The East Theater Street scenario is also imaginative, but for a number of reasons constitutes a more plausible, if less detailed, reconstructed setting: it represents one form of urban accommodation that existed during the time of Paul's visits to Corinth, a type likely to have been occupied by non-elite, though not the most impoverished, urban residents, and it fits well with the setting Luke depicts in Acts 20:9. Of course, this is only one plausible type of setting among a range of possibilities, but on a number of counts it is worth considering seriously, even though it means confessing that we are—and are likely to remain—unable to ascertain any architectural explanation for the Corinthian σχίσματα.

87. Questions about Luke's sources or accuracy concerning the historicity of this point are largely irrelevant: what is important is the indication that Luke—not averse to depicting Christianity spreading among the well-to-do (e.g., Acts 17:4, 12)—depicts a Christian meeting happening in such a setting, which was presumably therefore plausible, even "typical," for him.

88. On τρίστεγον (the neuter substantive from τρίστεγος), "the third story of a building," i.e., the second above ground level, see BDAG, 1016. For the use of τρίστεγος in the papyri of the first century CE and later, specifically in the phrase "οἰκίας τριστέγου," "of a three-storeyed house," see J. H. Moulton and G. Milligan, *The Vocabulary of the Greek Testament Illustrated from the Papyri and Other Non-Literary Sources* (1930; repr., Peabody, MA: Hendrickson, 2004), 642.

Chapter 3

Farewell to Another Wealthy Patron?

Reassessing Philemon in the Light of Recent Scholarly Discussion of Socioeconomic Level and Domestic Space

Introduction

The letter to Philemon has often been treated as if it were rather "useless" in studies of Pauline theology, since it appears to lack directly theological material and significant doctrinal reflection. While this judgment may be open to question,[1] it is at least clear that the letter became much more "useful" when the focus of scholarly attention shifted to the social aspects of earliest Christianity, with the development of what may broadly be labeled social-scientific criticism:[2] "once useless, now useful."[3] While Philemon's significance for discussions of early Christian attitudes to slavery has long

1. See, e.g., Michael Wolter, "The Letter to Philemon as Ethical Counterpart of Paul's Doctrine of Justification," in *Philemon in Perspective: Interpreting a Pauline Letter*, ed. D. Francois Tolmie, BZNW 169 (Berlin: de Gruyter, 2010), 169–79, who seeks to rectify the neglect, arguing that there are significant points of contact between Philemon and Paul's other letters, not least with regard to its "theological substructure" and Paul's doctrine of justification.

2. Under this broad label I intend to include both "sociohistorical" and "social-scientific" perspectives, which have sometimes been posed as competing alternatives. See further David G. Horrell, "Social Sciences Studying Formative Christian Phenomena: A Creative Movement," in *Handbook of Early Christianity: Social Science Approaches*, ed. Anthony J. Blasi, Jean Duhaime, and Paul-André Turcotte (Walnut Creek, CA: Alta Mira, 2002), 3–28; David G. Horrell, "Whither Social-Scientific Approaches to New Testament Interpretation? Reflections on Contested Methodologies and the Future," in *After the First Urban Christians: The Social-Scientific Study of Pauline Christianity Twenty-Five Years Later*, ed. Todd D. Still and David G. Horrell (London: T&T Clark, 2009), 6–20.

3. I owe this particular use of the letter's play on the name of Onesimus to John White, who wrote an essay during his MA at Exeter on the treatment of Philemon in social-scientific scholarship under the title, "Once Useless, Now Useful."

been recognized—and this important theme continues to be a focus for a good many contemporary studies—the revival of interest in the social character of the earliest Christian communities[4] has given Philemon new and considerable significance.[5] In the following essay, I shall offer an overview of two interrelated areas of recent scholarly discussion, seeking to show how Philemon both contributes to, and is differently construed by, changing perspectives. The two areas in question concern the socioeconomic level of the earliest Christians and their meeting places.

Socioeconomic Level: The New Consensus and Beyond

The modern phase of social-scientific criticism began in the early 1970s, through two particular developments.[6] One was the formation in 1973 of a Society of Biblical Literature group devoted to studying the social world of early Christianity. The second was a series of pioneering essays by Gerd Theissen, published in the early 1970s, on both the Jesus movement and the Pauline churches at Corinth, that decisively shaped much subsequent work.[7] One of those early essays was concerned with social stratification in the Corinthian community.[8]

4. For reasons discussed in ch. 1 above, I am inclined to avoid the label "Pauline church/community," since it too easily gives the impression that there were ideologically and geographically distinct "Pauline" churches, when the NT evidence suggests that Paul's competitors and rivals interacted with precisely the same groups. The label remains useful insofar as it functions as a "shorthand for those communities which were founded or addressed by Paul, together with those represented in later documents which appeal to the Pauline heritage" (John M. G. Barclay, *Pauline Churches and Diaspora Jews*, WUNT 275 [Tübingen: Mohr Siebeck, 2011], 9n18). In the case of Philemon, there is no direct evidence that Philemon and the assembly that meets in his house relate to any leader other than Paul; but the silence should not necessarily be taken as decisive.

5. As is clear, for example, in the groundbreaking study of Norman R. Petersen, *Rediscovering Paul: Philemon and the Sociology of Paul's Narrative World* (Philadelphia: Fortress, 1985). It is interesting that N. T. Wright's recent magnum opus begins with a lengthy discussion of Philemon: N. T. Wright, *Paul and the Faithfulness of God*, Christian Origins and the Question of God, 2 vols. (Minneapolis: Fortress, 2013), 1:3–36.

6. For an overview of the history, see Horrell, "Social Sciences."

7. The essays were initially collected in Gerd Theissen, *Studien zur Soziologie des Urchristentums*, 3rd ed., WUNT 19 (Tübingen: Mohr Siebeck, 1988).

8. Gerd Theissen, "Soziale Schichtung in der korinthischen Gemeinde: Ein Beitrag zur Soziologie des hellenistischen Urchristentums," *ZNW* 65 (1974): 232–72; cited from the ET in Gerd Theissen, *The Social Setting of Pauline Christianity: Essays on Corinth*, ed. and trans. John H. Schütz (Edinburgh: T&T Clark, 1982), 69–119.

Theissen's point of departure was the contrasting assessments of Adolf Deissmann and Edwin Judge. While Deissmann, according to Theissen, regarded earliest Christianity "as a movement within the lower strata,"[9] Judge, in a work that helped to stimulate the revival of interest in sociohistorical questions,[10] argued that the early Christians, at least at Corinth, may rather have come from among the wealthier and higher status members of society.[11] Through a detailed study of both groups and individuals in the Corinthian correspondence, Theissen concluded by agreeing, in a sense, with both Deissmann and Judge: "Both opinions are probably correct, because . . . the Corinthian congregation is marked by internal stratification. The majority of the members, who come from the lower classes [*aus den unteren Schichten*], stand in contrast to a few influential members who come from the upper classes [*aus der Oberschicht*]."[12] Theissen used four criteria—"statements about holding office, about 'houses,' about assistance rendered to the congregation, and about travel"—to determine the likelihood of someone's being of high social status.[13]

Theissen's study was fundamental in laying the groundwork for what came to be known as the "new consensus," perceived—not entirely accurately—as a contrast with a so-called old consensus associated with Deissmann's view that the early Christians were poor.[14] First to note the appar-

9. Theissen, *Social Setting*, 69. See, e.g., G. Adolf Deissmann, *Light from the Ancient East* (London: Hodder & Stoughton, 1910), 142. However, as Steven Friesen points out, Deissmann elsewhere sees a cross-section of social strata within the earliest Christian communities (Steven J. Friesen, "Poverty in Pauline Studies: Beyond the So-called New Consensus," *JSNT* 26 [2004]: 325). For example: "The people whose souls were moved by the mission of Paul and his faithful companions were—the overwhelming majority at least—men and women from the middle and lower classes. . . . On the other hand, Paul mentions by name certain fairly well-to-do Christians" (G. Adolf Deissmann, *Paul: A Study in Social and Religious History*, 2nd ed. [London: Hodder & Stoughton, 1926], 241, 243).

10. Note Theissen's remark on this book in *Social Reality and the Early Christians: Theology, Ethics, and the World of the New Testament*, trans. Margaret Kohl (Edinburgh: T&T Clark, 1993), 19n23: "This little book deserves a place of honor in the history of modern sociological exegesis."

11. Theissen, *Social Setting*, 69. In explicit contrast to Deissmann's view, Judge comments, "Far from being a socially depressed group . . . if the Corinthians are at all typical, the Christians were dominated by a socially pretentious section of the population of the big cities" (Edwin A. Judge, *The Social Pattern of Early Christian Groups in the First Century: Some Prolegomena to the Study of the New Testament Ideas of Social Obligation* [London: Tyndale, 1960], 60).

12. Theissen, *Social Setting*, 69; German from Theissen, *Studien*, 231. It is important to note the word *Schicht* (stratum), in contrast to "class."

13. Theissen, *Social Setting*, 73.

14. In both cases, talk of a consensus exaggerates the degree of unanimity and also

ently "emerging consensus" was Abraham Malherbe, in his *Social Aspects of Early Christianity*, published in 1977.[15] Theissen's perspective was influentially developed and extended by Wayne Meeks, in a chapter on "the social level of the Pauline Christians" in his book *The First Urban Christians*, a landmark in the study of the social world of Paul and the early Christians.[16] Meeks explicitly affirmed the emerging consensus reported by Malherbe, offering the summary claim that "a Pauline congregation generally reflected a fair cross-section of urban society."[17] In particular, this new consensus established the view that some of the named Christians in the Pauline letters could and should be regarded as "wealthy," "upper-class," high-status figures, whose patronage and hospitality were crucial to the success of the early Christian movement.[18]

Unsurprisingly, Philemon is among the figures referred to in such terms. For Meeks, Philemon "ranks high at least on the dimension of wealth," having "a house large enough to accommodate a meeting of Christians" and owning probably several slaves.[19] James D. G. Dunn is still more confident: "What we can deduce about him [sc. Philemon] is straightforward: . . . He was well-to-do. He had a house large enough to host the church in the city where he lived (v. 2) and to provide a guest room (probably more than one . . . v. 22). He was a slaveowner and we must assume owner of several

---

overlooks the degree of similarity between views expressed in both "old" and "new" consensus: as we have seen (n. 9 above), Deissmann's view is rather similar to that of Theissen and Meeks, regarding the cross-section of urban society included in the earliest churches. Note the comments of Friesen, "Poverty," 325, who stresses the similar perspectives of "old" and "new" viewpoints; and Gerd Theissen, "The Social Structure of Pauline Communities: Some Critical Remarks on J. J. Meggitt, *Paul, Poverty, and Survival*," *JSNT* 84 (2001): 66, who questions whether there was either an "old" or a "new" consensus.

15. Abraham J. Malherbe, *Social Aspects of Early Christianity*, 2nd ed. (Philadelphia: Fortress, 1983), 31.

16. Wayne A. Meeks, *The First Urban Christians: The Social World of the Apostle Paul* (New Haven: Yale University Press, 1983), 51–73; reprinted in David G. Horrell, ed., *Social-Scientific Approaches to New Testament Interpretation* (Edinburgh: T&T Clark, 1999), 195–232. For discussion of the developments since Meeks's book, see Todd D. Still and David G. Horrell, eds., *After the First Urban Christians: The Social-Scientific Study of Pauline Christianity Twenty-Five Years Later* (London: T&T Clark, 2009).

17. Meeks, *First Urban Christians*, 73.

18. Such a perspective is developed, e.g., in John K. Chow, *Patronage and Power: A Study of Social Networks in Corinth*, JSNTSup 75 (Sheffield: JSOT Press, 1992); Andrew D. Clarke, *Secular and Christian Leadership in Corinth: A Socio-Historical and Exegetical Study of 1 Corinthians 1–6*, AGJU 18 (Leiden: Brill, 1993).

19. Meeks, *First Urban Christians*, 60.

slaves. . . . He was probably a successful businessman." He may be described as "wealthy."[20] Other commentators express similar views.[21] Even when the descriptions are more cautious—as in Peter Arzt-Grabner's comment that "Philemon was wealthy enough, and his residence large enough, to accommodate the local Christian community when they held meetings"[22]—the terms are such as to suggest that Philemon may in some sense be ranked among the relatively "wealthy."[23]

Leaving Philemon aside for one moment, one may at least observe that the severe limitations of our evidence should undoubtedly have led to rather less far-reaching claims about the standing of certain early Christian figures. For example, Anthony Thiselton describes Chloe as "a wealthy Asian woman,"[24] a "businesswoman" who has sent her "middle managers to

20. James D. G. Dunn, *The Epistles to the Colossians and to Philemon*, NIGTC (Grand Rapids: Eerdmans, 1996), 300–301.

21. E.g., Michael Wolter, *Der Brief an die Kolosser. Der Brief an Philemon*, ÖTK 12 (Gütersloh: Gütersloher Verlagshaus; Würzburg: Echter, 1993), 227–28: "wir dürfen ihn [sc. Philemon] uns als recht wohlhabend vorstellen"; Joseph A. Fitzmyer, *The Letter to Philemon*, AB 34C (New York: Doubleday, 2000), 12; R. McL. Wilson, *A Critical and Exegetical Commentary on Colossians and Philemon*, ICC (London: T&T Clark, 2005), 365; Roger W. Gehring, *House Church and Mission: The Importance of Household Structures in Early Christianity* (Peabody, MA: Hendrickson, 2004), 154. Slightly more cautious is Klaus Wengst, *Der Brief an Philemon*, THKNT (Stuttgart: Kohlhammer, 2005), 30: "relativ wohlhabend."

22. Peter Arzt-Grabner, "How to Deal with Onesimus? Paul's Solution within the Frame of Ancient Legal and Documentary Sources," in *Philemon in Perspective*, ed. Tolmie, 119. Cf. Peter Arzt-Grabner, *Philemon*, PKNT 1 (Göttingen: Vandenhoeck & Ruprecht, 2003), 82; Peter Stuhlmacher, *Der Brief an Philemon*, 2nd ed., EKKNT 18 (Düsseldorf: Benziger; Neukirchen-Vluyn: Neukirchener Verlag, 1981), 71.

23. Markus Barth and Helmut Blanke, *The Letter to Philemon: A New Translation with Notes and Commentary*, Eerdmans Critical Commentary (Grand Rapids: Eerdmans, 2000), 137, give a somewhat more cautious depiction, though with broadly similar content: "Philemon . . . was a successful middle-class citizen, owner of a house large enough to host a house church and to have, in addition, at least one guest room available for a visitor. Also he owned, whether for work in his business or household, or as a status symbol, at least one slave." In a footnote (137n65) they remark: "Enthusiasm for class-struggle terminology might count the slave-owner Philemon among the 'bourgeoisie.' . . . But if Philemon had been very rich . . . he would rather have lived in Hierapolis, Laodicea, or farther west or east in an industry and trade center such as Ephesus or Apamea, than in the insignificant town of Colossae. Also he would hardly have had the opportunity for the close brotherly relation to Onesimus for which Paul is calling."

24. Anthony C. Thiselton, *The First Epistle to the Corinthians*, NIGTC (Grand Rapids: Eerdmans, 2000), 121.

Corinth," a city "humming with wealth."[25] Yet the sum total of our knowledge about Chloe is the three Greek words in 1 Cor 1:11: ὑπὸ τῶν Χλόης. Gaius, Erastus, Phoebe, and Philemon are among those often depicted in broadly comparable terms but about whom we have extremely limited information.

Indeed, the claims of the new consensus were strongly attacked in Justin Meggitt's 1998 monograph *Paul, Poverty, and Survival*. Meggitt sharply questions much of the evidence used to support the view that some of the early Christians were high-status, wealthy figures, and argues instead that they all shared in the poverty that 99 percent of the empire's population experienced.[26] Although Meggitt's overly binary depiction of a 1 percent elite and a 99 percent poor has rightly been criticized,[27] his questioning of the evidential basis for the new consensus view and his insistence that the majority of the early Christians endured lives not far above subsistence level seem persuasive.

Indeed, a broadly similar perspective, but with a more nuanced approach to the description of socioeconomic position, was presented by Steven Friesen in 2004. Friesen outlines a "poverty scale" for Roman urban society with seven categories ranging from the super-wealthy imperial elites (PS1) to those below subsistence level (PS7).[28] Friesen concurs with Meggitt that there is little if any evidence to place any of the Pauline Christians into the category of the wealthy elite (PS1–3), and that the vast majority of the empire's inhabitants, and of the early Christians, were poor, living around or not much above subsistence level (PS4–7).[29] Subsequent work has continued to refine the economic taxonomy,[30] but the general picture remains

25. Anthony C. Thiselton, *First Corinthians: A Shorter Exegetical and Pastoral Commentary* (Grand Rapids: Eerdmans, 2006), 6–7.

26. Justin J. Meggitt, *Paul, Poverty, and Survival*, SNTW (Edinburgh: T&T Clark, 1998).

27. See Dale B. Martin, "Review Essay: Justin J. Meggitt, *Paul, Poverty, and Survival*," *JSNT* 84 (2001): 54–57; Theissen, "Social Structure of Pauline Communities," 70–75; Friesen, "Poverty," 339; Bengt Holmberg, "The Methods of Historical Reconstruction in the Scholarly 'Recovery' of Corinthian Christianity," in *Christianity at Corinth: The Quest for the Pauline Church*, ed. Edward Adams and David G. Horrell (Louisville: Westminster John Knox, 2004), 261–66; Bruce W. Longenecker, "Exposing the Economic Middle: A Revised Economy Scale for the Study of Early Urban Christianity," *JSNT* 31 (2009): 243–78.

28. Friesen, "Poverty."

29. Friesen, "Poverty," 348.

30. See esp. Walter Scheidel and Steven J. Friesen, "The Size of the Economy and the Distribution of Income in the Roman Empire," *JRS* 99 (2009): 61–91, esp. 82–85; Bruce W. Longenecker, *Remember the Poor: Paul, Poverty, and the Greco-Roman World* (Grand

essentially similar: imperial, regional, and municipal elites constituted only around 1.5 to 2 percent of the population; middling groups, with a "moderate surplus," may have comprised around 6 to 15 percent of the population;[31] and the large majority of the population (c. 80 percent+) lived more or less at subsistence level.

As John Barclay has pointed out, this challenge to the new consensus has perhaps ended up in some respects not so very far away from it: there is broad agreement that the early Christian assemblies encompassed people from a range of socioeconomic levels; we simply lack the data to be more precise about numbers and relative wealth/poverty.[32] Meeks's assessment that the first urban Christians represented "a fair cross-section of urban society" is in general terms still convincing. Nonetheless, it is important to give due attention to the shift in language and perception: under the influence of the new consensus established by Theissen and Meeks, it became common to talk of certain early Christians as wealthy, upper class, high status, or elite.[33] The work of Meggitt, Friesen, and Bruce Longenecker should make us very wary of describing any of the early Christians in such elevated terms and much more conscious that the vast majority of people lived around or not far above subsistence level. Even Erastus (Rom 16:23), once hailed on the basis of inscriptional evidence as just such an elite figure,[34] may well have been a lower-level functionary, a public slave: recent work on the archaeological and inscriptional evidence has shown that the

---

Rapids: Eerdmans, 2010), 44–53. For further overview and discussion, see David G. Horrell, *Becoming Christian: Essays on 1 Peter and the Making of Christian Identity*, LNTS/Early Christianity in Context 394 (London: Bloomsbury T&T Clark, 2013), 100–102, 105–10.

31. Scheidel and Friesen estimate 6–12 percent for middling groups, whose income is between 2.4 and 10 times above bare subsistence, while Longenecker estimates about 15 percent in urban areas, where Scheidel and Friesen suggest they may have been more common. See previous note for references.

32. John M. G. Barclay, "Poverty in Pauline Studies: A Response to Steven Friesen," *JSNT* 26 (2004): 365. This is also broadly similar to the perspective articulated by Deissmann long ago; see n. 9, above.

33. In addition to those already cited, such terms are employed, e.g., by Clarke, *Leadership in Corinth*, 45, 59, 88, 130; David W. J. Gill, "In Search of the Social Elite in the Corinthian Church," *TynBul* 44 (1993): 323–37; Bruce W. Winter, *After Paul Left Corinth: The Influence of Secular Ethics and Social Change* (Grand Rapids: Eerdmans, 2001), 108–20.

34. Theissen, *Social Setting*, 75–83, followed, with some differences, by many subsequent studies, including Clarke, *Leadership in Corinth*, 46–56. In my own early work, I cautiously accepted that the identification of the Erastus of the inscription and Paul's Erastus was likely. See David G. Horrell, *The Social Ethos of the Corinthian Correspondence: Interests and Ideology from 1 Corinthians to 1 Clement*, SNTW (Edinburgh: T&T Clark, 1996), 97–98.

likelihood of Paul's Erastus being the aedile of Corinth who laid the pavement beside the theater is slim.[35]

Debate continues, however, about the likely socioeconomic implications of Erastus's status as οἰκονόμος τῆς πόλεως, though this looks likely to remain uncertain: John Goodrich, who argues for οἰκονόμος as equivalent to *quaestor*, and thus for Erastus as a person of considerable wealth and power, candidly notes that "significant data exist for reading the title οἰκονόμος τῆς πόλεως as either a servile position or a magistracy."[36] With the possible exception of Erastus, then, the cross-section of urban dwellers included in an early Christian assembly is unlikely to have included any elite or wealthy members from the top few percent of the economic scale (though this does not imply that they were illiterate or "ungebildet").[37]

How then, in the light of this discussion, should we assess the evidence about Philemon? Three pieces of evidence from the letter are relevant: Philemon's ownership of at least one slave (vv. 10–16), his οἶκος (v. 2), and his (assumed) ability to provide ξενία for Paul (v. 22). As already indicated above, commentators find in these references the basis for depicting Philemon as a person of wealth. Each item may be assessed in turn.

35. An early challenge to the identification was made by Justin J. Meggitt, "The Social Status of Erastus (Rom 16:23)," *NovT* 38 (1996): 218–23. More recently, on the basis of the archaeological evidence, including the field notebooks from the original excavations, Friesen has shown that the identification is highly unlikely: Steven J. Friesen, "The Wrong Erastus: Ideology, Archaeology, and Exegesis," in *Corinth in Context: Comparative Studies on Religion and Society*, ed. Steven J. Friesen, Daniel N. Schowalter, and James C. Walters, NovTSup 134 (Leiden: Brill, 2010), 231–56.

36. John K. Goodrich, "Erastus, *Quaestor* of Corinth: The Administrative Rank of ὁ οἰκονόμος τῆς πόλεως (Rom 16:23) in an Achaean Colony," *NTS* 56 (2010): 95. For the further debate, see Alexander Weiss, "Keine Quästoren in Korinth: Zu Goodrichs (und Theißens) These über das Amt des Erastos (Röm 16:23)," *NTS* 56 (2010): 576–81; John K. Goodrich, "Erastus of Corinth (Romans 16:23): Responding to Recent Proposals on His Rank, Status, and Faith," *NTS* 57 (2011): 583–93.

37. I do not therefore see this conclusion as standing in any significant tension with Udo Schnelle's recent argument for the earliest Christian communities as "Orte der Bildung," as evidenced particularly in their literary productivity. As Schnelle notes, "Bildung" was not confined to the highest socioeconomic levels, and levels of (at least elementary) literacy may have been significantly higher than sometimes estimated (Schnelle proposes 30–50 percent for "elementare Schreib- und Lesekenntnisse"). Schnelle sees Paul, for example, as a member of the "Mittelschicht," though his essay proceeds without any engagement with the recent energetic English-language discussion of socioeconomic level, reviewed above. See Udo Schnelle, "Das frühe Christentum und die Bildung," *NTS* 61 (2015): 113–43.

1. It is often assumed that "Philemon was the owner of a number of slaves."[38] According to Dunn, "had Onesimus been his only slave that would surely have been reflected in some way in what Paul says."[39] However, all that is clear from the letter—though even this has been (implausibly) questioned[40]—is that Philemon owned one slave.[41] Whether he had more is unknown.[42] That Paul describes Onesimus as previously ἄχρηστον (v. 11) need not imply that Philemon had other slaves, such that this particular one could be dismissed as unimportant and useless. More likely, not least given Onesimus's name itself—meaning "useful," and commonly used for slaves[43]—Paul's play on the contrasting perspectives, ποτε . . . ἄχρηστον νυνί . . . εὔχρηστον, refers to the breach in relationship between owner and slave and the positive change that the slave's conversion (v. 10) has made possible.[44] It is not impossible that Philemon did own many slaves, but it is equally plausible—and perhaps more likely—that he owned only one or two, which would by no means place him among the wealthy elite. Arzt-Grabner, for example, cites evidence from census declarations in Roman Egypt that shows that in urban areas around 21 percent of households declared slaves

38. Wilson, *Colossians and Philemon*, 365.

39. Dunn, *Colossians and Philemon*, 300.

40. By, e.g., Allen Dwight Callahan, *Embassy of Onesimus: The Letter of Paul to Philemon*, New Testament in Context (Valley Forge, PA: Trinity Press International, 1997), who revives an argument originally proposed by antebellum abolitionists, that Onesimus was not Philemon's slave but his actual physical brother. See further D. Francois Tolmie, "Tendencies in the Research on the Letter to Philemon Since 1980," in *Philemon in Perspective*, ed. Tolmie, 5; and, for criticisms, e.g., Fitzmyer, *Philemon*, 18–19; Arzt-Grabner, *Philemon*, 84–85.

41. So, rightly, Barth and Blanke, *Philemon*, 137 ("at least one slave").

42. That Paul requests Philemon to release Onesimus to assist Paul does not prove the contrary, though the implications of releasing his only slave would of course have been considerable: we cannot assume that only relatively undemanding requests were made.

43. See, e.g., Fitzmyer, *Philemon*, 107; Arzt-Grabner, *Philemon*, 86–87, who describes the name as "ein typischer Sklavenname, der auch unter den stadtrömischen Sklavennamen reich belegt ist" (86).

44. Cf. Fitzmyer, *Philemon*, 108–9. Rather than seeing Onesimus as a runaway, it seems more likely that he had left Philemon due to his owner perceiving himself to have been wronged in some way by his slave (Peter Lampe suggests that this might be something like Onesimus breaking something). Onesimus turned to Paul to mediate in the dispute and intercede for him. Cf. Peter Lampe, "Affects and Emotions in the Rhetoric of Paul's Letter to Philemon: A Rhetorical-Psychological Interpretation," in *Philemon in Perspective*, ed. Tolmie, 62–65. Influential in the rejection of the previously dominant "runaway" hypothesis is Peter Lampe, "Keine 'Sklavenflucht' des Onesimus," *ZNW* 76 (1985): 135–37. For an overview of discussion and other proposals, see Tolmie, "Research," 2–6.

(compared with 12 percent in villages, giving an overall figure of 16 percent). More crucially, around 60 percent of slaveholding households had only one or two slaves, and few households had more than six or seven.[45] Since Egypt is the only area for which such detailed census reports exist, it is difficult to determine how far this picture of the distribution of slave ownership is indicative for the empire as a whole. Walter Scheidel suggests that, overall, slaves may have comprised between 7 and 13 percent of the empire's total population, with a relatively small number of elite and wealthy persons owning very large numbers, and many more modest households owning just a few.[46] As Meggitt notes, "not only artisans, but soldiers, peasants, and even other slaves, owned slaves," and recovering an exposed infant was one relatively cheap way to acquire a slave, who could later be sold, potentially at a profit.[47] The most likely scenario, other indications notwithstanding, is therefore that Philemon owned one or two slaves, or perhaps a handful at most; this would place him in the top 20 percent or so of society, most likely among the middling groups who possessed some surplus resources, but not by any means among the wealthy or socially elite.

2. What we should deduce from the reference to Philemon's[48] οἶκος is also much more limited than is sometimes suggested. The crucial phrase is the established expression ἡ κατ᾽ οἶκον ἐκκλησία (cf. Rom 16:5; 1 Cor 16:19; Col 4:5). As is often noted, οἶκος here (as in the other uses of the phrase) may be taken to refer either to Philemon's household—"the church made up of members of the household or family of Philemon"—or to the physical

45. Arzt-Grabner, "How to Deal with Onesimus," 118, citing work by R. S. Bagnall and B. W. Frier; Arzt-Grabner, *Philemon*, 82n117. See also Walter Scheidel, "The Roman Slave Supply," in *The Ancient Mediterranean World*, ed. Keith Bradley and Paul Cartledge, vol. 1 of *The Cambridge World History of Slavery*, ed. Keith Bradley, Paul Cartledge, David Eltis, and Stanley L. Engerman, 4 vols. (Cambridge: Cambridge University Press, 2011–), 289–90.

46. Scheidel, "Slave Supply," 291–92. Among the famous examples is Tacitus's reference to the four hundred slaves of Pedanius Secundus (*Annals* 14.43).

47. Meggitt, *Paul*, 130–31.

48. There is little to be said for the suggestion of John Knox, that it is the house of Archippus, despite the fact that Douglas Campbell asserts this to be part of the "data" often ignored. See John Knox, *Philemon among the Letters of Paul* (London: Collins, 1960), 49–61; Douglas A. Campbell, *Framing Paul: An Epistolary Biography* (Grand Rapids: Eerdmans, 2014), 254n2. Knox also argues that Onesimus was Archippus's slave, though Campbell does not follow him on this point. The three phrases marked off by καί introduce three co-addressees alongside the main addressee, Philemon: Apphia, Archippus, and "the church in your house." The most likely referent of σου is Philemon. Cf. Fitzmyer, *Philemon*, 89: "the construction actually distinguishes Archippus, another addressee along with Apphia, from the person mentioned by *sou*."

space in which the assembly gathered.[49] Not infrequently both aspects are combined together, based on the conviction that the early church was constituted in an essentially household-based manner.[50] The household is seen as the crucial basis for mission, conversion, meetings, and meals, both in terms of the core social groups that constituted the church and in terms of the physical space in which it met.[51] However, there are good reasons—not least in relation to Philemon—to be wary of exaggerating this household focus and constitution.[52]

In terms of the specific referent of οἶκος here, it seems best to take it to refer to the physical space in which the church met. There are various reasons for this. A reason specific to the letter to Philemon is the case of Onesimus: converted only on meeting Paul (vv. 10–12), he proves that Philemon's household did not convert en bloc to Christianity. (This is, indeed, a significant point to observe: that the paterfamilias adopted a religion which was not required or expected of his slave[s], unless this in some way underlay their conflict—though since Onesimus specifically sought out Paul, this seems unlikely.[53]) Indeed, while it seems plausible that some of Philemon's household formed at least a part, perhaps the predominant part, of this particular ἐκκλησία, this is less than certain: Apphia is often seen as Philemon's wife, since she is named directly after him, perhaps reflecting her significant place in the household,[54] but this is nowhere stated, and remains only a plausible hypothesis.[55] Archippus may or may not be a member of this same

49. Fitzmyer, *Philemon*, 89, who opts for the latter. Contrast Wengst, *Philemon*, 27, 49, who refers to Paul as addressing Philemon's "Hausgemeinde."

50. Cf., e.g., Hans-Josef Klauck, *Hausgemeinde und Hauskirche im frühen Christentum*, SBS 103 (Stuttgart: Katholisches Bibelwerk, 1981), 12, 21: "die sich hausweise konstituierende Kirche"; cf. 101–2, etc.

51. Cf. Peter Müller, *Der Brief an Philemon*, KEK 9.3 (Göttingen: Vandenhoeck & Ruprecht, 2012), 48; Gehring, *House Church*.

52. This is a point stressed by Edward Adams, *The Earliest Christian Meeting Places: Almost Exclusively Houses?*, LNTS/Early Christianity in Context 450 (London: Bloomsbury T&T Clark, 2013), on which see further below.

53. It is conceivable that Philemon acquired Onesimus only after Philemon's own conversion (a suggestion I owe to Edward Adams), but there is nothing to indicate that this might have happened. Even if it had, notwithstanding its significance for understanding early Christian attitudes to slavery, it would remain significant that Onesimus was not immediately expected to adopt the religious commitments of the head of the household.

54. So Müller, *Philemon*, 88–89. Cf. also Arzt-Grabner, *Philemon*, 82; Stuhlmacher, *Philemon*, 30.

55. Cf. Wengst, *Philemon*, 49; Barth and Blanke, *Philemon*, 256, who comment regarding Apphia's (and Archippus's) identity and relation to Philemon: "Not even one of the

household; the possibility that he is the son of Philemon and Apphia is, as Peter Müller notes, "not verifiable."[56] His description as συστρατιώτης is hardly an obvious indication of his junior age, nor of his relationship to Philemon and Apphia.

Elsewhere in the NT, κατ' οἶκον is used to refer to the place where the disciples gather (Acts 2:46; 5:42). More broadly, while the phrase κατ' οἴκους πατριῶν is often used in LXX Numbers and 1–2 Chronicles of ancestral households (e.g., Num 1:2, 4, 20, 22; 1 Chr 5:13; 2 Chr 17:14), the most common meaning of κατ' οἶκον in other Greek literature is "in a house," or "at home," that is, of the physical location rather than the human group.[57] Arzt-Grabner comments that "the members of a household group are never addressed as οἱ κατ' οἶκον or similar in the Papyrus letters." The Pauline formulation thus most likely refers to "a community that met in Philemon's house, but to which not only members of Philemon's household belonged."[58] One must qualify the latter part of this statement, to the extent that we do not know how many (if any) members of Philemon's household shared his Christian allegiance. All we know for sure is that Onesimus, his slave, did not, prior to visiting Paul.

Further aspects of this issue will be discussed in the second major section below. But for now we may note that οἶκος can refer to various kinds of domestic and meeting space, and certainly does not itself indicate that Philemon owned a large or sumptuous *domus* or villa. The distinction between οἰκία and οἶκος seems largely to have disappeared by the time of the NT, and certainly the terms are overlapping in the NT itself; but it is worth noting the use in the papyri of οἰκία to denote the whole house, while οἶκος indicates an apartment, or set of rooms within it. A fine example is found in PTebt I.46 (113 BCE), where "a certain Menches complains that a raid has been made on his house—ἐπὶ τὴν ὑπάρχουσάν μοι οἰκίαν, and that the

---

various hypotheses can be solidly proven." They go on to give some reasons why Apphia may not have been his wife (nor Archippus their son).

56. Müller, *Philemon*, 89 ("nicht nachweisbar"). Cf. also Arzt-Grabner, *Philemon*, 83; Stuhlmacher, *Philemon*, 30–31.

57. See, e.g., Thucydides, *History* 2.14.1; Euripides, *Hippolytus* 639; *Andromache* 57, 563, 804, 1052; *Iphigenia in Tauris* 1310; Plutarch, *Lycurgus* 17.2; Athenaeus, *The Dinner Sophists* 4.19.30.

58. Arzt-Grabner, *Philemon*, 166 ("die Mitglieder eines Hausverbandes in Papyrusbriefen nie als οἱ κατ' οἶκον o.ä. angeredet werden. . . . Eine Gemeinde . . . die sich im Haus des Philemon traf, der aber nicht nur Angehörige aus dem Hausverband des Philemon angehörten").

raiders had burst open the lock of his mother's apartment—ἐκκρούσαντε[ς] τὸ χελώνιον τοῦ οἴκου τῆς μητρός μου."[59] Indeed, οἶκος is regularly used to refer to a room, some part of a house, or an apartment, a place of lodging, including workshops, which often served as accommodation for their owners or tenants.[60] It is also used to denote the meeting place of associations.[61] The view that Philemon owned a relatively large house depends on assumptions about both the kind of space needed to accommodate a meeting of the ἐκκλησία and the likely numbers involved. As we shall see below, these assumptions are open to serious question. We may reasonably deduce that Philemon is responsible—whether as owner or through some other form of occupancy—for an οἶκος, meaning some kind of physical space in which a Christian assembly took place. But there are no firm grounds here for taking this to indicate that Philemon was "wealthy."

3. One last piece of evidence in the letter is often taken to indicate that Philemon was among the relatively wealthy: Paul's request that he prepare for him ξενία. Dunn, for example, takes this reference to what he renders as "a guest room" to indicate "that he [Philemon] was a man of means with a house capable of hosting more than one visitor at a time." According to Dunn, the lack of the article before ξενία suggests more than one guest room.[62]

The main philological question is whether to take ξενία concretely ("guest room," or "lodging") or in a more abstract sense ("hospitality").[63]

59. J. H. Moulton and G. Milligan, *The Vocabulary of the Greek Testament Illustrated from the Papyri and Other Non-Literary Sources* (1930; repr., Peabody, MA: Hendrickson, 2004), 441, and see other examples cited there. Also quoted by Geneviève Husson, *OIKIA: Le vocabulaire de la maison privée en Égypte d'après les papyrus grecs*, Papyrologie 2 (Paris: Publications de la Sorbonne, 1983), 213. Moulton and Milligan also cite a number of NT texts (Matt 5:15; Luke 15:8; John 12:3; 2 Tim 2:20) where they suggest that the larger sense of οἰκία is apparent, indicating the whole "house," though in none of these cases does οἰκία necessarily imply a *large* house.

60. Cf. LSJ, 1204–5; Husson, *OIKIA*, 211–15; O. Michel, *TDNT* 5:119–20.

61. See Richard S. Ascough, Philip A. Harland, and John S. Kloppenborg, *Associations in the Greco-Roman World: A Sourcebook* (Berlin: de Gruyter, 2012), §§47, 52, 121, 203, 224, 319; and used for the association itself, §§81, 94, 267.

62. Dunn, *Colossians and Philemon*, 346; cf. also 300.

63. Despite spending over five hundred pages exclusively on Philemon, Barth and Blanke do not attempt to resolve this question, though elsewhere they appear to favor the concrete (*Philemon*, 137, quoted in n. 23 above). The entirety of their comments on ξενία in v. 22 run as follows: "The expression *hetoimaze xēnian* [*sic*] occurs outside the New Testament as well (Ps-Clement, *Hom.* 12.2, cited by Stuhlmacher, *Philemon*, 54). *Xēnian* [*sic*] means 'shelter,' 'guest room,' or in the abstract, 'hospitable reception.' It remains open

The latter is more often found in literature of the period, not infrequently paired with φιλία (e.g., Plutarch, *Solon* 5.2.3; 5.3.1; Josephus, *Jewish Antiquities* 1.259).[64] But the concrete sense also appears, as in Josephus, *Jewish Antiquities* 5.147 (ἐπὶ τὴν ξενίαν) and the later Pseudo-Clementine Homilies, where a closely parallel phrase is used (τὰς ξενίας ἑτοιμάζοντες. *Hom.* 12.2.5–6; cf. also *Hom.* 14.1: ἐπὶ τὴν ξενίαν ἐλθεῖν), as well as in the papyri.[65] The concrete meaning is most likely also implied in Acts 28:23 (εἰς τὴν ξενίαν), the only other place where this word occurs in the NT. In the context of Philemon, the request ἑτοίμαζέ μοι ξενίαν may also imply the sense "guest room" or "lodging," as most commentators conclude,[66] though the sense "prepare hospitality for me" is by no means impossible, particularly given the lack of the article.[67]

However we understand the word, we should again be very cautious of presuming that the ability to provide ξενία indicates wealth and a sizable house. Such presumptions—perhaps like the "new consensus" more generally—too easily reflect modern Western assumptions about the kind of space that one would need to have in order to accommodate a guest: a "spare bedroom," as it were, preferably with en suite facilities! Even without considering the ancient context, those familiar with informal gatherings and the provision of hospitality in less developed countries will rapidly challenge any presumption that one needs to be relatively wealthy in order to offer such things. After all, even if ξενία is to be taken concretely, it need imply no more than some kind of lodging, space to

---

whether Philemon is to prepare a guest room in his house or to provide for Paul's maintenance with a fellow member of the house community" (493).

64. Cf. BDAG, 683; Arzt-Grabner, *Philemon*, 257; Thucydides, *History* 8.6.3; Euripides, *Medea* 359; Philo, *On the Life of Moses* 2.33; Josephus, *Jewish Antiquities* 1.200.

65. See Arzt-Grabner, *Philemon*, 257, for examples.

66. See, e.g., Stuhlmacher, *Philemon*, 54; Wilson, *Colossians and Philemon*, 365; Fitzmyer, *Philemon*, 122; Dunn, *Colossians and Philemon*, 346; Arzt-Grabner, *Philemon*, 253–58; Müller, *Philemon*, 134n307; also BDAG, 683. The opposite claim is made by Moulton and Milligan, *Vocabulary of the Greek Testament*, 433. On the basis of the common use of ξενία to mean "hospitality" and the specific use of τὰ ξένια "for the gifts provided on the occasion of the visit of a King or other high official to a district," they suggest that this "seems to make it practically certain that the word is to be understood in the same sense in Ac 28[23], Philem[22], rather than of a *place* of lodging."

67. Note the article in the concrete uses cited above, contrasted with the anarthrous phrases (where the meaning seems to be "hospitality") in Philo, *On the Life of Moses* 2.33; and Josephus, *Jewish Antiquities* 1.200 (both with ἐπὶ ξενίαν). It is less likely that the absence of the article implies that Philemon had more than one guest room, as Dunn suggests (see above with n. 62).

sleep, and so on. That Paul requests this be prepared does not necessarily indicate a lavish level of anticipated provision but more likely reflects the rhetorical aims of the letter: Paul wants Philemon to know that he plans to come and check on progress, so requests hospitality in advance of doing so. The obliqueness of Paul's request does not seem likely to reflect Philemon's high social status, but rather Paul's general tendency to avoid direct commands (1 Cor 7:6) and to prefer muted yet rhetorically powerful appeals (e.g., 2 Cor 8:8–11).[68]

Overall, then, there is nothing in the letter that constitutes firm evidence of Philemon's wealth and high social status. He may or may not have been in such a position, but there is nothing that requires this to be the case. Indeed, the paucity of explicit evidence is partly why perceptions of his socioeconomic status—as of other named figures in the Pauline letters—tend, inevitably, to be shaped by broader perspectives on the likely socioeconomic composition of the early Christian communities. Given the rather different picture that has emerged in recent scholarship, it is time to reassess our portrait of Philemon. Our conclusions as to whether he was "wealthy" or "upper class" have to depend on what seems a broadly plausible picture of the socioeconomic location of the earliest Christians, and, indeed, of the empire's population as a whole, in which wealth was heavily concentrated in the hands of a very small percentage of its members. On that basis, it would seem better to place Philemon into a "middling" group whose members live significantly above subsistence level but still with only modest resources, and quite probably among what would in more general terms be regarded as the urban non-elite.[69]

Domestic Space and Meeting Places

Conclusions about Philemon's socioeconomic status relate closely to assumptions about the kind of οἶκος space in which this particular ἐκκλησία

68. Cf. Dunn, *Colossians and Philemon*, 324–25, who suggests that Philemon's social status may have been a reason to avoid strong commands and threats, but also notes that Paul's general style was to avoid such assertions of authority.

69. The description of Philemon given by Barth and Blanke, *Philemon*, 137 (quoted above in n. 23), is therefore nearer to the mark, though the picture of a "successful middle-class citizen," with a relatively large house and "at least one guest room," may still convey a picture of a situation more lavish than need have been the case, not to mention the question over whether the terminology of "middle-class" is apposite to the period.

would have met. Once again, broader perspectives in scholarship have tended to set the contours for the depictions. It has long been a matter of consensus that the early Christians met "almost exclusively" in houses; and these domestic contexts are seen as crucial for understanding the mission and character of the early Christian movement.[70] Until relatively recently, the dominant form of "house" presumed as the context for early Christian meetings was the *domus* or villa, with its triclinium for dining. As David Balch has remarked: "the current consensus is based on elite Roman *domus* that have triclinia. . . . Non-elite spaces for dining are rarely considered."[71] This setting has been seen as helping to explain how, for example, divisions arose at the Lord's Supper. Many scholars and commentators, particularly in English, have followed Jerome Murphy-O'Connor's influential reconstruction (see ch. 2 above).[72] Outlining the archaeological evidence for a particular villa at Corinth, and comparable elite housing elsewhere, which he sees as typical of the kind of house in which the whole church may have met, Murphy-O'Connor explains that only nine or fewer diners—the "first class believers" of higher social status—could have been accommodated in the triclinium. The others would have had to remain outside, in the inferior conditions of the atrium.[73] Thus the architectural configuration of the house helps to explain how the divisions between the "haves" and the "have-nots" arose.[74]

70. Gehring, *House Church*, 1.

71. David L. Balch, "The Church Sitting in a Garden (1 Cor 14:30; Rom 16:23; Mark 6:39–40; 8:6; John 6:3, 10; Acts 1:15; 2:1–2)," in *Contested Spaces: Houses and Temples in Roman Antiquity and the New Testament*, ed. David L. Balch and Annette Weissenrieder, WUNT 285 (Tübingen: Mohr Siebeck, 2012), 204–5. In an essay from 2004, Balch explicitly corrects his own earlier focus on the *domus* (in Carolyn Osiek and David L. Balch, *Families in the New Testament World: Households and House Churches* [Louisville: Westminster John Knox, 1997]). See David L. Balch, "Rich Pompeian Houses, Shops for Rent, and the Huge Apartment Building in Herculaneum as Typical Spaces for Pauline House Churches," *JSNT* 27 (2004): 28.

72. Jerome Murphy-O'Connor, *St. Paul's Corinth: Texts and Archaeology*, 3rd rev. and exp. ed. (Collegeville, MN: Liturgical Press, 2002), 178–85. Commentators who have followed Murphy-O'Connor include Gordon D. Fee, *The First Epistle to the Corinthians*, NICNT (Grand Rapids: Eerdmans, 1987), 533–34n10; Richard B. Hays, *First Corinthians*, IBC (Louisville: Westminster John Knox, 1997), 196; Raymond F. Collins, *First Corinthians*, SP 7 (Collegeville, MN: Liturgical Press, 1999), 418–19; Thiselton, *First Epistle*, 860–61.

73. Murphy-O'Connor, *St. Paul's Corinth*, 183.

74. Cf. similarly, following Murphy-O'Connor on this point, Peter Lampe, "Das korinthische Herrenmahl im Schnittpunkt hellenistisch-römischer Mahlpraxis und paulinischer Theologia Crucis (1 Kor 11, 17–34)," *ZNW* 82 (1991): 197n43, 201; Osiek and Balch, *Families*,

Alternative meeting places have also been proposed. Murphy-O'Connor himself indicates that workshops, such as those excavated on the north side of the forum in Corinth, may also have provided a venue for small Christian groups to assemble.[75] Robert Jewett points to the possibility of "tenement churches" meeting in multistory apartment blocks, arguing that 2 Thess 3:10 implies just such an assembly; more recently he proposes a similar locale for some of the Roman Christian groups.[76] In an article from 2004 (ch. 2 above) I also challenged the plausibility of Murphy-O'Connor's proposal concerning meeting places for "the whole church" (Rom 16:23) and divisions at Corinth, partly due to the uncertainty concerning the date and character of the archaeological evidence he uses and partly on the basis that the *domus* space in question is undoubtedly characteristic of the wealthy. As an alternative, I proposed that the buildings excavated east of the theater in Corinth, where domestic accommodation of a less luxurious kind was evident, offered a plausible kind of setting for early Christian meetings, assuming that the members were more likely to be from the various strata of the urban non-elite. More generally, my point was to argue that "NT studies should pay more attention to the varieties of domestic space in the urban setting of Corinth and other cities of the Roman Empire, and consider these as possible settings for early Christian meetings" (p. 48, above). Indeed, in a review of Roger Gehring's book on the house churches of early Christianity, Alastair Campbell cites this article as an indication that the consensus which Gehring's book represents—regarding the type of domestic space in which we should imagine the early Christians meeting—"may be about to crumble."[77] More recently, Peter Oakes and David Balch are among those who have discussed a wider range of domestic settings in which Christians may have assembled.[78] Indeed,

200–201. Osiek and Balch do, however, also point to the possibility of meeting in gardens (203), where much larger numbers could have been accommodated—a point developed in Balch's subsequent work. See esp. Balch, "Church Sitting."

75. Murphy-O'Connor, *St. Paul's Corinth*, 192–98.

76. Robert Jewett, "Tenement Churches and Communal Meals in the Early Church: The Implications of a Form-Critical Analysis of 2 Thessalonians 3:10," *BR* 38 (1993): 26. Jewett refers to these four- or five-story apartment blocks (such as are famously found at Ostia) as *insulae* (26), though one should note that the term *insula* does not necessarily denote high-rise apartment blocks; see n. 80 below. See Robert Jewett, *Romans*, Hermeneia (Minneapolis: Fortress, 2007), 64–69.

77. R. Alastair Campbell, review of Roger W. Gehring, *House Church and Mission*, *JTS* 58 (2007): 671.

78. Balch, "Rich Pompeian Houses"; Balch, "Church Sitting"; Peter Oakes, *Reading*

a “key argument” of Oakes’s book “is that scholars have generally been looking at the wrong houses when looking for types of house in which a typical early Christian group would have met . . . they will not generally have met in elite houses.”[79] Oakes presents a detailed analysis of some units excavated at Pompeii, including an extensive *insula* containing craftworkers’ homes;[80] these illustrate something of the range of domestic accommodation occupied by the non-elite.

Detailed responses to my earlier proposals have been offered by Daniel Schowalter and by Murphy-O’Connor, and I offer here some brief replies which may, I hope, help to further the ongoing discussion.[81] The most important point Schowalter makes regarding my use of the archaeological evidence for the buildings east of the theater is to point out that the latest thinking among the archaeologists, in contrast to the earlier published articles, is to doubt the likelihood of there having been upper floors with accommodation in these buildings.[82] If correct, these buildings cannot themselves have offered the specific kind of space I suggested as plausible, namely some kind of room(s) on an upper floor. That does not, however, render the evidence from East Theater Street irrelevant, since the various buildings here include apartment rooms as well as shops serving cooked meat (in which owners, workers, or meetings could have been accommodated). Nor does it make it unlikely that comparable kinds of domestic space existed elsewhere

Romans in Pompeii: Paul’s Letter at Ground Level (Minneapolis: Fortress, 2009). See also Bradly S. Billings, “From House Church to Tenement Church: Domestic Space and the Development of Early Urban Christianity—The Example of Ephesus,” *JTS* 62 (2011): 541–69, who, drawing on social network theory, proposes that Christians may gradually have come to dominate certain *insulae*, renting or owning their various units within the block, after the earliest phase of house churches.

79. Oakes, *Romans in Pompeii*, 70.

80. It may be helpful to note that the term *insula*, here and throughout this essay, refers, as is standard in the archaeological literature, to the (often roughly rectangular) blocks (of houses, apartments, shops, etc.) formed in the (usually) gridlike pattern of streets. They are not necessarily “high-rise,” like the famous examples from Ostia, though those Oakes studies in Pompeii often have an upper story of some kind. See also n. 76 above.

81. Jerome Murphy-O’Connor died in November 2013 after a long and distinguished career in biblical studies. While continuing the discussion—in which he can no longer himself participate—I would like to pay tribute to his life and work.

82. Daniel N. Schowalter, “Seeking Shelter in Roman Corinth: Archaeology and the Placement of Paul’s Communities,” in *Corinth in Context*, ed. Friesen, Schowalter, and Walters, 333–34.

in Corinth (and other cities of the empire),[83] whether on ground floors or floors above.[84]

Schowalter also criticizes me for making the comparison with Acts 20:9, on the basis that "some will undoubtedly see his analysis of the supposed second floor space on East Theater Street as archaeological evidence proving the accuracy or even inerrancy of the Acts 20 account."[85] However, quite apart from the fact that the meeting depicted in Acts 20:7–12 is in Troas, not Corinth, it is clear and explicit in the article that to picture "the first Christians in Corinth meeting in an upper-story room in East Theater Street is . . . entirely imaginative" and that the aim is to use such information to enable precisely such historically disciplined imagination about the *kinds* of possible settings for early Christian meetings.[86] Schowalter's concern with the inappropriate use of archaeology to prove biblical accuracy is entirely understandable, but it would be an enormous leap from my imaginative scenario to a potential validation of the inerrancy of the historical information in Acts 20:7–12. The point of the citation of Acts 20:9, which I continue to regard as valid, is that an early Christian writer (even if writing some decades after Paul's letters) found it plausible to imagine such a meeting place. Such verisimilitude in literary works has value for historical reconstruction; but it does not of course say anything about the historical veracity of the specific events and locations narrated.

Murphy-O'Connor raises a number of points in response. He insists that the villa at Anaploga, his key Corinthian example, lay inside the city walls

83. Indeed, Peter Oakes makes a fair point in criticizing me (as well as Murphy-O'Connor) for "overlocalizing" the issue, particularly in terms of questions about the dating of the dining room in the villa at Anaploga: "since the aim of the exercise is imaginative interpretation by use of a typical setting, it is beside the point to worry about the structure of the rooms at a particular date." See Peter Oakes, "Methodological Issues in Using Economic Evidence in Interpretation of Early Christian Texts," in *Engaging Economics: New Testament Scenarios and Early Christian Reception*, ed. Bruce Longenecker and Kelly Liebengood (Grand Rapids: Eerdmans, 2009), 25.

84. The idea that upper stories were avoided in Corinth due to the danger of earthquakes (so Schowalter, "Seeking Shelter," 334n20) is at least open to question, as Annette Weissenrieder points out, given evidence from Pompeii and elsewhere. See Annette Weissenrieder, "Contested Spaces in 1 Corinthians 11:17–33 and 14:30: Sitting or Reclining in Ancient Houses, in Associations and in the Space of the *ekklēsia*," in *Contested Spaces: Houses and Temples in Roman Antiquity and the New Testament*, ed. David L. Balch and Annette Weissenrieder, WUNT 285 (Tübingen: Mohr Siebeck, 2012), 81.

85. Schowalter, "Seeking Shelter," 335.

86. P. 47, above. The imaginative construction of characters as part of disciplined historical enquiry is particularly prominent in Oakes, *Romans in Pompeii.*

in Roman times.[87] Clearly it lay inside the area enclosed by the old Greek city walls,[88] but in Roman times there were, according to Mary Hoskins Walbank, large areas of open and probably cultivated ground within the Greek walls; and the late Roman walls enclosed a significantly smaller area.[89] The important point, which Murphy-O'Connor does not address, is that the villa may have been a working farm, and so hardly representative or typical of urban accommodation in Roman Corinth.[90] I accept his response that he labeled the villa at Anaploga, his key example from Corinth, as "typical" not in the sense that most believers at Corinth lived in such houses, but rather in the sense that it was "typical of *the sort of house required to host the whole church.*"[91] Whether this latter claim is plausible, however, is precisely open to question, depending on what socioeconomic level we find likely for such hosts, the likely size of the groups meeting there, and the (other) kinds of domestic spaces available for meetings. The villa excavated at Anaploga is most likely a residence owned by a member of the aristocratic, landowning elite.[92] Unfortunately, in discussing the socioeconomic level of the Corinthian Christians, and of hosts such as Gaius in particular, Murphy-O'Connor quotes lines from my article as if they reflected my own claims, when they are clearly reporting the argument of Meggitt.[93] Indeed, I immediately go

87. Jerome Murphy-O'Connor, *Keys to First Corinthians: Revisiting the Major Issues* (Oxford: Oxford University Press, 2009), 191.

88. See David Gillman Romano, "Post-146 B.C. Land Use in Corinth, and Planning of the Roman Colony of 44 B.C.," in *The Corinthia in the Roman Period*, ed. Timothy E. Gregory, JRASup 8 (Ann Arbor: Journal of Roman Archaeology, 1993), 11.

89. Cf. Mary E. Hoskins Walbank, "The Nature and Development of Roman Corinth from 44 BCE to the End of the Antonine Period" (PhD diss., Open University, 1986), 315–23; Hoskins Walbank, "The Foundation and Planning of Early Roman Corinth," *JRA* 10 (1997): 95–130 (esp. 107–11), with the plan of the city area in the early Roman period on 108. More generally on villas as working farms, see Simon P. Ellis, *Roman Housing* (London: Duckworth, 2000), 13–14.

90. See Murphy-O'Connor, *Keys to First Corinthians*, 191, where in responding to the point he cites the work of Romano but not that of Hoskins Walbank.

91. Murphy-O'Connor, *Keys to First Corinthians*, 191 (italics original). The relevant section in Murphy-O'Connor, *St. Paul's Corinth*, 178–82, is entitled "A Typical House."

92. Cf. Ellis, *Roman Housing*, 22–72, 73, 112.

93. Murphy-O'Connor, *Keys to First Corinthians*, 191, attributes the following claim to me, quoting from my article: "Paul and the early Christians shared in the absolute poverty which was the fate of the vast majority of the population of the Roman empire." This is a rather obvious and unfortunate misreading. The quoted sentence runs as follows: ". . . Justin Meggitt's *Paul, Poverty, and Survival*, in which Meggitt argues that the evidence used to identify named Corinthian Christians as members of the wealthy elite cannot sustain this

on to offer some critical reactions to Meggitt's view and to suggest a more "cautious" version of the "new consensus," one that accepts some socioeconomic diversity but is hesitant to label any of the early Christians known to us as wealthy, elite, or upper class.[94] And a mere citation of 1 Cor 1:26 does not sufficiently prove the contrary.[95]

The most significant question Murphy-O'Connor raises about my alternative scenario is that it would require people to eat "sitting knee to knee with their food on their laps! To what extent that would have been socially acceptable in any Graeco-Roman city of the period is up to Horrell to explain."[96] How crowded any particular meeting was would of course depend on the numbers as well as the size of venue, and we can only guess at the numbers who gathered at Gaius's home, or indeed at Philemon's. But a degree of crowding seems to be plausible for such a meeting (cf. Acts 20:9; Mark 2:2–4).

More significantly, however, the question about sitting to eat, as opposed to reclining, has precisely been addressed in recent work by David Balch and Annette Weissenrieder. Challenging "the virtual consensus that Pauline assemblies were always centered in dining rooms (triclinia)," Balch explores a wide range of evidence, particularly from the archaeology and art of Pompeii, to "demonstrate . . . that Romans sat in taverns, open gardens, and peristyle gardens."[97] He concludes: "Romans did not always recline when eating, nor did they always eat in a triclinium. The non-elite typically drank and ate sitting on stools or benches in taverns, and they reclined/sat on cushions on the ground in open gardens."[98] The numbers of worshipers who might gather in such spaces, particularly in gardens, could potentially be large.[99] Similarly, Weissenrieder presents evidence from literary, visual, and archaeological sources to show that sitting to eat was not uncommon, particularly in lower-class settings.[100]

---

conclusion, and that Paul and the early Christians shared the absolute poverty that was the fate of the vast majority of the population of the Roman empire, a conclusion also supported in Steven Friesen's recent work" (p. 36, above).

94. Pp. 36–38, above.

95. *Pace* Murphy-O'Connor, *Keys to First Corinthians*, 191: "This [sc. Meggitt's view, attributed to me] is clearly contradicted by 1 Cor 1:26, which asserts that *some* members of the community were well off by human standards."

96. Murphy-O'Connor, *Keys to First Corinthians*, 192.

97. Balch, "Church Sitting," 205.

98. Balch, "Church Sitting," 229.

99. See Balch, "Church Sitting," 205, 226–28; Osiek and Balch, *Families*, 202–3.

100. Weissenrieder, "Contested Spaces," esp. 66–79.

If, then, we shift our perspective from the conventional patterns of elite dining in a plush triclinium to the more plausible depictions of patterns of eating among the non-elite, it is not at all unrealistic to imagine members of an early Christian assembly sitting to eat, perhaps in quite crowded surroundings.

An even more radical questioning of the "house-church" consensus has recently been presented by Edward Adams.[101] Without denying that the early Christians did meet in homes, Adams shows, in the first part of his book, that the evidence for this is less extensive than is often supposed. There is scope to question the conviction that the home was "almost exclusively" the venue for such meetings. In the second part of his book, Adams therefore explores other possible meeting places: shops and warehouses, rented dining rooms, baths, and open-air spaces such as gardens, watersides, and burial places. He distinguishes carefully between direct evidence for Christians meeting in such places and wider evidence that indicates (only) the possibility of such places functioning in this way. His conclusions suggest that the predominant focus on the house as the only significant meeting place for the early Christians, and as the basis for the eventual development of ecclesial architecture, may need to be significantly revised, and replaced by a model of much greater diversity.

What does all this suggest about the kind of place in which Philemon's ἐκκλησία met? It is important to recall, as noted above, that the term οἶκος can refer to a wide variety of types of space. In other words, reference to Philemon's οἶκος does not in itself tell us anything about the size or type of space he made available for the ἐκκλησία. Its description as "his" οἶκος (κατ' οἶκόν σου) does indicate that this is most likely domestic space of some kind: this *is* an instance where the evidence points clearly to a meeting in a home. But our sense of what kind of domestic space this is likely to have been can only be further informed by broader hypotheses concerning: (1) the likely socioeconomic level of Philemon; (2) the numbers that are likely to have assembled; and (3) the range of plausible spaces suggested by the wider historical and archaeological evidence.

1. We have already seen that there are good reasons to question any presumption that Philemon must be "wealthy" in order to have a slave and have some kind of οἶκος space in which he could offer Paul ξενία. The most plausible picture would seem to be that Philemon was among the middling groups in urban society—not destitute but with some surplus resources.

101. Adams, *Meeting Places*.

Where exactly we place him on the economic scale depends in part on assumptions about what is necessary to provide what he does for Paul and the ἐκκλησία, so there is a risk of circularity here.

2. It is very difficult to say with any precision how large the group is likely to have been that met in Philemon's οἶκος; we are given very little indication about the size of the ἐκκλησία. The relevant names mentioned in the letter, Apphia and Archippus, do not of course constitute a group of any great size, though there are clearly other members besides them, who together form the ἐκκλησία. Peter Stuhlmacher estimates around 10–40 as the usual range for a Christian *Hausgemeinde*.[102] Murphy-O'Connor calculates an estimate of around 40–50 for the Christian community at Corinth,[103] but stresses that this is a number for "the whole church" that met on occasion with Gaius as host (Rom 16:23). He suggests that this gathering should be contrasted with the smaller subgroups that assembled on other occasions, as indicated elsewhere in the phrase ἡ κατ' οἶκον ἐκκλησία.[104] The assembly in Philemon's house, therefore, may well have been quite small, perhaps fewer than ten people, though we cannot tell for sure.

3. The smaller the group, the smaller the space needed for a meeting, and the assembly of a small number of Christians would not have required a large or luxurious dwelling. Even if the group were somewhat larger than ten it would be perfectly possible to meet in a workshop, or in a room or apartment, and there is no reason to imagine that non-elite diners would have expected to recline for the eucharistic meal on couches in a triclinium. We do not know the location of Philemon's house, so cannot use archaeological evidence to be more specific about what was locally likely. It is generally presumed to have been in Colossae, which is yet to be excavated, but this conclusion hangs largely on the names mentioned in both letters. If Colossians is pseudonymous, then these connections may simply indicate the literary dependence of Colossians on Philemon, and more specifically an attempt to give the former the aura of authen-

102. Stuhlmacher, *Philemon*, 72. Barth and Blanke, *Philemon*, 261, suggest that "in view of the average size of first-century houses owned by persons of some means, no more than forty persons may have assembled in one room." But this comment begs a number of questions.

103. Murphy-O'Connor, *St. Paul's Corinth*, 182; Murphy-O'Connor, *Keys to First Corinthians*, 183.

104. Murphy-O'Connor, *St. Paul's Corinth*, 183; Murphy-O'Connor, *Keys to First Corinthians*, 184. Cf. also Robert Banks, *Paul's Idea of Community: The Early House Churches in Their Historical Setting*, rev. ed. (Peabody, MA: Hendrickson, 1994), 38.

ticity.[105] In any case, as Oakes has pointed out, it is better to use a wider range of comparative evidence from across the empire, with appropriate caution, than to depend too much on evidence from one locality alone.[106] And recent work based on various locations has highlighted the range of forms of domestic space, refocusing away from the villas and large houses that had previously attracted the most attention, and exploring (inter alia) the range of apartment-type units, the mix of residents of various socioeconomic levels within larger *insulae*, and the use of workshops for accommodation.[107] We can therefore very plausibly imagine Philemon's ἐκκλησία meeting in an apartment, room, or workshop.

Conclusions

The first conclusion to be drawn from this study is negative and limited, though nonetheless significant. We must confess that we know very little about the concrete social circumstances of Philemon and the κατ' οἶκον αὐτοῦ ἐκκλησία. This means that depictions of these circumstances inevitably tend to depend on the dominant hypotheses concerning the early Christians' socioeconomic status and associated meeting places. The era of the so-called new consensus has shaped such depictions, so that we commonly read in commentaries and elsewhere of Philemon as a person of wealth who owned a number of slaves and possessed a large house. At the very least, it

105. See further Angela Standhartinger, *Studien zur Entstehungsgeschichte und Intention des Kolosserbriefs*, NovTSup 94 (Leiden: Brill, 1999), 81–85, developing a suggestion by Eduard Lohse, *Die Briefe an die Kolosser und an Philemon*, 2nd ed., KEK 9.2 (Göttingen: Vandenhoeck & Ruprecht, 1977), 246–47. Philemon may perhaps have seemed a suitable choice, despite its short length, if part of the aim of Colossians was to develop and "correct" the Pauline teaching on slavery, in a kind of *fiktive Selbstauslegung* on the part of "Paul." Cf. Annette Merz, *Die fiktive Selbstauslegung des Paulus: Intertextuelle Studien zur Intention und Rezeption der Pastoralbriefe*, NTOA 52 (Göttingen: Vandenhoeck & Ruprecht; Fribourg: Universitätsverlag, 2004), esp. 245–67, who considers 1 Tim 6:1–5 and Titus 2:9–10 as "corrective" reinterpretation of "die sozialen Folgen der Geschwisterschaft von SklavInnen," intertextually related to Phlm 16.

106. Cf. Oakes, "Methodological Issues," 25, quoted in n. 83 above.

107. See, e.g., Ellis, *Roman Housing*, 73–113; Andrew Wallace-Hadrill, *Houses and Society in Pompeii and Herculaneum* (Princeton: Princeton University Press, 1994), esp. 65–117; Ray Laurence and Andrew Wallace-Hadrill, eds., *Domestic Space in the Roman World: Pompeii and Beyond*, JRASup 22 (Portsmouth, RI: Journal of Roman Archaeology, 1997); Oakes, *Romans in Pompeii*, 1–45; Dirk Jongkind, "Corinth in the First Century AD: The Search for Another Class," *TynBul* 52 (2001): 139–48; Meggitt, *Paul*, 62–67.

should be clear that such deductions are open to serious doubt. It is by no means necessary for Philemon to have been any of these things in order to do what Paul's letter depicts him as doing.

Recent work on both the socioeconomic level of the early Christians and the range of spaces (domestic and other) available for meetings indicates reasons for serious doubts about this prominent depiction and also suggests a much more likely scenario, which constitutes a positive and constructive conclusion. Given the very small numbers who were really wealthy, owning many slaves and large villas, it is much more plausible, in the absence of any contrary evidence, to imagine Philemon as a member of the "middling" groups in the urban non-elite, with relatively modest resources—perhaps an artisan like Paul, Prisca, and Aquila, who employed a slave or two in his workshop, or perhaps owned or rented an apartment in an *insula*. This does not mean he lacked some resources that he used to support and host the local Christian community, nor does it imply that he was not cultured or educated enough to receive and understand a rhetorically powerful and in some ways sophisticated letter. But it should nonetheless change the kind of picture we have of Philemon and the assembly that met in his οἶκος, and might also change our perception of the implications of his relationship with Onesimus. It is significant, in such a small-scale setting, that Onesimus had not previously been required to convert along with his owner; and the potential economic impact on Philemon of the loss of a slave—perhaps his only slave—could be very considerable. Fundamentally, the results of recent scholarship should lead us to be more realistic—and also much more cautious—about picturing life in small Christian assemblies in the preindustrial Roman Empire.

Chapter 4

From ἀδελφοί to οἶκος θεοῦ

Social Transformation in Pauline Christianity

> *Unser Leben geht hin mit Verwandlung*, Rilke says: Our life passes in transformation. This is what I seek to grasp in the theory of structuration.
>
> ANTHONY GIDDENS, *Central Problems in Social Theory*

> The purpose of our journey is to attempt to construct a kind of ethnography of Christian beginnings.
>
> WAYNE MEEKS, *The Origins of Christian Morality*

Introduction

One of the aspects of social structure commonly investigated by anthropologists is that of kinship.[1] This is true not only of anthropological studies based on the traditional method of "participant observation," but also of those based on the study of particular literary or historical texts: the Anglo-Saxon epic *Beowulf*, or the novels of Jane Austen, for example.[2]

1. See, e.g., Roger M. Keesing, *Cultural Anthropology: A Contemporary Perspective*, 2nd ed. (New York: Holt, Rinehart & Winston, 1981), 212–50; Thomas H. Eriksen, *Small Places, Large Issues: An Introduction to Social and Cultural Anthropology* (London: Pluto, 1995), 82–94. A brief introduction related to NT studies is given by K. C. Hanson, "Kinship," in *The Social Sciences and New Testament Interpretation*, ed. Richard L. Rohrbaugh (Peabody, MA: Hendrickson, 1996), 62–79.

2. John M. Hill, *The Cultural World in Beowulf*, Anthropological Horizons (Toronto: University of Toronto Press, 1995); Isaac Schapera, *Kinship Terminology in Jane Austen's Novels*, Royal Anthropological Institute Occasional Paper 33 (London: Royal Anthropological

Investigation of the language used to describe kinship patterns and family relationships is important not just because it enables a picture to be sketched of who relates to whom and how, but also because the specific language used both reflects and shapes patterns of social relationships. In the process of what Anthony Giddens calls "structuration"—the "structuring of social relations across time and space," with structure as both "the medium and outcome of the conduct it recursively organizes"—kinship language shapes social relationships and is simultaneously reproduced in the context of those relationships.[3] Over time, both language and patterns of relationships may evolve and change. That sons in Jane Austen's novels always address their father as "sir," for example, reveals something about the moral ideals of deference and obedience expected among children in that author's era.[4] Contemporary British terms of address are generally different, and both reflect and construct correspondingly different patterns of social and moral interaction.

In this essay I want to consider how some aspects of kinship and household language contribute to the shaping of social relationships within the Pauline churches, and how, if at all, the patterns of language and relationships change over time in the NT period. In line with general, though by no means unanimous, scholarly judgment, I shall include as genuine epistles of Paul: Romans, 1 and 2 Corinthians, Galatians, Philippians, 1 Thessalonians, and Philemon.[5] Colossians and Ephesians will be taken as early and closely

---

Institute of Great Britain and Ireland, 1977). Stanley R. Barrett notes the recent upsurge in archival and historical research in anthropology in *Anthropology: A Student's Guide to Theory and Method* (Toronto: University of Toronto Press, 1996), 194n4.

3. See Anthony Giddens, *The Constitution of Society: Outline of the Theory of Structuration* (Cambridge: Polity, 1984), 374, 376, further xiii–xxxvii, 1–40; Anthony Giddens, *Profiles and Critiques in Social Theory* (London: Macmillan, 1982), 28–39. For further references, and an introduction to Giddens's structuration theory in relation to NT studies, see David G. Horrell, *The Social Ethos of the Corinthian Correspondence: Interests and Ideology from 1 Corinthians to 1 Clement*, SNTW (Edinburgh: T&T Clark, 1996), 45–59, 313; Horrell, "The Development of Theological Ideology in Pauline Christianity: A Structuration Theory Perspective," in *Modelling Early Christianity*, ed. Philip F. Esler (London: Routledge, 1995), 224–36.

4. See Schapera, *Kinship Terminology*, 2.

5. 2 Thessalonians, the authenticity of which is often doubted, is not taken directly into consideration, though the relevant statistics are included for information on the table in the appendix. Ἀδελφός terminology appears somewhat more frequently in 2 Thessalonians than in what I have counted as pseudo-Pauline epistles; but if 2 Thessalonians is pseudonymous, as seems to me most likely, it is in a somewhat unique position, being clearly based upon 1 Thessalonians. That would make the reduction in references to believers as ἀδελφοί (19

related examples of post-Pauline pseudepigraphy, the Pastoral Epistles as somewhat later additions to the Pauline corpus, written probably around the end of the first century.

There are many familial and household terms used in the Pauline correspondence, and while a number are mentioned briefly in the discussion below, my main focus is upon the language of brother- or sisterhood (ἀδελφός, ἀδελφή, etc.)[6] and of house or household (οἶκος, οἰκία, οἰκεῖος, etc.).[7] My particular interest in this essay is in the metaphorical uses of these terms to describe and to construct the Christian community and the relationships between its members. In other words, the focus is on what has often been termed "fictive kinship" language and on the designation of the church community as a household (of God), and not on the relations between natural siblings or within actual households. While the language of brother-/sisterhood and of house/household are clearly closely related and overlap in terms of that which they generally describe, they should not simply be treated together as varied forms of familial terminology.[8] We need to consider how

---

times in 1 Thessalonians, 8 times in 2 Thessalonians) notable, an observation that coheres with the overall argument of this essay.

6. I have wrestled with the problem of inclusive terminology in this paper, though I am conscious that—lacking in imagination perhaps—I have not satisfactorily solved it. What is clear is that a strategy such as that adopted by the NRSV, where ἀδελφός and אח are regularly translated "neighbor," "member of the community" (e.g., Deut 15:2–3, 7–11), "believer" (e.g., 1 Cor 6:6–8; 7:12; 8:11; etc.), would be entirely inappropriate for this paper. As Scott Bartchy points out, this leads to the original terminology being obscured such that modern readers miss seeing the extent to which siblinglike bonds are being encouraged among the communities addressed by the biblical writers (S. Scott Bartchy, "Undermining Ancient Patriarchy: The Apostle Paul's Vision of a Society of Siblings," *BTB* 29 [1999]: 70). Since the masculine terms ἀδελφός and ἀδελφοί are those most often used (generically) by Paul, I have also written them frequently. Leaving the terms untranslated may perhaps help to stress that this is ancient (patriarchal!) language that raises problems for modern inclusive translation. To some extent I have followed Bartchy and Aasgaard in using the term "sibling," though I am conscious that this term is much less common in contemporary English than "brother" or "sister." See Reidar Aasgaard, *"My Beloved Brothers and Sisters!": Christian Siblingship in Paul*, JSNTSup 265 (London: T&T Clark, 2004).

7. On the familial terms in particular, see Daniel von Allmen, *La famille de Dieu: La symbolique familiale dans le Paulinisme*, OBO 41 (Fribourg: Éditions Universitaires; Göttingen: Vandenhoeck & Ruprecht, 1981).

8. As (understandably) in the brief survey by Robert Banks, *Paul's Idea of Community: The Early House Churches in Their Historical Setting*, rev. ed. (Peabody, MA: Hendrickson, 1994), 50–51; and in Philip F. Esler, "Family Imagery and Christian Identity in Gal 5:13 to 6:10," in *Constructing Early Christian Families*, ed. Halvor Moxnes (London: Routledge, 1997), 122–23. Note the comments of Karl Olav Sandnes, "Equality within Patriarchal Struc-

the distribution of sibling and household language varies within the Pauline corpus and to take account of the ways in which the different terms may reflect *different* ideals with regard to the construction of social relationships in the Christian communities.

The Meaning of the Terms ἀδελφός/אח and οἶκος/בית

The term ἀδελφός,[9] like its Hebrew equivalent, אח, first of all signifies "a person's own blood brother,"[10] but was also used of various relationships where there was some emotional and social bond:[11] between spouses,[12] kinsfolk (see n15), tribe members, colleagues, fellow members of an association,[13] and even between a king and a hoped-for ally.[14] In view of the frequent description of the members of the Christian community as ἀδελφοί in the

---

tures: Some New Testament Perspectives on the Christian Fellowship as a Brother- or Sisterhood and a Family," in *Constructing Early Christian Families*, ed. Moxnes, 150; and K. Schäfer, *Gemeinde als "Bruderschaft": Ein Beitrag zum Kirchenverständnis des Paulus*, Europäische Hochschulschriften 23/333 (Frankfurt: Lang, 1989), 18–19.

9. Similar things could be said about the term ἀδελφή, "sister," but because masculine language was used generically, occurrences of ἀδελφός (often plural) are much more common in the NT and elsewhere. Cf., e.g., Job 42:11 LXX; n. 11, below.

10. H. Ringgren, *TDOT* 1:188; cf. LSJ, 20: "son of the same mother."

11. For more detailed investigation of the diversity of usage sketched here see K. H. Schelke, "Bruder," *RAC* 2 (1954): 631–40; Aasgaard, *"My Beloved Brothers and Sisters!,"* 107–16.

12. E.g., P.Lond. 42; and for the term ἀδελφή used by a husband of his wife, see P.Oxy. 120, 528, 744. Cf. also G. H. R. Horsley, *Review of the Greek Inscriptions and Papyri Published in 1976*, *NewDocs* 1 (North Ryde, NSW: Ancient History Documentary Research Centre, Macquarie University, 1981), 58, who notes: "Letters in the papyri containing ἀδελφός as an address between spouses are commonplace." Sometimes, however, it is impossible to tell whether it is a spouse or a sibling who is being addressed (letters are also frequently exchanged between siblings); and given the practice of intersibling marriage in Egypt, it is possible that spouses are sometimes literally a brother or sister (see C. K. Barrett, *The New Testament Background: Selected Documents*, rev. ed. [London: SPCK, 1987], 29).

13. On the use of ἀδελφός terminology in associations, see LSJ, 20 (ἀδελφός); G. H. R. Horsley, *Review of the Greek Inscriptions and Papyri Published in 1977*, *NewDocs* 2 (North Ryde, NSW: Ancient History Documentary Research Centre, Macquarie University, 1982), 49–50; Dennis C. Duling, "The Matthean Brotherhood and Marginal Scribal Leadership," in *Modelling Early Christianity*, ed. Esler, 159–82. On the terminology in Greco-Roman religious contexts, see Schelke, "Bruder," 632–34.

14. Josephus, *Jewish Antiquities* 13.45; cf. 1 Kgs 9:13; Jdt 7:30 LXX. See further LSJ, 20; Ringgren, *TDOT* 1:188–93; H. F. von Soden, *TDNT* 1:144–46.

NT, it is important to note that the Hebrew Bible often uses the term אח, rendered ἀδελφός in the LXX, for kinsfolk and fellow Israelites (members of an extended kin group).[15] This usage in Judaism is continued into NT times and beyond.[16] Despite the widely varied uses of the term its basic meaning throughout remains that of "brother" (and likewise for ἀδελφή, "sister"). Thus, in its varied contexts, it reflects the existence of, or the desire for, a sibling-like bond between speaker and addressee(s).[17] The term itself conveys no sense of hierarchy or superiority, though that may of course be assumed or stated elsewhere in the context where it appears.[18]

The Greek terms οἶκος/οἰκία[19] and the Hebrew term בית are even more wide-ranging in meaning and use. In both languages the terms are used

15. E.g., Gen 13:8; Exod 2:11; Lev 25:35–36; Deut 15:7, 9, 11–12; 22:1–4. Cf. 2 Macc 1:1; Philo, *On the Virtues* 82; Ringgren, *TDOT* 1:188–93; von Soden, *TDNT* 1:145: "There can be no doubt, however, that ἀδελφός is one of the titles of the people of Israel taken over by the Christian community."

16. See, e.g., Josephus, *Jewish War* 2.122 (on the Essenes); 1QS 6.10; 6.22; CD 6.20; 7.2; Str-B 1:276; Aasgaard, *"My Beloved Brothers and Sisters!,"* 113–15.

17. Bartchy seems to overlook the extent to which sibling language was widely used outside family contexts and in the extended kinship group of an *ethnos* like Israel, thus ignoring the extent to which this siblinglike bond was meant to characterize a wide range of relationships. Bartchy suggests that in ancient Mediterranean culture, in relationships outside the family, "both boys and girls were socialized to expect . . . that every male should seek to dominate as many other men as possible . . . traditional male socialization produced human beings who were programmed to pursue a never-ending quest for greater honor and influence" ("Undermining Ancient Patriarchy," 68). Both the widespread use of ἀδελφός terminology and the qualities ascribed to friendship suggest that extrafamily relationships were frequently characterized by more than an agonistic contest for honor. Indeed, authors who describe fraternal relations often draw parallels with the qualities and characteristics of friendship. Cf., e.g., Terence, *Brothers* 707–8: "si frater aut sodalis esset, qui magis morem gereret?" ("if he were a brother or a friend, how could he do more to gratify me?"); the well-known saying κοινὰ τὰ τῶν φίλων (Plato, *Phaedrus* 279C; Terence, *Brothers* 803–4; Plutarch, *On Brotherly Love* 490E). For a comparison between Paul and Plutarch on "brotherhood" see Reidar Aasgaard, "Brotherhood in Plutarch and Paul: Its Role and Character," in *Constructing Early Christian Families*, ed. Moxnes, 166–82; and further Aasgaard, *"My Beloved Brothers and Sisters!"*

18. Cf. Sandnes, "Equality within Patriarchal Structures," 150; Schäfer, *Gemeinde als "Bruderschaft,"* 37.

19. The distinction between these two Greek terms (e.g., in Attic law οἶκος designated the whole of a deceased person's estate, οἰκία simply his residence; Xenophon, *Economics* 1.5) is largely lost in the NT (cf. 1 Cor 1:16; 16:15). Cf. O. Michel, *TDNT* 5:131; LSJ, 1203. Note, however, Craig S. de Vos, "The Significance of the Change from οἶκος to οἰκία in Luke's Account of the Philippian Gaoler (Acts 16:30–4)," *NTS* 41 (1995): 292–96, who explores the different nuances of the two words in that specific Lukan context.

for both the building (part or whole) in which people live and the human members or material contents that comprise the household.[20] בית and οἶκος may thus designate physical locations such as house, palace, and temple, or rooms or halls within these,[21] and also human groups ranging in scope from the immediate or extended family to the clan, dynasty, tribe, or tribal league,[22] hence the frequent Hebrew Bible expression "house of Israel" (בית ישראל).[23] A particularly interesting and relevant example of the use of οἶκος is in the late-second or early-first-century BCE inscription from Philadelphia in Lydia, discussed by Stephen Barton and Greg Horsley. The inscription sets out the regulations for members of a private Hellenistic cultic association, and uses the word οἶκος to denote both the (private) meeting room or building and the association (of people) itself.[24]

A number of other related Greek terms also need to be included along with οἶκος/οἰκία in a consideration of the use of household language to describe the Christian community in the Pauline letters. Some of these relate more to the notion of the οἶκος as a building—οἰκοδομή and οἰκοδομέω for example—others to οἶκος as household, such as οἰκεῖος and οἰκέτης. When and where these words are relevant to a metaphorical description of the Christian community as a household has to be decided according to context.

Since there is a range of potentially relevant terms and a basic distinction between οἶκος used of physical locations and the same word used of human groupings, it is more difficult than in the case of ἀδελφός to say something basic about what the term or terms convey and imply. However, it would seem fair to say that when οἶκος is used to describe the human household it often denotes some kind of structured and stratified

20. Cf. Carolyn Osiek and David L. Balch, *Families in the New Testament World: Households and House Churches* (Louisville: Westminster John Knox, 1997), 6: "The Greek *oikos, oikia*, Hebrew *bayit*, and Latin *domus* can all refer to the physical building but can all just as well, and more often do, mean: household, including material goods and slaves; immediate blood family; or family lineage."

21. E.g., H. A. Hoffner points out that בית can designate a building or part of a building, including house, palace, temple, or room or hall within these (*TDOT* 2:107–16). Michel, *TDNT* 5:119–20, mentions house, cave, temple, treasure-house, dwelling, etc., as meanings of οἶκος; cf. also LSJ, 1204–5.

22. Cf. Gen 17:12, 27; 24:27, 38; 34:19; Exod 6:14; Num 2:34; Josh 17:17; 22:14, etc.

23. Exod 16:31; Lev 10:6; Num 20:29; Josh 21:45; Isa 5:7; Jer 2:4, etc. The phrase is often rendered οἶκος Ισραηλ in the LXX (e.g., Lev 10:6; Num 20:29; Ruth 4:11), though sometimes υἱοὶ Ισραηλ, etc. (e.g., Exod 16:31; Josh 21:45).

24. S. C. Barton and G. H. R. Horsley, "A Hellenistic Cult Group and the New Testament Churches," *JAC* 24 (1981): 7–41, esp. 15–16, 31–32.

group.[25] Despite the diversity of real family structures at the time,[26] which often deviated from the "ideal" of an extensive household headed by a κύριος or paterfamilias, there are clearly distinctions between husbands and wives, parents and children, owners and slaves.[27] Precisely what size or kind of οἶκος is in view, however, can only be determined from the context of each particular reference. Indeed, it is most important to stress that an assessment of the implications of sibling and household language for the structuring of social relationships can only be undertaken by examining the context of specific occurrences, the discourse in which the terms are embedded.

The Language of Kinship and Household and the Structuring of Social Relationships

The Authentic Pauline Letters

Let us then turn to a survey of the occurrences of sibling and household language in the authentic Pauline letters and first to the use of the terms ἀδελφός/ἀδελφή to denote fictive kinship relations between fellow Christians (see appendix).[28] As is well known, Paul uses the term ἀδελφοί fre-

25. Cf. again Sandnes, "Equality within Patriarchal Structures," 150.

26. See the important article by Dale B. Martin, "The Construction of the Ancient Family: Methodological Considerations," *JRS* 86 (1996): 40–60. On household structures around the time of Christian origins, see David C. Verner, *The Household of God: The Social World of the Pastoral Epistles*, SBLDS 71 (Chico, CA: Scholars Press, 1983), 27–81; more generally, Osiek and Balch, *Families*; Suzanne Dixon, *The Roman Family* (Baltimore: Johns Hopkins University Press, 1992).

27. Verner, *Household of God*, 79: "in both [Greek and Roman] societies the household was conceived as a patriarchal institution, whose male head (κύριος, *paterfamilias*) exercised sweeping, although not entirely unrestricted authority over the other members. These members fell into three main categories, namely, wife, children, and slaves." Hoffner (*TDOT* 2:111) outlines the similar structure of the οἶκος/בית in ancient Greek, Semitic, and Hittite traditions; it comprised "a father, his wife, his own and adopted children, dependent relatives, clients, and domestic servants (i.e., male and female slaves)."

28. The figures given for the Pauline epistles here differ slightly from those given by Bartchy, "Undermining Ancient Patriarchy," 70, for "Paul's Use of Surrogate Kinship Language." This appears to be due to the fact that Bartchy has wrongly included all appearances of the term ἀδελφός/ἀδελφή, even when they clearly describe a biological kinship relation and not the surrogate kinship of Christian believers (i.e., Gal 1:19; 1 Cor 9:5; and probably Rom 16:15). I have also excluded Rom 9:3, where Paul uses ἀδελφοί of Israel rather than

quently in addressing the congregations to which he writes; and he refers to individual believers, specific or nonspecific, as ἀδελφός or ἀδελφή.[29] Robert Banks rightly observes that the designation ἀδελφοί "is far and away Paul's favorite way of referring to the members of the communities to whom he is writing."[30] Leaving aside the uses of ἀδελφός or ἀδελφή to refer to biological kinship relations or to the people of Israel (Rom 9:3), Paul uses ἀδελφοί (and, less frequently, the singular form, both masculine and feminine) to refer to Christian believers 112 times in the seven authentic letters; that is, on average fractionally over once per page of the Nestle-Aland Greek text (26th edition).[31] The prominence of this kinship description would seem to imply that Paul both assumes and promotes the relationship between himself and his addressees, and among the addressees themselves, as one between equal siblings, who share a sense of affection, mutual responsibility, and solidarity. In most of these places, the term ἀδελφοί appears simply as an apparently standard and common—though not for that reason insignificant—designation of the Christians Paul is addressing: "I do not want you to be ignorant, ἀδελφοί" (Rom 1:13; 11:25); "I appeal to you, ἀδελφοί" (Rom 15:30; 1 Cor 1:10; 16:15; cf. 1 Thess 5:14); and so on. That ἀδελφός is a basic identity designation of those who are members of the Christian communities is also indicated in 1 Cor 5:11, where Paul warns the Corinthians against association with any so-called brothers (ἀδελφὸς ὀνομαζόμενος) who are shown by their immorality not to be truly ἀδελφοί, like the sexually immoral man who is to be shunned and expelled from the church (5:1–8).

While the various nuances and variations among these many instances could no doubt profitably be explored,[32] the texts that seem especially sig-

---

of the Christian community. See also the table provided by von Allmen, *Famille de Dieu*, xxvii, discussion on 156–65.

29. Unsurprisingly, Paul uses ἀδελφός much more frequently than ἀδελφή. The lack of parallel in 1 Cor 7:12–13 is striking (εἴ τις ἀδελφὸς . . . καὶ γυνὴ εἴ τις), but no great significance can be attached to this given the phrase ὁ ἀδελφὸς ἢ ἡ ἀδελφή in v. 15.

30. Banks, *Paul's Idea of Community*, 50–51. Despite this fact, the notion of the church as "family" is seen only as one of a number of "descriptions" of the church in Paul, and not as a significant "model" of the church, by Helen Doohan (*Paul's Vision of Church*, GNS 32 [Wilmington, DE: Glazier, 1989], 137–69). She privileges the more theological "models" of the church—"new creation," "body of Christ," etc.—thus bearing out Bartchy's point that the importance of sibling language in Paul has generally been neglected ("Undermining Ancient Patriarchy," 69–70).

31. Taking the data from the 27th or 28th editions would make no significant difference.

32. For a comprehensive study, see Schäfer, *Gemeinde als "Bruderschaft,"* 330–52. It is notable, for example, that 1 Thessalonians—addressed to a community with which Paul is

nificant for our purposes are those where sibling language is used with an apparently deliberate and repeated emphasis and where it expresses a particularly ethical concern. The passages most worthy of note in this regard are Rom 14:10–21 (where there are five occurrences in eleven verses); 1 Cor 6:5–8 (four occurrences in four verses); and 1 Cor 8:11–13 (four occurrences in three verses).[33]

In each of these places Paul is challenging his readers to give to their fellow Christians a degree of consideration, respect, and care that is currently lacking but that should follow from their identity as ἀδελφοί—hence the reason for the emphatic use of sibling language. In 1 Cor 6:1–8 Paul criticizes those among the Corinthian community who are taking their fellow believers to court; indeed, he explicitly aims to put them to shame (6:5). For Paul their behavior shows a scandalous lack of appreciation both of their status as ἅγιοι amid the "unrighteous" of the world (6:1–3), and also of the fact that those whom they accuse in court are ἀδελφοί (6:5–8). An emphasis on the identity of their opponents as ἀδελφοί is especially clear in v. 8: "But you yourselves wrong and defraud, and brothers and sisters at that [καὶ τοῦτο ἀδελφούς]."

In 1 Cor 8:1–13 Paul begins his discussion of food sacrificed to idols by seeking to change the basis on which "the strong" make their ethical decision on this matter (see further ch. 6 below). Rather than base their decision—which is currently an assertion of their right to eat without restriction—on their theological knowledge ("there is no idol in the world"; v. 4), Paul wants them to base it upon love, on a concern for the other who may be offended

pleased and on good terms (1 Thess 1:2–10; 4:9–12)—has the highest incidence of ἀδελφός language among the genuine Paulines, 2 Corinthians the lowest, reflecting perhaps the fraught and difficult relationship between Paul and the Corinthians after the painful visit (2 Cor 2:1). However, the variations between Paul's letters in their uses of ἀδελφός language cannot be consistently explained on this basis alone, and other factors would have to be explored in any attempt to explain the variations. Cf. further John M. G. Barclay, "Thessalonica and Corinth: Social Contrasts in Pauline Christianity," *JSNT* 47 (1992): 49–74; Craig S. de Vos, *Church and Community Conflicts: The Relationships of the Thessalonian, Corinthian, and Philippian Churches with Their Wider Civic Communities*, SBLDS 168 (Atlanta: Scholars Press, 1999).

33. See further the detailed discussions in Aasgaard, *"My Beloved Brothers and Sisters!,"* 118–303. The list of passages worthy of consideration could of course be expanded considerably. Note, e.g., 1 Cor 7:12–15, where the marital relationship between an ἀδελφός or ἀδελφή and their non-Christian spouse is the matter of concern; and 1 Thess 4:6, where, like 1 Cor 6:1–8, Paul's concern is that no one should wrong or exploit an ἀδελφός. On Phlm 16 see below.

or damaged through their conduct (vv. 1–3, 7–13).[34] He warns them against "destroying" one of "the weak" (v. 11), and strongly insists upon the consideration that should be shown towards even these "weak" members of the community. Here, as elsewhere, the ethical appeal of the sibling language is intensified by using the singular form:[35] each single individual is "ὁ ἀδελφός for whom Christ died" (8:11). In that concise phrase both sibling language and the central Christian confession concerning Christ's self-giving death serve as ethical foundations for an "other-regarding" morality that gives equal value to each member of the community (cf. 1 Cor 12:25–26).[36] Both aspects of that ethical appeal are intensified further in the following verses (vv. 12–13): sinning against οἱ ἀδελφοί is a "sin against Christ"—this is the only time Paul ever uses this stern and serious phrase. Finally Paul illustrates the lengths to which he would go in order not to cause a sibling to stumble: he would never eat meat again rather than cause such offense. Notable for our investigation here is his twice-repeated description of such a person as ὁ ἀδελφός μου.[37]

The pattern of ethical argument Paul developed in 1 Cor 8:1–11:1 is drawn on again in the related but different context addressed in Rom 14:1–15:13. Here too Paul wants to persuade Christians with different convictions regarding prohibited foods and special days not to judge but to accept and welcome one another (προσλαμβάνεσθε ἀλλήλους—Rom 15:7).[38] Again there is a repeated insistence that those who are judged and despised are ἀδελφοί: this in itself should apparently reveal such antagonism as utterly inappropriate. Also notable once again is the use of the singular form of the noun to focus and personalize the appeal: all five occurrences of ἀδελφός in Rom 14:10–21 are singular, four of them followed by σου—ὁ ἀδελφός

34. For a detailed consideration of Paul's ethical argument in these chapters, see David G. Horrell, "Theological Principle or Christologial Praxis? Pauline Ethics in 1 Cor 8:1–11:1," *JSNT* 67 (1997): 83–114.

35. See esp. Rom 14:10–21; also 1 Cor 6:5–6; 1 Thess 4:6.

36. On this christologically based pattern of "other-regarding" morality in Pauline ethics, see David G. Horrell, "Restructuring Human Relationships: Paul's Corinthian Letters and Habermas's Discourse Ethics," *ExpTim* 110 (1999): 321–25.

37. Note the singular; see n. 35 above.

38. On the context addressed here see John M. G. Barclay, "'Do We Undermine the Law?' A Study of Romans 14:1–15:6," in *Paul and the Mosaic Law*, ed. James D. G. Dunn, WUNT 89 (Tübingen: Mohr Siebeck, 1996), 287–308; and Mark Reasoner, *The Strong and the Weak: Romans 14:1–15:13 in Context*, SNTSMS 103 (Cambridge: Cambridge University Press, 1999). However, I am not always convinced that the parallels Reasoner finds in Roman literature are very close to the concerns of Paul and his addressees.

σου, "*your* brother or sister." One of Paul's very rare references to Christian believers as members of a metaphorical household appears here in support of the same ethical argument: judgment of a fellow believer is inappropriate not only because he or she is an ἀδελφός, but also because he or she is an οἰκέτης (again, Paul uses the singular form) belonging to the κύριος, and the right to judge them is therefore his alone (14:4). Moreover, alongside the emphatic use of sibling language and this one example of "household" language, in both the Romans and the 1 Corinthians passages, Paul also uses the language of building as part of his appeal for mutual regard and solidarity among the ἀδελφοί of the congregation.[39]

One final example deserves to be considered, not least because of the comparison it facilitates with a significant passage in 1 Timothy: Paul's letter to Philemon. Paul strengthens the emotional intensity of his appeal to Philemon by twice addressing him directly as ἀδελφέ (vv. 7, 20). Equally significant is Paul's direct appeal that Philemon receive back his slave, without regard for any wrong he may have committed (v. 18), "no longer as a slave, but more than a slave, a beloved brother" (v. 16).[40] That this is meant to imply a real change in the social relationship between slave and owner, and not merely a spiritual revaluation in the sight of God, is strongly suggested by Paul's declaration that their brotherhood exists "both in the flesh and in the Lord" (v. 16).[41]

In all these instances it would seem right to conclude that Paul uses sibling language to promote the solidarity and mutual regard among members of the congregations.[42] His emphatic use of such language when confronting

39. οἰκοδομέω: 1 Cor 8:1, 10 (used ironically); cf. 10:23. οἰκοδομή: Rom 14:19; 15:2. For the same terms elsewhere in Paul see Rom 15:20; 1 Cor 14:3–5, 12, 17, 26; 2 Cor 5:1; 10:8; 12:19; 13:10; Gal 2:18; 1 Thess 5:11.

40. On the implications of this see further Norman R. Petersen, *Rediscovering Paul: Philemon and the Sociology of Paul's Narrative World* (Philadelphia: Fortress, 1985), 266–70, 288–89. Allen Dwight Callahan rightly notes: "Fraternal love is a leitmotiv of the epistle" (*Embassy of Onesimus: The Letter of Paul to Philemon*, New Testament in Context [Valley Forge, PA: Trinity Press International, 1997], 49). I find less convincing Callahan's argument that Onesimus was not actually a slave (see 4–19, 44, 47, 69, etc.). See further ch. 3 above.

41. It is the phrase καὶ ἐν σαρκί that is especially noteworthy: it seems intended to oppose explicitly any notion that this "brotherhood" applied only to some nonworldly realm in the sight of God. For comparable uses of ἐν κυρίῳ see 1 Cor 7:22, 39; 11:11.

42. Also significant, of course, are Paul's appeals for φιλαδελφία and ἀγάπη among members of the congregations (e.g., Rom 12:9–10; 13:8–10; 1 Cor 13:1–13; 1 Thess 4:9). See further Schäfer, *Gemeinde als "Bruderschaft"*; Sandnes, "Equality within Patriarchal Structures," 150–65; Aasgaard, "Brotherhood in Plutarch and Paul."

situations in which there is currently a lack of such concern indicates that he sees sibling bonds as implying precisely that mutualism which he seeks to foster. In Scott Bartchy's words, "his readers were challenged to practice the general reciprocity and mutual support that characterized the relations among siblings at their best."[43]

However, that should not be taken to imply that Paul's vision is unambiguously that of an egalitarian community. It seems to me that that *is* essentially what Paul implies with the designation ἀδελφοί, but of course that is not the only designation Paul uses, either of himself or of his congregations.[44] For example, Paul describes the Corinthians as his beloved children (ὡς τέκνα μου ἀγαπητά) and himself as their father (πατήρ), a position from which he can threaten them with the rod (1 Cor 4:14–15, 21).[45] His calling by God to proclaim the gospel to the gentiles, and his role as "founding father," give him (he believes) some power and authority over his churches (cf. 2 Cor 10:8; 13:10).[46] What seems clear, nonetheless, is that the frequent use of ἀδελφός language reflects both an established designation for the members of the Christian assemblies and Paul's efforts to ensure that social relationships ἐν ἐκκλησίᾳ are structured in a manner appropriate to their description as groups of equal siblings. Yet distinctions

43. Bartchy, "Undermining Ancient Patriarchy," 77. Bartchy, however, strongly disagrees with the labeling of such relations as "egalitarian," largely because sibling language belongs within the sphere of kinship whereas the term *egalitarian* belongs within the sphere of politics. However, given the use of kinship language in various social and political settings (see above, with nn. 11–17) this distinction in the spheres to which the two respective sets of terminology belong seems to me hard to sustain. Cf. also Plutarch, *On Brotherly Love* 484B–E.

44. The status differentiations that might be introduced between elder and younger brothers and between brothers and sisters are largely excluded because Christ is himself the firstborn son (Rom 8:29) and both male and female believers acquire the status υἱοὶ θεοῦ (Rom 8:14; Gal 3:26).

45. Cf. also 2 Cor 12:14; Gal 4:19; 1 Thess 2:11. His juxtaposed descriptions of Onesimus as his child (Phlm 10) and as a brother (Phlm 16) show that these labels are not a fixed description of a certain pattern of relations but a field of metaphors, used to shape relationships in various ways. Nonpatriarchal images are also found, such as when Paul describes himself as the Thessalonians' wet nurse (τροφός, 1 Thess 2:7; cf. 1 Cor 3:2).

46. Ernest Best raises some important questions concerning the common assumption that Paul's authority is basically to be understood as "apostolic authority." Best argues that "Paul claimed to be an apostle. . . . But he only used the title when others disputed it or might dispute it. Basically, he considered himself the parent of those to whom he wrote." A better term than *parent*, Best suggests, is founding father ("Paul's Apostolic Authority—?," *JSNT* 27 [1986]: 17).

can be, and are, made among the ἀδελφοί (cf. Gal 6:6; 1 Thess 5:12), and Paul certainly does not restrict himself to a role as an ἀδελφός among equal siblings.

The use of οἶκος/οἰκία language in Paul's letters is hard to assess in any meaningful way with statistics, since there is a range of relevant terms that may or may not be used in a manner relevant for our present concern. As indicated above, the terms and their uses fall into two broad groups (not always clearly distinguishable), according to whether they are describing the act or object of building, on the one hand, or the human beings who comprise a household on the other. Paul not infrequently urges the "building up" of the members of the congregation (e.g., Rom 14:19; 15:2; 1 Cor 14:3–5, 26; 1 Thess 5:11) and refers to the community as a building or a temple (1 Cor 3:9, 16–17; 2 Cor 6:16).[47] However, none of these references conveys the image of the church as a human household.

There are a number of references to actual households (1 Cor 1:16; 16:15), or to the assembly that meets in so-and-so's house (Rom 16:5; 1 Cor 16:19; Phlm 2), but the terms οἶκος and οἰκία are never used by Paul to describe the Christian community.[48] Despite the appearance of the word οἰκία, 2 Cor 5:1–2 does not seem strictly relevant, since Paul is there describing the contrast between an earthly home (i.e., the human body) in which we dwell and a heavenly home not made with hands; he indicates the longing he has to inhabit the latter. The concern is with death and the transformation that then occurs, and with the assurance that despite the body's death, the Christian will not be naked or homeless.

The image of believers as members of a spiritual or fictive household is glimpsed briefly on two occasions, one of which we have already mentioned: in Rom 14:4 a Christian is portrayed as an οἰκέτης belonging to the Lord and in Gal 6:10 Paul describes fellow believers as οἰκεῖοι τῆς πίστεως. There is, then, little evidence of the household image providing a structuring model

47. On this imagery in the Corinthian letters see John R. Lanci, *A New Temple for Corinth: Rhetorical and Archaeological Approaches to Pauline Imagery*, Studies in Biblical Literature 1 (New York: Lang, 1997).

48. Cf. Georg Schöllgen, "Hausgemeinden, οἶκος-Ekklesiologie und monarchischer Episkopat," *JAC* 31 (1988): 74–90, esp. 82. The distinction between assemblies meeting in houses and the church as modeled on the household is too frequently blurred, as Schöllgen makes clear (77–84). See, e.g., Hans-Josef Klauck, *Hausgemeinde und Hauskirche im frühen Christentum*, SBS 103 (Stuttgart: Katholisches Bibelwerk, 1981), 12, 21: "die sich hausweise konstituierende Kirche"; cf. 101–2, etc; Barton and Horsley, "Hellenistic Cult Group," 31 with n112.

for relationships ἐν ἐκκλησίᾳ.[49] That is not to deny, however, that there were people in positions of leadership and power, both resident members of the congregations and itinerant leaders such as Paul himself.[50]

Colossians and Ephesians

The frequency of sibling language is strikingly low in Colossians and Ephesians, compared with the authentic Pauline epistles: ἀδελφός terminology appears only seven times in Colossians and Ephesians (that is, on average 0.36 times per NA[26] page). Every one of the seven letters of Paul, including Philemon, has more uses of fictive sibling language applied to Christians than either Colossians or Ephesians. Indeed, leaving aside the references to named and prominent believers as ἀδελφοί—Timothy, Tychicus, and Onesimus[51]—the members of Christian congregations are described as ἀδελφοί only three times in the two epistles (Col 1:2; 4:15; Eph 6:23). No particular ethical implications are drawn from the sibling language.

Language connected with the image of building appears once in Colossians (ἐποικοδομούμενοι ἐν αὐτῷ [2:7]) and a number of times in Ephesians (2:20–21; 4:12, 16, 29), almost always connected with the depiction of the Christian community as a body or building in which Christ is central—either as head, or as cornerstone (Eph 4:15–16; 2:20–22). The image of the congregation as a household appears only once, in Eph 2:19, where the image is used to give the addressees a real sense of belonging: instead of being strangers and aliens (πάροικοι), they are now citizens (συμπολῖται) with the saints and members of the household of God (οἰκεῖοι τοῦ θεοῦ; cf. Gal 6:10: πρὸς τοὺς οἰκείους τῆς πίστεως).[52]

49. Cf. Schöllgen, "Hausgemeinden," 82.

50. On leadership patterns see David G. Horrell, "Leadership Patterns and the Development of Ideology in Early Christianity," in *Social-Scientific Approaches to New Testament Interpretation*, ed. David G. Horrell (Edinburgh: T&T Clark, 1999), 309–37. Schäfer (*Gemeinde als "Bruderschaft,"* 335, 369–85, 407–18, etc.) is rather too concerned to downplay the evidence concerning the exercise of power and authority: in his thorough investigation of the "brotherhood" language and concept, he overstresses the extent to which "brotherly" equality characterized the Pauline congregations.

51. See Col 1:1; 4:7, 9. The reference to Tychicus in Col 4:7 reappears verbatim in Eph 6:21.

52. Cf. also 1 Pet 1:17; 2:5; 2:11; 4:17. On this theme in 1 Peter, see John H. Elliott, *A Home for the Homeless: A Sociological Exegesis of 1 Peter, Its Situation and Strategy* (London: SCM, 1982); though note the criticisms raised by Schöllgen, "Hausgemeinden," 83–84.

An important and relevant feature of Colossians and Ephesians is their interest in the proper structuring of the household, an interest expressed in the so-called household codes (Col 3:18–4:1; Eph 5:21–6:9). While these codes are concerned with relations in actual individual households and not with the church itself as a household,[53] their explicit concern with the management of relations between parents and children, masters and slaves, is a significant innovation for which there is little precedent in Paul. Paul is certainly concerned with sexual morality, and therefore with the issues of sexual relations in and outside marriage, with divorce, betrothal, remarriage, and so on (cf. 1 Thess 4:1–8; 1 Cor 5:1–13; 6:12–20; 7:1–40), and also with issues concerning the identity and relations of men and women (1 Cor 11:2–16).[54] However, he seldom, if ever, gives any direct instruction concerning the "appropriate" behavior required from other social groups within the household (slaves-masters, fathers-children), as is clear in the household codes.[55] Paul's ethical concern is with relations among ἀδελφοί, and between ἀδελφοί and outsiders (e.g., 1 Cor 6:1–8; Rom 13:1–7); it is fundamentally as relations among ἀδελφοί that he seems to envisage the relationships among the members of the congregations (cf. 1 Cor 7:12–15). Colossians and Ephesians, however, demonstrate a concern to give ethical instruction to these ἀδελφοί (as they are still occasionally called) according to their social position within the human household.

The Pastoral Epistles

As in Colossians and Ephesians, so too in the Pastoral Epistles, the use of sibling terminology to describe the members of the Christian community is

53. So Schöllgen, "Hausgemeinden," 83.

54. I take 1 Cor 14:34–35 to be an interpolation; for detailed argument see Horrell, *Social Ethos*, 184–95.

55. If authentic, 1 Cor 14:34–35 would be the only place where Paul calls for the subordination of one social group (women or wives to men or husbands), though a secondary place in a created hierarchy may well be implied for women in 1 Cor 11:2–9. In 1 Cor 7:17–24, Paul gives his general advice that people should stay as they are; they do not need to change their social position (an argument that relates to the wider discussion of being married or single). In the case of slaves, however, they are urged to take the opportunity of freedom if it comes their way (for this interpretation of 7:21, see Horrell, *Social Ethos*, 162–66). On all these passages and the wider issues, see Horrell, *Social Ethos*, 158–98. In Philemon, Paul of course gives instruction to a slave owner (though not to any slaves), but this is a specific and personal request.

comparatively rare: there are five such occurrences in the three epistles (that is, on average 0.28 times per NA[26] page) of which three represent a general description of all believers as ἀδελφοί (see 1 Tim 4:6; 6:2; 2 Tim 4:21). In the case of the Pastoral Epistles, this might be thought to be attributable to the fact that these letters are, at least ostensibly, addressed to individual church leaders—Timothy and Titus—rather than to whole congregations. However, comparison with Paul's short letter to Philemon, which has more uses of ἀδελφός terminology than all three Pastoral Epistles added together, indicates that this is not a complete or satisfactory explanation. Nevertheless, statistics can provide only a crude and cursory overview of the picture, and examination of the ways in which such language is used in context is most important for determining its significance for the structuring of Christian social relationships.

Of particular note are the places in 1 Timothy where some qualification of the basic designation of all believers as ἀδελφοί is evident. In 1 Tim 5:1–2, Timothy is urged, presumably because of his young age (1 Tim 4:12) to exhort an elder man as a father, younger men as ἀδελφοί, elder women as mothers, and younger women as ἀδελφαί.[56] The elder figures in the community—senior in faith as well as age and perhaps social standing[57]—are set above those whose junior status enables Timothy to address them as ἀδελφοί. In terms of familial terminology, these elders, like Paul before them, are in the position of fathers and mothers within the congregations.

A clear acknowledgment of the fact that Christian slaves and Christian masters are ἀδελφοί is found in 1 Tim 6:2, but in contrast to the appeal Paul made to Philemon on behalf of Onesimus (see above), here slaves are warned *against* drawing from this fact any ideas about the restructuring of the social relationship between slaves and masters (δεσποταί).[58] They are not to "despise" (μὴ καταφρονείτωσαν) their masters "because they are ἀδελφοί" but

56. Even if—as seems to me likely—the address to Timothy is part of the device of pseudepigraphy, the pattern of relationships according to seniority within the church is nonetheless presented as exemplary.

57. See further R. Alastair Campbell, *The Elders: Seniority within Earliest Christianity*, SNTW (Edinburgh: T&T Clark, 1994).

58. Clearly some of the differences may be explicable on the grounds of the different situations and addressees. Nevertheless, it remains significant that in Philemon Paul does not make any comments (or promises) about Onesimus's return as an obedient and submissive slave (and Phlm 16 may imply quite the opposite), whereas the author of 1 Timothy makes no comments about the obligations of slave owners (e.g., to treat their slaves decently; cf. Col 4:1; Eph 6:9).

rather to serve them all the more (ἀλλὰ μᾶλλον δουλευέτωσαν) because they are beloved fellow believers. The verb καταφρονέω here clearly expresses a view from above, from the perspective of the slave-owners: what Christian slaves are likely to do specifically on the basis that their masters are ἀδελφοί (ὅτι ἀδελφοί εἰσιν) is not exactly to despise them, but rather to act in a way subversive of the master-slave relationship, treating them more like equal siblings, as ἀδελφοί. For the author of the Pastorals this is in effect to treat them—or rather, their social position—with contempt: it is the opposite of serving them well.

The contrast with Paul's use of ἀδελφός language should be clear. Paul on several occasions, not least in his letter to Philemon, urges Christians to consider the fact that they and their fellow believers are ἀδελφοί, to draw from this fact appropriate conclusions and to restructure their social relationships accordingly. The author of the Pastoral Epistles does not (and could hardly) deny the firmly established belief that fellow Christians are ἀδελφοί. But he does warn slaves *not* to draw social consequences from this. On the contrary, he adds Christian legitimation to the notion that slaves should serve Christian owners willingly and well (ὅτι πιστοί εἰσιν καὶ ἀγαπητοί).

This concern for the "proper" and traditional structuring of social relations between household members—the concern central to the household codes of Colossians and Ephesians—appears elsewhere in the Pastoral Epistles, though nowhere is there a concise and complete domestic code comparable to those found in Col 3:18–4:1 and Eph 5:21–6:9. Notable in the Pastoral Epistles is the emphasis on teaching directed towards the subordinate social parties, women and slaves; teaching that urges these people to remain quietly and submissively in their place (1 Tim 2:9–15; 6:1–2; Titus 2:1–10). The male heads of households are urged to govern their households well—keeping their children submissive, and so on—and thus to qualify as potential leaders over the church itself (1 Tim 3:4–5, 12–13).

The imagery of building does not appear prominently in the Pastoral Epistles,[59] but the image of the church as a household clearly does. It is true that the description of the church as an οἶκος, specifically the οἶκος θεοῦ, appears only once (1 Tim 3:15). But the context in which that statement is made reveals that the hierarchical household model has become an impor-

59. Ὀικοδομέω and οἰκοδομή do not appear. Note, however, στῦλος and ἑδραίωμα in 1 Tim 3:15; these terms show that the οἶκος image in that verse contains the idea of the house building as well as of the household members. Cf. also 2 Tim 2:20.

tant one for the structuring of church life.[60] The preceding verses have discussed the qualifications necessary for leadership in the church and have repeatedly made clear that those who seek to be ἐπίσκοποι and διάκονοι must be male heads of households who manage their own households well (see 1 Tim 3:4–5, 12).[61] Women are permitted a leadership role only in relation to other women (1 Tim 2:11–15; cf. Titus 2:3–5).[62] Competent leadership of the human household is an essential prerequisite for competent leadership of God's household, and only those who are in a position to do the former can legitimately undertake the latter. The image of the church as a household also appears in 2 Tim 2:20–21. Urging his readers to rid themselves of wickedness, the author speaks of a μεγάλη οἰκία in which there are various kinds of vessels for various uses, some honorable, some dishonorable. Applying this metaphor to the church, the author assures his readers that those who cleanse themselves from evil will become honorable vessels, useful to the master (δεσπότης). The οἶκος θεοῦ is an οἶκος that, like its earthly counterparts, is hierarchically ordered and stratified, with God as its supreme δεσπότης.[63]

So then, while the designation of believers as ἀδελφοί is represented in the Pastoral Epistles, the model of the household has become significantly more important as a model for the structuring of social relationships within the church.[64] The socially subordinate are specifically

60. Norbert Brox describes 1 Tim 3:15 as "die zentrale ekklesiologische Stelle der drei Briefe" (*Die Pastoralbriefe*, RNT 7 [Regensburg: Pustet, 1969], 157). Quoted with approval by Klauck, *Hausgemeinde und Hauskirche,* 67 (see 66–68). See further Verner, *Household of God*, 147, 186, passim.

61. Cf. also Titus 1:7, where it is said that the ἐπίσκοπος must be ὡς θεοῦ οἰκονόμον. Since the term οἰκονόμος originally designated a person with responsibility for household management, this passage may also reflect the model of the church as household. However, the term οἰκονόμος has a rather wider meaning in NT times and cannot by itself be said to convey a specific link with a household: cf. Rom 16:23; 1 Cor 9:17; Gal 4:2; BAGD, 560; Ceslas Spicq, *Theological Lexicon of the New Testament*, trans. and ed. James D. Ernest, 3 vols. (Peabody, MA: Hendrickson, 1994), 2:568–75.

62. The exhortation to younger widows οἰκοδεσποτεῖν (1 Tim 5:14) seems, in context, to be an instruction that they should take up their proper place in the household structure ("bear children, etc.") rather than gadding about as idle gossips (5:13). They should "manage their own households," or "keep house" (cf. Titus 2:5 [οἰκουργός]; see I. Howard Marshall, *The Pastoral Epistles*, ICC [Edinburgh: T&T Clark, 1999], 604).

63. Notably, in his desire to strengthen the position of the bishop, Ignatius declares that the bishop is the "type" of God the Father, the earthly embodiment of divine leadership (see Ignatius, *Ephesians* 6:1; *Magnesians* 6:1). See further Schöllgen, "Hausgemeinden," 87–88. The term δεσπότης does not appear in the genuine Pauline epistles, nor in Colossians and Ephesians.

64. Both Georg Schöllgen and Ulrike Wagener argue convincingly, "daß der οἶκος als

warned against expecting their identity as ἀδελφοί to have an impact on conventional social relations. The church is a stratified and hierarchical community led by those men who lead their human households well. The hierarchy of social relations found in the human household is presented as the structuring ideal for the church too: slaves should serve their masters well, especially if they are believers (1 Tim 6:1–2; Titus 2:9–10); women should be submissive to their husbands and good workers in the home (Titus 2:5).

Conclusions

What conclusions can we then draw from this investigation? First, it is clear, both from the relative frequency with which the designation ἀδελφός appears and from the ways in which this terminology is used, that the prominence of sibling language as a model for social relationships in the churches decreases notably in the pseudo-Pauline epistles compared with those by Paul himself.[65] Paul on a number of occasions stresses repeatedly the believers' identity as ἀδελφοί, in order to appeal for a degree of solidarity and mutual care that is currently lacking. None of the pseudo-Pauline letters contains anything comparable; indeed, almost the opposite is found in 1 Tim 6:2, where slaves are warned against drawing social consequences from the fact that all believers are ἀδελφοί.

---

ekklesiologisches Leitmodell weder bei Paulus noch in den Deuteropaulinen Kolosser- und Epheserbrief eine entscheidende Rolle spielt. Die Pastoralbriefe erweisen sich so als das älteste Zeugnis für die Erhebung des οἶκος zu ekklesiologischen Leitmetapher" (Ulrike Wagener, *Die Ordnung des "Hauses Gottes": Der Ort von Frauen in der Ekklesiologie und Ethik der Pastoralbriefe*, WUNT 2/65 [Tübingen: Mohr Siebeck, 1994], 236; cf. Schöllgen, "Hausgemeinden," 82–85).

65. Von Allmen ignores the significant variations among the Pauline epistles when he writes: "le sens 'figuré' de ces mots [sc. ἀδελφός/ἀδελφή] est extrêmement fréquent, et son usage est assez régulièrement réparti sur l'ensemble des épîtres, à l'exception de Tite" (*Famille de Dieu*, 156). This conclusion also raises some questions over Bartchy's suggestion (drawing on the work in a dissertation by Joseph Hellerman) that "both the brother-sister rhetoric and sibling values continued to characterize a wide variety of Christian groups throughout the Roman Empire for more than 250 years" and that it was Constantine who was essentially responsible for introducing "a virulent form of hierarchy and patriarchy" into Christianity ("Undermining Ancient Patriarchy," 76–77). The significant changes evidenced within the Pauline corpus indicate that, in at least some strands of early Christianity, moves in this direction should be traced back into the NT period.

Second, alongside the decreased emphasis on the reality and consequences of being ἀδελφοί, it is clear that the model of the hierarchically structured household becomes increasingly significant as the structuring pattern for the church community. An important moment in this ongoing process of the structuration of the early Christian communities would seem to be the introduction of the household codes in Colossians and Ephesians. These codes do not reflect a model of the *church* as household, but are an important step in enabling that model to emerge; they formalize a concern for the proper ordering of the human household, which in the Pastorals becomes a model for the proper ordering of the church itself.[66]

We might then broadly characterize this change as one from the model of an egalitarian community of ἀδελφοί towards the model of a hierarchical household community, a community with masters and subordinates, structured according to the relative positions of different social groups. However, it would be misleading not to qualify that conclusion somewhat, for it is also clear that the genuine Pauline letters do both assume and urge the recognition of certain people—primarily Paul himself—as being in positions of power and authority. If the Pauline churches develop, as they seem to do, from a loosely organized sectarian-type movement where the language of brotherhood predominates, into one which is more structured and "church-like," which mirrors the conventional household hierarchy in its own internal organization, then we should perhaps speak of changes in the *form* of authority and power, rather than implying that we simply move from egalitarianism to authoritarianism. In Weberian terms, we move from a charismatic form of domination towards a traditional form.[67] Nevertheless, this transformation does imply both that the Pauline churches become more hierarchically structured over time, and—crucially—that this structure increasingly mirrors the established and conventional social order, following the stratified household model.

Giddens's structuration theory requires, however, that we appreciate the intertwining of continuity and change, rather than simply emphasizing one or the other: "Every act which contributes to the reproduction of a structure is also an act of production, a novel enterprise, and as such may

66. On this, see further Horrell, "Development of Theological Ideology," 230–35.

67. The language of sect and church here owes much to the typology formulated by Ernst Troeltsch (see Ernst Troeltsch, *The Social Teaching of the Christian Churches*, trans. Olive Wyon, 2 vols. [London: Allen & Unwin, 1931], 1:331–43). On these broader perspectives and their implications, see Margaret Y. MacDonald, *The Pauline Churches: A Socio-historical Study of Institutionalization in the Pauline and Deutero-Pauline Writings*, SNTSMS 60 (Cambridge: Cambridge University Press, 1988); Horrell, "Leadership Patterns."

initiate change by altering that structure at the same time as it reproduces it—as the meaning of words change in and through their use."[68] Continuity is evident in that the designation ἀδελφοί is used of Christian believers in all of the Pauline epistles, and also in that the image of believers as members of a household appears occasionally throughout. However, as this language and imagery are taken up and reproduced in new contexts, significant changes are also apparent, changes that have considerable implications for the structuring of social relationships among the members of the Pauline congregations. Without forgetting, then, that believers are described both as siblings and as household members throughout the Pauline corpus, the character of this significant degree of transformation may nevertheless be epitomized in the phrase "from ἀδελφοί to οἶκος θεοῦ."

68. Anthony Giddens, *New Rules of Sociological Method: A Positive Critique of Interpretative Sociologies* (London: Hutchinson, 1976), 128. Cf. Anthony Giddens, *Central Problems in Social Theory* (London : Macmillan, 1979), 210: "with a conception of structuration, the possibility of change is recognized as inherent in every circumstance of social reproduction."

Appendix

Ἀδελφός/ἀδελφή as fictive kinship terms referring to fellow Christians

Letter	Plural, or nonspecific	Concerning a specific (usually named) believer	Total
1 Thessalonians	18	1	19
Galatians	10	0	10
1 Corinthians	37	2	39
2 Corinthians	4	8	12
Romans	16	2	18
Philippians	8	1	9
Philemon	0	5	5
Totals	93	19	112
Colossians	2	3	5
Ephesians	1	1	2
Totals	3	4	7
1 Timothy	4	0	4
2 Timothy	1	0	1
Titus	0	0	0
Totals	5	0	5
2 Thessalonians (see n. 5 above)	7	1	8

Frequency of fictive sibling terminology (given as average number of occurrences per page of NA^{26} text)

Paul's undisputed letters	1.00
Colossians/Ephesians	0.36
Pastoral Epistles	0.28

Part II

Pauline Ethics in Historical Context

Chapter 5

Particular Identity and Common Ethics

Reflections on the Foundations and Content of Pauline Ethics in 1 Corinthians 5

Introduction: Indicative-Imperative and Beyond

As in so many areas of modern NT studies, so in the study of Pauline ethics the contours of current debate are still shaped by the early contributions of Rudolf Bultmann. In his classic essay of 1924, "Das Problem der Ethik bei Paulus," Bultmann highlighted a crucial and central issue in Pauline ethics, namely the relationship between the indicative and the imperative. In Paul, Bultmann noted, indicative and imperative "are very closely tied together and form an antinomy," as in Gal 5:25: "If we live by the Spirit, let us also walk by the Spirit" (ESV; εἰ ζῶμεν πνεύματι, πνεύματι καὶ στοιχῶμεν).[1] Such expressions, Bultmann suggested, appear "self-contradictory";[2] they are commonly epitomized in the concise phrase "be what you are." Bultmann rejected the notion that the indicatives described a real or objective change in a person while the imperatives called for empirically distinct and identifiable behavior. Rather, "for the believer, the moral demand has acquired *no new content*, and his moral conduct is distinguishable from that of others only in that it bears the character of obedience."[3] "The indicative gives expression to the new self-understanding of the believer," while the imperative shows that their action is done *as* obedience.[4]

1. Rudolf Bultmann, "Das Problem der Ethik bei Paulus," *ZNW* 23 (1924): 123; Bultmann, "The Problem of Ethics in Paul," in *Understanding Paul's Ethics: Twentieth Century Approaches*, ed. Brian S. Rosner (Grand Rapids: Eerdmans, 1995), 195.

2. Bultmann, "Ethik bei Paulus," 123; Bultmann, "Ethics in Paul," 195.

3. Bultmann, "Ethik bei Paulus," 138; cf. Bultmann, "Ethics in Paul," 213.

4. Rudolf Bultmann, *Jesus Christ and Mythology* (London: SCM, 1960), 76.

Bultmann's solution to the "problem" he had so well identified bears all the hallmarks of his existentialist hermeneutic, and fails to convince in a number of respects. For example, as Wolfgang Schrage pointed out in his important study *Die konkreten Einzelgebote in der paulinischen Paränese*, specific commands and exhortations are integral to the Pauline ethic, and Paul's theological ethics cannot be reduced to a new self-understanding and an obligation to love.[5] Schrage agreed, however, that the distinctiveness of Pauline ethics lay not so much in their content (*Was*) as in the sense and motivation (*Wie*) that Paul provides.[6] Nonetheless, Bultmann succeeded in focusing attention on this issue, so much so that Victor Paul Furnish, in what remains a landmark study, could insist that "no interpretation of the Pauline ethic can be judged successful which does not grapple with the problem of indicative and imperative in Paul's thought."[7] Indeed, much more recently, in the context of an attempt to move "beyond indicative and imperative," Ruben Zimmermann notes that the formulation is "still prominent as a foundational pattern right up to the present."[8]

I have already suggested elsewhere, as Zimmermann notes, that a focus on *identity* can offer an alternative way to understand and conceptualize the indicative-imperative antinomy in Paul.[9] It is this proposal I would like to develop here, through an examination of a significant and intriguing ethical text in Paul: 1 Cor 5. This text invites a consideration of the relationship between identity and ethics, and also, I shall argue, shows how a strong sense of distinctive group identity does *not* necessarily imply a distinctive set of ethical norms. We shall thus find relevant material to consider one of the aspects of the study of Pauline ethics cataloged by Zimmermann, namely the question of the "scope of validity of a norm" ("Geltungsbereich einer Norm"), a question concerned with the "relationship between particularism and universalism."[10] Such observations, to be developed in what follows,

5. Wolfgang Schrage, *Die konkreten Einzelgebote in der paulinischen Paränese* (Gütersloh: Mohn, 1961).

6. Schrage, *Einzelgebote*, 200–209.

7. Victor Paul Furnish, *Theology and Ethics in Paul* (Nashville: Abingdon, 1968), 279.

8. Ruben Zimmermann, "Jenseits von Indikativ und Imperativ: Entwurf einer 'impliziten Ethik' des Paulus am Beispiel des 1. Korintherbriefes," *TLZ* 132 (2007): 259–84 (259: "doch als Begründungsmuster bis in die Gegenwart hinein maßgeblich").

9. David G. Horrell, *Solidarity and Difference: A Contemporary Reading of Paul's Ethics* (London: T&T Clark, 2005), 93–95; Zimmermann, "Jenseits von Indikativ und Imperativ," 264.

10. Zimmermann, "Jenseits von Indikativ und Imperativ," 276.

are highly relevant in the context of modern debates about the character of Christian ethics, and the relationship between "church" and "world"; I shall connect my interpretation of 1 Cor 5 with these contemporary debates at the close of this essay.

Identity and Ethics: Towards an Alternative Framework

A first point to note about the indicative-imperative formulation is that, insofar as it expresses an intrinsic and intimate connection between "is" and "ought," it is by no means unique to Pauline, or even Christian, thought. Anthropologist Clifford Geertz, on the basis of the study of diverse (and non-Christian) religious cultures, distinguishes between worldview ("the assumed structure of reality") and ethos ("the approved style of life"),[11] but also insists that these are closely related together: "The powerfully coercive 'ought' is felt to grow out of a comprehensive factual 'is,' and in such a way religion grounds the most specific requirements of human action in the most general contexts of human existence."[12]

The subsuming of the "indicative" into the much broader category of worldview begins to suggest that what is in view here can readily and appropriately be regarded as the foundations of identity: a worldview establishes crucial aspects of "the way things are" and, in doing so, provides a strong sense of "who we are."[13] In this sense, Bultmann was not wrong to speak of the gospel bringing a "new self-understanding"; what is unfortunate in Bultmann's mode of interpretation is his focus on the existential orientation of the individual, the "I" who is addressed and challenged by the Word.[14] Instead, we should see the "indicatives" that constitute a worldview as constructing and maintaining the identity of a group, community, or society.

11. Clifford Geertz, *The Interpretation of Cultures* (New York: Basic Books, 1973), 129; see 126–29.

12. Geertz, *Interpretation of Cultures*, 126.

13. Cf. the classic sociological work of Peter L. Berger and Thomas Luckmann, *The Social Construction of Reality: A Treatise in the Sociology of Knowledge* (Garden City, NY: Doubleday, 1966).

14. Among those who criticize the individualism of Bultmann's hermeneutic and call for its development in a more social and political direction, see Dorothee Sölle, *Political Theology*, trans. John Shelley (Philadelphia: Fortress, 1974); Christopher Rowland and Mark Corner, *Liberating Exegesis: The Challenge of Liberation Theology to Biblical Studies*, Biblical Foundations in Theology (London: SPCK, 1990), 69–74; Gareth Jones, *Bultmann: Towards a Critical Theology* (Cambridge: Polity, 1991), 185–92, 203–8.

Correspondingly, "imperatives" indicate "what we (should) do"; that is, they express the norms and patterns of practice that should characterize those who share a certain identity. Indicative and imperative deal, respectively, with who we are and what we do.

What begins to complicate the distinction, however, is the fact that "what we do" is not merely an *expression* of "who we are," but crucial to and *constitutive* of that identity, at least insofar as we are dealing with aspects of social and personal identity that are not simply fixed but rather constructed and changeable. For example, while I cannot change (except, perhaps, through radical surgery) various physical aspects of my identity (sex, race), my membership of social, religious, or political groupings, while equally tied up with my upbringing and sociogeographical location, is much more obviously changeable, and, crucially, intrinsically bound up with my *acting* in certain ways. While identity should be, indeed unavoidably is, expressed in action, it is equally true, at least in some respects, that action constitutes identity.[15]

Some of these latter aspects of the construction of identity have been the focus of studies by social identity theorists for many years.[16] What interests these theorists in particular are the ways in which groups define and distinguish themselves, and how groups maintain a positive sense of social identity for those who belong to them. This is crucial in order to sustain membership of the group, at least in situations where leaving the group is an option. Indeed, social identity theorists have concluded that it is "a psychological requirement that groups provide their members with a positive social identity," and, moreover, that such positive aspects of social identity

15. Such a close relationship between identity and action is also characteristic of the virtue ethics tradition, in which emphasis falls more on the formation of character than on ascertaining the solution to ethical quandaries. Cf. Stanley Hauerwas, *Character and the Christian Life* (Notre Dame: University of Notre Dame Press, 1975); Alasdair MacIntyre, *After Virtue* (Notre Dame: University of Notre Dame Press, 1981); Horrell, *Solidarity*, 65.

16. See esp. Henri Tajfel, *Social Identity and Intergroup Relations* (Cambridge: Cambridge University Press, 1982); William Peter Robinson, ed., *Social Groups and Identities: Developing the Legacy of Henri Tajfel* (Oxford: Butterworth Heinemann, 1996). This work has been applied to biblical texts in a series of studies by Philip Esler: *Galatians*, New Testament Readings (London: Routledge, 1998); *Conflict and Identity in Romans* (Minneapolis: Fortress, 2003); see also David G. Horrell, "'Becoming Christian': Solidifying Christian Identity and Content," in *Handbook of Early Christianity: Social Science Approaches*, ed. Anthony J. Blasi, Jean Duhaime, and Paul-André Turcotte (Walnut Creek, CA: Alta Mira, 2002), 309–35; Alistair S. May, *"The Body for the Lord": Sex and Identity in 1 Corinthians 5–7*, JSNTSup 278 (London: T&T Clark, 2004).

are "inherently comparative in nature, deriving from evaluative comparisons between social groups."[17]

These theoretical reflections on the recasting of the indicative-imperative concept in terms of social identity and the close connections between who we are and what we do may begin to be suggestive for an analysis of Pauline ethics. But in order to consider whether and how they might prove insightful it is necessary to turn to our chosen text, 1 Cor 5.

The πόρνος and the νέον φύραμα: 1 Cor 5

First Corinthians 5 deals with a notorious case of incest: a man who "has his father's wife." Whether the relationship is one of formal marriage or not,[18] it is clear from the wording of the text that it is a sexual relationship (ἔχειν)[19] between a man and his stepmother (γυνὴ τοῦ πατρός).[20] We shall return to the ethical judgment on this specific relationship later. What is interesting, though, is that having briefly described this situation—with some evident attempt to convey his horror at it (ὅλως ἀκούεται . . . οὐδὲ ἐν τοῖς ἔθνεσιν)—Paul immediately turns his attention to the community, censuring them for their arrogant complacency (πεφυσιωμένοι ἐστε, v. 2; cf. v. 6a) and for failing to cast out from their midst (ἀρθῇ ἐκ μέσου ὑμῶν) the one who has done this (ὁ πράξας). It is the community that is criticized and instructed, not the man himself. Paul proceeds to explain the sentence that he has already pronounced, as if present with them, and that

17. John C. Turner, "Henri Tajfel: An Introduction," in *Social Groups and Identities*, ed. Robinson, 16. Cf. Rupert Brown, "Tajfel's Contribution to the Reduction of Intergroup Conflict," in *Social Groups and Identities*, ed. Robinson, 179.

18. The commentators discuss the uncertainty on this point; see, e.g., Wolfgang Schrage, *Der erste Brief an die Korinther (1 Kor 1,1–6,11)*, EKKNT 7.1 (Zurich: Benziger; Neukirchen-Vluyn: Neukirchener Verlag, 1991), 369; Anthony C. Thiselton, *The First Epistle to the Corinthians*, NIGTC (Grand Rapids: Eerdmans, 2000), 386.

19. The verb, in sexual or marital contexts, is, as Gordon D. Fee notes, "a euphemism for an enduring sexual relationship" (*The First Epistle to the Corinthians*, NICNT [Grand Rapids: Eerdmans, 1987], 200) and an "idiom . . . common in biblical Greek" (278 and n49). Discussing the use in 1 Cor 7:2, Fee cites eight examples from the LXX (Exod 2:1; Deut 28:30; 2 Chr 11:21; 1 Esdr 9:12, 18; Tob 3:8; Isa 13:16; 54:1) and nine from the NT (Mark 6:18; 12:23 [// Luke 20:33; Matt 22:28]; Luke 20:28; John 4:18 [*bis*]; 1 Cor 5:1; 7:29).

20. Note the distinction drawn in Lev 18:7–8 between the mother (μήτηρ) and the father's wife (γυνὴ πατρός σου). Cf. Maria Pascuzzi, *Ethics, Ecclesiology and Church Discipline*, Tesi Gregoriana, Serie Teologia 32 (Rome: Gregorian University Press, 1997), 47.

they should, as a community (συναχθέντων ὑμῶν), enact: "to hand over this man to Satan for the destruction of the flesh, so that his spirit may be saved on the day of the Lord" (v. 5).[21] What exactly this sentence is meant to imply has long been debated: Is it effectively a death sentence,[22] or only a matter of exclusion from the community?[23] Whatever the answer to this difficult question, it is absolutely clear that Paul demands and expects the expulsion of the offender (vv. 5, 7, 11, 13).

The reason why Paul considers this expulsion so vital becomes clear in the analogy he proceeds to develop, citing a proverbial saying he also uses at Gal 5:9: "a little leaven leavens the whole lump" (v. 6). Leaven (not "yeast," as many modern translations have it)[24] is a portion of previously made dough that, when incorporated into a new batch of dough, enables the raising effect of yeast to be transferred and reproduced.[25] While this was a valuable technique, given the difficulty of cultivating fresh yeast, it was also risky, since any impurities or infection in the old lump would, of course, be transferred into the new. Hence, as Leslie Mitton points out, in the NT "leaven is used symbolically to symbolize (*sic*) an evil influence which spreads like an infection."[26] The Israelites' Feast of Unleavened Bread (Exod 12:15–20) thus served (among other things) a practical function: to ensure that, periodically, a fresh start was made. Paul alludes to this festival in his instruction to "clean out the old leaven, so that you may be a new lump, just as you are unleavened" (v. 7a)—here we have another example of the indicative and imperative closely bound together—and in his following references to Christ as the Passover sacrifice (v. 7b) and the need to "celebrate the feast" (ἑορτάζωμεν) "with the unleavened bread of sincerity and truth" (v. 8). The offender, embodying κακία and πονηρία, acts like an infection, polluting the whole lump.[27]

21. On the various possible construals of the syntax of vv. 3–5, see Pascuzzi, *Ethics*, 110–14.

22. As is suggested by Ernst Käsemann, *New Testament Questions of Today*, trans. W. J. Montague (London: SCM, 1969), 71.

23. As argued by James T. South, *Disciplinary Practices in Pauline Texts* (Lewiston, NY: Mellen, 1992), 23–88; May, *Body for the Lord*, 76–77.

24. E.g., NRSV, NIV. German translations more accurately use *Sauerteig* here, not *Hefe*.

25. See C. Leslie Mitton, "New Wine in Old Wineskins: IV. Leaven," *ExpTim* 84 (1973): 339–43; May, *Body for the Lord*, 68–69; Timothy and Barbara Friberg, *Analytical Lexicon to the Greek New Testament* (Grand Rapids: Baker, 2000), s.v. ζύμη.

26. Mitton, "Leaven," 342.

27. On the significance of Paul's depiction of the community as a φύραμα, see Pascuzzi, *Ethics*, 151–55.

Referring to an earlier letter,[28] Paul next reminds the Corinthians of his instruction μὴ συναναμίγνυσθαι πόρνοις (v. 9). He explains that he did not mean that the Corinthians should not associate with such people "of this world," since this would require a withdrawal from the world (v. 10). What he meant, he now clarifies (νῦν δὲ ἔγραψα), was that they should not associate with someone who claims to be an ἀδελφός but is actually a πόρνος, or any other kind of sinner (v. 11). The instruction not even to eat with such persons (τῷ τοιούτῳ μηδὲ συνεσθίειν) suggests a general social disassociation, and more specifically their exclusion from the Lord's Supper, *the* act of communal eating together in early Christianity (cf. 1 Cor 11:17–34).[29] Finally, Paul insists that his responsibility is to judge insiders, not outsiders, whom God (alone) will judge (vv. 12–13). Quoting Deut 17:7 (LXX) he reiterates the key pronouncement: "cast out the evildoer from among you."

Particular Identity

Among the many features of this rich and striking passage, two may be highlighted here. One is that the focus of Paul's concern is not with the individual's conduct—Paul nowhere bothers to explain *why* it might be wrong to "have his father's wife"—but with the character of the community, and the impact of this man's presence upon it. Indeed, while the man is evidently censured for his conduct, Paul's criticism is directed at the community (vv. 2, 6).[30] The second, as Alistair May has pointed out, is that Paul effectively *identifies* the man as a πόρνος (or, more generally, a πονηρός [v. 13]):[31] the vice

28. Generally thought to be lost, though sometimes identified with 2 Cor 6:14–7:1, e.g., by John C. Hurd, *The Origin of 1 Corinthians* (London: SPCK, 1965), 235–37.

29. So, e.g., Judith M. Gundry Volf, *Paul and Perseverance: Staying in and Falling Away*, WUNT 2/37 (Tübingen: Mohr Siebeck, 1991), 115, 117.

30. Cf. Pascuzzi, *Ethics*, 146–67, 183–200, who sees the implication of Paul's focus on the community as a challenge to contemporary "radical individualism." Also Gerald Harris, "The Beginnings of Church Discipline: 1 Corinthians 5," in *Understanding Paul's Ethics: Twentieth Century Approaches*, ed. Brian S. Rosner (Grand Rapids: Eerdmans, 1995), 140: "Paul's concern was not so much a sexual ethic as it was the purity of the Christian community."

31. Peter S. Zaas, "'Cast Out the Evil Man from Your Midst' (1 Cor 5:13b)," *JBL* 103 (1984): 259–61, suggests that the citation from Deut 17:7 was chosen partly because of the wordplay between πόρνος and πονηρός. Cf. also Brian S. Rosner, *Paul, Scripture, and Ethics: A Study of 1 Corinthians 5–7*, AGJU 22 (Leiden: Brill, 1994), 61–93.

lists in vv. 10–11 (and 6:9) list types of sinful *people* (πόρνος, εἰδωλολάτρης), not abstract types of sin (πορνεία, εἰδωλολατρία, as in Gal 5:19–21).[32]

These features combine to indicate that the main thrust of Paul's reaction to this situation is that the community is polluted by the presence of this evildoer in their midst.[33] They are supposed to be a pure, holy community, standing in contrast to a dirty, sinful world, as the depictions in vv. 10–11 clearly show. The πόρνος in their midst does not belong here. In terms derived from Mary Douglas's classic treatment of purity, he is "dirt," matter in the wrong place, and needs to be removed to the "right" place—in the world of sinners—in order to restore the boundaries and identity of the community.[34] As Paul makes clear in vv. 9–11, it is not the existence of πόρνοι and other such sinners that threatens the purity of the community, nor even social interaction with such sinners (v. 10; cf. 1 Cor 10:27; 14:23). Rather, it is interaction with a so-called brother (ἀδελφὸς ὀνομαζόμενος) who is *really* a πόρνος that destroys the purity of the νέον φύραμα.

All of this represents what I have elsewhere called the rhetoric of distinction, namely, the depiction of the ἐκκλησία as a pure and holy community standing in stark contrast to a sinful, unholy world.[35] Clearly, as Bultmann rightly perceived, this does not merely *describe* some supposed empirical contrast between the church and the world, whatever Paul might wish: the notorious Corinthian sinner proves as much, since he is precisely an ἀδελφός who has acted just as badly as anyone "in the world." But neither does it make much sense to see Paul here as insisting that the only distinctive

32. May, *Body for the Lord*, 66–68, 71–74. Pascuzzi, stressing Paul's vision of the community as a "sinless" entity, fails sufficiently to consider why it is that it is only in this particular case that Paul calls for the expulsion of a "sinner" (Pascuzzi, *Ethics*, 162–65). Evidently, as May shows, there is something about *this* case that makes the sin such as to redefine the offender's *identity*, not so in other cases. May argues that sexual sin is particularly significant for Paul, since it concerns (or negates) the believer's "bodily" identification with Christ. See May, *Body for the Lord*, 110, 266–67.

33. Cf. Dale B. Martin, *The Corinthian Body* (New Haven: Yale University Press, 1995), 168: "Paul's primary concern in this passage is the purity of the church, the body of Christ, and his anxieties center on the man as a potentially polluting agent within Christ's body, an agent whose presence threatens to pollute the entire body." William Countryman's argument that Paul formulates sexual ethics on the basis of property rules, not purity concerns, fails to do justice to this text; see L. William Countryman, *Dirt, Greed, and Sex: Sexual Ethics in the New Testament and Their Implications for Today* (Philadelphia: Fortress, 1988), 109, 197–202, 213, etc.

34. Mary Douglas, *Purity and Danger: An Analysis of Concepts of Pollution and Taboo* (London: Routledge & Kegan Paul, 1966).

35. See Horrell, *Solidarity*, 133–65.

aspect of Christian conduct is that it is done "as obedience." Rather, in terms of social identity theory, Paul is constructing and reinforcing a positive sense of group identity for his readers who, though once as dirty and sinful as those in the world (1 Cor 6:11), are now washed, redeemed members of the new, holy, righteous community. This is, as social identity theorists predict, a positive and inherently comparative notion of group identity, built on the idea that these new converts have a superior moral status (1 Cor 5:10–11). The presence of the πόρνος threatens this identity, so Paul uncompromisingly calls for his immediate expulsion. The language and concepts with which this identity is constructed are, here as elsewhere in the Pauline writings, profoundly rooted in Jewish scripture and tradition, reconfigured through a christological lens.[36] As we have seen, the dominant images in this passage are those of leaven and unleavened bread, of Christ as Passover sacrifice, and of the holy community in which evildoers have no place. These are the motivational foundations for Pauline ethics here.

Common Ethics

But, at the same time as we notice how forcefully Paul depicts the contrast between the holy community and the unholy world, and motivates the believers' conduct with scriptural motifs, we should also pause to observe that the ethical norm that underlies Paul's discourse is not distinctively Christian. Paul explicitly indicates this in his comment that the kind of πορνεία found in the Corinthian ἐκκλησία is οὐδὲ ἐν τοῖς ἔθνεσιν (v. 1).[37] Whatever verb Paul intended to imply here,[38] commentators agree that a relationship be-

36. On the use of scriptural imagery and texts here, see Rosner, *Paul, Scripture, and Ethics*, 61–93.

37. Cf. Pascuzzi, *Ethics*, 107: "Paul essentially insinuates that there exists a societal consensus that incest is wrong. . . . This universal moral value is set out as a standard against which Corinthian judgement and behavior is initially critiqued." She sees this as part of the first rhetorical "proof" to the Corinthians that this situation is wrong and must be rectified, one intended to "shame" them (see 101–9). It needs to be stressed, though, that in none of these "proofs" does Paul attempt to demonstrate why the man's relationship should be regarded as sinful, except insofar as he indicates that everyone agrees this to be so.

38. Essentially the two options are (1) "not found" or "heard of" (so, e.g., NRSV: "not found"; Schrage, *Korinther [1 Kor 1,1–6,11]*, 367, 369: "nicht . . . vorkommt"; Hans Conzelmann, *1 Corinthians: A Commentary on the First Epistle to the Corinthians*, trans. James W. Leitch, Hermeneia [Philadelphia: Fortress, 1975], 94: "unheard of") or (2) "not tolerated" or "accepted" (so, e.g., Thiselton, *First Epistle*, 385; Pascuzzi, *Ethics*, 104n42).

tween a man and his mother-in-law was forbidden under both Jewish and Roman law.[39]

For example, the *Institutes* of Gaius, an important second-century CE source for Roman law, record that "I may not marry a woman who was previously my mother-in-law or daughter-in-law or stepdaughter or stepmother. We have said 'previously,' because if the marriage establishing such a relationship is still in being there is another reason why she cannot be married to me; the same woman cannot be married to two men, nor the same man have two wives" (1.63).[40] Cicero also indicates the clear disapproval of such a relationship, referring to just such a case in the course of his defense of Cluentius (*For Cluentius* 5–6). Cicero's comments, like Paul's, emphasize the scandal by inferring that such immorality was very rarely seen: "Oh! to think of the woman's sin, unbelievable, unheard of in all experience save for this single instance" ("O mulieris scelus incredibile et praeter hanc unam in omni vita inauditum!").[41] Cicero's report also indicates, though, that such cases were not "unheard of" ἐν τοῖς ἔθνεσιν, though they clearly were not tolerated or accepted—making this latter an attractive option for Paul's implied verb (see n38).

Jewish proscription stems from Lev 18:7–8; 20:11; Deut 22:30; and 27:20, where the sin of lying with one's father's wife is prohibited because it constitutes an uncovering of one's father's nakedness, that is, a dishonoring of the father and a violation of his sexual rights: "Cursed be anyone who lies with his father's wife, because he has uncovered his father's nakedness" (Deut 27:20). Amos 2:7 cites this as an example of the kinds of sin that profane the name of God, and the book of Jubilees expands the story of Reuben's liaison with his father's mistress (Gen 35:22), presenting this as a reason for the laws against a man lying with his father's wife (Jubilees 33:1–17; cf. also Testament of Reuben 3:11–15). The Torah's regulations are also reiterated by Josephus (*Jewish Antiquities* 3.274), for whom "lying with the father's wife" is one instance of "abominable wickedness," and by Philo (*On the Special Laws* 3.20–21), for whom this regulation demonstrates how carefully the Jewish law guards against incest. The Mishnah lists sex with one's mother, or one's father's wife, among those sexual crimes worthy of

39. See, e.g., Fee, *Corinthians*, 200n24; Thiselton, *First Epistle*, 385–86; also Andrew D. Clarke, *Secular and Christian Leadership in Corinth: A Socio-Historical and Exegetical Study of 1 Corinthians 1–6*, AGJU 18 (Leiden: Brill, 1993), 77–80.

40. Translation from William M. Gordon and Olivia F. Robinson, *The Institutes of Gaius* (London: Duckworth, 1988).

41. *For Cluentius* 6.15 (Hodge, LCL).

stoning to death (m. Sanhedrin 7:4). Such a liaison is forbidden both because the woman is his father's wife and because she is a married woman (cf. the *Institutes* of Gaius, cited above), though the prohibition applies after the father's death as well as in his lifetime (cf., similarly, b. Sanhedrin 54a).

This evidence confirming the widespread agreement on this point is significant. It indicates—as Paul briefly acknowledges in his opening comment—that the substantive ethical norm on which Paul's reaction is based is one that is commonly held. It is not a distinctively Christian or Jewish norm, but one shared and supported ἐν τοῖς ἔθνεσιν. Moreover, Paul nowhere explains or argues for the immorality of this particular kind of sexual relationship. His discussion is focused on showing the Corinthian Christians why they should not tolerate the presence of a πόρνος among them; but this discussion is entirely premised on the assumption that the man *is* a πόρνος, because of his conduct in this matter. In other words, Paul simply assumes and accepts the general ethical norm—that a sexual relationship with one's stepmother is unacceptable—and proceeds to argue on this basis.[42] His argument for the distinct and holy identity of the Christian community is, at the same time, built on a point of shared moral consensus.

Conclusions: Indicative and Imperative, Identity and Ethics, Particular and Universal

Standing back from the details of this particular passage, we may draw out some wider reflections and conclusions relevant to our understanding of Pauline ethics, and to contemporary debates in Christian ethics. I shall begin with some reflections on the indicative-imperative categories, arguing that the concept of identity provides a much better framework within which to make sense of what Paul is saying here. Next, I shall comment on the significance of the distinction I have drawn between particular identity and common ethics. Finally, I shall offer some reflections on the significance of these findings for the contemporary construal of the character of Christian ethics.

42. It is similar with Paul's treatment of sex with prostitutes and with one's spouse, in 1 Cor 6–7: he presumes, rather than argues for, the immorality of the former and the legitimacy of the latter (even when the spouse is an unbeliever) and builds his argument on the basis of this presumption. See Horrell, *Solidarity*, 149, 153–64.

Beyond Indicative and Imperative?

As we have briefly noted, there is one place in our passage where the indicative and imperative are closely bound together: "Cleanse out [ἐκκαθάρατε] the old leaven that you may be [ἦτε] a new lump, as you really are unleavened [ἐστε ἄζυμοι]" (v. 7, ESV). This does not, *pace* Zimmermann, constitute evidence that the content of the Pauline texts contradicts the form of the indicative-imperative schema, since it is precisely such close antinomies to which Bultmann drew attention (e.g., in Gal 5:25) and placed at the center of his reflections.[43] Indeed, one might also agree with Bultmann that here, in a sense, "the indicative calls forth the imperative," since it is the fact that the community "is" the new, unleavened lump that generates the imperative to purge it of the old leaven. However, it is questionable whether Bultmann's notion of the indicative as an expression of the new self-understanding of the believer and the imperative as an expression of the character of their action as obedience is illuminating in this particular case. The passage contains a number of imperatives and implicitly imperatival instructions (vv. 2, 5, 7–8, 11, 12, 13), all of which are focused on the need to expel the evildoer from the community. I have suggested that a focus on identity provides a better perspective with which to make sense of such material. From this angle, the indicatives express the terms in which the identity of the community is defined, while the imperatives call for action to reflect and sustain that identity. In particular, the antinomy of v. 7 can be explained as a tacit reflection of the fact that social identity is constructed and precarious, and thus requires affirmation and action to sustain it: the community members need both to be reminded that they *are* the new and holy community of God—this is the positive identity that members enjoy—and that, as such, they must *be* that holy community, and take the action necessary to maintain that identity, since it is threatened by the πόρνος among them.

There is another respect in which the content of this passage subverts the usual understanding of the relationship between indicative and imperative and is once again better understood in terms of notions of identity.[44] This relationship is usually seen, in Bultmann's words, as one in which "the

43. Zimmermann, "Jenseits von Indikativ und Imperativ," 264: "Das Indikativ-Imperativ-Schema ist ein Forschungskonstrukt, das dem Textbefund widerspricht. . . . Die Klassifikation bestimmter Inhalte in die Sprachmodi 'Indikativ' und 'Imperativ' lässt sich nicht am Text nachweisen. Die gleichen Aussagen können von Paulus sowohl indikativisch als auch imperativisch formuliert werden."

44. I am indebted to Alistair May for the idea expressed in this paragraph.

indicative calls forth the imperative," or, as Michael Parsons puts it, one where "being precedes act": the believer's identity in Christ is expressed in certain patterns of behavior.[45] However, in this text the relationship between identity and action is more complex and interesting, with action much more determinative of identity than the usual formulations of the indicative-imperative relationship would suggest. There can be little doubt that the man at the center of this scandal is—or up to this point, has been—a member of the Corinthian church, an ἀδελφός.[46] Yet his action, in engaging in a relationship with his stepmother, (re)defines his identity, and reveals him truly to be a πόρνος. In other words, it is his action that defines his identity. It is this labeling of his identity that then requires him to be relocated, to be "placed" where his identity indicates he belongs, among the sinners of the world.[47] Paul's concern, as is indicated by the consistent thrust of all the explicit instructions in this passage, is with the purity of the community, with sustaining its positive identity through the prompt removal of a pollutant that threatens to destroy its essential character and whose identity is not congruent with belonging. Compared, then, with traditional theological ap-

45. Michael Parsons, "Being Precedes Act: Indicative and Imperative in Paul's Writing," in *Understanding Paul's Ethics*, ed. Rosner, 247: "The indicative speaks of that which has been accomplished by God in and through Christ. . . . The imperative is grounded on the reality that has been given, appeals to it and is intended to bring it to full development."

46. To argue, as Judith Gundry Volf does, that he is "not a genuine Christian" and so cannot represent a case where a Christian has lost their salvation, fails to consider the crucial question of the man's status prior to his sexual liaison. See Gundry Volf, *Paul and Perseverance*, 119–20, further 113–20. Paul shows no interest in whether the man was ever truly an ἀδελφός. But since it is his immoral sexual *activity* that identifies him as a "so-called brother," a false believer, it is difficult to see any way in which the man could ever have been identified as (only) a "so-called" ἀδελφός except now, and retrospectively, based solely on the fact of his illicit sexual activity. Just as Paul's (re)definition of the man as an outsider is a theological judgment intended to protect the privileged identity of the church, so Gundry Volf's position would seem to reflect a theologically driven conviction that true believers *cannot* fall away: *ex hypothesi*, any believer who does fall away was not a real believer in the first place. So, her study concludes: "We have uncovered clear and abundant evidence that for Paul sure continuity characterizes the salvation of individual believers" (283). "Whereas ethical failure does not exclude true Christians [!] from salvation, according to Paul there is no salvation for those who stand outside the gospel of grace" (285).

47. Cf. May, *Body for the Lord*, 75: "By virtue of Paul's argument, the immoral man is *already* an outsider: he is leaven existing illegitimately in the unleavened bread. . . . Prior to the church's act, Paul has already passed judgment (5:3), but even this judgment merely recognizes the state of affairs revealed by the man's action. . . . The man's sin, and status as a sinner, defines his status as an outsider."

proaches focused on the indicative-imperative scheme or on questions of the security of salvation that are outside Paul's focus of concern,[48] an approach to this passage from the perspective of identity seems to me to make better sense of the dynamics and content of Paul's instruction.

Particular Identity and Common Ethics

In the analysis of the passage above, a key distinction was drawn between the particular identity that Paul is at pains to sustain for the community and the common ethical norm on which his judgment is based. Much of the rhetoric of the passage reflects the sense of distinction Paul seeks to underscore between the holy community and the unholy world. And the motivations for Paul's ethical instruction are drawn from the traditions on which this distinct sense of identity is based: the Jewish scriptures, interpreted christologically (τὸ πάσχα . . . Χριστός).[49] Yet the actual ethical *norm* that Paul assumes as the basis for his judgment is not justified or motivated with resources from this particular tradition; indeed, it is not justified or explained here at all. It is simply presumed, and—as Paul's comment in v. 1 and the findings of historical study together confirm—was evidently accepted as a common ethical norm shared by Jews, Christians, and τὰ ἔθνη.

What this shows, significantly, is that the distinctive sense of particular group identity Paul seeks to construct and sustain for his converts, in Corinth and elsewhere, does *not* depend on a distinct set of ethical norms. In this case at least, we might partially affirm Bultmann's comment that the ethics required of the believer have acquired "no new content." However, while Bultmann sees no empirical distinction between the conduct of believers and unbelievers, only the invisible distinction that the believers' action is done *as obedience*, Paul bases the distinctive identity of the community in part precisely on an empirical and comparative distinction: the Christians do better at meeting these moral standards than those in the world. He does not say this in so many words, of course, but this is the implication of his

48. As in Gundry Volf, *Paul and Perseverance*, 113–20. Paul here simply shows no interest in the question about whether the man was ever truly "saved," prior to his sin, though he evidently holds open the possibility of his final salvation.

49. Pascuzzi, *Ethics*, 139, observes that "Christ's death is the only 'because' (*gar*, v. 7c) in the entire chapter." This is not entirely correct (see v. 3), but rightly identifies v. 7c as an important "explanation" for why the Corinthians are the unleavened lump, and should therefore cast out the evildoer.

insistence that there are πόρνοι in the world, but not in the church, based (at least in this instance) on a commonly agreed norm as to what constitutes πορνεία. This is, in part, why the offender's presence in the church is so dangerous, since it threatens the validity of Paul's empirical claim. Redefining him as an outsider, purely on the basis of his immoral action, theoretically restores the validity of the identification of the community as pure and holy, while at the same time risking its long-term plausibility (How long can one sustain the claim that the community is holy by simply identifying anyone who is unholy as not "really" a member?).

In terms of the foundations and content of Pauline ethics, we should also draw a careful distinction. In this text at least, the ethical *norm*—the substantive ethical *content*—is a commonly accepted one, though Paul evidently expects a higher level of compliance with such norms within the community, compared with people in the world. But the foundations and *motivations* for Pauline ethics here are part of a distinctively scriptural and Christian discourse, focused on the identity of believers as a pure and holy community in Christ. To put this in terms that already suggest a connection with issues in contemporary ethical theory: the community has a distinct and tradition-specific basis to undergird its identity and motivate ethical action, but the content of the invoked ethical norm is tradition-transcendent and held in common by all.

Particular and Universal: Issues in Contemporary Christian Ethics

These observations may valuably be related to what has been described as one of the most significant debates in political theory since the 1980s: that between liberals and communitarians.[50] Put briefly, and in general terms, liberals argue for the possibility of a rational basis for an agreed public morality and system of justice in which individuals can pursue their own freely chosen visions of the good, visions which vary according to religion, culture, identity, and so on. Communitarians, on the other hand, insist that the liberal notion of a tradition-transcendent, rational basis for morality is an impossible and pernicious dream, since it is only by location within a particular tradition, embodied in communities, that people's identity and

50. Cf. Daniel Bell, *Communitarianism and Its Critics* (Oxford: Clarendon, 1993), 2, 27–28; Stephen Mulhall and Adam Swift, *Liberals and Communitarians*, 2nd ed. (Oxford: Blackwell, 1996), xii. See further ch. 8 below.

moral values are formed. The liberal view not only empties such traditions of their integrity by making them merely possible "options" in a forum of free choice but also obscures the extent to which liberalism is itself a particular tradition, which imposes its own moral values, sometimes forcibly.[51]

This debate is played out in particular ways in important disagreements about the character of Christian ethics. Stanley Hauerwas, for example, is probably the most influential and outspoken representative of a kind of Christian communitarianism, since he insists that the task of Christian ethics is to show how the church is called to *be* a particular people, based on a particular story that shapes moral character and sustains specifically Christian virtues.[52] By contrast, other writers, such as David Fergusson, stress the value of a more liberal vision, in which Christians might seek "common cause" with others in the task of building the kind of "moral consensus which alone can sustain a pluralist culture."[53] The debate, in other words, concerns the way in which the church's existence in, and distinction from, the world is to be understood, and the implications of this for Christian ethics.

While a reading of one text in Paul can hardly make a major contribution to resolving such debates, it can at least provide some fruitful stimulus to our thinking in this crucial area. On the one hand, Paul's clear and uncompromising—indeed, rather ominously threatening—call for the expulsion of the offender in order to sustain the character of the distinct Christian community finds an echo in Hauerwas's polemical call for the church to be different from the world, to sustain a distinct identity with correlative ethical practices.[54] Yet on the other hand it is important to note that Paul's attempt to sustain the particular identity of the Christian community does not depend on a distinctive set of ethical norms, but here assumes and invokes a common and taken-for-granted standard. The ethical norm is not distinctive, nor is it generated by the specific tradition whose resources Paul

51. For a more extensive sketch of these positions, and their specific representation in the work of Jürgen Habermas and Stanley Hauerwas, see Horrell, *Solidarity*, 47–82.

52. See, e.g., Stanley Hauerwas, *The Peaceable Kingdom: A Primer in Christian Ethics* (Notre Dame: University of Notre Dame Press, 1983), 99–100.

53. David Fergusson, *Community, Liberalism and Christian Ethics* (Cambridge: Cambridge University Press, 1998), 73, 75.

54. Jeffrey Stout, in a powerful (though not unsympathetic) critique of Hauerwas's work, notes that "Hauerwas likes to shock first and qualify later" (149), and examines the way in which Hauerwas's rhetoric serves to sharpen the sense of opposition between church and world. See Jeffrey Stout, *Democracy and Tradition*, New Forum Books (Princeton: Princeton University Press, 2004), 147–61.

uses to construct the community's identity. The material Paul uses to motivate the community's ethical action and to undergird their distinct identity is tradition-specific; but the ethical norm is not.

Cast in terms of a broader ethical theory, what this suggests is that the maintenance of distinct identities within a framework of shared moral norms—a key facet of the liberal vision—is perhaps not impossible. Put differently, a communitarian focus on the importance of specific traditions for the construction of identity and the motivation of moral action does not necessarily negate the liberal goal of establishing what John Rawls calls an "overlapping consensus" on ethical norms.[55] Paul's discourse in 1 Cor 5 is, of course, in many ways distant from the world of modern political life. His notion of community purity and his uncompromising call for the offender's expulsion (perhaps even his death) are unlikely to be appealing to liberals who like to think that the values of tolerance, liberty, and diversity are foremost in our contemporary public morality. Nonetheless, without denying these clear and significant cultural differences, the historical study of Pauline ethics can perhaps offer some insights relevant to the pressing contemporary task of discerning a way to accommodate and sustain particular identities while seeking and sharing some common ethics.

55. John Rawls, *Justice as Fairness: A Restatement*, ed. Erin Kelly (Cambridge: Harvard University Press, 2001), 32–38.

Chapter 6

Idol Food, Idolatry, and Ethics in Paul

Introduction

In Paul's earliest letter, his brief summary of the Thessalonians' response to the gospel describes how they "turned to God from idols" (1 Thess 1:9). This phrase forms part of what Howard Marshall calls "a classic description of what it meant for a group of Gentiles to become Christians."[1] The language used, commentators often note, is "not characteristically Pauline," and the summary statements in 1 Thess 1:9–10 have often been seen as an echo of earlier Christian material, perhaps derived from the context of gentile mission.[2] Morna Hooker argues to the contrary, that these verses are best seen as a concise summary of the themes Paul will go on to discuss in the letter, and not as a resume of his, or others,' earlier preaching.[3] For our purposes here, resolving this debate is not crucial: whether the phrasing is Paul's or that of his predecessors, it seems certain that Paul shares with other early Christian missionaries the conviction that conversion for gentiles entails "turning from idols."

Elsewhere, Paul describes the fundamental change undergone by gentile converts in terms of a past characterized by involvement with "dumb

1. I. Howard Marshall, *1 and 2 Thessalonians*, NCB (London: Marshall, Morgan & Scott, 1983), 56.

2. Marshall, *Thessalonians*, 56–57; cf. also Ernest Best, *The First and Second Epistles to the Thessalonians*, BNTC (London: Black, 1972), 86–87.

3. Morna D. Hooker, "1 Thessalonians 1:9–10: A Nutshell—But What Kind of Nut?," in *Frühes Christentum*, ed. Hermann Lichtenberger, vol. 3 of *Geschichte—Tradition—Reflexion: Festschrift für Martin Hengel zum 70. Geburtstag*, ed. Hubert Cancik, Hermann Lichtenberger, and Peter Schäfer, 3 vols. (Tübingen: Mohr Siebeck, 1996), 435–48.

idols": "when you were gentiles [ἔθνη]," he reminds the Corinthians, "you were enticed and led astray to idols [εἴδωλα] that could not speak" (1 Cor 12:2, NRSV). The incompatibility of "the temple of God" and "idols" is forcefully stressed in 2 Cor 6:16, while in a number of places "idolaters" (εἰδωλολάτραι) or "idolatry" (εἰδωλολατρία) are included in lists of types of sinner or sin: those who are guilty of idolatry, Paul warns, will not inherit the kingdom of God (1 Cor 6:9; Gal 5:20; cf. 1 Cor 5:10–11).

In fact, nineteen of the thirty-two NT uses of words from the εἰδωλ- word-group—εἴδωλον, εἰδωλεῖον, εἰδωλολατρία, εἰδωλολάτρης, and εἰδωλόθυτον—are in the seven undisputed letters of Paul,[4] not to mention passages like Rom 1:19–32, where idolatry is clearly a key theme in the story of humanity's turn from God (note v. 23), though the word-group itself is not used. Other clusters are in Acts, in passages citing the Apostolic Decree (15:20, 29; 21:25; see also 7:41), and in Revelation (2:14, 20; 9:20; 21:8; 22:15). Most of Paul's uses (fifteen) are clustered in 1 Corinthians, especially in chs. 8–10, the section on εἰδωλόθυτα, where eleven of the Pauline occurrences are found, five being occurrences of the word εἰδωλόθυτον.

It is clear that Paul's treatment of idols and idolatry is, like that of the NT generally, firmly rooted in the biblical tradition. The word εἴδωλον, in Greek literature generally, has a wide range of meanings, including image, representation, ghost, unreal thing, and is used, as Derek Newton notes, "in a positive, neutral, or merely factual manner . . . [and] only very rarely . . . to indicate a representation of the divine. . . . It indicated something which was an image or representation of a real thing but not the real thing itself."[5] The LXX uses εἴδωλον to translate a range of Hebrew words in various contexts.[6] Of particular influence, of course, are the Torah's prohibitions against making idols or images, where various Hebrew terms are translated by εἴδωλον in the LXX,[7] along with the warnings and threats against those among the people who refuse to obey God and who turn to idols (e.g., Lev 26:30; Deut 32:19–21; 2 Kgs 17:9–12) and the violent or ridiculing polemic against the idols of other nations (e.g., Num 33:52;

4. The references are: Rom 2:22; 1 Cor 5:10, 11; 6:9; 8:1, 4 (*bis*), 7 (*bis*), 10 (*bis*); 10:7, 14, 19 (*bis*); 12:2; 2 Cor 6:16; Gal 5:20; 1 Thess 1:9.

5. Derek Newton, *Deity and Diet: The Dilemma of Sacrificial Food in Corinth*, JSNTSup 169 (Sheffield: Sheffield Academic Press, 1998), 131; see 128–34.

6. E.g., the references to Laban's household gods, stolen by Rachel: התרפים; τὰ εἴδωλα, Gen 31:19, 34, 35; cf. θεούς in 31:30. Often אלהים is the Hebrew word translated, e.g., Num 25:2; 1 Kgs 11:8.

7. Exod 20:4; Deut 5:8 (פסל); Lev 19:4 (אליל).

Deut 29:16; Isa 46:1–7[8]). Worshiping idols or images is plainly prohibited for the people of God (cf. Ps 97:7; Dan 3:1–18; Bel 5). This is essentially the perspective on idols and idolatry that Paul shares, along with other Jewish writings from before and around his time (e.g., Wis 13–15; 1 Macc 1:41–64; Bel 1–22; etc.).[9]

The word for idol food, εἰδωλόθυτον—literally, "something sacrificed to an idol"—which recurs frequently throughout 1 Cor 8–10, does not, however, occur in pre-Pauline literature and may be a word of Christian coinage.[10] There are clear precursors and near equivalents, however, in phrases like αἱ θυσίαι τῶν εἰδώλων (Num 25:2; cf. Exod 34:15; Lev 17:7). The only precisely relevant LXX text is 4 Macc 5:2, which may well postdate Paul's letters.[11] The text describes Antiochus compelling every Hebrew "to eat pork and food sacrificed to idols" (κρεῶν ὑείων καὶ εἰδωλοθύτων); elsewhere in 4 Maccabees the verb μιαροφαγέω (to eat defiling food) is used (4 Macc 5:3, 19, 25; 8:2, 12, 29; 11:16; 13:2). As in 4 Maccabees, characteristic of many Jewish writings is the conjunction of concerns about idolatry and about unclean food.[12]

Idols, Idolatry, and Idol Food: 1 Cor 8–10

However, while it is clear that "turning from idols" is definitive of gentile conversion, and that "idolatry" belongs in a list of key vices excluded from the kingdom, it is only in 1 Cor 8–10 that we gain any concrete view of what, in Paul's view, "turning from idols" might mean. Here Paul responds in some detail to an issue most likely raised by the Corinthians, "concerning idol food" (περὶ δὲ τῶν εἰδωλοθύτων—1 Cor 8:1).[13]

8. Here the LXX has γλυπτά, "carved images," not εἴδωλα, translating Heb. עצב.

9. See further Alex T. Cheung, *Idol Food in Corinth: Jewish Background and Pauline Legacy*, JSNTSup 176 (Sheffield: Sheffield Academic Press, 1999), 39–81.

10. See Cheung, *Idol Food*, 43 with n12; Newton, *Deity and Diet*, 179–83.

11. There is disagreement over the date, some arguing for an early date, pre–50 CE, and others for a date around the end of the first century CE; the latter is perhaps more likely. For a brief summary see John M. G. Barclay, *Jews in the Mediterranean Diaspora: From Alexander to Trajan (323 BCE to 117 CE)* (Edinburgh: T&T Clark, 1996), 449.

12. See esp. Cheung, *Idol Food*, 39–81; e.g., 1 Macc 1:41–64 (note v. 62); Daniel provides a clear OT example: cf. Dan 1:8; 3:8–12, etc.

13. See further John C. Hurd, *The Origin of 1 Corinthians* (London: SPCK, 1965), 65–74; though note the cautions of Margaret M. Mitchell, "Concerning περὶ δέ in 1 Corinthians," *NovT* 31 (1989): 229–56.

This long and complex passage raises many difficulties and has been much discussed. Derek Newton rather underestimates the extent of this discussion when he writes (in 1998) that "judging by current output, 1 Corinthians 8–10 remains the least considered section of Paul's First Letter to the Corinthians"; Alex Cheung is more accurate when he reports (in 1999) that "a plethora of studies on 1 Corinthians 8–10 has been produced in the last decade."[14] At least some of the scholarly discussion is generated by the key difficulty of discerning exactly what Paul's stance was regarding the eating of idol food and participating in non-Christian meals and cultic acts in various settings. The diversity of scholarly views at least reveals for certain that Paul's instruction is less than crystal clear on these matters! There are also difficulties arising from the apparent contrasts between different sections of the passage: ch. 8 and the latter parts of ch. 10 (10:23–30) seem at least theoretically to accept a Christian's right to eat idol food, even in an εἰδωλεῖον, while 10:1–22 is full of stern warnings against idolatry. And ch. 9 appears in some respects a digression from the main topic. These literary difficulties have led to various partition hypotheses, in which certain sections of the passage are assigned to different letters,[15] and to a range of studies that leave some parts of the passage out of consideration.[16] Most recent work, however, has affirmed the unity of the passage, and indeed of 1 Corinthians as a whole, a conclusion with which I fully concur: compelling grounds for

14. Newton, *Deity and Diet,* 26; Cheung, *Idol Food,* 17. Besides Newton and Cheung, monographs include Wendell L. Willis, *Idol Meat in Corinth,* SBLDS 68 (Chico, CA: Scholars Press, 1985); Hermann Probst, *Paulus und der Brief,* WUNT 2/45 (Tübingen: Mohr Siebeck, 1991); Peter D. Gooch, *Dangerous Food: 1 Corinthians 8–10 in Its Context,* Studies in Christianity and Judaism 5 (Waterloo, Ont.: Wilfred Laurier University Press, 1993); Paul D. Gardner, *The Gifts of God and the Authentication of a Christian* (Lanham, MD: University Press of America, 1994); Khiok-khng Yeo, *Rhetorical Interaction in 1 Corinthians 8 and 10* (Leiden: Brill, 1995); Joop F. M. Smit, *"About the Idol Offerings": Rhetoric, Social Context and Theology of Paul's Discourse in First Corinthians 8:1–11:1* (Leuven: Peeters, 2000); John Fotopoulos, *Food Offered to Idols in Roman Corinth,* WUNT 2/151 (Tübingen: Mohr Siebeck, 2003).

15. See, e.g., Johannes Weiss, *Der erste Korintherbrief,* KEK 5 (Göttingen: Vandenhoeck & Ruprecht, 1910), xl–xliii, 210–13; Jean Héring, *The First Epistle of Paul to the Corinthians,* trans. A. W. Heathcote and P. J. Allcock (London: Epworth, 1962), xiii–xiv, 75; Walter Schmithals, *Gnosticism in Corinth* (Nashville: Abingdon, 1971), 90–96; Robert Jewett, "The Redaction of 1 Corinthians and the Trajectory of the Pauline School," *JAAR* 44.4, Supplement B (1978): 396–404; Gerhard Sellin, "Hauptprobleme des ersten Korintherbriefes," *ANRW* 25.4:2964–82.

16. E.g., Willis, *Idol Meat*; Jerome Murphy-O'Connor, "Freedom or the Ghetto (1 Cor.,VIII,1–13; X,23–XI,1.)," *RB* 85 (1978): 543–74; Yeo, *Rhetorical Interaction.*

partition are lacking, and the form of the argument (a broadly chiastic ABA pattern with an apparent digression in the center), along with its tensions and internal variety, seem established features of some of Paul's most extended arguments (cf. 1 Cor 12–14; Rom 1:18–3:20; Rom 9–11).[17]

The challenge to interpreters, then, is to understand the complex argument of the whole passage, and the relations of its various parts. Since I have previously published a detailed exegetical study of this text,[18] I shall avoid repeating that work here and will restrict myself to drawing out some key points concerning Paul's instructions on the issue of idolatry and idol food.[19]

One of the things that makes this passage interesting and important in revealing the character of Pauline ethics is its focus on relational concerns as crucial to moral decisions: in a situation where different (and permissible) convictions are held, an orientation to the interests of the other is fundamental. However, Paul does set down some absolute, as well as some relational, instructions in this passage. Two clear imperatives, one permissive, one prohibitive, establish absolute limits for conduct.

The permissive imperative is to "eat everything sold in the market without making inquiries to reach a judgment because of conscience" (πᾶν τὸ ἐν μακέλλῳ πωλούμενον ἐσθίετε μηδὲν ἀνακρίνοντες διὰ τὴν συνείδησιν),[20] an instruction given scriptural justification through the immediately following citation of Ps 24:1 (1 Cor 10:25–26). No concessions are made to the possible concerns or sensibilities of others.[21] Here there is an absolute limit on the extent to which the concerns of others, elsewhere in this passage so crucially determinative, can be allowed to control one's freedom. But the Christian's own self-awareness, or moral consciousness—perhaps the best renderings of συνείδησις—is not to be an issue in such matters

17. See David G. Horrell, "Theological Principle or Christological Praxis? Pauline Ethics in 1 Corinthians 8:1–11:1," *JSNT* 67 (1997): 84.

18. Horrell, "Theological Principle."

19. It is worth noting that this particular focus leaves aside many other potentially interesting questions, such as the ontological status and relation of εἴδωλα and δαιμόνια in Paul's thought-world.

20. Anthony C. Thiselton, *The First Epistle to the Corinthians*, NIGTC (Grand Rapids: Eerdmans, 2000), 779, translates μηδὲν ἀνακρίνοντες, "without asking about it to reach a judgment"; see his comments on 785. On συνείδησις see below with n. 22.

21. The instruction in v. 28 to desist from eating if someone mentions the origins of the food seems most likely to be linked only with the immediately preceding scenario in v. 27 (on which see below), not with v. 25 also. Verses 27 and 28 describe a situation in hypothetical terms (though an entirely realistic and likely one)—εἴ τις καλεῖ . . . ἐὰν δέ τις ὑμῖν εἴπῃ—while v. 25 gives a straightforward imperative.

either.[22] The instruction certainly concerns a real and everyday situation for the Corinthians; the existence of at least one meat and fish market in Corinth in Paul's time is confirmed by inscriptional evidence, although the location of this *macellum* is not entirely certain.[23] Contrary to some earlier suggestions, still supported by some, it does not seem likely that virtually all meat on sale would have come from sacrificial offerings and thus counted as εἰδωλόθυτα.[24] Nevertheless, Paul's instruction is unequivocal—note the emphatic πᾶν and the imperative ἐσθίετε—no food need be regarded as unclean or unacceptable for the Christian.

The prohibitive imperative is to "flee from idolatry" (1 Cor 10:14). It is important to note the word Paul uses here: not εἰδωλόθυτα but εἰδωλολατρία. Worship of idols is clearly prohibited, but what is left unclear is when, if at all, eating εἰδωλόθυτα per se constitutes idolatry.[25] Had Paul meant plainly to prohibit the eating of idol food he could have done so quite simply, thus making his instruction on the matter clear to the Corinthians and other early Christians and depriving modern scholars of one interpretive conundrum.[26] A phrase such as is used in Didache 6:3 would have been unambiguous:

22. Cf. Thiselton, *First Epistle*, 785. For further literature on this term, see David G. Horrell, *The Social Ethos of the Corinthian Correspondence*, SNTW (Edinburgh: T&T Clark, 1996), 147n110.

23. Cf. C. K. Williams II, "Roman Corinth as a Commercial Center," in *The Corinthia in the Roman Period*, ed. Timothy E. Gregory, JRASup 8 (Ann Arbor: Journal of Roman Archaeology, 1994), 39–46. For the relevant inscriptions, see A. B. West, *Corinth 8.2: Latin Inscriptions 1896–1926* (Cambridge: Harvard University Press, 1931), 100–104, §§124–25; John H. Kent, *Corinth 8.3: The Inscriptions 1926–50* (Princeton: ASCSA, 1966), 127–28, §321.

24. *Pace* Thiselton, *First Epistle*, 783. See esp. Dietrich-Alex Koch, "'Alles, was ἐν μακέλλῳ verkauft wird, eßt . . .': Die *macella* von Pompeji, Gerasa und Korinth und ihre Bedeutung für die Auslegung von 1Kor 10,25," *ZNW* 90 (1999): 194–219, though Koch is not correct in suggesting that the North Market at Corinth is the most likely candidate to be identified as the *macellum* of Paul's time (209; cf. Williams, "Roman Corinth"). Cooked meats were also sold at Corinth in Paul's time from the buildings immediately east of Theater Street; see C. K. Williams II and O. H. Zervos, "Corinth 1985: East of the Theater," *Hesperia* 55 (1986): 146–48; also ch. 2 above.

25. *Pace* Markus Bockmuehl (*Jewish Law in Gentile Churches* [Edinburgh: T&T Clark, 2000], 168n101), it is not sufficient to cite this verse as an indication that "idol food is certainly *not* a matter of indifference for Paul." Due weight must be given to the fact that Paul chose the word εἰδωλολατρία, and not εἰδωλόθυτα, in the midst of a discussion primarily concerned with the latter (8:1, 4).

26. Origen, *Against Celsus* 8.24, perhaps implies that Paul's words were not exactly clear on this matter and that others may have understood them differently; see his comment that Paul proves the harm of eating idol food (a harm caused to one's ἀδελφοί) "to those able to understand his words" (τοῖς ἀκούειν τῶν ἐκεῖ δυναμένοις); more generally, cf. 2 Pet 3:15–16.

"keep strictly from that which is offered to idols" (ἀπὸ δὲ τοῦ εἰδωλοθύτου λίαν πρόσεχε). But he did not. Hence we are left with the difficult task of determining how this prohibition against idolatry, and the wider section of warning in which it is located (1 Cor 10:1–22), relate to the apparently more permissive instruction elsewhere in chs. 8 and 10.

Derek Newton's detailed study of the sociohistorical background to the issue of sacrificial food at Corinth offers new and significant illumination here. Most scholars have been unable to see how there could be any difference between eating in a temple setting, as depicted in ch. 8, and participating in the table of demons, as depicted, and apparently prohibited, in 10:1–22.[27] In terms of the activity depicted in ch. 8, "reclining ἐν εἰδωλείῳ," Newton shows what a variety of settings could be included in such a designation, and how those partaking in meals in such contexts might or might not be eating food that had been directly taken from the sacrificial act.[28] In many cases, only a small group of worshipers or cultic officials took part in the sacrificial act and ate of the sacrificial offerings; others might eat other food, and might do so in adjacent rooms, or in the open air, or in other settings that evinced no close connection with the cultic act itself.[29] In 10:1–22, Newton argues, a different degree of participation is in view. Here Paul talks of those who participate in sacrifice (note θύω; 10:20) and share "the table of δαιμονίων" (10:21); "Paul's emphasis is thus very much on those involved in the actual act of making and eating sacrifices."[30] Thus the difference be-

27. E.g., Cheung, *Idol Food*, 28–32, in comments on eating in the sanctuary of Demeter and Kore.

28. Newton, *Deity and Diet*, 79–257, 298–305. Newton includes funerary meals, imperial cult, and athletic games in his consideration of the types of meals that might be relevant to Paul's concerns in this passage, as well as those more frequently mentioned by scholars, those associated with the sanctuary of Demeter and Kore, the Asclepeion, etc.

29. See, e.g., Newton, *Deity and Diet*, 198–99, 202, 230, 233–39, etc. Cheung's work, by contrast, deals briefly with the sociohistorical and archaeological evidence, largely following Gooch in this respect, and thus makes a number of questionable assumptions that affect the range of possible conclusions, most importantly that there could not be any plausible distinction between idolatry and eating idol food (which begs the key question), nor between eating ἐν εἰδωλείῳ and sacrificing to demons (*Idol Food*, 36–38, 92–94, etc.). *Pace* Cheung (28–32), it is actually unclear whether sacrificial eating took place in the sanctuary of Demeter and Kore in Roman times, though dining of some sort evidently did, and it is entirely possible that a distinction could be drawn between participating in the cult itself and eating in some area around the sanctuary. See further Nancy Bookides and Ronald S. Stroud, *The Sanctuary of Demeter and Kore: Corinth 18.3* (Princeton: ASCSA, 1997), 273ff. esp. 434–45; Newton, *Deity and Diet*, 91–96.

30. Newton, *Deity and Diet*, 338.

tween the two sections of the passage is that "1 Corinthians 8 dealt with the issue of temple *eating*, whereas 1 Cor 10:1–22 tackled the problem of actual sacrificial acts accompanied by eating."[31] This latter case represents the level of participation that Paul without exception prohibits.[32]

Inside the limits framed by these instructions are situations where it is the concerns of the other that are crucial: there is no absolute or intrinsic reason why certain actions are sinful, but they should be avoided if they are a cause of stumbling to others. In this category there appear to be two activities, about which Paul gives instruction, that may or may not overlap in any given case.

One activity is that of eating εἰδωλόθυτα, in settings that may include an εἰδωλεῖον (8:10: the verb κατακείμενον, "reclining," implies the activity of dining/eating). Here Paul essentially accepts as legitimate the theological principles by which the so-called strong justify their freedom to eat idol food—"there is no idol in the world and there is no God but one" (8:4)—and thus agrees that they have a legitimate ἐξουσία to act in this way. But the exercise of this ἐξουσία is very firmly limited by the offense it may cause to the weak. This "offense" or "stumbling," it should be noted, is not to be understood in terms of their being outraged or angered by the conduct of the strong, but rather that they too may be emboldened to eat idol food even though their weak consciousness connects such food closely with an idol (8:7–10). As in Rom 14:23, whether a practice is ethically legitimate or not can depend, it seems, on the stance of the actor: "everything that is not from faith is sin." The danger, as Paul perceives it, is that the weak will be led to destruction by the boldness of the strong, and this act of causing the destruction of "an ἀδελφός for whom Christ died" (1 Cor 8:11) amounts to a "sin against Christ" (8:12)—a phrase of stern warning that Paul uses only here in his letters.[33] Only by accepting that Paul regards the ἐξουσία of the strong as entirely legitimate, yet nevertheless calls for it to be renounced out of concern for the weak, can we make proper sense of ch. 9 within the wider argument.

In this somewhat digressive yet crucial section, after insisting firmly and somewhat defensively that he is a genuine apostle (9:1–3)—an essential basis

31. Newton, *Deity and Diet*, 198–99; see further 331–71.

32. Cf. Newton, *Deity and Diet*, 365. This provides some detailed evidence to support my earlier argument, that Paul prohibits participation in "cultic sacrificial gatherings" but not necessarily all occasions or activities in temples and their precincts (Horrell, "Theological Principle," 101, 103).

33. Cf. Murphy-O'Connor, "Freedom or the Ghetto," 563.

for the argument that follows—Paul proceeds to pile up reasons to justify the legitimacy of his right to material support from the church. Arguments from everyday life, from scripture, from temple and cult, and even—climactically—from a command of the Lord, all combine to demonstrate that Paul has a right, an ἐξουσία, that is unquestionably legitimate (9:7–14). Yet Paul sets aside his right for the sake of the gospel, and particularly for the sake of the weak, enslaving himself to all, and hyperbolically asserts that he would rather die than be deprived of his boast in this regard (9:15–23).[34] This, then, is the imitation to which Paul calls the Corinthian strong at the end of the whole passage and which he sees as an imitation of Christ (11:1). They may have the "right" to eat idol food but must be prepared to set this right aside out of concern for others, especially for their "weaker" siblings in the church.

A second activity is attending dinners or banquets when invited by an unbeliever (10:27–29). In attempting to understand the relationship between the various sections of 1 Cor 8–10, especially between 10:1–22 and the material in ch. 8 and later in ch. 10, many scholars regard these invitations as those to a private home and see 10:1–22 as concerned with, and prohibiting, any meals in temple settings.[35] However, there is nothing explicit to indicate such a delimitation, and as Newton has shown, not all eating in the context of an εἰδωλεῖον need fall into the category of participating in cultic sacrifice, despite the assumptions of most scholars to the contrary. Given too that Paul does not dispute in absolute terms the legitimacy of eating εἰδωλόθυτα and even reclining ἐν εἰδωλείῳ, and given the widespread use of temples and their wider precincts (not to mention other places that might also count as εἰδωλεῖα) for social, economic, political, and religious purposes, it is quite possible that various kinds of social and celebratory occasions at both private homes and in more public settings are in view.[36] As Wolfgang Schrage notes, this rather wider interpretation of the contexts that are included here makes better sense of the reticence Paul expresses in the phrase "and [if] you wish

34. On this passage see David G. Horrell, "'The Lord Commanded . . . But I Have Not Used . . .': Exegetical and Hermeneutical Reflections on 1 Cor 9:14–15," *NTS* 43 (1997): 587–603.

35. Cf., e.g., Gordon D. Fee, "Εἰδωλόθυτα Once Again: An Interpretation of 1 Corinthians 8–10," *Bib* 61 (1980): 172–97; Fee, *The First Epistle to the Corinthians*, NICNT (Grand Rapids: Eerdmans, 1987), 357–63; Ben Witherington III, *Conflict and Community in Corinth* (Grand Rapids: Eerdmans, 1995), 188; N. T. Wright, *The Climax of the Covenant* (Edinburgh: T&T Clark, 1991), 134–35.

36. See further John E. Stambaugh, "The Functions of Roman Temples," *ANRW* 16.1:554–608.

to go" (καὶ θέλετε πορεύεσθαι), which contrasts with the straightforward and unqualified imperative expressed in 10:25—"because here the limits of what is permitted threaten to become rather blurred."[37] However, as in the case already outlined by Paul in ch. 8, here too it is the consciousness of the other that is crucial for determining legitimate practice. If someone points out that the food is ἱερόθυτον—a more positive term, denoting "sacrificed to a divinity," than the implicitly negative εἰδωλόθυτον—then one should desist from eating, for the sake not of one's own consciousness, but that of the other. It is difficult to determine whether this hypothetical "someone" (τις) is a Christian or a non-Christian;[38] but if the latter may at least be included among those in view, then unlike in ch. 8, here Paul's concerns are with the impact of Christians' actions *outside* as well as inside the church (see further below).

In practice, then, in both of these cases, Paul's instruction (if heeded) could well be to restrict Christians' conscious eating of idol food and their full participation in meals with unbelievers where such food would be served. But it is important to stress that any such avoidance is entirely conditional on the awareness or concerns of others and does not rest on any intrinsic grounds related to the action itself. Moreover, in each case the scenario of others being harmed or imparting information is depicted as a hypothetical situation: a real possibility, but not one to be assumed as routine or inevitable.[39] Since the so-called weak appear to be a reality in the congregation at Corinth, *pace* John Hurd and Peter Gooch,[40] the presence of people on any given occasion who might be caused to stumble by the strong's actions, or might point out that some food was "sacrificed food," is certainly to be reckoned with. Given that possibility, Paul's instruction here does not seem to fit the "love-patriarchal" pattern suggested by Gerd Theissen, where the socially weak show "subordination, fidelity and esteem" to

37. Wolfgang Schrage, *Der erste Brief an die Korinther (1 Kor 6,12–11,16)*, EKKNT 7.2 (Zurich: Benziger; Neukirchen-Vluyn: Neukirchener Verlag, 1995), 469: "Zudem paßt dann auch die Zurückhaltung (εἰ θέλετε) besser, weil die Grenze des Erlaubten hier eher zu verschwimmen droht."

38. For the range of opinions, see Horrell, *Social Ethos*, 147n109.

39. ἐὰν γάρ τις ἴδῃ σέ (8:10); ἐὰν δέ τις ὑμῖν εἴπῃ (10:28). Cf. Thiselton, *First Epistle*, 652, 787.

40. Hurd, *Origin*, 117–25; Gooch, *Dangerous Food*, 61–72. Cheung is somewhat inconsistent on this point, agreeing with Hurd that there was no "weak" party at Corinth and that Paul was therefore fighting on "one front" only (*Idol Food*, 87–89), but later rejecting the view that the "weak" were merely hypothetical (though still maintaining that they did not form a "party") (124–26).

the socially strong, and where the equality asserted before God ἐν ἐκκλησίᾳ does not impinge upon the activities of everyday life.[41] Rather, whether or not the weak and the strong are divided on socioeconomic lines, as argued by Theissen,[42] Paul gives considerable power, at least in theory, to the so-called weak in determining the conduct of the strong: any member of the community, however insignificant, can embody sufficient reason for others to forgo important social involvement in the city.[43] On the other hand, however, it is important to note that Paul presents no absolute reason why εἰδωλόθυτα should be avoided, except in the context of cultic sacrificial acts; the basis for its avoidance elsewhere is entirely relational.

What, then, are the implications for our understanding of Pauline ethics that emerge from these various instructions, and from the general Pauline rhetoric against idolatry? I shall explore these under three headings: relational morality and its christological basis; identity and boundaries, food and the body; and rhetoric and social practice.

Relational Morality and Its Christological Basis

While Paul does appear to set down some absolute limits in terms of what is permitted and prohibited regarding idolatry and idol food, it is also clear that a substantial amount of his argument in 1 Cor 8–10 is focused on promoting a form of relational morality. In other words, the moral practice he urges on the Corinthians is not specified as some particular stance regarding idol food but rather as a pattern of relating, a "looking to the interests of the other" (10:24). It is this "other-regard" that is morally imperative. Inside the limits of the absolutes Paul sets down, what is right or wrong in terms of one's conduct cannot be specified in absolute or abstract terms relating to the substantive issue of idol food, but only in terms of relational moral imperatives that encapsulate one's duties in relation to the others with whom one is placed.

41. Gerd Theissen, *The Social Setting of Pauline Christianity*, ed. and trans. John H. Schütz (Edinburgh: T&T Clark, 1982), 107. See also Ernst Troeltsch, *The Social Teaching of the Christian Churches*, trans. Olive Wyon, 2 vols. (London: Allen & Unwin, 1931), 1:69–89 (from whom Theissen derives the idea of "love-patriarchalism").

42. Theissen, *Social Setting*, 121–43; note the criticisms in Justin J. Meggitt, *Paul, Poverty and Survival*, SNTW (Edinburgh: T&T Clark, 1998), 107–16; Meggitt, "Meat Consumption and Social Conflict in Corinth," *JTS* 45 (1994): 137–41.

43. See further Horrell, *Social Ethos*, 148–49.

These relational moral imperatives have a clear christological grounding: it is the identity of the "other" as a sister or brother for whom Christ died (8:11) that renders any action that leads to their destruction as a "sin against Christ" (8:12)—an extremely strong indication of its seriousness. And it is Christ's self-giving for others, his taking the form of a slave and humbling himself even to death, that evidently provides the paradigm for Paul's practice of renouncing his own rights, becoming weak and slavelike, for the sake of the gospel and in imitation of Christ (9:15–19; 11:1; etc.). This pattern of conduct is one to which he calls the Corinthian "strong," urging them to place a christologically grounded concern for others above any theologically legitimated rights they may justifiably consider themselves to have.[44]

Given this major focus on an "other-regarding" morality, those who focus on attempting to elucidate "Paul's position regarding idol food,"[45] whatever their conclusions, fail to appreciate one of the key features of Paul's moral argument here. In trying to pin down clearly what Paul thought about the rights and wrongs of eating idol food, it is all too easy to ignore the extent to which Paul refuses to approach the issue in this way.[46] To be sure, there are some reasonably clear absolutes, which Paul legitimates and undergirds theologically (10:26) and christologically (10:16–17), but much of his argument is based on the presumption that "right" practice can only be determined in relation to the context of human relationships in which one is enmeshed, the possible injury that one's actions may cause to others. Even if this communal context were to be such that eating idol food would often need to be avoided, it is nonetheless important to appreciate the basis on which Paul argues for its (conditional) avoidance and the relational concerns on which he focuses. Also worth noting is that while Paul's concerns are very

44. The christological basis for Paul's ethics here is emphasized and explored in further detail in Horrell, "Theological Principle"; and in Thomas Söding, "Starke und Schwache: Der Götzenopferstreit in 1Kor 8–10 als Paradigma paulinisher Ethik," *ZNW* 85 (1994): 69–92, who focuses rather heavily on 8:11 (see, e.g., 88).

45. The phrase is from Cheung (*Idol Food*, 171), for whom it is self-evident that the early church needed "a clear-cut answer to the rightness or wrongness of the act of consumption of idol food" (168), and who sees "Western secular materialism" as the reason why commentators have underestimated "the sinfulness of eating idol food" (303). But other writers approaching the issue from non-Western contexts have stressed the ambiguities and complexities that make any "clear-cut" position difficult to elucidate and justify; see, e.g., Newton, *Deity and Diet*; Yeo, *Rhetorical Interaction*, 217–20; Khiok-khng Yeo, "The Rhetorical Hermeneutic of 1 Corinthians 8 and Chinese Ancestor Worship," *BibInt* 2 (1994): 294–311.

46. Cf. further Wayne A. Meeks, "The Polyphonic Ethics of the Apostle Paul," *Annual of the Society of Christian Ethics* (1988): 17–29.

much focused on the others within the church, they are not exclusively so: seeking the benefit of "the many" outside the community is also imperative (10:32–33). The significance of this is something to which we shall return.

Identity and Boundaries, Food and the Body

Given the clear indications that turning from idols is for Paul definitive of gentile conversion, and in view of the treatment of practical issues concerning idol food and idolatry in 1 Cor 8–10, we may ask: How are the Corinthians to "mark" their transfer from the worship of idols to the service of the one true God, to indicate to themselves and to the world their distinctive identity as those "called" by God? Or, to put the issue in broader terms, how does Paul envisage that the boundaries of the church are to be maintained, the identity of its members confirmed and sustained?

One of the major contributions of the anthropologist Fredrik Barth in his work on ethnic groups and boundaries was to insist, on the basis of wide-ranging empirical studies, that ethnic identities and distinctions

> do not depend on an absence of mobility, contact and information but do entail social processes of exclusion and incorporation whereby discrete categories are maintained *despite* changing participation and membership in the course of individual life histories . . . ethnic distinctions do not depend on an absence of social interaction and acceptance . . . cultural differences can persist despite inter-ethnic contact and interdependence.[47]

Previous studies of ethnicity, in Barth's view, had begged "all the critical questions" by assuming that "boundary maintenance" was "unproblematical" and followed from the *isolation* that the key characteristics of ethnic identity were taken to imply: "racial difference, cultural difference, social separation and language barriers, spontaneous and organized enmity."[48]

Barth thus sought to shift the focus of attention onto the boundaries that define groups. He argued that only "some cultural features are used by the actors as signals and emblems of differences, others are ignored, and in some

47. Fredrik Barth, "Introduction," in *Ethnic Groups and Boundaries*, ed. Fredrik Barth (London: Allen & Unwin, 1969), 9–10.

48. Barth, "Introduction," 11.

relationships radical differences are played down and denied."[49] In other words, the maintenance of distinct identity does not depend on distinctiveness or, still less, isolation in all aspects of social life, but only in certain areas that are taken to be definitive and salient. Barth divides such key signals of difference into two main categories, "overt signals or signs," such as dress, language, and house-form, and "basic value orientations," "the standards of morality and excellence by which performance is judged."[50] The persistence of ethnic groups does not imply or require an absence of interaction with other groups; it does imply "not only criteria and signals for identification, but also a structuring of interaction which allows the persistence of cultural differences."[51]

Clearly, Barth's ideas cannot be unproblematically applied to the early Christian groups as Paul portrays them, which are not exactly "ethnic" groups in the usual sense, not being "largely biologically self-perpetuating"[52] and with their members remaining conscious of possessing other ethnic identities, as Jew or Greek, that continue in some sense to inform their sense of self-identity (in Paul's case, see Rom 9:3; 2 Cor 11:22; Gal 2:15). At this early stage, a sense of "Christian" identity is only beginning to develop and solidify, and that "Christian" identity in any case owes a great deal, of course, to the Jewish traditions out of which it grew.[53] However, Barth's reflections are relevant insofar as they concern ethnic groups as "a form of social organization" in which the "critical feature" is that the group "has a membership which identifies itself, and is identified by others, as constituting a category distinguishable from other categories of the same order," what Barth calls "the characteristic of self-ascription and ascription by others." "A categorical ascription," he continues, "is an ethnic ascription when it classifies a person in terms of his basic, most general identity, presumptively determined by his origin and background."[54] While early "Christian" identity, as an identity associated with a newly founded movement requiring voluntary conversion to join, is not "determined by origin and background," it is, at least as Paul

49. Barth, "Introduction," 14; see 14–15.

50. Barth, "Introduction," 14.

51. Barth, "Introduction," 16.

52. See Barth, "Introduction," 10.

53. See further David G. Horrell, "'Becoming Christian': Solidifying Christian Identity and Content," in *Handbook of Early Christianity: Social Science Approaches,* ed. Anthony J. Blasi, Jean Duhaime, and Paul-André Turcotte (Walnut Creek, CA: Alta Mira, 2002), 309–35.

54. Barth, "Introduction," 11, 13.

sees it, one's "basic, most general, identity": it is being "in Christ," to use the key Pauline phrase, that fundamentally describes and determines one's identity and establishes the boundary between insider and outsider (1 Cor 7:39; 12:12–13; 2 Cor 5:17; 12:2; Gal 3:26–29; etc.). In relation to this key self- and group-designation, all other identity descriptors are relativized or negated (the distinction between circumcised and uncircumcised, for example, is now "nothing," οὐδέν, 1 Cor 7:19; Gal 5:6; cf. also Phil 3:4–8; etc.).[55]

But if it is, at least in Paul's terms, being "in Christ" that crucially demarcates and identifies Christians as a distinct human group, an ethnic-religious "category," then what are the cultural features—the "overt signals" or "basic value orientations"—that are taken to be significant, or "organizationally relevant"?[56]

Paul, it seems to me, sets out a distinction of principle, making clear that *food* is not a relevant marker of group distinctiveness while the *body* is; or in ethical terms, that food per se is morally irrelevant while the body is highly relevant.[57] The clearest expression of this notion is in 1 Cor 6:13: "Foods for the stomach and the stomach for foods, and God will destroy both one and the other. The body not for sexual immorality but for the Lord, and the Lord for the body." In 1 Cor 8:8 Paul insists that "food will not bring us close to God. We are no worse off if we do not eat, and no better off if we do" (NRSV).[58] In both of these cases, as elsewhere in 1 Corinthians, commentators frequently regard parts of these phrases as quotations of Corinthian slogans.[59] Identifying such quotations is, however, inevitably uncertain, and perhaps not as crucial for interpreting the text as is often supposed. It is indeed probable that Paul does echo phrases and ideas of the Corinthians, given the nature of 1 Corinthians, where Paul is responding to issues, reports,

55. See further David G. Horrell, "'No Longer Jew or Greek': Paul's Corporate Christology and the Construction of Christian Community," in *Christology, Controversy and Community: New Testament Essays in Honour of David R. Catchpole*, ed. David G. Horrell and Christopher M. Tuckett, NovTSup 99 (Leiden: Brill, 2000), 321–44.

56. Barth, "Introduction," 14.

57. *Pace* Cheung, *Idol Food*, 16, 133–35. Cf. Newton, *Deity and Diet*, 343, 375–76; Alistair S. May, *"The Body for the Lord": Sex and Identity in 1 Corinthians 5–7*, JSNTSup 278 (London: T&T Clark International, 2004), 106–10.

58. As Cheung notes (*Idol Food*, 134–36), this formulation reflects a context where Paul is essentially wanting to induce caution about the prospect of eating, compared with the more positive formulation in Rom 14:6, though it is not necessarily intended to imply a categorical "do not eat," as Cheung suggests.

59. Cf. Hurd, *Origin*, 68; Newton, *Deity and Diet*, 293; Thiselton, *First Epistle*, 462, 647–48.

and even a letter from Corinth (7:1). But it is also evident that he agrees, or at least does not disagree, with the phrases he writes, though he wishes to add to them, to qualify them, so as to spell out his own priorities and instructions (cf. also 6:12; 10:23); it is notable that Paul does not negate any of these so-called Corinthian slogans with his characteristic μὴ γένοιτο (cf. Rom 3:4, 6, 31; 1 Cor 6:15; Gal 2:17, etc.).

In the case of 1 Cor 6, Paul wants to stress that sexual immorality matters ethically, because it is something done in the body and the individual's body is a member of Christ's body.[60] A sexually immoral union is incompatible with union with Christ. One does not have to think for long to pick holes in Paul's logic: the stomach is also part of the body, so one could equally well make a case that allowing unclean food to contaminate the body (via the stomach) is incompatible with the body's union with Christ. Nor does Paul's argument *demonstrate* why sex with a πόρνη is wrong; it merely proceeds on this assumption. The parallel drawn between sexual union and union with Christ *could* serve as an argument against all sexual activity and certainly against union with an unbeliever. But although Paul's views on sex show some leaning towards asceticism (7:34), he does not wish to pursue the logic this far. Rather, *because* sex with a prostitute is sinful (for reasons Paul does not elucidate), uniting one's body with her is incompatible with union with Christ, whereas union with one's wife or husband, whether believer or unbeliever, is not (7:4–5, 12–13).

The forceful and clear imperative of 6:18, φεύγετε τὴν πορνείαν, is closely parallel with a key imperative in 10:14: φεύγετε ἀπὸ τῆς εἰδωλολατρίας. Indeed, there are some notable parallels in terms of the arguments Paul makes.[61] Idolatry is fundamentally wrong because it involves κοινωνία with δαιμόνια,[62] a participation (μετέχειν) at their table, which is incompatible with belonging to the body of Christ. Participation in the Lord's Supper is a κοινωνία in the blood and body of Christ, the bread in particular a demonstration of the identity of the Christian congregation as "one body" (ἓν σῶμα—10:17). Far from the rites of Christian belonging (baptism and Lord's Supper) protecting the Corinthians against danger, they imply a requirement of loyalty, an avoidance of any competing or incompatible participation, with the threat of punishment arising from divine jealousy (10:1–13, 22).

60. Cf. further May, *Body for the Lord*, 92–143.

61. On these parallels see Cheung, *Idol Food*, 112–14.

62. Semi-divine beings, divinities, spirits, powers, etc. (BDAG, 210), not necessarily hostile or regarded negatively, though clearly so in this context, as in other Jewish and Christian writings; see further Newton, *Deity and Diet*, 349–62.

Indeed, the Corinthians' failure with regard to the Lord's Supper can be summarized as a failure to "discern the body" (11:29), a failure to appreciate the identity of the community as the body of Christ, demonstrated as it shares the bread that is the body of Christ.[63]

In terms of "overt signals" or "basic value orientations," then, it is the christologically grounded notions of participation in the body and of self-giving for others that function for Paul as key bases for distinctive Christian values and practice and that undergird the construction of distinct group identity and boundaries between inside and outside. These are signaled positively through participation in baptism, which marks incorporation into the body, and in the Lord's Supper, which confirms and reaffirms the members' participation in Christ, specifically in his body and blood, and negatively through the avoidance of what are seen as competing unions, whether in the realm of sex or of idolatry. In terms of actions that are in themselves morally neutral, notably those regarding food, there is a general principle of not causing offense to anyone (1 Cor 10:32; 1 Thess 4:12) and especially to one's ἀδελφοί; seeking the benefit of others can require a sacrificial renunciation of one's own rights, in imitation of Christ.

Idol food, then, is in an ambiguous category and hence receives somewhat ambivalent treatment in Paul's discussion. Insofar as it is food, it is, in itself, though not necessarily in its consequences and its impact on others, morally neutral (1 Cor 8:8; Rom 14:14). But insofar as it is idol worship, seen as participation in a κοινωνία incompatible with union with Christ,[64] then it is dangerous, and forbidden.

In one sense, then, with his focus on the body and on preserving its purity (cf. 5:7), Paul well exemplifies Mary Douglas's view that the human body serves as a symbol of society. Concern for the boundaries of the body, for the substances that enter and exit from its orifices, Douglas argues, mirrors a wider social concern for the (often precarious) boundaries of society.[65] Yet in terms of this model Paul is surprising for his lack of concern about food, simply declaring all foods "clean" (Rom 14:20) for the one with faith to regard them so. Returning to Barth, it appears that Paul does not regard food per se, even food that may have been offered to idols, as an area of

63. On the ambiguous phrase, μὴ διακρίνων τὸ σῶμα, see Horrell, *Social Ethos*, 152–53.

64. Note the striking references to Christ in 10:4 and 9, where Paul retells the story of Israel in the wilderness.

65. Mary Douglas, *Purity and Danger* (London: Routledge & Kegan Paul, 1966), 115; cf. also 14–28. See also Dale B. Martin, *The Corinthian Body* (New Haven: Yale University Press, 1995).

cultural practice in which the Christian groups are to indicate their distinctive identity.[66]

Rhetoric and Social Practice

This raises the wider question as to how the distinct identity so strongly affirmed by Paul and signaled on the basis of certain values and practices impinges on and shapes the social interaction of members of the Christian communities. Specifically, I am interested in the relationship between what we may call the rhetoric against idolatry on the one hand and the implications for social practice on the other.

A number of scholars have suggested that the Corinthian Christians are rather comfortably and unproblematically integrated within their wider society and that part of Paul's aim in 1 Corinthians is to draw boundaries more tightly around the church. John Barclay's article on "Thessalonica and Corinth" has been an important stimulus to such views. In contrast to the Thessalonians, Barclay sees the Corinthian church as characterized by an

66. This seems to be a point of difference from Jewish norms, in which food serves as a key marker of cultural distinctiveness—though this is not, let me stress, to claim that Paul has somehow been "liberated" from such cultural constraints, or has a more "radical" view, or other such expressions of Christian superiority. Barth's work should suggest a less loaded description: it is simply that there is some difference in the areas of cultural practice that are deemed to be relevant in terms of defining group identity. In relation to the Jewish evidence regarding attitudes to idol food Cheung's valuable and important study needs some nuancing in terms of the implications Cheung draws from his survey. He concludes that "a negative attitude toward idol food was pervasive . . . the idol food prohibition was held as the *sine qua non* of Jewish faith" (Cheung, *Idol Food*, 296). But, as he reports, neither Philo nor Josephus, for example, actually deals with the topic of idol food as such (Cheung, *Idol Food*, 56–60, 65–69). What is evident in the material Cheung surveys is a consistent opposition both to defiling food and to idolatry. In many cases, these concerns are linked: avoiding gentile food is at the same time a deliberate attempt to avoid participation in idolatry (cf. 1 Macc 1:41–64). Since food is such an important marker of social identity and a test case of loyalty (cf. Aristeas 139, 142; 4 Macc 5:5–8; Philo, *On the Embassy of Gaius* 361–63), this helps to explain "why the Rabbis took a more stringent attitude toward idol food than toward images and idols": as Cheung suggests, the importance of the dietary laws is the likely reason (Cheung, *Idol Food*, 74). If Paul comes to deem food *in itself* a matter of indifference with regard to purity and the demarcation of community boundaries, then the coalescence of concerns about food and idolatry becomes less clear. Paul remains implacably opposed to idolatry, but sees no reason, at least in theory, why any food should not be eaten (πάντα καθαρά, Rom 14:20; cf. 1 Tim 4:3–4). Hence the ambiguity that surrounds εἰδωλόθυτα.

"absence of conflict in the relationship between Christians and 'outsiders' ... Paul is somewhat uneasy about the degree of integration which the Corinthian Christians enjoy ... he has a much more sectarian and separatist expectation of the social standing of the church than the Corinthians."[67] Edward Adams argues on similar lines that the "dominant issue" in 1 Corinthians is that of group boundaries: the Corinthians define the lines of demarcation between church and society too loosely for Paul, and "1 Corinthians may be interpreted as a sustained attempt by Paul to strengthen the social and ideological boundaries of the church."[68] Adams therefore suggests: "The overarching problem in Corinth was thus a failure to maintain clear lines of distinction between the Christian group and the wider society: the Corinthians were not sufficiently differentiating themselves in terms of their practices, beliefs and attitudes and their social and religious participation outside the church. This is clearly Paul's diagnosis of the Corinthian aberrations."[69]

However, it is important to do justice to a distinction between Paul's rhetoric and the social practice that he encourages, or, in Adams's terms, between "social" and "ideological" boundaries. Certainly it is clear, in rhetorical or ideological terms, that Paul draws a stark distinction between the church and the world, the former inhabited by those who have turned from idols to serve the one true God—the definitive transition made by gentile converts—and who have been washed clean in baptism; the latter characterized by those who are idolaters, sexually immoral, greedy, and so on. Paul can express a strong appeal for separation: "come out from the midst of them and be separate, says the Lord, touch nothing unclean, and I will welcome you" (2 Cor 6:17, based on Isa 52:11 and Ezek 20:34). Indeed, despite the variations among Paul's letters,[70] he consistently reflects the assumption that the gentile world is one of godlessness, idolatry, immorality, and vice, in

67. John M. G. Barclay, "Thessalonica and Corinth: Social Contrasts in Pauline Christianity," *JSNT* 47 (1992): 57–59.

68. Edward Adams, *Constructing the World: A Study in Paul's Cosmological Language*, SNTW (Edinburgh: T&T Clark, 2000), 87.

69. Adams, *Constructing the World*, 93. Similar views are also expressed by Craig S. de Vos, *Church and Community Conflicts: The Relationships of the Thessalonian, Corinthian, and Philippian Churches with Their Wider Civic Communities*, SBLDS 168 (Atlanta: Scholars Press, 1999), 205–32; and Timothy L. Carter, *Paul and the Power of Sin: Redefining "Beyond the Pale,"* SNTSMS 115 (Cambridge: Cambridge University Press, 2001).

70. Differences explored with regard to their portrayal of "the world" by Adams, *Constructing the World*; cf. also de Vos, *Church and Community Conflicts*.

stark contrast to the Christian communities, whose members are distinct, holy, elect, and washed clean from the dirt of the world.[71] In terms of identity description, this draws a clear distinction between Christians and the gentile world at large, just as in different ways Paul draws a boundary between the church and Judaism, despite the extensive degree to which the church claims the identity-defining language of Judaism as its own.[72]

Yet we must also consider how this identity-defining rhetoric translates into social practice, where, interestingly, the degree of distinction seems somewhat less, the boundaries between church and world less tightly drawn, than the rhetoric might lead us to expect. Here the nature of Paul's arguments in 1 Cor 8–10, so strongly oriented to the interests and concerns of the other, makes it difficult to be precise. The two absolute instructions that frame Paul's more relationally oriented advice suggest certain clear limits and opportunities. Christians may eat whatever they like from the market, without worrying about its origins or idolatrous connections, so in this context their social interaction and participation is entirely open. They are forbidden, however, from direct involvement in gentile cultic sacrifice, so here a strict limit on social involvement is placed. Other situations are placed under the rubric of not causing offense to others, especially to those within the church of God (10:32), so cannot be categorically ruled in or out on their own intrinsic terms. Eating ἐν εἰδωλείῳ or at a variety of meals hosted by unbelievers is theoretically permissible, but must be curtailed if others raise concerns, for the sake of those others; and whatever is served at such meals may be eaten, unless someone present points out the sacrificial connections of some dish or other. In some sense Paul has therefore left open, at least in terms of their inherent ethical acceptability, a considerable range of occasions for social interaction with those outside the church, yet at the same time has insisted that those opportunities must be renounced if they are a cause of stumbling to any member of the church, however socially insignifi-

71. Cf. John M. G. Barclay, "Paul among Diaspora Jews: Anomaly or Apostate?," *JSNT* 60 (1995): 107.

72. Cf. Philip F. Esler, *Galatians* (London: Routledge, 1998), 90–91: "From the perspective of social identity theory these Christ-followers constitute an ingroup *vis-à-vis* two outgroups, Israelites and gentiles. . . . The principal focus of Paul's concern in this letter is the boundary represented by the line AB [see Esler's fig. 3.2, p. 90], which separates his Christ-followers from Israel." This has also been the principal focus, for understandable reasons, of much Pauline scholarship, though the nature of the boundary drawn between gentiles and Christians deserves careful consideration.

cant—not causing ἀδελφοί to stumble is a higher ethical priority than continuing interaction with outsiders.

While concern for other members of the church is paramount, and despite the strong rhetoric against idolatry, Paul also makes explicit a concern for smooth relations with all, outside as well as inside the church (9:19–22; 10:32–33). Part of his concluding exhortation is the instruction to be ἀπρόσκοποι καὶ Ἰουδαίοις . . . καὶ Ἕλλησιν καί τῇ ἐκκλησίᾳ τοῦ θεοῦ (10:32). It is often noted that this formulation already expresses embryonically the notion that would later develop into the explicit description of Christians as a third race, sociologically distinct from both Jews and Greeks.[73] But the expressed desire for peaceful coexistence with outsiders is less frequently discussed (cf. 1 Thess 4:12). In this particular context Paul's comment may reflect his sense in dealing with the dilemma of idol food that he is treading an awkward path amid the customs and convictions of various groups and that his ideal would be for Christians' practice in this regard to offend no one (see esp. v. 33). This brief instruction clearly echoes Paul's earlier and more famous description of his accommodatory missionary stance, becoming all things to all people (9:19–22), and is explicitly part of the imitation to which he calls the Corinthians (10:32–11:1). The same three basic categories are present in both passages: the Jews in 10:32 correspond to the Jews and those under the law in 9:20; the Greeks in 10:32 to those outside the law in 9:21; and the church of God in 10:32 to the weak in 9:22, since this is the particular grouping within the church that is affected by the actions of the so-called strong. Acting so as not to cause offense to others within the church has been a dominant theme throughout the passage.

But it may also have been part of Paul's aim—however unrealistic—to encourage the Corinthians to act with regard to idolatry and idol food in such a way that they accommodated themselves as far as possible to those among whom they lived, and did not offend either their Jewish or their Greek neighbors; hence, perhaps, Paul's solution of eating whatever is served at meals, *unless* anyone points out that it is sacrificial food. That this could imply a rather flexible, even (to some) offensively vacillating practice with regard to food should not cause surprise, in view of Paul's own description of his variously being to the Jews "like a Jew" (note the ὡς) and to those outside the law, ὡς ἄνομος, an indication that his identity and practice are no longer defined by these categories, but rather by a "being in Christ," which

73. See, e.g., E. P. Sanders, *Paul, the Law and the Jewish People* (London: SCM, 1983), 171–79; Horrell, "No Longer Jew or Greek," 341.

Paul understands to demand precisely this chameleon-like flexibility, with its missionary and community-building purpose (9:19–23).[74]

Further relevant and important material on the relationship between rhetoric and social practice emerges in 1 Cor 5 (see ch. 5 above). In the context of pronouncing judgment on a "brother" who has committed gross sexual immorality, of a kind not tolerated among Jews or gentiles, Paul urges the Corinthians not even to eat with such a person (τῷ τοιούτῳ μηδὲ συνεσθίειν, 5:11). Paul here refers back to his earlier letter (5:9), which evidently warned the Corinthians not to "mix" (συναναμίγνυσθαι) with the sexually immoral (πόρνοι) and with other sinners. The kind of stark warnings against being "yoked" with unbelievers, and about the incompatibilities of light and dark, such as are found in 2 Cor 6:14–7:1, could exemplify the kind of material that Paul wrote,[75] even though it is difficult (but not impossible) to envisage how a fragment of this former letter could end up in the middle of 2 Corinthians. In any case, Paul now makes clear that he did *not* mean them to avoid contact with these immoral people in the world, "since then you would need to come out of the world" (5:10). He evidently does not envisage the church as a community with boundaries closed to social interaction with the sexually immoral, the greedy, robbers, and idolaters. Rather, what he objects to is social interaction with fellow Christians who by their sinful conduct reveal their identity to be other than truly Christian: the sinner here is "named" a "brother" (ἀδελφὸς ὀνομαζόμενος) but he is *actually* a πόρνος (5:11)—note that it is types of person, not types of sin, that are listed here.[76] It is people such as this, rather than outsiders, who are a dangerous threat to the holiness of the church.

Mary Douglas's well-known reflections on "dirt" are apposite here: "dirt is essentially disorder. There is no such thing as absolute dirt: it exists in the eye of the beholder."[77] The classification of things as dirty or clean, Douglas argues, represents a human attempt to order and structure experience. Dirt

74. Paul's references to gaining (κερδαίνω) and saving (σῴζω) people in these verses have both a missionary reference and also, I would argue, a reference to the continuing process of sustaining and unifying the community's membership (around the gospel as Paul understands it); cf. Matt 18:15. So also, rightly, Gardner, *Gifts*, 99; otherwise David A. Black, "A Note on 'the Weak' in 1 Corinthians 9,22," *Bib* 64 (1983): 240–42; David A. Black, *Paul, Apostle of Weakness* (New York: Lang, 1984), 118–19.

75. Cf. the suggestion of Hurd, *Origin*, 235–37.

76. On this passage in 1 Cor 5 see further May, *Body for the Lord*, 58–80, from whose work (originally a 2001 Glasgow PhD dissertation) I have learned a great deal.

77. Douglas, *Purity and Danger*, 2.

is matter that is out of place, which has transgressed a boundary and thus threatens to pollute. So in 1 Cor 5, the brother who is actually a πόρνος threatens to pollute the whole church (5:6–7); he does not belong in the community and must be expelled (5:13). Fellowship with such persons, even eating with them, is to be avoided; but by implication, social interaction, including commensality, with "sinners" outside the church does not raise the same problems of contamination.

It is notable that this is the only case where the conduct Paul criticizes is so bad that it "redefines" the identity of the offender such that he no longer belongs in the community of the church (though even here some hope for the man's final salvation remains [5:5]). From the point of view of Pauline ethics this is interesting because the man's actions are such as to be regarded as unacceptable from the perspectives of Roman law and Jewish tradition as well as from Paul's Christian point of view (cf. 5:1).[78] In other words, the action that is so bad as to require expulsion from the church is action that Paul's wider society agrees in defining as sinful—so while the rhetoric with which Paul's judgment is expressed is based on the notion of the church as a pure entity from which polluting evil must be expelled, the moral judgment is one that conforms to that of the wider society and does not set "church" in contrast to "world."

Other material worth noting includes the highly positive theological grounds Paul offers for remaining in "mixed" marriages (1 Cor 7:12–16): children in such marriages are sanctified by the Christian spouse and there is always the hope of the other partner's salvation. Certainly there is no need for Christians to withdraw from such relationships. Endogamy, marriage to another believer, is the preferable course of action, given the choice (1 Cor 7:39), but the rejection of divorce forms a higher ethical principle than the ideal of unions only among those who belong to Christ. It is interesting too that Paul envisages unbelievers being present during the church's worship meetings (1 Cor 14:23), an important though neglected indication that these were not expected to be the meetings of an entirely exclusivist sect.

In a nutshell, Paul effectively says, "you are a pure and holy community, and the world is full of wicked, idolatrous people . . . but of course you can still go and share meals with them, remain married to them, and generally accommodate yourselves to the world so as not to cause offense." Within certain rather wide but important absolute limits, this social interaction is

78. See Thiselton, *First Epistle*, 385–86, and the primary and secondary sources mentioned there; also ch. 5 above.

limited above all by an overriding concern for the well-being of others, fellow believers in particular, for whose sake extreme renunciation may be called for.

This conjunction of strong and stark ideological distinction and relatively open social interaction might to some extent be illuminated using the distinctions John Barclay draws between assimilation, acculturation, and accommodation. When related to diaspora Jews, including Paul, these represent, respectively, the extent of social interaction with gentiles (assimilation); the degree of Hellenistic linguistic, educational, and cultural influence (acculturation); and the use to which acculturation was put, with either integrative or oppositional tendencies (accommodation). Because of his extensive and intimate contacts with gentiles, Paul ranks high on the scale of assimilation; but because of his scripturally based and apocalyptically strengthened portrayal of the gentile world in starkly negative terms, he ranks low in terms of accommodation, presenting an antagonistic stance towards gentile culture.[79] However, viewing Paul from the perspective of diaspora Judaism, it is mainly the contacts Paul enjoys with gentile *Christians* that Barclay adduces as evidence for this high assimilation.[80] Yet, as Barclay notes, from Paul's perspective this high degree of intimate contact is explained by the fact that Paul moves "the chosen few among the Gentiles into territory traditionally ascribed to Jews"—they are now children of Abraham, God's children, his temple, even the Israel of God, and so on.[81] From the point of view of other Jews, it is understandable that this was regarded as a dangerous and apostatizing level of intimacy with gentiles; but from Paul's point of view these gentiles have now become part of the community of God's people, defined as all who are in Christ.

What is striking, however, from the evidence we have surveyed in 1 Corinthians, especially on the idolatry and idol food issues, is the extent to which Paul's starkly antagonistic rhetoric contrasting church and world goes hand in hand with a policy of quite open interaction with *outsiders*, albeit circumscribed by certain clear limits. There is, then, in this case a distinction to be drawn between the rhetoric that constructs a strong sense of group identity and distinction, and the ways in which social interaction is structured. A strong sense of ideological distinction does not necessarily translate into strongly separatist or antagonistic social practice. Rather, returning

79. Barclay, "Paul among Diaspora Jews"; Barclay, *Jews*, 92–98, 381–95.
80. Barclay, "Paul among Diaspora Jews," 103–4; Barclay, *Jews*, 384–87.
81. Barclay, *Jews*, 388; and further 388–89; Horrell, "No Longer Jew or Greek," 341–42.

again to Barth, it translates into specific aspects of social practice, defined in certain ways—for Paul in terms of avoiding incompatible unions—and not into blanket isolation or antagonism.

Conclusions

In our brief exploration of Paul's general statements about idolatry and his specific treatment of the issue in 1 Cor 8–10, a number of points have emerged that are significant in understanding Paul's ethics. They may be summarized as follows.

1. While Paul sets some clear and absolute limits in terms of what is permitted and prohibited regarding idolatry and idol food, much of his focus is on the relational moral concerns that arise because of the interests and concerns of others, especially others within the ἐκκλησία.
2. Paul bases his arguments on theological, and especially christological, grounds. In substantive terms, Christology provides a basis for Paul's focus on the body, both individual and collective, as the key foundation for group identity and distinctiveness, and also for his emphasis on the need for self-giving and other-regard.
3. In terms of the construction and preservation of a distinct group identity, food does not serve for Paul as a marker of religio-cultural distinctiveness, while the body does, specifically as perceived in relation to ideas of union, κοινωνία, participation, and so on. The group's identity is marked on the positive side by the practices of baptism and Lord's Supper that initiate and confirm this union, and on the negative side by the avoidance of incompatible unions in sexual immorality and idolatry.
4. There is in Paul a collocation of on the one hand a strong rhetoric of difference, with its stark contrasts between the idolatrous world and the pure ἐκκλησία, which underpins a strong sense of group identity and separation, and on the other hand a concern for accommodation and peaceful coexistence that permits a considerable degree of social integration and open interaction.

This last point may bear some moral significance. What Barth relates as an empirical observation—that distinct ethnic identities can be sustained along with interethnic interaction and cooperation—is also a pressing moral task, the task of allowing ethnic and cultural difference to be treasured while at the same time building human solidarity and reducing interethnic hostility.[82] In relation to this task, we might judge Paul negatively, as someone who rants against a hostile and sinful world while sharing more of its moral values and participating more in its life than he admits. Or we might see in Paul, though not, of course, uniquely, some potential for the coexistence of a strong sense of distinct group identity alongside a considerable degree of social integration.

82. On this theme in Pauline studies, see Daniel Boyarin, *A Radical Jew: Paul and the Politics of Identity* (Berkeley: University of California Press, 1994); David G. Horrell, "Solidarity and Difference: Pauline Morality in Romans 14–15," *Studies in Christian Ethics* 15.2 (2002): 60–78.

Chapter 7

Imitating the Humility of Christ

Paul's Philippian Christ-Hymn and the Making of Christian Morality

Introduction: The Influence and Interpretation of Phil 2:6–11

One passage in Paul's letter to the Philippians has exerted enormous influence in the history of Christian theology and liturgy: the so-called Christ-hymn in Phil 2:6–11. It is, as Markus Bockmuehl remarks, "easily the most important [paragraph] in this letter."[1] Whether or not this passage originated as a hymn, it has certainly become one, contributing rich and memorable phrases to the vocabulary of Christian devotion. Moreover, as Bockmuehl notes, it "has been the subject of an uncontainable deluge of scholarly debate, quite possibly more than any other New Testament text."[2]

Some of this debate has been generated by the specific words and phrases of the passage; these are often crucial for understanding early Christology, yet equally enigmatic and subject to varying interpretations. What does it mean for Christ to be ἐν μορφῇ θεοῦ? What is the sense to be given to the word ἁρπαγμός? Are there parallels to the story of Adam here, and how would these affect the understanding of the passage?[3]

More broadly, two crucial landmarks in the scholarly discussion of the passage set the agenda for much subsequent work. The first of these is Ernst Lohmeyer's proposal, first published in 1928, that the passage represents an

1. Markus N. A. Bockmuehl, *The Epistle to the Philippians*, BNTC (London: Black, 1998), 115.

2. Bockmuehl, *Philippians*, 115.

3. For a valuable introduction to the issues and debates in the history of interpretation, see Ralph P. Martin and Brian J. Dodd, eds., *Where Christology Began: Essays on Philippians 2* (Louisville: Westminster John Knox, 1998).

early Christian hymn that Paul adopted in his letter.[4] Subsequent scholarship has included various attempts to reconstruct the original form of this hymn, and to identify its likely poetic structure.[5] There have also been those skeptical of the prospects for any such reconstruction,[6] and a number of more recent commentators have insisted, whatever the possibility of the hymn existing in some form prior to Paul's including it in his letter, that the exegete must interpret the text in its context in Philippians.[7] Some prior formulation remains most likely—given that the hymn goes far beyond what Paul needs to say in order to make his point, and given the poetic (or at least, rhythmic) language—though Paul quite evidently affirms and adopts the hymn's content, whether or not he first composed it, and it plays an important function in its current epistolary context.[8] We may be reasonably confident that the hymn is in some form "pre-Philippians," though whether it is "pre-Pauline" is more difficult to say.

The second landmark is Ernst Käsemann's critical analysis of the passage, first published in 1950.[9] One of Käsemann's central arguments concerned v. 5, and specifically the phrase ἐν Χριστῷ Ἰησοῦ. In essence, Käsemann argued against the ethical interpretation of the passage, which saw in v. 5 an appeal to the Philippians to have in themselves the same mind that was in Christ. From this perspective, the Christ-hymn that follows sets out an ethical example, which Paul urges the Philippians to follow. By contrast, Käsemann

4. Ernst Lohmeyer, *Kyrios Jesus: Eine Untersuchung zu Phil. 2,5–11* (Darmstadt: Wissenschaftliche Buchgesellschaft, 1961). For an overview and discussion of Lohmeyer's influential work, see Colin Brown, "Ernst Lohmeyer's *Kyrios Jesus*," in *Where Christology Began*, ed. Martin and Dodd, 6–42.

5. See esp. Otfried Hofius, *Der Christushymnus Philipper 2,6–11: Untersuchungen zu Gestalt und Aussage eines urchristlichen Psalms*, 2nd ed., WUNT 17 (Tübingen: Mohr Siebeck, 1991), who details the OT precursors and influences, and demonstrates that the phrases often seen as additional to the hymn (vv. 8c and 11c) belong coherently to its original structure.

6. See, e.g., Bockmuehl, *Philippians*, 116–17; Michael Peppard, "'Poetry,' 'Hymns' and 'Traditional Material' in New Testament Epistles or How to Do Things with Indentations," *JSNT* 30 (2008): 319–42.

7. E.g., Morna D. Hooker, "Philippians 2:6–11," in *Jesus und Paulus: Festschrift W. G. Kümmel*, ed. E. Earle Ellis and Erich Gräßer (Göttingen: Vandenhoeck & Ruprecht, 1978), 152; N. T. Wright, *The Climax of the Covenant: Christ and the Law in Pauline Theology* (Edinburgh: T&T Clark, 1991), 97–98; Gordon D. Fee, *Paul's Letter to the Philippians*, NICNT (Grand Rapids: Eerdmans, 1995), 193n3; Bockmuehl, *Philippians*, 119.

8. I shall continue to use the term "hymn" to refer conveniently to the passage in question, without implying any firm conclusions concerning its origins and use.

9. Ernst Käsemann, "Kritische Analyse von Phil. 2,5–11," *Exegetische Versuche und Besinnungen*, 2 vols. (Göttingen: Vandenhoeck & Ruprecht, 1960–1964), 1:51–95.

proposed that the elliptical phrase should rather be understood to imply an exhortation to have the mind that it is necessary for those "in Christ Jesus" to have (assuming that the verb[s] to be supplied in v. 5b were φρονεῖν δεῖ, or similar, hence: ὃ καὶ φρονεῖν δεῖ ἐν Χριστῷ Ἰησοῦ).[10] The following hymn would not then function as an ethical example—not least since incarnation and exaltation are hardly the subjects for the Christian's imitation—but rather as the mythical depiction of the salvation event, the basis for the Philippians' life in Christ. Subsequent scholarship, however, has largely rejected Käsemann's argument on this particular point and reaffirmed the ethical function of the hymn in its epistolary context.[11] Nonetheless, Käsemann was right to insist that the hymn must not be reduced to the status of moral example, as if the story of Christ merely illustrated a pattern of commendable behavior.[12] Rather, it sets out the paradigmatic pattern of Christ's journey—with a basic "down-up" movement at its heart—as the determining myth by which the Philippians' identity should be formed. It is a story to which they, like Paul and his coworkers, should be conformed. As such it has profoundly soteriological and eschatological implications, as well as ethical ones; and these various facets of its significance are inextricably woven together.

The Ethical Function of Phil 2:6–11

Philippians as a whole, and 2:1–5 in particular, displays an unusual concentration of words from the φρον- group, suggesting that Paul's goals in the

10. See Käsemann, *Kritische Analyse*, 90–91. Similarly, Joachim Gnilka, *Der Philipperbrief*, HThKNT 10.3 (Freiburg: Herder, 1968), 108–10.

11. E.g., Hooker, "Philippians 2:6–11"; Larry Hurtado, "Jesus as Lordly Example in Philippians 2:5–11," in *From Jesus to Paul: Studies in Honour of Francis Wright Beare*, ed. John C. Hurd and Peter Richardson (Waterloo, Ont.: Wilfred Laurier University Press, 1984), 113–26; Stephen E. Fowl, *The Story of Christ in the Ethics of Paul: An Analysis of the Function of the Hymnic Material in the Pauline Corpus*, JSNTSup 36 (Sheffield: Sheffield Academic Press, 1990), 49–101; Bockmuehl, *Philippians*, 122–23; Peter Oakes, *Philippians: From People to Letter*, SNTSMS 110 (Cambridge: Cambridge University Press, 2001), 188–93; Joseph H. Hellerman, *Reconstructing Honor in Roman Philippi*, SNTSMS 132 (Cambridge: Cambridge University Press, 2005), 202–3n2.

12. Cf. Wayne A. Meeks, "The Man from Heaven in Paul's Letter to the Philippians," in *The Future of Early Christianity: Essays in Honor of Helmut Koester*, ed. Birger A. Pearson (Minneapolis: Fortress, 1991), 331. See the valuable discussion of Käsemann's essay and its influence by Robert Morgan, "Incarnation, Myth, and Theology: Ernst Käsemann's 'Interpretation of Philippians 2:5–11,'" in *Where Christology Began*, ed. Martin and Dodd, 43–73.

letter bear close comparison with the moral philosophical concern with φρόνησις, or practical wisdom, as Wayne Meeks and others have noted.[13] Also evident are words and motifs from the Greco-Roman vocabulary of friendship, suggesting to many that this letter deliberately reflects a relationship of friendship between Paul and the Philippians, and an attempt by Paul to strengthen such bonds. For example, the appeals for ἀγάπη, κοινωνία, and harmony (τὸ αὐτὸ φρονῆτε, τὸ ἓν φρονοῦντες) all reflect the kind of qualities that were thought to characterize friendship at its best.[14]

Particularly notable as the most explicit connection between 2:1–5 and the hymn itself in 2:6–11 is the appeal for humility (ταπεινοφροσύνη). Paul urges the Philippians: "in humility, consider others above yourselves," an appeal expanded in the following request "not to look to your own interests but to those of others" (vv. 3–4). This is explicitly the φρόνησις embodied by Christ, who does not take consideration for what he himself might gain (v. 6) but rather empties (ἐκένωσεν, v. 7) and humbles himself (ἐταπείνωσεν ἑαυτόν, v. 8) even to the point of death. This narrative of self-lowering culminates in the phrase that many see as the crux of the hymn—θανάτου δὲ σταυροῦ (v. 8), which emphasizes the extent of Christ's degradation, at the same time highlighting the central symbol of the early Christian faith.[15] Furthermore, the active verbs ἐκένωσεν and ἐταπείνωσεν, along with the reflexive ἑαυτόν, emphasize Christ's willing and active commitment to this path.[16] Indeed, we may contrast the first half of the hymn, where Christ is subject, actively and obediently following the way of self-emptying and self-

13. Meeks, "Man from Heaven."

14. See, e.g., L. Michael White, "Morality Between Two Worlds: A Paradigm of Friendship in Philippians," in *Greeks, Romans, and Christians: Essays in Honor of Abraham J. Malherbe*, ed. David L. Balch, Everett Ferguson, and Wayne A. Meeks (Minneapolis: Fortress, 1990), 201–15; Stanley K. Stowers, "Friends and Enemies in the Politics of Heaven," in *Thessalonians, Philippians, Galatians, Philemon*, ed. Jouette M. Bassler, vol. 1 of *Pauline Theology*, ed. Jouette M. Bassler, David M. Hay, and E. Elizabeth Johnson, 4 vols. (Minneapolis: Fortress, 1991–1997), 105–21. In an extensive consideration of friendship language and the genre of Philippians, John Reumann concludes that the letter does indeed reflect the language and topoi of friendship, but cannot confidently be placed within a "friendship letter" genre. See John Reumann, "Philippians, Especially Chapter 4, as a 'Letter of Friendship': Observations on a Checkered History of Scholarship," in *Friendship, Flattery, and Frankness of Speech: Studies on Friendship in the New Testament World*, ed. John T. Fitzgerald, NovTSup 82 (Leiden: Brill, 1996), 83–106.

15. Hellerman, *Reconstructing Honor*, 129–48, sees the first part of the Christ-hymn as setting out a *cursus pudorum*, a three-stage process in which Christ descends from equality with God to the status of a slave and the public humiliation of his death on the cross.

16. Cf. Bockmuehl, *Philippians*, 138.

abasement, with the second half, where God is the active subject, exalting and bestowing upon Christ the honor of the highest position of all (vv. 9–11).

This pattern of conduct—self-lowering for the sake of others—is one that Paul reiterates elsewhere in his letters, grounding it in the paradigmatic story of Christ (e.g., Rom 15:2–3). He also presents himself (and his coworkers) as embodiments of this pattern of self-lowering and self-giving for others, and thus as models to be imitated (1 Cor 4:8–16; 10:24–11:1; Gal 4:12–14; 1 Thess 1:6). Indeed, in Philippians specifically, Paul presents himself, as well as Timothy and Epaphroditus, as representing this same paradigm. Paul defines his own identity fundamentally in terms of Christ (1:20–21; 3:7–9); he is "conformed" to the pattern of Christ's death in hope of sharing also in his resurrection (3:10, 21); like Christ, he puts the Philippians' interests above his own (1:24–25); and, following the down-up pattern of the hymn, he strains *upwards* (ἄνω) towards the heavenly prize (3:14). Similarly, Timothy is concerned for the Philippians' welfare, unlike "those who seek their own interests" (οἱ . . . τὰ ἑαυτῶν ζητοῦσιν; 2:19–21); thus he embodies precisely the pattern of conduct to which Paul calls the Philippians in 2:4. Epaphroditus too represents the same Christlike pattern: he has served Paul's needs and ministered to him when the Philippians could not (2:25–30), specifically giving himself to the point of death (μέχρι θανάτου, 2:30; cf. 2:8) for the work of Christ. The Philippians are explicitly called to follow these and similar examples—ἔχετε τύπον ἡμας—to become together imitators of Paul, as he in turn embodies the paradigm of Christ (3:17). Furthermore, in 3:20–21 we find what Meeks has called an "inclusive description of Paul and the letter's recipients" that again "echoes the hymn" of 2:6–11: as Christ was in the form of God, yet humbled himself to death and was subsequently exalted, so he will transform the body of those who have followed his pattern of self-lowering humility (ταπείνωσις), conforming (σύμμορφον) them to his glory.[17] Indeed, 3:21 provides a concise summary of the pattern of transformation from humiliation to glory, and—contrary to those who insist that Christ's glorification is a unique and nonimitatable event—depicts the future hope of Paul and the Philippians precisely in terms of a conformity to the glory of Christ's body.[18] It is not that Paul's self-description (3:2–16) and

17. Meeks, "Man from Heaven." See further William S. Kurz, "Kenotic Imitation of Paul and of Christ in Philippians 2 and 3," in *Discipleship in the New Testament*, ed. Fernando F. Segovia (Philadelphia: Fortress, 1985), 103–26.

18. On the meaning and interpretation of τὸ σῶμα τῆς ταπεινώσις in 3:21, see Peter Doble, "'Vile Bodies' or Transformed Persons? Philippians 3:12 in Context," *JSNT* 86 (2002): 3–27.

his depiction of Christ (2:6–11) are parallel at all specific points of detail, but rather, as Meeks again sagely puts it, "that the dramatic structure of the two 'plots' is analogous, though not the same."[19] Stephen Fowl summarizes the point well: "the story of Christ narrated in 2:6–11 functions as an exemplar, a concrete expression of a shared norm from which Paul and the Philippians can make analogical judgments about how they should live."[20]

Humility and the Moral Norms of Pauline Ethics

I have argued in detail elsewhere that this pattern of conduct—a self-giving and self-lowering modelled on the pattern of Christ's self-giving which constitutes in essence an "other-regard"—is, along with the norm of corporate solidarity, one of the central moral norms of Pauline ethics.[21] (It should be clear that "Christ's self-giving" shapes ethics not in the sense of supplying specific resolutions to particular ethical quandaries but rather in the "metamoral" sense of shaping human relations and values, forming the character and ethos of communities.[22]) Both these norms are grounded in Christology. Paul can use a variety of terms to describe this self-giving, depending in part on the specific appeal he is wanting to make: becoming poor (2 Cor 8:9), not pleasing oneself (Rom 15:2–3), and (fundamentally) looking not to one's own concerns but to those of others (1 Cor 10:24; Phil 2:4).[23]

One term would seem to encapsulate this moral virtue, particularly in the literary context of Phil 2: "humility" (ταπεινοφροσύνη). The positive valuation of humility is evident across a range of early Christian sources (e.g., Matt 18:4; Matt 23:12//Luke 14:11//18:14; 1 Pet 3:8), often connected with a theme of reversal of fortunes, brought about by God (e.g., Jas 1:9–10; 4:6, 10//1 Pet 5:5–6). Indeed, this reversal language fits well with the im-

19. Meeks, "Man from Heaven," 333. Cf. Oakes, *Philippians*, who sees a "three-fold parallel between Christ, Paul and the Philippians" as the "main thematic structure of the letter" (xiii; see 103–28, 175–210).

20. Stephen E. Fowl, "Christology and Ethics in Philippians 2:5–11," in *Where Christology Began*, ed. Martin and Dodd, 145–46; cf. Fowl, *Story of Christ*, 92–101.

21. David G. Horrell, *Solidarity and Difference: A Contemporary Reading of Paul's Ethics* (London: T&T Clark, 2005).

22. Cf. my comments in Horrell, *Solidarity*, 3, 274–76.

23. In both these texts, where a very similar phrase is used, Paul does not specify a noun (concerns, interests, rights, etc.) but simply contrasts τὸ ἑαυτοῦ/τὰ ἑαυτῶν with τὸ ἑτέρου/τὰ ἑτέρων.

plied depiction of humility in Phil 2, where self-lowering and self-abasement—ἐταπείνωσεν ἑαυτόν—is followed by exaltation and honoring by God. However, we need to note that Paul (and the Pauline tradition) uses the word-group in a variety of ways. The adjective, rather than the noun, is used most in the undisputed Pauline letters, where it generally refers to those who are lowly, or humiliated (Rom 12:16; 2 Cor 7:6; 12:21). In some cases this is evidently a pattern of being brought low—whether by one's own volition or involuntarily—that coheres well with the pattern of self-humiliation depicted in the first half of the Christ-hymn (2 Cor 11:7; Phil 4:12).[24] The noun ταπεινοφροσύνη, interestingly, apart from Phil 2:3, appears only in texts that represent the later Pauline tradition (Acts 20:19;[25] Eph 4:2; Col 2:18, 23; 3:12; 1 Pet 5:5[26]). In Col 3:12 and Eph 4:2 it is evidently one among a list of Christian virtues (cf. 1 Pet 3:8; 1 Clement 30:8; 44:3).[27] Philippians would therefore seem to hold a place of special importance and influence in terms of establishing this concept as one of the central virtues of the Christian tradition.

It has been widely accepted that such humility—specifically the social humility of lowering or abasing oneself for the sake of other (lower-status) people—is not a virtue in the traditions of Greek and Roman ethics.[28] However, this is by no means a unanimous or uncontentious position, as we shall see. I wish to consider in particular two recent challenges to the idea that the

24. Cf. Klaus Wengst, *Humility: Solidarity of the Humiliated* (London: SCM, 1988), 45–47.

25. A text that represents a kind of Pauline farewell speech, summarizing the pattern of Paul's apostolic activity.

26. The extent to which 1 Peter stands in the Pauline tradition is a matter of some debate, but it seems clear that there are some points of connection with the Pauline letters. See further David G. Horrell, "The Product of a Petrine Circle? A Reassessment of the Origin and Character of 1 Peter," *JSNT* 86 (2002): 29–60.

27. The two references in Col 2:18 and 23 are more difficult, but probably refer to practices of self-abasement or self-denial, which form part of the "empty philosophy" (cf. 2:8) that the author here opposes.

28. Note, e.g., the opening comments of Stephen B. Dawes, "Humility: Whence This Strange Notion?," *ExpTim* 103 (1991): 72; and John P. Dickson and Brian S. Rosner, "Humility as a Social Virtue in the Hebrew Bible?," *VT* 54 (2004): 459n3. See further Wengst, *Humility*, 4–15; Gudrun Guttenberger Ortwein, *Status und Statusverzicht im Neuen Testament und seiner Umwelt*, NTOA 39 (Göttingen: Vandenhoeck & Ruprecht, 1999), 77–84. There has been more disagreement about the extent to which this notion finds precedents in pre-Christian Jewish tradition. See, for example, the contrasting arguments of Dawes, "Humility"; Stephen B. Dawes, "'*ănāwâ* in Translation and Tradition," *VT* 41 (1991): 38–48; and Dickson and Rosner, "Humility."

self-humbling for the sake of others depicted in the Philippian hymn represents a distinctive development in the context of Greco-Roman morality.

Humility, Self-Giving, and Friendship in Lucian's *Toxaris*?

The first such challenge is found in essays by L. Michael White and Stanley Stowers, both of whom locate Philippians (and the hymn specifically) within Greek traditions about friendship.[29] They seem to me to make a strong case for seeing Philippians as a letter suffused with the language of (ideal) relations between friends. More specifically, Stowers suggests that the "behavior which the Christ hymn warrants is described in the traditional language of ideal friendship"—"thinking the same thing," "having the same love," "united in soul," and so on (2:2).[30] When it comes to the self-giving or self-lowering demonstrated by Christ, White comments, appealing to Aristotle, that "the model of selflessness, the willingness to give up one's own status and share another's troubles, is the ultimate sign of true friendship."[31] The good man, Aristotle remarks, "does many acts for the sake of his friends [τῶν φίλων] and his country [τῆς πατρίδος], and if necessary dies for them" (*Nicomachean Ethics* 9.8.9 [1169a]).[32]

Both White and Stowers (referring to White) point to the description of friendship in Lucian's *Toxaris* to illustrate how the kind of self-giving Paul depicts in Phil 2:6–8 exemplifies what ancient Greeks would recognize as "the supreme virtue of friendship."[33] The context is a conversation in which Toxaris, a Scythian, and Mnesippus, a Greek, discuss friendship; each attempts to demonstrate with stories they swear to be authentic that the ideals of friendship are better embodied by their people than by the other's. The context, then, leads one to expect tales that depict the extremes to which friends might go.[34] The particular story in view concerns two life-

29. White, "Morality"; Stowers, "Friends."

30. Stowers, "Friends," 112.

31. White, "Morality," 212–13.

32. Greek text from LCL; translation from W. D. Ross, *The Works of Aristotle*, vol. 9 (Oxford: Oxford University Press, 1915). Cf. White, "Morality," 212–13.

33. White, "Morality," 213.

34. Though the extremes, along with other features, may suggest that the stories are "preposterous and absurd," there are indications that they constitute "an often subtle parody of the kinds of sentimental views of Greek male friendship depicted in romantic novels," as Richard Pervo argues in "With Lucian: Who Needs Friends? Friendship in the *Toxaris*," in

long friends, Greeks named Demetrius and Antiphilus (*Toxaris* 27–34[35]). Demetrius goes away on a trip, on which Antiphilus preferred not to go (*Toxaris* 27). During Demetrius's absence, disaster befalls Antiphilus due to the behavior of his slave, Syrus, who joins certain temple robbers, and ends up storing the stolen goods at Demetrius's house (*Toxaris* 28). Both slave and master are subsequently imprisoned, despite Antiphilus's protesting his innocence. Antiphilus suffers badly in the terrible prison conditions (*Toxaris* 28–29). On his return, Demetrius discovers what has happened and immediately runs to the prison. Eventually he gains entry and finds Antiphilus, leading to an emotional reunion (*Toxaris* 30).[36] Demetrius then tears his cloak in half, giving half to his friend, and attends to his needs in prison, returning each day and sleeping at night outside the prison (*Toxaris* 30–31). When, later on, his visits are stopped, Demetrius deliberately incriminates himself, so that he too can be imprisoned and be alongside his dear friend, caring more for his friend's needs than his own (*Toxaris* 32). In a scene much like that of Acts 16:22–40,[37] Demetrius and Antiphilus have an opportunity to escape from prison, but choose not to run away, detaining Syrus the slave also. The two friends are then given their freedom by the prefect of Egypt, who praises them for not running away (*Toxaris* 33). However, Demetrius is not content to let the injustice of their imprisonment be ignored, and insists on a proper investigation, which results in compensation being paid to both Antiphilus and Demetrius (*Toxaris* 33). The friends eventually go their separate ways—a feature that may point to a rather ironic parody being presented here[38]—though the final comments in the story refer to Demetrius's courtroom speech, in which he defended his friend rather than himself, until Syrus the slave confessed "under the lash" (μαστιγούμενος) and exonerated them both (*Toxaris* 34).

White describes this story as one concerning "the relationship between a certain young noble, named Demetrius, and his slave Antiphilus."[39] Similarly, Stowers describes the story as one in which "the slave of a young aristocrat is wrongfully imprisoned." According to Stowers, "His master, Deme-

Greco-Roman Perspectives on Friendship, ed. John T. Fitzgerald, RBS 34 (Atlanta: Scholars Press, 1997), 165.

35. Not *Toxaris* 29–34, as White, "Morality," 213, states.

36. Both friends are said to faint (*Toxaris* 30). Pervo comments that this is a common topos in romantic novels: Pervo, "With Lucian," 171n44.

37. So White, "Morality," 213n56, though he gives the reference as Acts 17.

38. Cf. Pervo, "With Lucian," 173.

39. White, "Morality," 213.

trius, displays his true friendship by attending to his slave in the wretched prison. . . . Demetrius thus demonstrated the highest ideals of Greek friendship by giving up his status, honor, wealth, and freedom for a slave. As in the Christ hymn, Demetrius lowers himself to a humble status for the sake of another."[40]

However, as far as I can see, this crucial claim is simply mistaken. Antiphilus is not Demetrius's slave, but rather "his friend from boyhood [ἑταίρος ἐκ παίδων] and comrade in their military training [συνεφήβος]" (*Toxaris* 27). The only reference to a slave is to Syrus, the slave (οἰκέτης) of Antiphilus (*Toxaris* 28, etc.).

This somewhat changes the scenario: Demetrius does not humiliate and lower himself for the sake of someone of lower social status, a slave, but for a lifelong friend and companion. Nor does the specific language of humility appear. Richard Pervo's suggestion that this story is an ironic parody on the part of Lucian would also change the picture.[41] One might also point out that Christ is (elsewhere) depicted as dying for the sake of his (and God's) *enemies*, though this is not the concern in Philippians, where the self-giving of Christ serves as a moral paradigm for the ἀδελφοί in the Philippian community—it is (here) an ethic for relationships among siblings and friends. The parallel does remain significant, but not to the extent claimed by White and Stowers. Stowers notes that "Greek writings usually suppose that such comrades will be social and moral equals," seeing both Lucian's and Paul's as stories that "stretch to the limit but do not break the logic of Greek friendship."[42] Since Demetrius and Antiphilus are indeed "social and moral equals," it should be apparent from the discussion above that this latter comment applies to Paul's depiction of Christ but not to Lucian's of Demetrius.

The Distinctiveness of Christian Social Humility?

A more recent challenge to the notion that social humility is a distinctively Christian virtue not evident in Greek or Roman ethics is found in Runar Thorsteinsson's important study of Roman Christianity and Roman Sto-

40. Stowers, "Friends," 119–20.

41. Pervo comments that the stories of friendship presented by Lucian "exude a sentimentality so effectively demolished by Lucian that his ridicule of it has made a substantial contribution to his literary immortality" ("With Lucian," 173).

42. Stowers, "Friends," 120.

icism.[43] Without rejecting this viewpoint entirely, Thorsteinsson nonetheless queries the contrast drawn in a number of ways.

First, he urges against overgeneralizing about the contrast between Judeo-Christian and Greco-Roman perspectives on the terms ταπεινός and ταπεινοφροσύνη: the adjective often has a negative sense in the LXX as well as in "non-Judeo-Christian texts"; Paul can also use it in a negative or derogatory way (citing 2 Cor 10:1; 11:7; 12:21); and non-Judeo-Christian texts can use ταπεινός positively. Thus "there are more 'grey areas' here than usually assumed," and we should be wary of taking, say, Epictetus's admittedly negative stance towards the terms as indicative of a general Stoic stance, let alone the general stance of "Greco-Roman" ethics.[44]

Second, Thorsteinsson cautions against drawing "generalizations about basic conceptions from the use of particular words." In other words, "even if Epictetus and other (non-Stoic) philosphers use the words ταπεινός and ταπεινοφροσύνη in a negative sense, that does not necessarily mean that the basic conception of 'social humility' . . . was totally lacking in (all cases of) 'Graeco-Roman ethics.'"[45]

Third, Thorsteinsson argues that Seneca's argument for the exercise of *clementia* on the part of the emperor Nero represents an appeal for "social moderation" that corresponds closely to the "social humility" that Christian sources treat as a virtue.[46]

Thorsteinsson is right to note that the LXX's uses of ταπεινός and (especially) ταπεινόω are often negative, as are some of Paul's—with the sense of humiliated, lowly, or violated—an observation that calls into question any straightforward contrast between a supposedly positive evaluation of humility in the Judeo-Christian tradition and a negative evaluation in other Greco-Roman writings (e.g., Gen 15:13; 34:2; Exod 1:12; Amos 2:7; Jdt 16:11; Dan 3:37; Sir 25:22). The positive attitude of God towards those who are lowly, oppressed, or humiliated, and the promise to reverse the positions of the high and the low, is what begins to make this social position one that has moral and religious value (see, e.g., Pss 17:28; 137:6; Prov 3:34; Job 5:11; Isa 66:2; Ezek 21:26). The positive references to humility in non-Judeo-Christian Greek writings are also part of this picture, even though, as Thorsteinsson notes, these positive references seem to denote the virtues

43. Runar M. Thorsteinsson, *Roman Christianity and Roman Stoicism: A Comparative Study of Ancient Morality* (Oxford: Oxford University Press, 2010).

44. Thorsteinsson, *Roman Christianity*, 182.

45. Thorsteinsson, *Roman Christianity*, 183.

46. Thorsteinsson, *Roman Christianity*, 183–85.

of modesty or obedience, rather than the kind of social humility in view in Paul's Philippian hymn.[47]

It is also valuable to be reminded that comparison of concepts cannot validly proceed merely on the basis of the use of particular terms—a point also made in the much earlier treatment of the subject by Stefan Rehrl.[48] Yet in the example Thorsteinsson offers as a close comparison to the Christian virtue of social humility, the differences remain significant: Seneca's argument, addressed to the new emperor Nero, that a virtuous ruler should be characterized by mercy (*clementia*) is very different from the self-emptying and self-abasement Paul presents as the paradigm of Christian virtue.[49] In particular, the *clementia* for which Seneca argues contains no notion of self-abasement or lowering but is rather a noble virtue appropriately displayed by someone of noble position. The *princeps* should model himself on the gods; and humans need gods who will be merciful, in view of their errors and sins (*On Clemency* 1.7.1). Moreover, being merciful to others is, for the emperor at least, a way of being merciful to oneself, given the conviction that he is the soul (*animus*) of the state, which is his body (*corpus*).[50] Some

47. Thorsteinsson, *Roman Christianity*, 182n229, citing W. Grundmann, *TDNT* 8:4. For example, in Xenophon, *Agesilaus* 11.11, being ταπεινός is clearly virtuous, but the practices in view are those of what we would probably call modesty: simplicity of dress, limitation of one's own needs, and generosity towards friends. An example where ταπεινός means something like obedience or submission to authority is found in Isocrates, *Nicocles* 56 (cf. also Plato, *Laws* 4.716A; Aeschylus, *Prometheus* 320; Plutarch, *How to Tell a Flatterer from a Friend* 60F). Cf. 1 Clement 56:1 for this sense in Christian literature. See further the detailed studies of Stefan Rehrl, *Das Problem der Demut in der profan-griechischen Literatur im Vergleich zu Septuaginta und Neuem Testament*, Aevum Christianum 4 (Münster: Aschendorff, 1961); and Guttenberger Ortwein, *Status und Statusverzicht*, esp. 77–80.

48. Rehrl, *Problem der Demut*. Rehrl argues against the common position that humility (*Demut*) was not regarded as a positive moral virtue by the ancient Greeks, despite the generally negative use of terms like ταπεινόω (199) and the nonappearance of the noun ταπεινοφροσύνη (197). Other words, Rehrl suggests, such as αἰδώς, φόβος, ἡσυχία, and σωφροσύνη, were used to characterize essentially the virtue that came to be known as humility (cf. 145, 199): "Zusammenfassend können wir sagen, daß die Griechen doch ein umfassenderes Verständnis für das Wesen der Demut gehabt haben als man häufig annimmt" (200).

49. As Thorsteinsson himself notes, "it would almost certainly be a mistake to claim that Seneca is here calling for social 'humility' on the part of the emperor" (Thorsteinsson, *Roman Christianity*, 184). Cf. also the comments of Wengst, *Humility*, 12–14.

50. For one example, see *On Clemency* 1.5.1: "For if . . . you are the soul of the state and the state your body, you see, I think, how requisite is mercy [tu animus rei publicae tuae es, illa corpus tuum, vides, ut puto, quam necessaria sit clementia]; for you are merciful to yourself when you are seemingly merciful to another" (Basore, LCL).

parallels with Pauline Christology should not be denied here, but the differences in terms of the depiction and valuing of self-humbling remain clear.

It would seem to be a specific kind of humility—the social humility that entails a renunciation of status, a self-lowering for the sake of those who are socially inferior—that seems difficult to parallel as a praiseworthy and virtuous practice in the non-Christian Greek and Roman sources and appears to be a distinctively Christian emphasis.[51] One should, however, immediately stress the word "emphasis" rather than innovation, as if there were no parallels or precedents whatsoever. For example, Gudrun Guttenberger Ortwein, despite her general thesis that social humility and renunciation of status came to prominence in early Christianity and was not on the whole positively regarded in Greco-Roman literature, notes indications that point towards the valuing of certain kinds of renunciation of status in non-Christian sources, including Seneca.[52]

In *On Clemency*, Seneca does depict leadership as a kind of servitude (*servitus*)—though on the grounds that the emperor is in effect enslaved because of the public visibility of his deeds and his need for self-protection. Like the gods, he is unable to leave the heights; this is unlawful for the gods, but unsafe for him. Thus he is effectively "nailed to [his] pinnacle" ("fastigio tuo adfixus es").[53] In his forty-seventh letter, famous for its humane stance towards slaves, though written, of course, from the perspective of the slave-owning class, Seneca declares that slaves are in effect "our fellow-slaves, if one reflects that Fortune has equal rights over slaves and freemen alike" (*Letters* 47.1).[54] Moreover, slave and free come from the same "stock" (*semen*): "It is just as possible for you to see in him a free-born man as for him to see in you a slave" (*Letters* 47.10). There is a corresponding ethical imperative, albeit one that assumes the enduring positions of higher and lower: "treat your inferiors as you would be treated by your betters" (*Letters* 47.11). There is also a practical implication that Seneca articulates,

51. See esp. Guttenberger Ortwein, *Status und Statusverzicht*. For example, she comments on Rehrl's "breit angelegten Untersuchung": "Die Forderung nach Statusverzicht hat er nicht nachweisen können" (15; see also 77, 84, 87, 317–20). Cf. also Hellerman, *Reconstructing Honor*. Gerd Theissen identifies this renunciation of status as one of the two "basic values" of early Christian ethics: see *A Theory of Primitive Christian Religion*, trans. John Bowden (London: SCM, 1999), 71–80.

52. Guttenberger Ortwein, *Status und Statusverzicht*, 70–71, 81, 87. For her broader thesis, see the preceding note.

53. *On Clemency* 1.8.1–3 (Basore, LCL).

54. Gummere, LCL.

as he rejects the common idea that it is debasing to associate in a kindly and affable way with one's slave (*Letters* 47.13).[55]

Seneca also displays a certain kind of humility in his efforts to be frugal, and to make do with only what is necessary when traveling—though it is telling that this entails taking "only" one carriage load of slaves and having a lunch that takes not more than an hour to prepare! He also confesses to some discomfort at what others make of this frugality, revealing some struggle to put into practice an attitude of which he approves (*Letters* 87.2–5).

These limited moves in the direction of a positive ethos of social humility indicate the need for a balanced and careful assessment of the evidence. Nonetheless, there seems good reason to hold on to the view that the *emphasis* on social humility and renunciation of status as moral virtues emerges distinctively in early Christian sources, albeit with the kind of cautious nuances and qualifications that Thorsteinsson rightly stresses as important. There are certainly precursors and partial parallels in Greco-Roman (as well as Jewish)[56] sources, though neither the appeal to the depiction of friendship in Lucian's *Toxaris* nor the suggestion of a parallel in Seneca's notion of *clementia* provides anything quite like the model of humility as self-emptying and self-lowering found in the Philippian hymn.

Conclusions

Paul's Philippian hymn, and the literary context in which it is placed, can help us to see how and why it is that such humility (ταπεινοφροσύνη) comes to be a central Christian virtue. Being ταπεινός can indeed be positively valued in a range of pre- and non-Christian sources, particularly when it concerns being appropriately humble before God/the gods, or before rulers and superiors. It can also be used in a negative sense to refer to being humiliated

55. In a private response to this paper, for which I would like to record my thanks, Thorsteinsson suggests that Seneca here (in *Letters* 47) goes rather further than I suggest above, in encouraging practices such as dining with slaves, being friends with them, and kissing their hands—seeing such things as reflecting a certain social self-lowering. It seems we can at least agree that the differences regarding humility are more those of emphasis, rather than Christian innovation as such, and that exploring the extent of the differences in emphasis and expression requires nuanced and attentive interpretation of both Christian and non-Christian sources, as is exemplified in Thorsteinsson's book.

56. I have not here given consideration to the debate as to how far a notion of social humility develops in pre-Christian Judaism, on which see n. 28, above.

or degraded. This, of course, is precisely the fate of Christ, whose suffering and death was a public form of shameful degradation. Central to the early Christian faith was the attempt to revalue this shameful death, not only on the basis of the vindication represented by the resurrection, but also by seeing it as a salvific act, an expression of divine love and self-sacrifice. Christ's humiliation was reinterpreted, in a way that ran counter to the conventional evaluation of a criminal's death by crucifixion, and instead saw this humiliation as a positive model of virtuous action, one that Paul presents to the Philippians as a paradigm for inter-Christian relationships. Paul's Philippian Christ-hymn, placed in its literary context and used to frame an appeal for humility among members of the community, thus plays a significant part in the construction of Christian morality, at the point where this morality finds what is probably its most distinctive characteristic.

The legacy of this reevaluation of being ταπεινός is, as always, ambivalent. One of the important contributions of Thorsteinsson's book, it seems to me, is to challenge the kind of implicit sense of Christian superiority that leads scholars to depict early Christian ethics as evidently superior to Stoic ethics, making judgments reflective more of presupposition and bias than of careful historical and exegetical assessment. Thorsteinsson makes this challenge provocatively as he moves, finally, to offer his conclusions on what does distinguish Stoic from Christian ethics—given his finding that they share a great deal in common. The key difference, he suggests, is that the Stoic ethic was a genuinely universal one, concerned for all human beings, while the Christian ethic was an ethic for insiders, focused on love for those inside the community.[57] In other words, though Thorsteinsson does not directly say so, when we do find a point of significant difference, the Stoic option is probably more attractive to modern sensibilities than the Christian one.

I would not want this paper to be taken as an attempt to suggest that, because the strong focus on social humility and renunciation of status is, it seems, a distinctively Christian development, this demonstrates the superiority of Christian ethics over its ancient (and contemporary) rivals. Nor should it be taken in any way as a denial of the value of Stoic ethics and of their positive influence on Christian ethics, which has been recognized from the earliest times.[58] (At the same time, we should not, from some hy-

57. Thorsteinsson, *Roman Christianity*, 190–209.

58. E.g., in the apocryphal correspondence between Paul and Seneca, and in early Christian references to "our Seneca," etc. See, e.g., Tertullian, *The Soul* 20 ("saepe noster");

perliberal perspective, entirely reject the possibility that a certain tradition of ethics —whether Stoic, Christian, or something else—might prove itself superior in certain respects, because of the way in which it outnarrates its rivals.) There is a considerable positive legacy from the prominence of social humility in the Christian tradition, for example, in the notion that even the weakest, most vulnerable, despicable members of society are worthy of moral consideration—something strongly evident in Jewish sources too—and that this moral consideration may rightly call for sacrificial self-giving, even self-lowering, on the part of the more powerful. This may be part of the reason why charitable concern for the poor seems to have been particularly promoted with the rise of early Christianity, as Bruce Longenecker has shown.[59] Yet there is also the negative legacy, for example, in the use of the model of virtuous humility to legitimate and valorize the willing acceptance of abuse, the notion that accepting harsh treatment with meekness and silence is a Christian duty, done in imitation of Christ (cf. 1 Pet 2:18–3:6).[60] As always, moral virtues, exemplars, and paradigms are interpreted and enacted in diverse ways, requiring continual reflection and critical scrutiny. We may find reasons, then, both to welcome and to lament the prominence that Paul's letter to the Philippians placed on the virtue of social humility. But there is little doubt that the letter, and its Christ-hymn in particular, makes a crucial contribution to the emergence of humility as a central virtue in the Christian tradition.

Jerome, *Against Jovinianus* 1.49; further Abraham J. Malherbe, "Hellenistic Moralists and the New Testament," *ANRW* 26.1:269–70. For a recent study of the ways in which Paul's depiction in Philippians of life as aimed towards Christ draws on motifs and techniques from ancient moral philosophy, not least Stoic philosophy, see Bradley Arnold, *Christ as the* Telos *of Life: Moral Philosophy, Athletic Imagery, and the Aim of Philippians*, WUNT 2/371 (Tübingen: Mohr Siebeck, 2014).

59. Bruce W. Longenecker, *Remember the Poor: Paul, Poverty, and the Greco-Roman World* (Grand Rapids: Eerdmans, 2010).

60. For a scathing critique of 1 Peter on this basis, see Kathleen Corley, "1 Peter," in *A Feminist Commentary*, vol. 2 of *Searching the Scriptures*, ed. Elisabeth Schüssler Fiorenza (London: SCM, 1995), 349–60.

Part III

Pauline Ethics in Modern Contexts

Chapter 8

Paul among Liberals and Communitarians

Models for Christian Ethics

Introduction: The Liberal-Communitarian Debate and Its Relevance to Theology

The liberal-communitarian debate has been described as "the central debate in Anglo-American political theory during the 1980s,"[1] one that continues, "in one way or another, to inform a great deal of contemporary theory."[2] This is not, however, a debate in which two clearly defined positions battle out their differences. The label, rather, serves conveniently to identify on the one side a rather diverse range of arguments brought against liberalism, from critics such as Alasdair MacIntyre, Charles Taylor, Michael Walzer, and Michael Sandel, and on the other the responses and restatements from representatives of political liberalism such as John Rawls and Jürgen Habermas.[3] Nonetheless, certain key contrasts between the two broadly defined perspectives can be outlined; they will be illustrated here with specific reference to the work of Jürgen Habermas, described by Stephen Bronner as "*the* great exponent of political liberalism in Germany,"[4] and of Stanley

1. Susan Moller Okin, quoted with approval in Daniel Bell, *Communitarianism and Its Critics* (Oxford: Clarendon, 1993), 2.

2. Stephen Mulhall and Adam Swift, *Liberals and Communitarians*, 2nd ed. (Oxford: Blackwell, 1996), xii. Mulhall and Swift provide a thorough introduction to the perspectives and issues in this debate.

3. Although Rawls tends to dominate the Anglo-American discussions of liberalism, Arne Rasmusson is right to describe Rawls and Habermas as "the two leading liberal theorists" (*The Church as Polis: From Political Theology to Theological Politics as Exemplified by Jürgen Moltmann and Stanley Hauerwas* [Lund: Lund University Press, 1994], 269).

4. Stephen Eric Bronner, *Of Critical Theory and Its Theorists* (Oxford: Blackwell, 1994), 284.

Hauerwas, whose ecclesial ethics embodies a strident opposition to the presuppositions of political liberalism and shares much of communitarianism's theoretical basis.[5]

In his attempts to articulate what he calls a "discourse ethics" (*Diskursethik*), Habermas intends to fulfill a key liberal aim: to outline a morality for the public sphere with a rational, universally valid grounding, a *Vernunftmoral,* which transcends the specific justifications provided by particular traditions. In this, he stands firmly in the Kantian and deontological tradition, but seeks to reformulate Kant's categorical imperative such that it depicts the agent as situated in a communicative context rather than as monologically reflective: "Only those norms can claim to be valid that meet (or could meet) with the approval of all affected in their capacity as participants in a practical discourse."[6] For Habermas, at least in the public sphere, ethics can no longer be justified by appeal to "the authority of unquestioned traditions."[7] The only means by which ethical norms can be tested, and thus found valid (or not), is through rational argumentation. And the principles of discourse ethics are, Habermas argues, implicit in the very presuppositions of human argumentation: that communication and understanding are possible through participation in real discourse; that reasons can be presented for following certain courses of action; and that what alone should be persuasive is "the unforced force of the better argument."[8]

While traditions, and specifically the Judeo-Christian tradition, have been, and remain, immensely important in generating substantive moral values, the task of philosophy, Habermas argues, is to translate these moral claims into the language of public reason, such that they can be accepted and affirmed (or not) on the basis of rational insight.[9] Indeed, "every morality,"

5. Although Hauerwas does not want to be labeled a "communitarian" (see Stanley Hauerwas, *Dispatches from the Front: Theological Engagements with the Secular* [Durham, NC: Duke University Press, 1994], 156–63), since he sees his project as a specifically theological one, he does not deny the accuracy of his being aligned with the communitarian position: "I generally share their historicist starting point as well as their more communitarian and anti-liberal political and social theory" (Stanley Hauerwas, "Will the Real Sectarian Stand Up?," *ThTo* 44 [1987]: 92).

6. Jürgen Habermas, *Moral Consciousness and Communicative Action* (Cambridge: Polity, 1990), 66.

7. Jürgen Habermas, *Justification and Application: Remarks on Discourse Ethics* (Cambridge: Polity, 1993), 151.

8. Habermas, *Justification*, 23.

9. Cf. Jürgen Habermas, *Religion and Rationality: Essays on Reason, God, and Modernity* (Cambridge: Polity, 2002), 162–63; Jürgen Habermas, "Transcendence from Within, Tran-

Habermas suggests, "revolves around equality of respect [*Gleichbehandlung*], solidarity, and the common good [*allgemeines Wohl*]," given the requirement simultaneously to protect both the individual and the well-being of the community to which they belong.[10] "To these two aspects correspond the principles of justice and solidarity"; the first principle "postulates equal respect and equal rights for the individual whereas the second postulates empathy and concern for the well-being of one's neighbour."[11] The crucial argument Habermas then makes is that these moral principles are fundamental ideas that can be traced back to the conditions of symmetry and expectations of reciprocity basic to communicative action, that is to say, that they are already implicit in the presuppositions of human communication and can be discerned in everyday practices oriented to understanding.[12]

Hauerwas, by contrast, is clearly and polemically opposed to the "false universalism of liberalism"[13] and to any notion that liberal political democracy represents a kind of social order that Christians should seek to legitimate and sustain.[14] Far from being a regime in which Christianity can flourish—protected in the name of "freedom of religion"—liberalism requires an acceptance that religious convictions are essentially a private matter and subject to legitimate freedom of choice, which in effect empties Christianity of its integrity, while making the liberal worldview determinative. Hauer-

---

scendence in This World," in *Habermas, Modernity, and Public Theology*, ed. Don Browning and Francis Schüssler Fiorenza (New York: Crossroad, 1992), 237.

10. Habermas, *Moral Consciousness*, 201; Jürgen Habermas, *Erläuterungen zur Diskursethik* (Frankfurt: Suhrkamp, 1991), 17.

11. Habermas, *Moral Consciousness*, 200.

12. Habermas, *Erläuterungen*, 17: "Alle Moralen kreisen um Gleichbehandlung, Solidarität und allgemeines Wohl; das sind aber Vorstellungen, die sich auf die Symmetriebedingungen und Reziprozitätserwartungen des kommunikativen Handelns zurückführen, d.h. in den wechselseitigen Zuschreibungen und gemeinsam Unterstellungen einer verständigungsorientierten Alltagespraxis auffinden lassen."

13. Stanley Hauerwas, *After Christendom? How the Church Is to Behave If Freedom, Justice, and a Christian Nation Are Bad Ideas*, reissued with a new preface (Nashville: Abingdon, 1999), 16.

14. Cf., e.g., Stanley Hauerwas, "Where Would I Be without Friends?," in *Faithfulness and Fortitude: In Conversation with the Theological Ethics of Stanley Hauerwas*, ed. Mark Nation and Samuel Wells (Edinburgh: T&T Clark, 2000), 325: "Christians have no stake in Western civilisation nor should we try to rescue the epistemological or political forms of liberalism. . . . The reason Christians should not underwrite the epistemology and politics of liberalism is very simple: they are not true." Similarly, Stanley Hauerwas, *After Christendom*, 35, passim. For a penetrating critique of Hauerwas's antiliberal rhetoric, see Jeffrey Stout, *Democracy and Tradition*, New Forum Books (Princeton: Princeton University Press, 2004), 140–61.

was's theological, ecclesial ethics represents a counterliberal project that embodies many of the characteristics of the communitarian critique of liberalism (Alasdair MacIntyre is an especially notable influence). Against the liberal notion of the "unencumbered self"—a self capable of free and rational reflection—Hauerwas insists, with other communitarians, that our identities and moral convictions are profoundly formed by our communities of nurture, by the stories and traditions that make us who we are.[15] In this respect, liberalism is subject to criticism on two counts: first, in that it insists that such traditions "do not matter," that they can and must be set aside insofar as they are trumped by the tradition-transcendent values of liberal democracy; second, in that it masks its own particular story about the character of human identity in a universal claim to rationality.

These comments already indicate how for Hauerwas, as for MacIntyre and others, narrative, or story, is crucial as the mode in which identity and community are formed. Moral virtue and moral character are defined in tradition-specific ways, and cultivated through participation in a story-formed community. What this means for Christians is, negatively, that they have, according to Hauerwas, allowed their values and character to be decisively formed by the story that liberalism offers, and positively, that their task is to be a community whose practices and ethics are shaped by its own (true) story, the story of God's redemption of the world in Jesus Christ. "The church is where the stories of Israel and Jesus are told, enacted, and heard, and it is our conviction that there is literally nothing more important we can do. But the telling of that story requires that we be a particular kind of people if we and the world are to hear the story truthfully. That means that the church must never cease from being a community of peace and truth in a world of mendacity and fear."[16] The church's task, indeed, is to stand as a

15. See discussion in, e.g., Seyla Benhabib, *Situating the Self: Gender, Community and Postmodernism in Contemporary Ethics* (Cambridge: Polity, 1992), 3, 71–76; Mulhall and Swift, *Liberals and Communitarians,* 11; Bell, *Communitarianism*, 4–6. Hence it is relevant for Hauerwas to mention, in illustrating this point, that he is a Texan: "Because I was raised Texan . . . I knew I was never free to be 'modern' and 'self-creating.' I would always be, for better or worse, Texan. It was my first lesson in particularity; as some would put it, being Texan made me realize early that the foundationalist epistemologies of the Enlightenment had to be wrong. . . . I prefer simply to have a Texan epistemology" (Stanley Hauerwas, "The Testament of Friends," *ChrCent* 107 [1990]: 214). See further Gloria H. Albrecht, *The Character of Our Communities: Toward an Ethic of Liberation for the Church* (Nashville: Abingdon, 1995), 29–32, where she discusses Hauerwas's "Texan Epistemology."

16. Stanley Hauerwas, *The Peaceable Kingdom: A Primer in Christian Ethics* (Notre Dame: University of Notre Dame Press, 1983), 99–100.

"political alternative," "an alternative politics to the politics that so dominate our lives."[17]

These contrasting approaches, and the debate they represent, are important for theology since they concern the different ways in which the political and ethical tasks of theology might be conceived, or, put differently, the different models by which theology might understand its relationship and engagement with "the world." The alternatives are perhaps most concisely represented in Arne Rasmusson's terms as "political theology" versus "theological politics," where the former envisages the theological task as one of engaging with the wider political context, mediating the Christian message to the wider world, while for the latter, the position represented by Hauerwas, "it is the politics of the church and not the politics of the world that forms the primary context."[18] On the former model, theologians might expect to make a contribution to public debate on ethics, with their claims, like all others, on Habermas's model, being subject to rational testing through public processes of argumentation. They might hope, even expect, to discern areas of common ground in ethics, which might form part of what John Rawls calls an "overlapping consensus," the kind of public consensus that can sustain the common political and social life of groups of people committed to diverse traditions and visions of the good.[19] On the latter model, a model that Rasumsson labels a Radical Reformation theology, the incommensurability, even opposition, between church and world is much more forcefully stressed. Liberal visions of public consensus, to which theologians might make some contribution, represent a secular politics, in which theology allows its fundamental orientation to be determined by the story of secular reason and thus compromises its own story about the church and the world.[20] Hauerwas rejects the notion that Christian social ethics might involve a search for "moral generalities . . . that provide the basis for common moral commitment and action" and challenges "the very idea that Christian social ethics is primarily an attempt to make the world more peaceable or just." The task of the church is not so much to contribute to some form of public social ethics, but rather, as Hauerwas puts it, "to be the church," to be itself "a social ethic."[21]

17. Hauerwas, *After Christendom*, phrases from 35 and 6, respectively.

18. Rasmusson, *Church as Polis*, 377.

19. John Rawls, *Justice as Fairness: A Restatement*, ed. E. Kelly (Cambridge: Harvard University Press, 2001), 32–38.

20. Here, of course, I echo briefly the thesis of John Milbank, *Theology and Social Theory: Beyond Secular Reason* (Oxford: Blackwell, 1990).

21. Hauerwas, *Peaceable Kingdom*, 99.

Readings in Paul: Models for Christian Ethics

With these debates and issues in mind, we turn to Paul, and to three different readings in Pauline ethics, in the hope that such readings may help to generate fruitful reflection.[22] The interpretive process is, then, two-way: on the one hand, the contemporary debate shapes the kinds of questions with which our readings are concerned; on the other hand, the engagement with Paul's thought is intended to generate critical and constructive reflection on the issues raised in this debate. The hermeneutical stance that is thereby presupposed requires, I think, no more long and sophisticated justification than the pithy and felicitous description given by Francis Watson: "in the last resort, to interpret is *to use the texts to think with*."[23] The function of the canon, Watson insists, is not to restrict or foreclose thought, but to generate it.

I do not, let me stress, intend to imply that Paul might somehow supply a definitive resolution of the issues of debate, or a systematic model for Christian ethics. Only a naïvely biblicistic approach would pretend either that the Bible alone could supply such a model, or that a biblical perspective could somehow trump contemporary critical debate. All I presume is that at the very least theologians regard the Bible as a primary source for the Christian tradition, one with which they engage in order to further develop that tradition in response to contemporary dilemmas and issues. I should also make clear that by presenting three different readings in Paul's ethics, I do not intend to imply that three (or more) distinct "models" for ethics can be identified in Paul. Rather, by sampling the Pauline material, I aim to illustrate some of its diverse facets and potential for contemporary appropriation.

22. Insofar as I seek to develop a conversation between Paul and these contemporary approaches in ethics, my project shares aims in common with the recent work of Douglas Harink (*Paul among the Postliberals* [Grand Rapids: Brazos, 2003]). Harink brings postliberal theologians, notably Hauerwas (along with Barth and Yoder), into conversation with Paul, and concludes that Paul thoroughly affirms postliberal theology: it is "a genuine recovery of the authentic Pauline gospel" (18). What I miss in his book is any sense that engaging with Paul might raise some critical questions for Hauerwas's ecclesial ethics or that Paul's thought might resonate in some ways with liberal concerns or with other approaches. The idea that liberalism might find some points of connection with Paul is sharply dismissed (cf. 84n29, 92). But Harink is selective in what he takes from Pauline theology and ethics (and from contemporary Pauline scholarship) and thus excludes some of the contrasting perspectives that might be considered. For further thoughts on this stimulating and significant book, see my review in *JTS* 55 (2004): 663–68.

23. Francis Watson, *Agape, Eros, Gender: Towards a Pauline Sexual Ethic* (Cambridge: Cambridge University Press, 2000), viii.

The Story-Formed Community: Ecclesial Ethics in Phil 2

Philippians 2:5–11 is among the most influential and theologically rich passages in the NT. It is also, as Markus Bockmuehl remarks, "a passage which in the twentieth century has been the subject of an uncontainable deluge of scholarly debate, quite possibly more so than any other New Testament text."[24] The crucial question for our purposes is whether, and how, the hymn of Christ functions in Paul's ethics. Ernst Käsemann famously argued that the hymn did not have an ethical function: v. 5 should be interpreted not as suggesting a parallel between the attitude the Philippians should have and the attitude Christ had, but as calling the Philippians to adopt the attitude that is fitting "in Christ Jesus."[25] The hymn that follows presents the mythical scheme of the salvation event, and it is this which forms the basis for Paul's paraenesis—not some depiction of Christ as ethical *Vorbild*. Verses 9–11, Käsemann insisted, add weight to this thesis, since they can hardly serve as an outline of an example to be imitated. Thus, according to Käsemann, "it becomes clear that the hymn conveys eschatology and soteriology, not ethics."[26] Käsemann's interpretation was widely followed in the 1950s and 60s, but subsequent work has on the whole reaffirmed an ethical reading of the hymn, and insisted, against Käsemann, that v. 5 *is* to be understood precisely as proposing a parallel between the attitude of the Philippians and that of Christ.[27]

In his opposition to what he calls the "ethical idealism" of most previous interpretations,[28] Käsemann is surely right, however, to insist that the ethical function of the Christ-hymn cannot be merely to set out an ethical example, a pattern to be copied. As a rich and compact expression of the Christian myth, shared and proclaimed, whether "liturgically" or otherwise, in the

24. Markus N. A. Bockmuehl, *The Epistle to the Philippians*, BNTC (London: Black, 1998), 115.

25. Ernst Käsemann, "Kritische Analyse von Phil. 2,5–11," *Exegetische Versuche und Besinnungen*, 2 vols. (Göttingen: Vandenhoeck & Ruprecht, 1960–1964), 1:51–95.

26. Käsemann, "Kritische Analyse," 94.

27. Among many examples, see Morna D. Hooker, "Philippians 2:6–11," in *Jesus und Paulus: Festschrift W. G. Kümmel*, ed. E. Earle Ellis and Erich Gräßer (Göttingen: Vandenhoeck & Ruprecht, 1978), 151–64; Larry Hurtado, "Jesus as Lordly Example in Philippians 2:5–11," in *From Jesus to Paul: Studies in Honour of Francis Wright Beare*, ed. John C. Hurd and Peter Richardson (Waterloo, Ont.: Wilfrid Laurier University Press, 1984), 113–26; Stephen E. Fowl, *The Story of Christ in the Ethics of Paul*, JSNTSup 36 (Sheffield: Sheffield Academic Press, 1990), 49–101.

28. Käsemann, "Kritische Analyse," 57.

context of Christian gatherings, this text shapes the beliefs, identity, and behavior of those who affirm it. In this sense, it is about soteriology, eschatology, *and—pace* Käsemann—ethics. Verses 9–11 are not then problematic for an ethical interpretation along these lines, though they are for a "mere example" ethic. They belong in the text since they depict a crucial part of the story, which cannot end simply with death on a cross. But more than this, while Christ's "story" is in one sense unimitatable, the pattern of faithful endurance through suffering leading to resurrection glory is precisely one to which Paul points the Philippians and sees mirrored in his own, as well as Christ's, experience (Phil 3:10–11, 21).[29]

Looking back to vv. 3–4, it becomes clear that the specific pattern of moral conduct that Paul sees exemplified in Christ is one characterized by "humility" (ταπεινοφροσύνη)—a self-lowering in which each person considers others before themselves, and looks not to their own [things][30] but to those of others.[31] This self-lowering other-regard is paradigmatically demonstrated in the central story of the faith, in Christ Jesus himself, whose self-lowering takes the extreme form of a movement from the form of God (and equality with God) to the form of a slave, a person "bereft of rights and social status."[32] This "social humility," that is, the lowering of oneself before (and for the sake of) those who are socially equal or inferior, is not, it is widely agreed, seen as positive or morally commendable in Greco-Roman ethics (see further ch. 7 above),[33] nor

29. See further Wayne A. Meeks, "The Man from Heaven in Paul's Letter to the Philippians," in *The Future of Early Christianity: Essays in Honor of Helmut Koester*, ed. Birger A. Pearson (Minneapolis: Fortress, 1991), 329–36.

30. As in 1 Cor 10:24, a closely parallel phrase, Paul does not specify a noun here (interests, concerns, rights, etc.) but speaks simply of τὰ ἑαυτῶν/τὰ ἑτέρων (cf. 1 Cor 10:24: τὸ ἑαυτοῦ/τὸ ἑτέρου).

31. Cf. also Rom 15:2–3. On the theme of Christ's self-giving as a paradigm for other-regard, see Horrell, *Solidarity and Difference*, ch. 7. This central norm of Pauline ethics is also stressed by Richard B. Hays, *The Moral Vision of the New Testament: A Contemporary Introduction to New Testament Ethics* (San Francisco: HarperCollins; Edinburgh: T&T Clark, 1997), 27–32.

32. Frank J. Matera, *New Testament Ethics: The Legacies of Jesus and Paul* (Louisville: Westminster John Knox, 1996), 179.

33. Cf., e.g., Wolfgang Schrage, *Die konkreten Einzelgebote in der paulinischen Paränese* (Gütersloh: Mohn, 1961), 204–5; W. Grundmann, *TDNT* 8:1–5; and esp. Gudrun Guttenberger Ortwein, *Status und Statusverzicht im Neuen Testament und seiner Umwelt*, NTOA 39 (Göttingen: Vandenhoeck & Ruprecht, 1999), for a major study of "renunciation of status" (*Statusverzicht*) as a value in the NT and its environment (cf. also Gerd Theissen, *A Theory of Primitive Christian Religion*, trans. John Bowden [London: SCM, 1999], 71–78, on this value as central to early Christian ethics). Guttenberger Ortwein comments: "Demut wird in der paganen Antike

does it exist with any degree of prominence as a virtue in pre-Christian Jewish tradition—though it has clear precedents and precursors there.[34] Yet it comes to prominence as a central Christian virtue, not least in Paul, precisely because it is demonstrated paradigmatically in the story of Christ's self-giving for others—his shameful and ignominious death becoming for Paul a positive model for imitation. As the Christians in Philippi affirm and celebrate the story of Christ's descent and ascent, humiliation and exaltation, so they are to conform their character and practice to this moral paradigm, and thus cultivate the virtues embodied by Christ—humility, self-giving for others, confidence and joy in suffering, and so on.

This description should already make clear how closely this text resonates with the approach of Hauerwas's ecclesial ethics: the central Christian story, told and retold in the context of communal worship, inculcates the practice of certain kinds of moral virtue (humility, above all), through nurturing a particular kind of character, one conformed to that of Christ. Given this similarity it is not insignificant to note that here Paul's ethics finds its most distinctive emphases, compared with his non-Christian contemporaries, namely the prominence of social humility, self-lowering, and renunciation of status.

Ethics in the Church and the World: Distinct Identity and Shared Ethics in 1 Cor 5

Paul's most extended treatment of sex and sexual ethics is in 1 Cor 5–7, three chapters dominated by this theme. Chapter 5 deals with what Paul regards

---

nur sehr selten positiv bewertet." The few positive references are to humility before the gods or under the law. "Als Haltung vor den Menschen wird sie als Haltung der Unterlegenen den Überlegenen gegenüber gefordert, mit einer Ausnahme (Agesilaios) aber negativ bewertet. Als Haltung der Überlegenen gegenüber den Unterlegenen läßt sie sich m.W. nicht nachwiesen" (87).

34. The extent to which the virtue of humility is evident in pre-Christian Judaism is debated, with, e.g., Klaus Wengst (*Humility: Solidarity of the Humiliated* [London: SCM, 1988]) and Stephen B. Dawes ("*'ănāwâ* in Translation and Tradition," *VT* 41 [1991]: 38–48; Dawes, "Humility: Whence This Strange Notion?," *ExpTim* 103 [1991]: 72–75) arguing for its Hebrew Bible origins (though Dawes rejects Wengst's view that it originated in the solidarity of the oppressed poor = the humiliated). John P. Dickson and Brian S. Rosner have argued that, while some kinds of humility are certainly evident, humility as *social* humility—the lowering of oneself before a lesser or equal—appears positively only in Sir 4:8 ("Humility as a Social Virtue in the Hebrew Bible?" *VT* 54 [2004]: 459–79). On the developments towards humility as a social virtue in Jewish tradition, Guttenberger Ortwein, *Status und Statusverzicht*, again offers a full survey (see the conclusions in this regard on 156–58, 320–22).

as a shocking case of immorality within the congregation—a certain man in a relationship with his stepmother (5:1)—shocking not least because of the failure of the community to sense and to judge the sinner among them (5:2–3, 12–13).

As Alistair May has persuasively and incisively shown, Paul does not deal with this scandal in terms of an immoral *act*, but rather in terms that connect much more with issues of identity, with the offender as an immoral *person*, a πορνός.[35] (Indeed, it is noteworthy, as May observes, that the so-called vice catalogs in 5:10, 5:11, and 6:9–11 list types of sinful people, not actual vices themselves.) His action is such as to (re)define him as a πορνός and not an ἀδελφός (cf. 5:11). "The one who has done this" (5:2) is in the midst of the community when he should be outside, since by definition πόρνοι belong in the world (cf. 5:9–10) and not in the church. Paul's explicit concern, moreover, is not with what we might call "individual ethics," but rather with the effect of such a misplaced person on the identity and purity of the group. Drawing clearly on the language and imagery of the Jewish scriptures,[36] he describes the presence of the offender as "old leaven" that leavens the whole lump (5:6–7), quoting a proverbial saying that he also repeats verbatim in Gal 5:9: "a little leaven leavens the whole lump (of dough)." Leaven—not simply "yeast," despite many modern translations (e.g., NRSV)[37]—comprises a portion of previously made dough that enables the raising effect of yeast to be reproduced through the incorporation of a piece of the old dough into a new batch. At the same time as this was a useful technique it was also risky, since any impurities or pollutants in the leaven would be transferred into the new dough, where they would come to permeate and infect the whole.[38] The Israelites' Feast of Unleavened Bread thus served, at one level, periodically to start afresh and thus avoid the risk of contamination (Exod 12:15–20). This explains why in the NT "leaven is used symbolically to symbolize (*sic*) an evil influence which spreads like an infection."[39] The intimate connection between the festival of the Passover lamb and the period of eating unleavened bread (see Exod 12; cf., e.g., Mark

35. Alistair S. May, *"The Body for the Lord": Sex and Identity in 1 Corinthians 5–7*, JSNTSup 278 (London: T&T Clark International, 2004), 58–80.

36. See esp. Brian S. Rosner, *Paul, Scripture, and Ethics: A Study of 1 Corinthians 5–7*, AGJU 22 (Leiden: Brill, 1994), 61–93.

37. See esp. C. Leslie Mitton, "New Wine in Old Wineskins: IV. Leaven," *ExpTim* 84 (1973): 339–43.

38. Mitton, "Leaven," 339–40.

39. Mitton, "Leaven," 342.

14:1, 12) explains the link Paul draws here, between the imagery of the pure unleavened lump that the community is meant to be, and the sacrifice of Christ as the Passover that marks and enables the beginning of this period of new life and purity (5:7–8). It is the identity and purity of the community with which Paul is fundamentally concerned, and with the offender insofar as he pollutes the whole.[40]

Paul's verdict on the offender is implicit in the imagery with which he describes the person and his effect upon the community. Old leaven, a pollutant in the lump, must be cast away, put outside; πόρνοι belong in the world, not in the church. Thus the offender must go where he belongs, that is, be expelled from the community (5:2, 5, 13; cf. Deut 17:7). What exactly Paul means to imply in condemning the man to be "handed over to Satan for the destruction of the flesh, so that his spirit may be saved on the day of the Lord" (5:5), is obscure and much disputed. Is it effectively, as Käsemann suggested, a death sentence on the offender?[41] Or does it refer only to his "exclusion from the fellowship of the Christian community,"[42] with an expression of hope for his conversion, which would involve a more metaphorical destruction of the flesh?[43] However ominous the pronouncement, it is clearly also imbued with some kind of hope for the man's eventual salvation, even though the necessary precursor to this is a negative judgment.

Running throughout this passage, then, is a strong sense of distinction between church and world: the church is (meant to be) a pure, holy community in the midst of an immoral world. Here again Paul's discourse finds an echo in Hauerwas's call for the church to be different, to be shaped by its own and not the world's story, to stand as "a community of peace and truth in a world of mendacity and fear."

Yet it is also to be noted that this sense of identity-distinction is found in conjunction with an explicit indication that the ethical norm to which Paul appeals is shared in common with the wider society: the reason the man's behavior is so shocking is that it is not tolerated "even among the gentiles"

40. Cf. Dale B. Martin, *The Corinthian Body* (New Haven: Yale University Press, 1995), 168: "Paul's primary concern in this passage is the purity of the church, the body of Christ, and his anxieties center on the man as a potentially [should we not say: actually?] polluting agent within Christ's body, an agent whose presence threatens to pollute the entire body."

41. Ernst Käsemann, *New Testament Questions of Today*, trans. W. J. Montague (London: SCM, 1969), 71.

42. James T. South, "A Critique of the 'Curse/Death' Interpretation of 1 Corinthians 5:1–8," *NTS* 39 (1993): 544.

43. So May, *Body for the Lord*, 76–77.

(5:1).[44] Commentators regularly note that indeed both Jewish and Roman law proscribed a relationship between son and stepmother.[45] Paul's purpose, of course, is not to appeal to shared ethical norms but to sharpen the sense of shame the congregation should feel. Yet at precisely this point—the only place in Paul's letters where an offender's sin is so grave as to require expulsion from the church[46]—Paul is making an ethical judgment that represents a point of moral agreement, shared "common ground," between him and his contemporaries outside the church. Indeed, Paul stresses that he is not calling for separation from the world, correcting a misunderstanding of his previous letter along these lines (1 Cor 5:9–11). Here we see, ironically, the juxtaposition of a sense of distinct identity and shared ethical norms (see further ch. 5).

Nor is this merely an isolated instance where Paul's ethics demonstrate points of contact and commonality with other contemporary ethical traditions. The so-called catalogs of vices and virtues, for example, again used by Paul to depict the distinct character of the Christian community (e.g., 1 Cor 5:10–11; 6:9–10; Gal 5:19–23), reflect both in their form and in their content a shared sense of what is good and bad.[47] In this case the extent of shared common ground is not acknowledged by Paul; historical criticism makes

44. A verb needs to be supplied here: the suggestions include "not found" (NRSV), "unheard of" (Hans Conzelmann, *1 Corinthians: A Commentary on the First Epistle to the Corinthians*, trans. James W. Leitch, Hermeneia [Philadelphia: Fortress, 1975], 94), and "not tolerated" (Anthony C. Thiselton, *The First Epistle to the Corinthians*, NIGTC [Grand Rapids: Eerdmans, 2000], 385). Neither of the first two renderings would reflect the true situation, objectively, since cases of such incest were both known and reported "among the Gentiles" (see, e.g., Martial, *Epigrams* 4.16; further May, *Body for the Lord*, 64–65; Thiselton, *First Epistle*, 385–86), making "tolerated" an attractive suggestion.

45. Cf., e.g., Jean Héring, *The First Epistle of Saint Paul to the Corinthians*, trans. A. W. Heathcote and P. J. Allcock (London: Epworth, 1962), 34, who mentions Lev 18:8 and Gaius, *Institutes* 1.63; Gordon D. Fee, *The First Epistle to the Corinthians*, NICNT (Grand Rapids: Eerdmans 1987), 200–201; James T. South, *Disciplinary Practices in Pauline Texts* (Lewiston, NY: Mellen, 1992), 29–30; Thiselton, *First Epistle*, 385–86, with further primary and secondary sources mentioned there.

46. The identification of the offender of 1 Cor 5 with the one referred to in 2 Cor 2:5–11 and 7:12, occasionally suggested (e.g., Geoffrey W. H. Lampe, "Church Discipline and the Interpretation of the Epistles to the Corinthians," in *Christian History and Interpretation: Studies Presented to John Knox*, ed. William R. Farmer, Charles F. D. Moule, and Richard R. Niebuhr [Cambridge: Cambridge University Press, 1967], 353–54), is unlikely. But there is no indication that the offender in 2 Corinthians was expelled from the church, still less that Paul ordered his expulsion.

47. Hans Dieter Betz, *Galatians*, Hermeneia (Minneapolis: Fortress, 1979), 282.

it evident. But in other places, as in 1 Cor 5, Paul's appeal to Christians to do good, and to do good to all, explicitly indicates that a sense of what is good constitutes common ground (Rom 12:17: προνοούμενοι καλὰ ἐνώπιον πάντων ἀνθρώπων). Indeed, crucial to Paul's argument for the universal condemnation of all humankind (Rom 1:18–3:20)—the necessary precursor to the announcement of good news (Rom 3:21–26)—is the conviction that all people can, and do, recognize what is good, even if they fail to live by its standards (Rom 2:14–15).[48] That this is not merely a negative conclusion is shown by Rom 13:1–7, where Paul strikingly—and in many ways problematically, for us—presumes that the secular authorities rightly recognize good and evil and act as God's servant accordingly, rewarding the one and punishing the other (vv. 3–4).

Thus we may suggest that the rhetoric of distinction can obscure the extent to which ethical norms and values are not so much distinctive as shared with the broader society. More specifically, 1 Cor 5 suggests that the claim to a sense of distinct and positive group identity is, at least in part, *dependent* on shared ethical values, since it essentially takes the form of the claim to moral superiority: "we" are moral, "they" are not—judged on the basis of shared norms, albeit "ours" are more rigorous. But then, such claims in a sense reduce to an "empirical" one—our tradition produces people of greater moral character than yours—that threatens to be falsified when someone like the Corinthian offender appears. Paul's attempt to redeem this claim by redefining the identity of the infamous sinner—he simply isn't really a Christian at all—is, at one and the same time, theoretically impregnable and profoundly unconvincing: the notion that the church is a moral community in an immoral world can always be sustained by (re)defining any sinner as "really" a member of the world and not the church. But then the claim about the character of the church threatens to lose any connection with the realities that might make such a claim convincing.[49]

48. Here and elsewhere (e.g., Rom 1:20; 12:1–2) Paul echoes Stoic language and concepts, also evident in, or filtered via, Hellenistic Judaism, thus giving another example of the way in which he uses the moral language of the surrounding world (cf. James D. G. Dunn, *Romans*, 2 vols., WBC 38A, 38B [Dallas: Word, 1988], 58; Brendan Byrne, *Romans*, SP 6 [Collegeville, MN: Liturgical Press, 1996], 90, 92–93, 363–65). For a comprehensive argument that Paul's thought follows an essentially Stoic model, see Troels Engberg-Pedersen, *Paul and the Stoics* (Edinburgh: T&T Clark, 2000).

49. Hauerwas is perhaps also vulnerable on this point, as, for example, when he makes such "empirical" claims in defense of Christian truth: "For those inclined to so dismiss my argument, I have no decisive response other than to ask if they represent

More constructively, we might suggest that despite the strong sense of distinction between church and world that characterizes Paul's ethics, the extent to which shared ethical norms are both presumed and accepted indicates, at least from a Pauline perspective, that the liberal goal of discerning some kind of "overlapping consensus" is by no means implausible or impossible.[50] In Paul's case, as generally, ethical norms are motivated in tradition-specific ways, but the norms themselves are in many cases more broadly accepted.[51] Furthermore, this example would also suggest the possibility for a sense of distinct identity and a commonly shared sense of what is good and bad to coexist. The former is, of course, a key focus for communitarianism in general and Hauerwas in particular—identity and moral character formed in community by a particular tradition—while the latter is a key liberal and Habermasian concern—how to sustain a common, tradition-transcending moral framework within which distinct identities and traditions may coexist.

practices that can produce a Dorothy Day" (Stanley Hauerwas, *With the Grain of the Universe: The Church's Witness and Natural Theology* [Grand Rapids: Brazos, 2001], 231). And pointing to examples of virtuous communities to show that "what Hauerwas commends can be done, has been done, and does produce people of virtue" (Samuel Wells, *Transforming Fate into Destiny: The Theological Ethics of Stanley Hauerwas* [Carlisle: Paternoster, 1998], 140) invites the kind of counterexample that Duncan Forrester presents, where "Christian" virtues are displayed in a community "far from the orbit of the church," while the church fails to embody such character (Duncan B. Forrester, "The Church and the Concentration Camp: Some Reflections on Moral Community," in *Faithfulness and Fortitude*, ed. Nation and Wells, 206). Hauerwas's acknowledgment that his depiction of the church is an ideal, a "task," not reality ("Where Would I Be," 326), empties the force from the claim that a certain tradition is better *because* it produces people of moral character.

50. By ignoring these aspects of Paul's thought, and the scholarship that highlights them, Harink (*Paul among the Postliberals*) fails to do justice to this point (cf. further Horrell, review of Harink, 666).

51. And sometimes Paul's "Christian" arguments simply presume certain (inherited) ethical convictions. For example, Paul's argument that sexual union with a prostitute (πόρνη) is incompatible with union with Christ (1 Cor 6:12–20), while union with an unbelieving spouse is not—indeed, in the latter case, the non-Christian spouse is brought into the sphere of the holy (1 Cor 7:12–16)—proceeds from the *presumption* that sex with a πόρνη is immoral while sex with a spouse is not. The arguments about union with Christ do not indicate why this should be the case, but build on the basis of this assumption.

Pauline Ethics and Societal Ethics: A Framework for Tolerance and Diversity in Rom 14–15

Romans 14:1–15:13, together with 1 Cor 8:1–11:1, constitute the longest passages of focused ethical argumentation in Paul. The passages are, moreover, related: the Romans text draws on and adapts material from 1 Corinthians. The subject of food provides the topical connection between the two texts, while the main difference is that Rom 14–15 does not deal with idolatry and idol food, the focus of concern in 1 Cor 8–10 (see ch. 6). The issue in Rom 14–15 concerns people who hold different convictions with regard to food and the observance of special days. Those Paul calls the "weak" eat only vegetables and keep certain days as special, while the "strong," among whom Paul counts himself, regard all foods as clean and all days as alike (Rom 14:1–2, 5; 15:1). While the two groups may each have contained both Jews and gentiles, the contrasting positions represent different stances towards the Jewish law, with the "weak" concerned to keep the dietary laws and avoid contamination, and the "strong" regarding all food and drink as clean and acceptable.[52]

Paul makes his own ethical convictions plain: "I know and am persuaded in the Lord Jesus that nothing is unclean in itself" (Rom 14:14); "all things are clean" (14:20). But he does not invest his argumentative energies into demonstrating why these convictions are correct and should therefore determine practice. Instead his energies go into outlining a basis for the tolerance of diversity within a united community.[53] The strong should not despise the weak, nor the weak judge the strong; each should instead welcome and accept the other, thus embodying the welcome already afforded them by God in Christ (14:1–3; 15:7). They belong together as siblings (ἀδελφοί)[54] and as such are called to demonstrate the same kind of costly regard for the other that has been paradigmatically exemplified by Christ (15:1–3). Paul also seeks to legitimate the validity of different patterns of conduct, and does so with a certain kind of ethical relativism: "nothing is unclean in itself, but to the one who reckons it unclean, to that one it is unclean" (14:14). What determines whether an act is legitimate or not is the "faith" (πίστις) of the actor: to act

52. See further John M. G. Barclay, "'Do We Undermine the Law?' A Study of Romans 14:1–15:6," in *Paul and the Mosaic Law*, ed. James D. G. Dunn (Tübingen: Mohr Siebeck, 1996), 287–308.

53. See in more detail, David G. Horrell, "Solidarity and Difference: Pauline Morality in Romans 14–15," *Studies in Christian Ethics* 15.2 (2002): 60–78.

54. This term is emphatically repeated in Rom 14:10–21, as in 1 Cor 8:11–13. See further ch. 4 above.

contrary to one's faith is to sin (14:23). In other words, as with his treatment of "moral consciousness" (συνείδησις) in 1 Cor 8:7–13, Paul argues that the rightness or wrongness of certain acts depends on the disposition of the actor. What is without question morally imperative is the demonstration of Christ-like other-regard; this, we may say, is the metanorm that provides the moral framework within which the toleration of diversity can operate.

At a general level it is clear, once again, that Paul's is an essentially ecclesial form of ethics. His concern is with the community of the church, with the character of relationships among its members, and he grounds his ethical arguments on the particular story from which this community derives its identity: God's welcoming act in Christ, Christ's self-giving death for others, his status as the believer's κύριος, and so on. It is notable, however, that rather than use the resources of this tradition to elucidate a substantive answer to the ethical dilemma at stake, Paul uses them to construct a framework to protect the diversity within the community while simultaneously sustaining its unity. Moreover, in this attempt there is a structural and substantive parallel with the ethics of contemporary liberalism, in which the individual's right to pursue their own (tradition-defined?) vision of the good is protected, and limited, by an "intolerant" framework of metanorms within which a circumscribed "tolerance" can be sustained.

The similarities, as well as some of the problems, can be illustrated by comparing the criticisms brought to bear against both Paul and liberalism. Daniel Boyarin, a Jewish scholar, criticizes Paul's vision of "human Oneness" in Christ, insofar as it relativizes differences of cultural identity and ethical conviction such that they are emptied of their integrity, becoming mere "matters of taste."

> What will appear from the Christian perspective as tolerance, namely Paul's willingness—indeed insistence—that within the Christian community all cultural practice is equally to be tolerated, from the rabbinic Jewish perspective is simply an eradication of the entire value system which insists that our cultural practice is our task and calling in the world and must not be abandoned or reduced to a matter of taste. The call to human Oneness, at the same time that it is a stirring call to equality, constitutes a threat as well to Jewish (or any other) difference.[55]

55. Daniel Boyarin, *A Radical Jew: Paul and the Politics of Identity* (Berkeley: University of California Press, 1994), 32; cf. also Barclay, "Do We Undermine the Law?," 303–8.

For Hauerwas, similarly, liberalism's apparent tolerance and guaranteed "freedom of religion" reduce Christianity to a matter of personal choice, and belief in God to something that fundamentally "does not matter."[56] Just as Boyarin argues that in Paul's thought religious and cultural differences are emptied of their integrity as they are brought within the encompassing (new) unity constituted in Christ, so, according to Hauerwas, the same happens to Christian integrity within the encompassing framework of liberalism: what Paul does to Judaism, liberalism does to Christianity.[57]

The closely parallel critiques illustrate the (in some ways) comparable structure of Pauline and liberal morality. The reasons why this structural similarity exists—aside from the possible *wirkungsgeschichtlichen* connections—may lie in the comparable social achievements that are sought in each case. Paul, like political liberalism, sought to unite diverse religious and social groups within a new form of human solidarity that at the same time transcended these differences. If we repudiate liberalism's attempts in this regard, in defense of Christianity's integrity, we should at least consider how the same arguments support a parallel repudiation of Paul, in defense of Judaism's integrity. More constructively, we might suggest that the ways in which Paul tries to deal with problems of solidarity and difference—sustaining both unity and diversity—could offer fruitful material for the development of a moral framework for contemporary plural societies. This, at least, is one possible mode in which the appropriation of Pauline ethics might proceed, one of a number we shall explore briefly below.

Towards the Appropriation of Pauline Ethics: Three Models

These three sample readings in Paul's ethics already indicate some of the ways in which the Pauline material might generate various perspectives, supporting various models of the church-world relationship. (I reiterate the caveat, however, that while reading Paul may be valuable in fostering our own reflection, this alone can neither resolve nor trump our contemporary debates.)

The first and most obvious model is, unsurprisingly, some form of ecclesial ethics: it is indisputable that Paul's is an ethic concerned primarily

56. Hauerwas, *With the Grain*, 231; Hauerwas, *After Christendom*, 8, etc.

57. Harink, to my mind, unconvincingly dismisses Boyarin's point about Paul here, and fails to see the parallel with Hauerwas's criticism of liberalism (*Paul among the Postliberals*, 91–92, 183–84n45; cf. Horrell, review of Harink, 667–68).

with the formation and development of the ecclesial community, and with individual Christians insofar as they are part of this "body." Moreover, Paul does not appeal, except in passing, to human rationality and reflection as significant means by which ethical norms can be tested (cf. Rom 12:2; 1 Cor 14:29; Gal 6:4; Phil 1:10; 1 Thess 5:21); his ethics, rather, are thoroughly grounded in his theology, his story about the redeeming work of God in Christ, as we saw in the case of Phil 2. While this does imply a strong sense of distinction between church and world, it does not, for Paul, imply a withdrawal from the world (1 Cor 5:10), but rather, to paraphrase Hauerwas, the obligation to be the church in the world.

Even when we read "with the grain" of Paul's discourse and thus affirm an ecclesially focused ethics, however, the study of Pauline ethics may nonetheless raise some suggestive considerations and issues. For example, the extent to which Paul invests his argumentative energies into constructing a framework for the toleration of diversity within the context of communal solidarity might raise important questions about the *priorities* for an ecclesial ethics of a Pauline kind. A second example may be drawn in part from 1 Cor 5: while Paul sees certain forms of practice as key for sustaining distinct Christian identity—primarily the avoidance of sexually immoral (or idolatrous) unions deemed incompatible with union with Christ[58]—his sense of what is ethical and unethical, say in the realm of sexual morality, derives to a considerable extent not from the Christian story as such but rather from his contemporary world. Thus, while an ecclesial ethics will be similarly concerned to foster a sense of distinct Christian identity, it need not reproduce the specific conventions Paul presumes, since these have no specifically Christian character. Indeed, to do so may lead to anachronistic attempts to reproduce ancient morality rather than a specifically Christian one.[59] Conversely, the example

58. In short, I think Paul sees union with Christ as the key marker of distinctive group identity, and thus proscribes especially other "unions" deemed to threaten or destroy this union. In this respect, his treatment of sexual morality in 1 Cor 6:12–20 and of idolatry in 1 Cor 10:14–22 are closely parallel.

59. For a comparable point in the context of a different argument, see Rudolf Bultmann's reasons why the mythology presumed by the NT writers should not and cannot be appropriated by modern Christians: in the first place, such mythology is not specifically Christian but merely ancient; in the second place, such "worldviews" cannot simply be believed or disbelieved at will (Rudolf Bultmann, *New Testament and Mythology and Other Basic Writings*, ed. and trans. Schubert Miles Ogden [London: SCM, 1985], 3). The same applies to ethical assumptions shared by NT and other ancient writers. Such anachronism is often discussed in the context of the homosexuality debate, in considering whether what Paul and other biblical writers had in view was anything like modern homosexuality. But

of Paul's ethics shows that a sense of distinct identity, based on a particular story, does not necessarily correlate with a distinct set of ethical values but may instead presume common standards of good and evil.

This begins to point towards a second model, one concerned not only with ecclesially focused ethics but with the possible contribution of these ethics to the formation of the kind of "moral consensus which alone can sustain a pluralist culture."[60] Such a model might build on the indications Paul gives that his substantive ethical convictions are widely shared, and that what is good and evil can be universally recognized and agreed. Even where Paul most strongly appeals to the notion of the purity of the ecclesial community (1 Cor 5), his appeal also intimates that the standard for ethical judgment is shared by all: in effect, his appeal is for the members of the Christian community to do better than their contemporaries at meeting common ethical standards. On this model, the challenge to Christian ethics (in a very different context) would be to go beyond Paul (and beyond Hauerwas?) in not only strengthening a sense of distinct identity and motivating ethics in specifically "Christian" ways but also in attempting an equally important task: to seek out and make explicit the extent to which the substance of ethical conviction forms (or could form) part of a broader moral consensus.

A third model might take a different approach to the possible contribution of Pauline ethics to contemporary social ethics, following the suggestions of Thomas Ogletree.[61] For Ogletree, Paul's treatment of diversity *within* the Christian communities, not least in Rom 14–15, provides valuable material for "the imaginative development of social thought in a modern

---

it is less often noted that this chronological and cultural divide equally affects subjects like marriage, where it is too easily presumed that Paul is addressing the same "ethical issue" as we do. Not only are the cultural presumptions vastly different (cf. further L. William Countryman, *Dirt, Greed, and Sex: Sexual Ethics in the New Testament and Their Implications for Today* [Philadelphia: Fortress, 1988]; Dale B. Martin, "Paul without Passion: On Paul's Rejection of Desire in Sex and Marriage," in *Constructing Early Christian Families*, ed. Halvor Moxnes [London: Routledge, 1997], 201–15), but even simple facts like the average age of marriage make straightforward comparison invalid. Girls in the Roman Empire often married at around twelve years of age, while husbands were generally somewhat older. For similar cautions about attempts to reproduce early Christian ethics, see Wayne A. Meeks, *The Origins of Christian Morality: The First Two Centuries* (New Haven: Yale University Press, 1993), 215–18.

60. David A. S. Fergusson, *Community, Liberalism and Christian Ethics* (Cambridge: Cambridge University Press, 1998), 75.

61. Thomas W. Ogletree, *The Use of the Bible in Christian Ethics* (Minneapolis: Fortress, 1983).

context of cultural pluralism."[62] A "Christian social ethic" can best be developed, according to Ogletree, not on the basis of the limited comments Paul and other NT authors make about wider societal institutions, but by taking Paul's ecclesial ethic as a model for an ethic for society—an approach that evidently presumes something like the "political theology" rather than the "theological politics" model. In effect, the distinctive identities of church and world are here blurred, and a Christian contribution to social ethics treats the (contemporary) world as analogous to the (early) church.[63]

On this model, the ways in which Paul deals with diversity in the early Christian assemblies might be suggestive for ways of dealing with diversity in contemporary societies, and so on. Paul's attempts to articulate an ethic in which diverse ways of life, dictated by a person's "faith," or "conscience," are respected within a framework of communal solidarity could provide generative material for our reflections on similar challenges. To some extent this is obviously to accept the liberal agenda, though the Pauline material would also suggest a certain kind of "communitarianization of liberalism":[64] rather than the focus on rational argumentation that Habermas's discourse ethics promotes, an approach that learned from Paul would presumably be one in which some kind of shared story, enacted in ritual, was an essential basis for a societal ethic. This might perhaps imply something like the project Nigel Biggar refers to as "recovering liberalism's lost theological horizon and rescuing it in non-secularist form."[65] More radically still, it might suggest some kind of post-Christian project in which the resources of the Pauline (and more broadly, Christian) tradition made a contribution to the formation of stories with which *human* solidarity, and difference, might be sustained.

However, while Paul was convinced of the need to read, reinterpret, and spiritualize his Jewish tradition in order for it to form the basis for a community in which Jews and gentiles took their place "without distinction" (cf. Rom 3:22; 10:12; 1 Cor 7:19; Gal 5:6; 6:15), he would no doubt have recoiled from the notion that his newly articulated Christian tradition might itself be subjected to a similar relativizing and reinterpretive exercise.[66] Contempo-

62. Ogletree, *Use of the Bible*, 158.

63. Cf. Ogletree, *Use of the Bible*, 192: "a Christian social ethic must proceed not on the basis of explicit New Testament commentary on economic and political institutions, but by analogy to developments within the early Christian communities themselves."

64. Cf. Bell, *Communitarianism*, 8.

65. Nigel Biggar, "Is Stanley Hauerwas Sectarian?," in *Faithfulness and Fortitude*, ed. Nation and Wells, 160.

66. Though there are, perhaps, hints that Paul could imagine the position of Christ

rary Christians too would no doubt find objectionable such a relativization of the truth of their particular story; though if this is so, they should perhaps be wary of celebrating the social achievement that Pauline Christianity represents, which called for precisely such a relativization of cultural and religious identity on the part of Jews.[67]

Conclusion

There are, then, a variety of ways in which a contemporary appropriation of Paul's ethics might fruitfully proceed, ways which imply quite different understandings of the possible relationships between church and world. Each model, however, brings problems as well as possibilities. With an ecclesial model, there is the question of how to avoid the negative stereotyping of all who are "outside"[68]—children of darkness, doomed for wrath and destruc-

---

being one day transcended by the all-supremacy of God (1 Cor 15:24–28). Cf. also Rom 10:17–11:36, where Paul conspicuously presents his view of God's mysterious plan to save all Israel as well as the full number of the gentiles without explicit reference to Christ.

67. Cf., e.g., the comments of James Dunn ("Paul: Apostate or Apostle of Israel?," *ZNW* 89 [1998]: 256–71): "Paul saw his own apostolic work not as a disowning of his heritage, but precisely as its fulfillment" (258); "Paul's criticism of Judaism was . . . a criticism of the xenophobic strand of Judaism, to which Paul himself had previously belonged. . . . Paul was in effect converting from a closed Judaism to an open Judaism" (261). And this involved rejecting the importance of the "trappings [*sic*] of Jewish identity"—circumcision and food laws especially—in favor of an "essence" of Jewishness "determined from within" (James D. G. Dunn, "Who Did Paul Think He Was? A Study of Jewish-Christian Identity," *NTS* 45 [1999]: 192). These positive comments confirm exactly the achievement that is for Boyarin a focus for criticism.

68. Again, this is at least a danger with what Fergusson refers to as Hauerwas's "over-concentration on the distinctiveness of the church" (David A. S. Fergusson, "Another Way of Reading Stanley Hauerwas?" *SJT* 50 [1997]: 244; cf. Fergusson, *Community*, 67). Fergusson elsewhere comments on Hauerwas's tendency "to depict secular arguments in the worst possible light. While not only unfair on much that is sane and decent outwith the church, this characterisation of an alternative position renders allies as foes and hinders the process of making common cause" (*Community,* 73). One example: Hauerwas does "not know why people who are not Christians have children," and sees no reason to investigate (Stanley Hauerwas, *A Community of Character: Toward a Constructive Christian Social Ethic* [Notre Dame: University of Notre Dame Press, 1981], 210–11); but he is able to assert that "from the world's perspective the birth of a child represents but another drain on our material and psychological resources" (228). Cf. also the critique of Hauerwas by Stout, *Democracy*, 140–61, where, inter alia, he sharply criticizes Hauerwas for his frequent offenses "against the vocation of charitable interpretation" (157).

tion (cf. 1 Thess 5:5, 9; 1 Cor 1:18, etc.)—while the model that looks to preserve a sense of distinct identity while building a broader moral consensus might be suspected, in that very move, of allowing the story of liberalism to become implicitly determinative.[69] The relativization of Christianity's integrity that might thereby be implied is more explicitly apparent in the third model, wherein the resources of the Christian tradition are used in the development of new forms of societal ethics—a radical idea that might well be felt to raise more problems than it could ever solve. So, while reading Paul in the context of our contemporary debates can be suggestive and fruitful, using Paul's texts "to think with" does not by any means suffice for the task of thinking about adequate models for Christian ethics, but only marks the beginning of that work.

69. I am grateful to Geoff Thompson for helping me to see another possible model, not mentioned above, which avoids this latter move, namely one in which the Christian story about the church and the world is construed such that the church is given a clear responsibility to attend to the truth (moral, theological, etc.) evident and revealed *extra muros ecclesiae*. This model, which Thompson develops through his work on Barth's "secular parables," may provide a fruitful route for Christian theologians to avoid both Hauerwas's ecclesiocentric polemic against "the world" and the ceding of priority to liberalism's secular story that my second model above may imply (see Geoff Thompson, "'As Open to the World As Any Theologian Could Be'? Karl Barth's Account of Extra-Ecclesial Truth and Its Value to Christianity's Encounter with Other Religious Traditions" [PhD diss., University of Cambridge, 1995]).

Chapter 9

A New Perspective on Paul?

Rereading Paul in a Time of Ecological Crisis

> Each successive epoch of theology found its own thoughts in Jesus; that was, indeed, the only way in which it could make him live.
>
> ALBERT SCHWEITZER, *The Quest of the Historical Jesus*

> Whenever he [the real Paul] is rediscovered—which happens almost exclusively in times of crisis—there issues from him explosive power.
>
> ERNST KÄSEMANN, "Paul and Early Catholicism"

Introduction: The "New Perspective on Paul" and Its Social Context

In confronting new problems we turn to the classic texts of our tradition, and for the tradition of Western thought, and not only within the church, Paul's letters are among those classic texts. They have been read and reread, inspiring and provoking other great thinkers to articulate new thoughts. This applies not only to the well-known giants of the history of Christian theology—Augustine, Luther, Wesley, Barth, to name but a few—but also to philosophers as diverse as Martin Heidegger and Alain Badiou. Even when expositors of Paul's thought have sought to be rigorously historical, aiming only to exegete Paul on his own terms, it is not hard to see how the context and agenda of the interpreter shapes the construction of Paul that is produced. Albert Schweitzer's comment about Jesus rings true for Paul too: each generation makes, and needs to make, its own portraits of Paul.[1]

1. It should be noted, though, that Schweitzer is critical of the way in which such theological influences shaped portraits of Jesus, hence his own rigorously historical "quest"

The emergence of the so-called new perspective on Paul may serve as an illustration. The label was coined by one of its most prominent representatives, James Dunn, in his 1982 Manson Memorial Lecture.[2] But, as Dunn makes clear, the main impetus for the new interpretation of Paul came from E. P. Sanders's book, *Paul and Palestinian Judaism*, published in 1977, and particularly from the revised view of first-century Judaism—the "*new perspective on Second Temple Judaism*," as Dunn calls it[3]—that Sanders presented. Sanders mounted a massive critique of what he saw as the Christian caricature of Judaism—as a religion of legalistic works-righteousness—that dominated the so-called Lutheran interpretation of Paul. On this view, Judaism was supposedly characterized by a misguided conviction that obedience to the law was the means by which to earn salvation, a convenient foil to Paul's gospel, understood as a message of justification for the guilty sinner, offered freely by God's grace, and appropriated by faith alone. In the wake of Sanders's study, this "Lutheran" reading of Paul, with its contrast between Judaism's supposed system of justification by works and Paul's message of justification by faith, has been widely denounced as a clear example where Paul was read, indeed misread, through the spectacles of a later age. As Dunn puts it:

> it is deceptively easy to read Paul in the light of Luther's agonized search for relief from a troubled conscience. Since Paul's teaching on justification by faith seems to speak so directly to Luther's subjective wrestlings, it was a natural corollary to see Paul's opponents in terms of the unreformed Catholicism which opposed Luther, with first-century Judaism read through the "grid" of the early sixteenth-century Catholic system of merit. To a remarkable and indeed alarming de-

(Albert Schweitzer, *The Quest of the Historical Jesus*, ed. John Bowden, 1st complete ed. [London: SCM, 2000], 6). Since the time when Schweitzer was writing we have come to be much more suspicious of any claim to present an objective historical account of Jesus (or Paul, or any historical figure), since it is now widely acknowledged that any historical portrait is inevitably shaped by the context, commitments, and presuppositions of the interpreter. Moreover, these influences, while they call for critical appraisal, generate fruitful and relevant engagements in ever-changing contexts and so are not to be regretted.

2. James D. G. Dunn, "The New Perspective on Paul," *BJRL* 65 (1983): 95–122, reprinted in James D. G. Dunn, *Jesus, Paul and the Law* (London: SPCK, 1990), 183–206; and James D. G. Dunn, *The New Perspective on Paul: Collected Essays*, WUNT 185 (Tübingen: Mohr Siebeck, 2005), 89–110; cited below from the 1990 reprint.

3. Dunn, *New Perspective*, 5 (italics original).

> gree, throughout this century the standard depiction of the Judaism which Paul rejected has been the reflex of Lutheran hermeneutic.[4]

E. P. Sanders makes a similar point:

> Luther, plagued by guilt, read Paul's passages on "righteousness by faith" as meaning that God reckoned a Christian to be righteous even though he or she was a sinner. . . . Luther sought and found relief from guilt. But Luther's problems were not Paul's, and we misunderstand him if we see him through Luther's eyes.[5]

Luther's concerns to find a merciful God in the context of late-medieval Catholic monasticism are thus seen, rightly or wrongly, to have driven his interpretation of Paul, and to have established a tradition of interpretation that not only skewed the reading of Paul's texts but also offered a degree of ideological underpinning for the anti-Judaism that reached its zenith in the Holocaust.

Indeed, despite the extent to which Sanders presents his study of Paul as an historical one, one that eschews any explicit interest in the contemporary theological agenda, the new perspective on Paul is, to a significant degree, the product of a post-Holocaust era, one in which Christian interpreters have rightly been pushed to reexamine the consequences, intended and unintended, of their readings of Paul and their assumptions about the Judaism contemporary with him.[6] After all, Jewish interpreters of Paul had made similar points to Sanders well before him; now, in a changed and differently sensitized social context, the time was ripe (indeed, well overdue) for Christian scholars to undertake a reassessment.[7] And even with his rig-

4. Dunn, *Jesus, Paul and the Law*, 185.

5. E. P. Sanders, *Paul* (Oxford: Oxford University Press, 1991), 49.

6. Cf. also the comments of Francis Watson, *Paul, Judaism and the Gentiles: Beyond the New Perspective*, rev. and exp. ed. (Grand Rapids: Eerdmans, 2007), 2: "After Auschwitz, new language and new conceptualities would have to be found. True to the traditions of their discipline, New Testament scholars looked to history and to historically informed exegesis to undermine the old paradigm and to establish a new one in its place. E. P. Sanders's two remarkable books achieved just that." For reflections on "the social and ideological milieu of the new perspective," see also John M. G. Barclay, "'Neither Jew Nor Greek': Multiculturalism and the New Perspective on Paul," in *Ethnicity and the Bible*, ed. Mark G. Brett (Leiden: Brill, 1996), 203–6.

7. See, e.g., Sanders's discussion of the work of George Foot Moore and others (E. P. Sanders, *Paul and Palestinian Judaism: A Comparison of Patterns of Religion* [London:

orously historical interests, Sanders's depiction of Judaism remains, for all its intended sympathy and refusal of any implicit Christian superiority, one cast in strongly Protestant terms, as Philip Alexander among others has pointed out.[8] In a highly revealing phrase, for example, Sanders declares that "the Judaism of before 70 kept grace and works in the right perspective,"[9] where "right," of course, must imply something like "the way it is in Protestantism," with grace given clear priority, and works seen as the appropriate response to the saving initiative of God. In a rare moment of faith-related candor near the close of his equally influential *Jesus and Judaism*, Sanders indicates his debt to a liberal, "social gospel" Protestantism[10]—thus revealing that his own attempts to create a sympathetic depiction of Judaism at the time of Christian origins are driven not solely by a concern for historical accuracy (though they are certainly that) but also by the moral convictions of an ecumenical post-Holocaust era. When proponents of the new perspective contrast Luther's "anachronistic" reading of Paul with their own more accurate historical interpretation, they accuse Luther of seeing Paul through sixteenth-century

SCM, 1977], 33–36). For a detailed review of Jewish engagement with Paul, see Daniel R. Langton, "Modern Jewish Identity and the Apostle Paul: Pauline Studies as an Intra-Jewish Ideological Battleground," *JSNT* 28 (2005): 217–58; and Daniel R. Langton, "The Myth of the 'Traditional View of Paul' and the Role of the Apostle in Modern Jewish-Christian Polemics," *JSNT* 28 (2005): 69–104.

8. In a review of Sanders's *Jesus and Judaism,* Alexander writes: "His [Sanders's] answer to the charge of 'legalism' seems, in effect, to be that Rabbinic Judaism, despite appearances, is really a religion of 'grace.' But does this not involve a tacit acceptance of a major element in his opponents' position—the assumption that 'grace' is superior to 'law'? The correct response to the charge must surely be: And what is wrong with 'legalism,' once we have got rid of abusive language about 'hypocrisy' and 'mere externalism'? It is neither religiously nor philosophically self-evident that a 'legalistic' view of the world is inferior to one based on 'grace.' If we fail to take a firm stand on this point we run the risk of seriously misdescribing Pharisaic and Rabbinic Judaism, and of trying to make it over into a pale reflection of Protestant Christianity" (Philip S. Alexander, review of E. P. Sanders, *Jesus and Judaism*, *JJS* 37 [1986]: 105). A similar point is made much more sharply by Jacob Neusner ("Mr Sanders' Pharisees and Mine: A Response to E. P. Sanders, *Jewish Law from Jesus to the Mishnah*," *SJT* 44 [1991]: 92–95), who criticizes Sanders's "Protestant theological apologetic for a Judaism in the liberal Protestant model" (92). These authors are cited by Barry Matlock, in a probing section on "a certain covert Protestantism" in the new perspective on Paul (R. Barry Matlock, "Almost Cultural Studies? Reflections on the 'New Perspective' on Paul," in *Biblical Studies/Cultural Studies: The Third Sheffield Colloquium*, ed. J. Cheryl Exum and Stephen D. Moore, JSOTSup 266; Gender, Culture, Theology 7 [Sheffield: Sheffield Academic Press, 1998], 444–47).

9. Sanders, *Paul and Palestinian Judaism*, 427.

10. E. P. Sanders, *Jesus and Judaism* (London: SCM, 1985), 334.

spectacles while sometimes failing to acknowledge the extent to which their own vision is shaped by twentieth- and twenty-first-century ones. Dunn, for example, claims that "Sanders has given us an unrivalled opportunity to look at Paul afresh, to shift our perspective back from the sixteenth century to the first century, to do what all true exegetes want to do—that is, to see Paul properly within his own context, to hear Paul in terms of his own time, to let Paul be himself."[11]

But if the "new perspective" on Paul is the product not only of historical study but also of a post-Holocaust context, with its ethical concerns and priorities, what further new perspectives on Paul might still newer issues of concern begin to generate? As pressing priorities emerge, and determine the central questions for our own time and place, so new issues and concerns arise for biblical exegetes: whether acknowledged or not, the contemporary context shapes the agenda of historical study, and not only, though especially, for biblical scholars who seek to connect their work with ongoing theological and ethical discussion.[12]

Pauline Studies and the Contemporary Context of Ecological Crisis

Among the many contemporary issues worthy of our concern, the environment has in the last few years come to the top of the list. While a "green" lobby has voiced concerns about the environment for some decades, it is only relatively recently that these have come to the center of political and ethical debate, primarily, of course, because of the now well-established scientific consensus about the reality and wide-ranging impacts of anthropogenic global warming and the urgent need to take decisive action on a global scale if the worst predictions are not to become reality. This is all reason enough to ask how Paul's letters, and other biblical texts, might resource a Christian response to our contemporary ecological crisis. But there are

11. Dunn, *Jesus, Paul and the Law*, 186. For a similar kind of comment, see N. T. Wright, *What Saint Paul Really Said* (Grand Rapids: Eerdmans, 1997), 23; though note elsewhere Wright's reflections on the ways in which all Pauline scholarship is the product, to a degree, of its social context (N. T. Wright, *Paul: Fresh Perspectives* [London: SPCK, 2005], 15–18).

12. The general point is well made by Walther Bindemann: "sachbezogene Theologie ist—selbst dort, wo sie mit dem Attribut 'historisch' versehen wird, das Abstand von der Gegenwart suggeriert—ein Seismograph für kulturelle und gesellschaftliche Vorgänge" (Walther Bindemann, *Die Hoffnung der Schöpfung: Römer 8,18–27 und die Frage einer Theologie der Befreiung von Mensch und Natur* [Neukirchen-Vluyn: Neukirchener Verlag, 1983], 9).

more specific reasons too. In 1967 the medieval historian Lynn White Jr. published a provocative article that has remained the most cited contribution to the ecotheological debate.[13] White argued that the Western Christian worldview, informed by the biblical creation stories, had established a dualism between humanity and nature, and encouraged the idea that nature was there to be exploited for human benefit. Christianity had thus provided the ideological foundations for the active conquest of nature in the modern technological project and as such, White claimed, bore "a huge burden of guilt" for our contemporary "ecologic crisis."[14]

Just as White raised serious questions about the impact of the biblical view of humanity's status in creation—made in the image of God and given dominion over the earth (Gen 1:26–28)—so questions have also been raised about the impact of biblical eschatology. In certain forms of fundamentalism and evangelicalism at least, it seems that Christian hope is construed in terms of an imminent return of Jesus, other-worldly salvation for the elect, and fiery destruction for the earth; attempts to preserve the earth are thus futile and contrary to God's purposes.[15] More generally, one may suspect that much traditional Christian eschatology has led believers to think in terms of individual spiritual salvation, and an end to the "old" material creation, in ways that run counter to the central concerns of environmental sustainability. There are good reasons, then, to address the topic of the environment in biblical studies, not only because of its urgent contemporary relevance, but also because of the suspicions that the biblical tradition may be partly culpable in generating the attitudes that have led to our crisis in the first place.

It is worth returning briefly here to White, and noting his insistence that a rejection of religion is not the solution: "What people do about their ecology depends on what they think about themselves in relation to things around them. Human ecology is deeply conditioned by beliefs about our nature and destiny—that is, by religion. . . . More science and more technology

13. Lynn White Jr., "The Historical Roots of Our Ecologic Crisis," *Science* 155 (1967): 1203–7.

14. White, "Ecologic Crisis," 1206.

15. For a nuanced discussion of these eschatological scenarios, their implications for attitudes towards the environment, and the recent "greening" of American fundamentalism, see Harry O. Maier, "Green Millennialism: American Evangelicals, Environmentalism, and the Book of Revelation," in *Ecological Hermeneutics: Biblical, Historical, and Theological Perspectives*, ed. David G. Horrell, Cherryl Hunt, Christopher Southgate, and Francesca Stavrakopoulou (London: T&T Clark, 2010), 246–65.

are not going to get us out of the present ecologic crisis until we find a new religion, or rethink our old one."[16]

The point is worth stressing, not least in the current context of competition for strictly limited research funding, that while scientific and technological responses to our environmental challenges are absolutely crucial, they are not by any means the whole story, nor alone the source of our salvation. It is equally crucial to analyze critically the ideological foundations of our cultural assumptions about the human relationship to the rest of the natural world and to consider constructively how our religious and moral traditions might be reconfigured in light of the challenges that now face us. White's answer was to propose Francis of Assisi as a "patron saint for ecologists."[17] My particular concern is to consider to what extent Paul of Tarsus might also have something to contribute to an ecological reconfiguration of Christian theology. Might Ernst Käsemann's claim that, in times of crisis, Paul is a source of "explosive power" ring true now?[18]

It is perhaps surprising that questions about the environment—or, put in more theological terms, about the status and future of the nonhuman creation—have scarcely yet registered on the agenda of contemporary Pauline scholarship. There are a few exceptions, though these are mostly found in publications whose primary focus is the subject of the environment, rather than in what we might call the mainstream of Pauline studies.[19] So, while

16. White, "Ecologic Crisis," 1205 and 1206.

17. White, "Ecologic Crisis," 1207.

18. The opening quotation using this phrase is found in Ernst Käsemann, "Paul and Early Catholicism," in *New Testament Questions of Today*, trans. W. J. Montague (London: SCM, 1969), 249. It comes in the context of an essay that is polemically critical of what Käsemann sees as the domestication of Paul in the developments towards "early Catholicism" evident in the deutero-Pauline letters.

19. Broadly speaking, there are two main approaches in biblical studies engaging the ecological agenda. The first, often though not always from an evangelical perspective, seeks to show how the Bible can be used to support the environmental agenda (e.g., R. J. [Sam] Berry, ed., *The Care of Creation: Focusing Concern and Action* [Leicester: InterVarsity Press, 2000]; Sam Berry et al., *A Christian Approach to the Environment* [Gloucester: John Ray Initiative, 2005]; Wesley Granberg-Michaelson, ed., *Tending the Garden* [Grand Rapids: Eerdmans, 1987]). The second is the more critical approach, focused around ecojustice principles and a hermeneutic of suspicion as well as retrieval, developed by the Earth Bible team. See Norman C. Habel, ed., *Readings from the Perspective of Earth*, Earth Bible 1 (Sheffield: Sheffield Academic Press, 2000); Norman C. Habel and Shirley Wurst, eds., *The Earth Story in Genesis*, Earth Bible 2 (Sheffield: Sheffield Academic Press, 2000); Norman C. Habel and Shirley Wurst, eds., *The Earth Story in Wisdom Traditions*, Earth Bible 3 (Sheffield: Sheffield Academic Press, 2001); Norman C. Habel, ed., *The Earth Story in the Psalms and*

Pauline studies has been explicitly and energetically engaged with post-Holocaust issues concerning Jewish-Christian relations, and with post-1960s issues about gender, sexuality, and the relative status of women and men, it has, to date, failed to register the environment as a significant issue for discussion.

A few selected examples from recent scholarship may serve to illustrate this lack of engagement. The examples are not simply chosen at random, but rather in order to demonstrate that even in those works where one might *most* expect to find some engagement with environmental issues this lack is evident.[20]

I begin with two more general works, focused on issues in NT ethics. Richard Hays's *Moral Vision of the New Testament* is rightly regarded as the most significant of recent studies of NT ethics, significant not least because of Hays's extensive discussion of hermeneutics and his attempts to apply the NT's teaching to a range of contemporary issues, from abortion and homosexuality to anti-Judaism, violence, and war.[21] While Hays's list of issues is of course consciously selective, the environment is absent, and the focus on issues in the areas of sexual ethics and violence mostly reflects a

---

the Prophets, Earth Bible 4 (Sheffield: Sheffield Academic Press, 2001); Norman C. Habel and Vicky Balabanski, eds., *The Earth Story in the New Testament,* Earth Bible 5 (London: Sheffield Academic Press, 2002); Norman C. Habel and Peter Trudinger, eds., *Exploring Ecological Hermeneutics,* SymS 46 (Atlanta: Society of Biblical Literature, 2008). The Exeter project has sought to develop an approach, put baldly, that fits somewhere between these two, and that includes a substantial attempt to read Paul from an ecological perspective; see David G. Horrell, Cherryl Hunt, and Christopher Southgate, "Appeals to the Bible in Ecotheology and Environmental Ethics: A Typology of Hermeneutical Stances," *Studies in Christian Ethics* 21 (2008): 219–38; David G. Horrell, "The Ecological Challenge to Biblical Studies," *Theology* 112 (2009): 163–71; David G. Horrell, Cherryl Hunt, and Christopher Southgate, *Greening Paul: Rereading the Apostle in an Age of Ecological Crisis* (Waco, TX: Baylor University Press, 2010). See further ch. 10 below. Among the notable exceptions in Pauline studies are Robert Jewett, "The Corruption and Redemption of Creation: Reading Rom 8:18–23 within the Imperial Context," in *Paul and the Roman Imperial Order*, ed. Richard A. Horsley (Harrisburg: Trinity Press International, 2004), 25–46; and Robert Jewett, *Romans*, Hermeneia (Minneapolis: Fortress, 2007), 508–20.

20. I should perhaps also include my earlier study of Paul's ethics in this category (David G. Horrell, *Solidarity and Difference: A Contemporary Reading of Paul's Ethics* [London: T&T Clark, 2005]): the focus there is on the political and social dimensions of Pauline ethics, in dialogue with the contemporary liberal-communitarian debate and the work of Stanley Hauerwas and Jürgen Habermas in particular.

21. Richard B. Hays, *The Moral Vision of the New Testament* (San Francisco: HarperCollins; Edinburgh: T&T Clark, 1996).

well-established agenda. Hays develops three “focal images” with which to formulate his NT ethics: community, cross, and new creation, images that, Richard Burridge has rightly suggested, derive primarily from Paul.[22] One question we might well ask is how these Pauline images might inform an ethical response to issues concerning the environment.

More recently, Willard Swartley has published a major work arguing that peace and peacemaking stand at the heart of the NT’s teaching and should be central to Christian ethics too. Paul is seen as a particularly strong exemplar. As Swartley puts it: “Paul, more than any other writer in the NT canon, makes peace, peacemaking, and peace-building central to his theological reflection and moral admonition.”[23] Engaging with Ralph Martin’s earlier work arguing for reconciliation as the heart of Pauline theology,[24] Swartley insists that peace and peacemaking should instead be the key terms.[25] Nonviolence and peacemaking are seen as the central moral virtues to be embodied in the church. Yet it is striking, in a work published as recently as 2006, that the relevance of these themes to environmental issues, or to relationships between God, humanity, and the nonhuman creation, is never entertained. Swartley simply reiterates the long-entrenched anthropocentrism of the tradition of Pauline interpretation, focusing only on relationships among humans, and between humans and God: “The notion of making peace *between humans and God and between formerly alienated humans* is so central to the core of Pauline doctrinal and ethical thought that it is impossible to develop a faithful construal of Pauline thought without peacemaking and/or reconciliation at the core.”[26]

As Brendan Byrne has noted, “The issue of justification by faith has dominated the interpretation of Paul in the Western theological tradition. This ensured that interpreters of Paul were engaged in a virtually exclusive preoccupation with relations between human beings and God. What Paul

22. Richard A. Burridge, review of *The Moral Vision of the New Testament: A Contemporary Introduction to New Testament Ethics* by Richard Hays, *JTSA* 102 (1998): 71–73. Hence Burridge’s own recent study of NT ethics places the historical Jesus at the center: see Richard A. Burridge, *Imitating Jesus: An Inclusive Approach to New Testament Ethics* (Grand Rapids: Eerdmans, 2007).

23. Willard M. Swartley, *Covenant of Peace: The Missing Peace in New Testament Theology and Ethics* (Grand Rapids: Eerdmans, 2006), 190.

24. Ralph P. Martin, *Reconciliation: A Study of Paul’s Theology* (Atlanta: John Knox, 1981).

25. Swartley, *Covenant of Peace*, 190–91.

26. Swartley, *Covenant of Peace*, 192, my emphasis.

thought or wrote about human relationship to the non-human created world scarcely entered the picture."[27] But what this comment also implies is that it is among those, like Swartley, who have stressed something *other* than "justification by faith" that we might expect to find some engagement with the wider concerns Byrne highlights. Indeed, I shall go on to argue that an approach to Paul focused on themes of participation and reconciliation rather than justification and acquittal offers fruitful resources for ecotheological reflection. Yet even among those who have most recently championed this particular side in a long-running debate about the center of Paul's theology—is it justification by faith or participation in Christ?—there has been no indication of the relevance of these themes to reflection on ecotheological and ecoethical concerns.

For example, in a brief but important work published in 2009, Michael Gorman offers a way beyond the justification versus participation impasse, arguing essentially for a participatory understanding of justification: justification by faith is "understood as co-crucifixion and participation in Christ."[28] Gorman sees at the heart of Paul's theology a "master story," best encapsulated in Phil 2:5–11.[29] This story of Christ, in which believers participate, leads from *kenosis* to *theosis*, that is, from self-emptying and self-giving to a form of divinization, becoming one with Christ and one with God.[30] Yet, despite what seems to me its rich ecotheological potential, there is no hint that this new construal of the heart of Paul's theology might have any relevance for our thinking about the place of the nonhuman world in the story of God's saving purposes.

While Gorman offers a participatory perspective that incorporates, rather than rejects, the theme of justification, Douglas Campbell launches an uncompromising and massive attack on the justification by faith tradition.[31] For Campbell, this tradition, with its contractual construal of the

27. Brendan Byrne, "Creation Groaning: An Earth Bible Reading of Romans 8:18–22," in *Readings from the Perspective of Earth*, ed. Norman C. Habel, Earth Bible 1 (Sheffield: Sheffield Academic Press, 2000), 194.

28. Michael J. Gorman, *Inhabiting the Cruciform God: Kenosis, Justification, and Theosis in Paul's Narrative Soteriology* (Grand Rapids: Eerdmans, 2009), 73.

29. Gorman, *Inhabiting the Cruciform God*; and Michael, J. Gorman, *Cruciformity: Paul's Narrative Spirituality of the Cross* (Grand Rapids: Eerdmans, 2001).

30. Gorman, *Inhabiting the Cruciform God*, 4. Gorman's definition of theosis is as follows: "Theosis is transformative participation in the kenotic, cruciform character of God through Spirit-enabled conformity to the incarnate, crucified, and resurrected/glorified Christ" (*Inhabiting the Cruciform God*, 7).

31. Douglas A. Campbell, *The Deliverance of God: An Apocalyptic Rereading of Justifica-*

process of human salvation, is disastrously flawed theologically and needs to be exegetically outmaneuvered. In its place, Campbell proposes what he terms a pneumatologically participatory martyrological eschatology as the most adequate framing of the heart of Paul's theology.[32] Yet despite the enormous detail in which this proposal is now worked out, and despite the potential in the participatory model, there is, as far as I can see, no indication that this might have relevance to questions about humanity's relationship to the nonhuman creation, or about the place of nonhuman as well as human creatures in the eschatological and soteriological story Paul tells.

Towards an Ecological Reading of Paul

Exploring why there is this lack of interest in the relevance of Paul's theology to thinking about the environment is not my purpose here—though I suspect that it is at least partly due to the simple fact that no one has yet squarely placed it onto the agenda of Pauline studies, and, like most academic disciplines, this area of biblical studies mostly proceeds through discussion and debate on issues already part of the established discourse. More relevant is to ask whether there is much real potential for what we may call an ecological reading of Paul. Can this be done with historical and exegetical seriousness, or will it be merely a faddish interest, driven solely by some new and trendy concern? Part of the point of the opening section of the essay was to show that, even where scholars eschew any direct connection with contemporary issues, these issues—however "faddish" in the eyes of some—do shape the questions exegetes ask and the implicit convictions that shape their answers.

Yet there is a more serious set of objections, namely that Paul shows very little direct interest in the subject of the nonhuman creation, and knows nothing of modern ecological awareness. These are serious points that should instill a certain caution. If an ecological reading of Paul is to get far, it must move beyond the one or two favorite texts, but must do so in ways that are exegetically cogent. It must also do so in ways that remain conscious of the risks of anachronism and clear about the extent to which theological

tion in Paul (Grand Rapids: Eerdmans, 2009); and Douglas A. Campbell, *The Quest for Paul's Gospel: A Suggested Strategy*, JSNTSup 274 (London: T&T Clark, 2005).

32. Campbell, *Paul's Gospel*, 29–55.

interpretation is a necessarily constructive and creative exercise, one that entails, echoing words of Francis Watson, using the texts "to think with."[33]

There is one Pauline text that stands out very clearly, and for good reason, as a favorite text for those seeking biblical support for environmental concern: Rom 8:19–23.[34] Not only does this text seem to capture something of the mood of environmental crisis—all creation groaning—but it also presents a vision of hope that the whole creation will one day share in the glorious liberation that is already but not yet the experience of the children of God.[35] The text may not straightforwardly support the contemporary envi-

33. Francis Watson, *Agape, Eros, Gender: Towards a Pauline Sexual Ethic* (Cambridge: Cambridge University Press, 2000), viii. It is worth noting, though, that a certain lack of directly relevant material need not be too much of a hindrance: by comparison, in the undisputed letters, aside from mentions of named women, Paul offers *substantive* discussion of topics related to the equality or inequality of women and men only in three texts in 1 Corinthians (7:1–40; 11:2–16; 14:34–35), aside from the much-quoted five-word catchphrase in Gal 3:28. But that has not stopped the contemporary interest in such matters driving the production of any number of books and articles on the subject of Paul and women. And the risk of anachronism is relevant, mutatis mutandis, to all other topics in NT ethics too, even those (such as marriage and divorce) where there appears more continuity between the issues addressed then and now.

34. For detailed discussion of ecological engagement with Rom 8, see Cherryl Hunt, David G. Horrell, and Christopher Southgate, "An Environmental Mantra? Ecological Interest in Romans 8:19–23 and a Modest Proposal for Its Narrative Interpretation," *JTS* 59 (2008): 546–79. There are good reasons to take κτίσις here to refer to the whole (nonhuman) creation, whatever precisely is intended to fall within its scope. The use of κτίσις in v. 39 is somewhat different: not πᾶσα ἡ κτίσις but τις κτίσις ἑτέρα. Paul's point here seems to be that no creature/created thing can stand in the way of God's love and saving purposes.

35. Aside from readings of this crucial passage written in the context of ecotheological publications (e.g., Byrne, "Creation Groaning"), most historical-critical studies, including the most recent, make little or no reference to any ecological relevance in this text. See, e.g., Horst R. Balz, *Heilsvertrauen und Welterfahrung: Strukturen der paulinischen Eschatologie nach Römer 8, 18–39*, BEvT 59 (Munich: Kaiser, 1971); Olle Christoffersson, *The Earnest Expectation of the Creature: The Flood-Tradition as Matrix of Romans 8:18–27* (Stockholm: Almqvist & Wiksell, 1990); Harry Alan Hahne, *The Corruption and Redemption of Creation: Nature in Romans 8:19–22 and Jewish Apocalyptic Literature*, LNTS 336 (London: T&T Clark, 2006). Christoffersson's conclusions are revealing in this respect: Paul's purpose in this text is to present "an eschatological outlook which opens up an universal [*sic*] perspective of [*sic*] this new righteousness. As sin is universal, so is salvation in Christ. . . . Rom 8:18–27 thus plays an important part in the section of the letter which serves as the fundation [*sic*] of Paul's argument in favour of *the unity of mankind* in chapters 9–11" (144, my emphasis). He comments in a note that "Paul is not even speaking of solidarity between man and Creation as part of an ecological or political debate. It may be legitimate to use the text in discussion of such questions [though this is the only reference to such questions in

ronmental agenda, certainly not as easily as the frequent and passing appeals to it assume. For example, it is God who has subjected creation to bondage, and it is unclear whether ethical action on the part of the children of God is envisaged as playing any part in creation's coming to freedom. Moreover, it is clear that Paul's priorities and concerns are not focused on the need to help creation towards its eschatological hope; he is focused on encouraging the hard-pressed Christians at Rome, and uniting them in a common bond. Nonetheless, Paul does here present a vision of salvation in which the whole creation, πᾶσα ἡ κτίσις, is intimately bound up, groaning *with* humanity and the Spirit and sharing a common hope; creation is not merely the stage on which the drama of human redemption takes place. As such, this text makes an important contribution to an ecological theology.

The other favorite eco-text in the Pauline epistles is Col 1:15–20, a Christ-hymn that stresses the all-encompassing scope of Christ's work in both creation and reconciliation. The text may not be authentically Paul's, but this makes little difference to its status in one of the Pauline letters canonized as scripture. As long ago as 1961, in an address to the World Council of Churches, Joseph Sittler noted the gravity of the threat to nature, and saw in the cosmic Christology of Col 1 a doctrinal basis with which to draw all of creation into the orbit of God's redemption.[36] More recently, some commentators and many ecotheologians have agreed with Sittler in finding ecological relevance in this text.[37] Once again, the move from ancient

---

the book], but it is important to make clear that they lie far beyond Paul's horizon" (145n18). Notable exceptions are Bindemann, *Hoffnung der Schöpfung*, and the broader studies of John G. Gibbs (*Creation and Redemption: A Study in Pauline Theology*, NovTSup 26 [Leiden: Brill, 1971]; and "Pauline Cosmic Christology and Ecological Crisis," *JBL* 90 [1971]: 466–79); both authors connect their studies explicitly with contemporary ecological issues.

36. Joseph Sittler, "Called to Unity," in *Evocations of Grace: The Writings of Joseph Sittler on Ecology, Theology and Ethics*, ed. Steven Bouma-Prediger and Peter Bakken (Grand Rapids: Eerdmans, 2000), 38–50.

37. See, e.g., Dunn's comments on 1:15–20 (James D. G. Dunn, *The Epistles to the Colossians and to Philemon*, NIGTC [Grand Rapids: Eerdmans, 1996], 104), quoted in the context of ecotheological reflection by Steven Bouma-Prediger, *For the Beauty of the Earth: A Christian Vision for Creation Care* (Grand Rapids: Baker Academic, 2001), 108. Again, the early studies of Gibbs are important (see n. 35, above). Nonetheless, as with Rom 8, most exegetical studies of this text make little if any reference to its potential ecological relevance (cf., e.g., Christian Stettler, *Der Kolosserhymnus: Untersuchungen zu Form, traditionsgeschichtlichem Hintergrund und Aussage von Kol 1, 15–20*, WUNT 2/131 [Tübingen: Mohr Siebeck, 2000]; Michael Dübbers, *Christologie und Existenz im Kolosserbrief: Exegetische und semantische Untersuchungen zur Intention des Kolosserbriefes*, WUNT 2/191 [Tübingen: Mohr Siebeck, 2005]; Ian K. Smith, *Heavenly Perspective: A Study of the Apostle Paul's Re-*

hymn to modern ecology is by no means straightforward. For example, the author's focus is on principalities and powers (1:16; 2:15) and reflects an ancient cosmology not straightforwardly identifiable with modern ecological awareness. The language and imagery are also different from those of Rom 8. But there does seem considerable ecotheological significance in the author's insistence that all things, τὰ πάντα, were created in Christ and for Christ, that all things exist in him, and that all things are reconciled in him.[38] From its beginnings to its goal or telos, creation's story is (literally) incorporated into Christ—in him, through him, and for him (ἐν αὐτῷ, δι' αὐτοῦ, εἰς αὐτόν; v. 16)—whose all-encompassing story becomes the story of everything.

These two favorite texts, then, do offer significant resources to an ecological theology: they insist, in their different ways, that the whole creation is, or "all things" are, bound up in the story of salvation and included in the reconciliation God has wrought in Christ. But can they be any more than outlying prooftexts, remote from the more central theological concerns of the Pauline corpus? I suggest that they can, and that they offer a starting point for a rereading of Pauline theology in which the status and fate of the whole creation is given a central place.

Colossians 1 is important in stressing the role of Christ in creation, a move found also in other NT traditions (John 1:1–3; Heb 1:2): all things were made in him, ἐν αὐτῷ.[39] But this conviction is found elsewhere in Paul too, albeit in more theocentric formulations, notably in 1 Cor 8:6, a credal declaration in which God the Father is named as the origin of all things (ἐξ

---

sponse to a Jewish Mystical Movement at Colossae, LNTS 326 [London: T&T Clark, 2006]; Matthew E. Gordley, *The Colossian Hymn in Context: An Exegesis in Light of Jewish and Greco-Roman Hymnic and Epistolary Conventions*, WUNT 2/228 [Tübingen: Mohr Siebeck, 2007]).

38. For developed ecotheological reflections on this text, see Vicky Balabanski, "Hellenistic Cosmology and the Letter to the Colossians: Towards an Ecological Hermeneutic," in *Ecological Hermeneutics*, ed. Horrell, Hunt, Southgate, and Stavrakopoulou, 94–107; and Vicky Balabanski, "Critiquing Anthropocentric Cosmology: Retrieving a Stoic 'Permeation Cosmology' in Colossians 1:15–20," in *Exploring Ecological Hermeneutics*, ed. Habel and Trudinger, 151–59.

39. It is open to discussion how the ἐν should be taken here, whether as locative or instrumental. Douglas J. Moo (*The Letters to the Colossians and to Philemon*, PNTC [Grand Rapids: Eerdmans, 2008], 120–21) argues for the former, while Dübbers (*Christologie und Existenz*, 97–98) argues for the latter. A locative sense seems likely if the notion of the universe as Christ's body underlies the hymn, as the uses of ἐν in vv. 17–19 (and in 3:11) would suggest.

οὗ), Christ as the one through whom (δι' οὗ) all things came to be. A similar, albeit still more theocentric formulation is found in Rom 11:36: "for from him and through him and to him are all things" (ὅτι ἐξ αὐτοῦ καὶ δι' αὐτοῦ καὶ εἰς αὐτὸν τὰ πάντα). As in Colossians, though here in theocentric terms, both the origins (ἐξ) and the telos (εἰς) of all things are located in God. These are strikingly universal declarations, in which all things are brought within the scope of God's creating and redeeming purposes—this is emphatically not the story of the salvation of a few elect human beings, however much that contrasting motif may also be found in Paul.[40]

Paul's conviction about the origins of creation in God, through Christ, seems, for Paul, to imply the essential goodness of creation, in contrast to any view of the material world as intrinsically evil or corrupting. The credal confession of 1 Cor 8:6 stands at the beginning of a long and complex argument about food offered to idols, in which Paul's practical advice to "eat everything sold in the marketplace" (10:25) is based on the conviction that "the earth is the Lord's" (10:26, citing Ps 24:1); the earth's gifts, therefore, are not to be rejected, but received "with thanksgiving." A similar position, with a more explicit declaration of the goodness of all created things, is found in the Pastoral Epistles, where the author opposes any ascetic rejection of foods and sexual relations (1 Tim 4:4).[41]

Much of the focus of Pauline studies, at least insofar as they attempt to identify and describe the central motifs of Pauline soteriology, concerns the question as to how Paul understands the means by which human beings, enslaved as they are under the power of sin, living "in Adam" in the old evil age, come to be rescued from this parlous state and to live new lives in Christ. That formulation implies, of course, that the focus of discussion is on human beings, as indeed it is for Paul, whose overriding concern is to preach the gospel to gentiles, and to unite both Jews and gentiles in the church. The traditional alternatives, put rather baldly, are either to emphasize the function of Christ's death as an atoning sacrifice of some kind, which leads to the acquittal of the guilty sinner, or to understand Christ's death as something in which the believer participates, such that they die *with* Christ and, in him,

40. On these two contrasting strands in Paul, see Sven Hillert, *Limited and Universal Salvation: A Text-Oriented and Hermeneutical Study of Two Perspectives in Paul,* ConBNT 31 (Stockholm: Almqvist & Wiksell, 1999), who labels them the universal and limited views of salvation.

41. See Paul Trebilco, "The Goodness and Holiness of the Earth and the Whole Creation (I Timothy 4:1–5)," in *Readings from the Perspective of Earth,* ed. Norman C. Habel, Earth Bible 1 (Sheffield: Sheffield Academic Press, 2000), 204–20.

begin a new life in the power of the Spirit. I have already noted that the former view, characterizing Paul's theology in terms of forensic justification, seems to hold out little prospect of any ecological (re)interpretation, focused as it is on guilty humans and their fate before the righteous judge. Might the participatory view offer more promising potential? On this view, the means by which sinful humans are saved is through their incorporation into Christ, an identification with him that baptism enacts.[42] But the Pauline vision of this incorporation goes beyond the salvation of human beings.

Colossians 1 is once again important for its insistence that it is all things, not just humans, and not just a few elect humans, that are reconciled "in Christ." If *all things* hold together in him, and are reconciled in him, then that implies that the extent of the community of those incorporated into Christ is boundless, or, as the conclusion of the baptismal tradition in 3:11 puts it, τὰ πάντα καὶ ἐν πᾶσιν Χριστός, "Christ is all things and in all things." The author's focus in using this panenchristic vision is on overcoming the divisions among the human community, just as it is in the earlier occurrences of a similar baptismal formula in Gal 3:28 and 1 Cor 12:13. But the use of τὰ πάντα, as in the hymn itself, implies, and certainly allows, a cosmic all-encompassing reference, and this would seem to be how the author of Ephesians understands the telos of God's saving plan, "as a plan for the fullness of time, to gather up all things in Christ [ἀνακεφαλαιώσασθαι τὰ πάντα ἐν τῷ Χριστῷ], things in heaven and things on earth" (Eph 1:10).

This vision of the incorporation of all things into Christ is also found, though in a theocentric rather than christocentric form, in the undisputed Pauline letters, in 1 Cor 15. Here, in a lengthy attempt to show how the resurrection of Christ is fundamental to Christian hope, Paul sets out an order of events leading up to "the End" (τὸ τέλος). Notable here is one of his more universal and participatory statements: "As in Adam all die, so in Christ shall all be made alive" (v. 22; cf. Rom 5:12–21). While humans are clearly the focus of Paul's attention here, we should not simply assume that the nonhuman creation is excluded from his vision of hope. Indeed, Paul's depiction of the End is one in which "all things" (τὰ πάντα)—except God—are subjected (by God) to Christ (cf. Phil 3:21), after which Christ will be subjected to God, "so that God may be all in all" (πάντα ἐν πᾶσιν; v. 28).[43] The same conviction,

42. Important arguments for a participatory understanding of Paul's theology, specifically as a form of "interchange," are presented in a series of essays by Morna Hooker, one of which was also delivered as a Manson Memorial Lecture. See Morna D. Hooker, *From Adam to Christ: Essays on Paul* (Cambridge: Cambridge University Press, 1990), 13–69.

43. Cf. Sanders, *Paul and Palestinian Judaism*, 474: "1 Cor 15:27f. seems to support the

as we have already seen, is more briefly encapsulated in the doxological exclamation of Rom 11:36. Paul's view of the telos of all things, then, and not just human beings, is apparently panentheistic, a vision of their ultimate incorporation into God, who becomes and fills everything; this is the goal towards which all things are directed.[44]

But what of the means by which this incorporation happens? For the author of Colossians, as we have seen, the key is reconciliation. To be sure, this terminology does not occur in the Pauline corpus as frequently as the language of justification (or being made righteous). But both sets of terminology are concentrated in particular texts,[45] and there is a case to be made, following Ralph Martin, that reconciliation can be placed at the heart of Pauline theology, though not to the exclusion of other themes and motifs.[46] There are two reconciliation texts in the undisputed letters: Rom 5:10–11 and 2 Cor 5:18–20. In both texts it is difficult to deny that Paul's primary focus is on what Reimund Bieringer calls *die Menschenwelt*, the world of human beings,[47] and in Rom 5:9–10 justification/righteousness terminology is clearly placed in close parallel with the language of reconciliation. In 2 Cor 5:19 an anthropological focus is implicit in the awkward grammar: God's reconciliation of the κόσμος to himself is glossed as "not reckoning *to them*

---

view of the ultimate redemption of the creation, and there are no statements to the contrary. Once Colossians is excluded from consideration, the cosmos is seen to play a smaller role in Paul's thought than it appears to in the descriptions of scholars who take Colossians to be authentic, but one must allow that here Colossians is building on a genuine Pauline view: the cosmos will be redeemed. Paul's general focus, however, is on the world of men [*sic*]." On the extent to which a cosmic perspective is profoundly woven into Pauline theology, including its earliest layers, see esp. Gibbs, "Pauline Cosmic Christology." Gibbs's article opens with the claim: "Cosmic christology, far from being a late addendum, belongs to the core of the Pauline concept of the Lord, no less than does theology of the cross" (466).

44. There is here a significant parallel with the way in which Aquinas conceives the telos of all things, which also suggests ecotheological potential in Aquinas's theology. See Dominic Coad, "Creation's Praise of God: A Proposal for a Theology of the Non-Human Creation," *Theology* 112 (2009): 181–89; Mark Wynn, "Thomas Aquinas: Reading the Idea of Dominion in the Light of the Doctrine of Creation," in *Ecological Hermeneutics*, ed. Horrell, Hunt, Southgate, and Stavrakopoulou, 154–65.

45. Uses of δικαιόω are concentrated in Rom 2–8 (esp. Rom 3:21–28) and Gal 2–3, especially in the declaration encapsulated in Gal 2:16 (cf. Rom 3:28).

46. Martin, *Reconciliation*.

47. Reimund Bieringer, "2 Kor 5,19a und die Versöhnung der Welt," *ETL* 63 (1987): 318. More generally, on the different nuances that adhere to Paul's multivalent uses of κόσμος, see Edward Adams, *Constructing the World: A Study in Paul's Cosmological Language* (Edinburgh: T&T Clark, 2000).

[αὐτοῖς] their trespasses."[48] Yet without denying that this is Paul's focus, it goes with the grain of the text (and the wider context of Pauline theology) to take the divine act of reconciliation to have a wider compass.[49] Colossians remains, however, the key text where an emphatically cosmic and universal dimension is given to the reconciliation God has wrought in Christ.[50]

Second Corinthians 5 also contains one of the only two references in the Bible to the phrase "new creation," the other also found in Paul, in Gal 6:15—both occurrences being elliptical and terse. There are two key questions for our purposes: one is whether the phrase has a cosmic or only an anthropological reference; the second is whether the hope for a new creation implies that the present creation is devalued as merely a temporary and soon-to-pass sphere of existence, the preservation of which thus makes little theological sense (see further ch. 10, pp. 218–21, below).

Contemporary scholarship has given contrasting answers to the first question, with some, notably Moyer Hubbard,[51] arguing that Paul's focus is on the Spirit-wrought transformation of the individual convert. Others, like Ulrich Mell and most recently Ryan Jackson, have argued, more convincingly in my view, that "new creation" signals an all-encompassing "eschatologically infused soteriology"—involving "the individual, the community and the cosmos . . . inaugurated in the death and resurrection of Christ."[52] As Mell rightly notes, the "from now on" (ἀπὸ τοῦ νῦν) of 2 Cor 5:16 is not conversion terminology but eschatological terminology; a new world has been brought into existence in Christ.[53] In this new world, as Rom 8 also makes

48. The antecedent to αὐτοῖς can only be κόσμος; note too the parallel phrase in 5:18, where God reconciles *us* (ἡμᾶς) to himself.

49. For a more detailed treatment of this text in relation to an ecological reading of Paul, see ch. 10 below.

50. Perhaps, then, from an ecological perspective, some of the most theologically significant texts may come from the disputed Paulines, reversing the usual tendency in scholarship to see the authentic letters as the source of innovative theology and the deutero-Pauline and Pastoral letters as indicative of a more conservative and conformist stance. As the preceding sections have shown, however, the cosmic Christology of Colossians and Ephesians develops a cosmic theme found already in the undisputed letters, albeit in more theocentric forms. See esp. Gibbs, "Pauline Cosmic Christology."

51. Moyer V. Hubbard, *New Creation in Paul's Letters and Thought*, SNTSMS 119 (Cambridge: Cambridge University Press, 2002).

52. T. Ryan Jackson, *New Creation in Paul's Letters: A Study of the Historical and Social Setting of a Pauline Concept*, WUNT 2/272 (Tübingen: Mohr Siebeck, 2010; repr. Eugene, OR: Wipf and Stock, 2016), 6.

53. Ulrich Mell, *Neue Schöpfung: Eine traditionsgeschichtliche und exegetische Studie zu einem soteriologischen Grundsatz paulinischer Theologie*, BZNW 56 (Berlin: de Gruyter,

clear, human and nonhuman are together bound up; the whole creation is included in this thoroughly cosmic transformation.

Implicit in Paul's declaration that already, in Christ, there is new creation is an answer to the second question. If the new creation is, in a sense, already here, if only in some partly visible and not yet fulfilled way, if it is already transforming the lives of those who join the assemblies of those who are in Christ, then there cannot be a sharp discontinuity or abrupt disjunction between "old" and "new" creation; it must instead be a matter of transformation. Radical transformation to be sure, such that it can be envisaged as a process of dying and rising to new life. But once again, if this dying with Christ and walking in newness of life is, as Paul clearly sees it to be, a matter of the *present* experience of believers, then it is clearly a transformation *of* the here and now, not something that lies (only) beyond. In other words, the shape of the hoped-for future is visible and enacted in the here and now, and implies a responsibility to act in ways congruent with that future, with participation in God's new creation. That responsibility, it should be stressed, follows even if the ultimate future is conceived as something beyond the realm of present experience, and beyond what human action could possibly secure.[54]

Outlines of a Pauline Ecotheology and Ethics

To what extent, then, do these ideas provide the outlines of an ecological Pauline theology, and what, if any, would be their ethical implications? Without in any way denying that Paul's focus is firmly on human beings, and specifically on the small Christian communities to which he writes, we may nonetheless propose that Paul's theology may be seen to center around God's redemption of the whole cosmos in Christ. Despite the anthropological concerns that dominate, Paul's soteriological vision is literally all-encompassing, whether this is put in the theocentric terms of Rom 11 and 1 Cor 15 or the more christological terms of Col 1. Just as God, through Christ, is creator

---

1989), 366. Cf. 324: "Nicht der Mensch heißt 'neue Schöpfung,' sondern, im soteriologischen Verfassungsdanken, die Welt!"

54. To be sure, this only partly answers the difficult questions about the extent to which an eschatological vision of a world that is clearly utterly different from the world of our experience can function positively in an ecological ethics. For somewhat more extended reflections, see David G. Horrell, *The Bible and the Environment: Towards a Critical Ecological Biblical Theology* (London: Routledge, 2014), 138–40.

of all things, so God, in Christ, is the redeemer of all things. All things are bound up in the process by which God is bringing about the liberation of the whole creation, a process that in the present still involves suffering and pain, but yet is filled with hope. Such a cosmic vision suggests that the anthropological focus of much of the Christian tradition, and of much Pauline scholarship, should be radically recast. The center of Paul's theology is God's transformation of the world in Christ.[55]

Yet what role is there, if any, for human beings in this divinely wrought transformation? This is a crucial question, since if there is no corresponding human responsibility, then even this more cosmic Pauline vision cannot generate any sense of environmental-ethical imperative. Romans 8 once again provides an interesting place to start: here it is the revelation of the children of God that creation strains to see, their freedom and glory that it longs to share. While the emphasis is on the eschatological future that God will bring about, there are ethical dimensions to the freedom that already defines the character of Christian life, and one may suggest that the assemblies of Christian believers, as they live out their new life in Christ and fulfill the responsibilities that that implies, play some part in the story of creation's liberation.[56]

Perhaps a still stronger ecoethical mandate can be derived from Col 1. Here the reconciliation that God has achieved in Christ encompasses all things, and all things are incorporated in Christ. While the hymn itself de-

55. Cf. J. Christiaan Beker, *Paul the Apostle: The Triumph of God in Life and Thought* (Edinburgh: T&T Clark, 1980), who argues for a theocentric focus on the eschatological triumph of God as at the heart of Pauline theology. However, Beker, it should be noted, is concerned to assert this theocentrism against the more realized christocentrism of the later letters, regretting "the transformation of theology into Christology." Quoting Col 1:19 (and noting Eph 1:10 also) he writes: "When futurist, cosmic eschatology is minimized or neutralized, the final triumph of God at the end of history becomes so identified with the triumph of God in the Christ-event that the theocentric apocalyptic focus of Paul is absorbed into the Christocentric triumph of Christ. . . . Whenever the final victory of the reign of God becomes secondary to the present reign of Christ, the result is an ecclesiology that is no longer geared to the cosmic future triumph of God over his creation" (356). But despite the more realized and christocentric outlook of Colossians and Ephesians, especially of the Colossian hymn, there is still a future eschatology in these letters (see, e.g., Todd D. Still, "Eschatology in Colossians: How Realized Is It?" *NTS* 50 [2004]: 125–38). And for our purposes here, the more important contrast is between anthropocentrism on the one hand, and theocentrism or Christocentrism on the other.

56. Cf. Jewett, "Corruption and Redemption," 35–46; and Jewett, *Romans*, 515. For developed ecoethical reflections in terms of what it might mean for humans to live out their "freedom in Christ," see Christopher Southgate, *The Groaning of Creation: God, Evolution, and the Problem of Evil* (Louisville: Westminster John Knox, 2008), 92–133.

picts this reconciliation as already accomplished in Christ, the rest of the letter makes clear that this is also an ethical imperative, incumbent on those who are in Christ. To be sure, the author's focus is firmly on interhuman and interecclesial relationships—he does not, of course, share our sense of a need to address a wider set of relationships—but it goes with the grain of the text (and of 2 Cor 5:18–20) to extend its vision of what reconciliation might entail.

Another basis for ecoethical implications might be found in the indications that Christ literally incorporates everything. That implies, as George van Kooten has suggested, that Colossians reflects some notion of the cosmos as Christ's body.[57] If that is so, at least as some kind of telos to the story of redemption, then it encourages a move to broaden the community of others to whom moral regard is owed. The community of those who are "in Christ," and for whom Christ died, is boundless: *all things* exist and are reconciled in him. Paul's depiction of relations among the various parts of the body in 1 Cor 12 is striking, particularly in its insistence that God has given greater honor to the less honorable parts, reversing the usual hierarchies of status, and in its call for solidarity among all the members in sharing one another's joys and sufferings.[58] Once again, it is beyond dispute that Paul's primary focus here is on the church, and particularly on the fractious community at Corinth; but if the body of Christ is, ultimately, a much wider, indeed boundless entity, then such solidarity and generous regard are not merely a pattern for interhuman relationships. In *Solidarity and Difference* I argued that corporate solidarity and other-regard are the central metanorms in Pauline ethics, derived from the notions of incorporation into Christ and Christ's paradigmatic self-giving and self-lowering on the cross.[59] One key move in generating a Pauline ecological ethic may be precisely to extend these notions to apply to human relationships with all creatures, animate and inanimate, and not just other people.[60] This may initially sound like a move well beyond anything in the Pauline letters, and is certainly a move beyond Paul's explicit and conscious concerns—after all, he infamously sug-

57. George H. van Kooten, *Cosmic Christology in Paul and the Pauline School: Colossians and Ephesians in the Context of Graeco-Roman Cosmology with a New Synopsis of the Greek Texts*, WUNT 2/171 (Tübingen: Mohr Siebeck, 2003).

58. See Dale B. Martin, *The Corinthian Body* (New Haven: Yale University Press, 1995), 94–96; Horrell, *Solidarity and Difference*, 121–24.

59. Horrell, *Solidarity and Difference*. See n. 20 above.

60. Cf. Cherryl Hunt, "Beyond Anthropocentrism: Towards a Re-reading of Pauline Ethics," *Theology* 112 (2009): 190–98.

gests that God cares little for oxen (1 Cor 9:9)![61] Yet the cosmic dimensions of Pauline theology—and specifically the indications that Christ's self-giving death was an act done to bring about the reconciliation of all things, not just people, and that all things, not just people, find their purpose and goal in their incorporation into Christ, or ultimately into God—make this move one that is actually well-grounded in Paul's theology.[62] Once we broaden the community of others to whom costly regard is owed, we may also find fresh nuances in Paul's exhortations: Paul calls for self-giving particularly on the part of the strong and powerful, and that is, of course, precisely the position of humans vis-à-vis other species and life-forms.

We might here recall the three focal images with which Richard Hays frames his NT ethics: community, cross, and new creation. Hays describes these images, particularly "community" and "new creation," in strikingly ecclesiocentric terms. The focal image of community is introduced as follows: "*The church is a countercultural community of discipleship, and this community is the primary addressee of God's imperatives.*"[63] New creation is outlined in the following words: "*The church embodies the power of the resurrection in the midst of a not-yet-redeemed world.*"[64] Our ecologically oriented engagement with Paul would suggest that these images retain their value, but need to be reconfigured from a more cosmic perspective if they are to have purchase in the area of environmental ethics. Put differently, what is required in the context of the ecological crisis is an ecclesiology that is not so much about the countercultural distinction between church and world,[65] but more about the ways the church is called to embody and enact the transformation of the cosmos in which everything is already caught up and towards which all things are oriented. The community that is in Christ, as we have seen, is,

61. Unlike Philo, who, discussing the same scriptural text (Deut 25:4), sees this command, like others, as reflecting a humane concern for animals (*On the Virtues* 145–46). I am grateful to Roger Tomes for pressing the relevance of this contrast, which certainly shows that Paul is no self-conscious animal theologian. But Paul's comment here, I think, does not so much reflect a negative stance towards animals as a positive concern to apply this text to humans (δι' ἡμᾶς πάντως λέγει, v. 10). In any case, *we* can perceive ecological dimensions to the wider themes of Pauline theology whether or not Paul was conscious of those dimensions and whether or not he would have agreed with them.

62. Cf. Gibbs, *Pauline Cosmic Christology*.

63. Hays, *Moral Vision*, 196 (italics original).

64. Hays, *Moral Vision*, 198 (italics original).

65. Cf. Horrell, *Solidarity and Difference*, e.g., 268–72, on the ways in which Hays's (and Hauerwas's) ecclesiology overstresses the distinction between church and world and thus neglects points of common ground and shared moral values. See also ch. 8 above.

in the eschatological vision, no less than τὰ πάντα, "all things," even if the church is the community in which this vision is recognized and anticipated in action. The cross is a paradigm of self-giving for others, but the community of others to whom such regard is owed needs to be broadened not only beyond the church, but beyond the human community too. And finally, new creation is not only something glimpsed and enjoyed in the life of the church, but a hope and a mandate for the transformation of all creation.

What all of this might mean in concrete ethical terms is much less easy to discern. In all areas of contemporary ethics, but particularly in an area so recent and so dependent on scientific insight as environmental ethics, there is no straightforward move from biblical exegesis to contemporary application—despite the claims in some quarters that lining up the relevant biblical verses is more or less all that is needed.[66] For example, it is by no means obvious what reconciliation might mean in the realm of environmental ethics. It cannot mean expecting lions to nourish themselves on straw, or teaching wolves to refrain from harming lambs, though it might mean that humans choose to end, or at least drastically to reduce, their killing of animals for food, as a sign of commitment to the peaceable kingdom (and of commitment to reducing global warming).[67] It might perhaps mean working

66. See, e.g., Wayne Grudem's description of the tasks of systematic theology and Christian ethics: "systematic theology involves collecting and understanding all the relevant passages in the Bible on various topics and then summarising their teachings clearly so that we know what to believe" (Wayne Grudem, *Systematic Theology: An Introduction to Biblical Doctrine* [Leicester: InterVarsity Press, 1994], 21; cf. 26 for similar comments on Christian ethics). This kind of conviction is also embodied in the recently published *Green Bible* (New York: HarperOne, 2008), an edition of the NRSV in which texts relevant to caring for the earth are highlighted in green. For a critical review, see David G. Horrell, "*The Green Bible*: A Timely Idea Deeply Flawed," *ExpTim* 121 (2010): 180–86.

67. To the various good reasons to reduce (especially red-) meat consumption—animal ethics, human health, social justice—the contribution to global warming of methane-producing ruminants is now added. See the concise comments of Southgate, *Groaning of Creation,* 122–23; also John M. G. Barclay, "Food, Christian Identity and Global Warming: A Pauline Call for a Christian Food Taboo," *ExpTim* 121 (2010): 585–93. In one sense, the point made above runs counter to the anti-ascetic theme we noted earlier, in the context of Pauline affirmations of the goodness of creation. But this is not an ascetic avoidance of things deemed to be polluting but rather a kind of ascetic self-giving, what Southgate calls an "ethical kenosis" (see n. 69, below), for the sake of the other. Paul insists that food in itself does not pollute (Rom 14:14, 20), but nonetheless states his willingness never to eat it again if it is the cause of a sister or brother's stumbling (Rom 14:15; cf. 1 Cor 8:9–13). For further discussion of the issue of Christian vegetarianism, see David G. Horrell, "Biblical Vegetarianism? A Critical and Constructive Assessment," in *Eating*

to sustain (and, a fortiori, not to destroy) ecosystems in which there is room for all the diversity of creatures, such that none suffers a level of competition that drives it to extinction.[68]

Other-regard is equally challenging to relate to the concrete circumstances of real life, not least because it raises the sharp and contentious question about the relative value of human and nonhuman life. It need not be taken to mean, I would suggest, that human lives should be regarded as of less value than those of other animals, such that humans might effectively be sacrificed in the cause of another species' welfare. But it might well mean that humans would limit, and even sacrificially curtail, the indulgence of their own acquisitive desires out of a concern not only for social justice, crucial though that is, but also for ecological justice, a level of self-giving intended to enable the flourishing of others, nonhuman as well as human.[69] Having for too long regarded "nature" as a bounty of good gifts, given for human benefit, we might thus be challenged to emphasize equally our obligation of gift-giving to all other things, on whose sustaining provision we so demonstrably depend.[70]

---

and Believing: Interdisciplinary Perspectives on Vegetarianism and Theology, ed. Rachel Muers and David Grumett (London: T&T Clark, 2008), 44–59; Christopher Southgate, "Protological and Eschatological Vegetarianism," in *Eating and Believing*, ed. Muers and Grumett, 247–65.

68. There is, of course, a distinction to be drawn between "natural" extinctions and anthropogenic extinctions, the latter of which are most clearly to be avoided from an environmental-ethical perspective. However, Southgate argues, on the basis of Rom 8 and his sense of what the "freedom of the children of God" means at this point in the eschatological story, that both forms of extinction should, as far as possible, be brought to an end. See Southgate, *Groaning of Creation*, 124–32.

69. Cf. Southgate, *Groaning of Creation*, 101–3, on an ecological ethical kenosis as entailing kenosis of appetite, aspiration, and acquisitiveness on the part of humans.

70. This sentence is an inadequate attempt to gesture towards a theme that John Barclay has rightly suggested to me might be both important and fruitful in this area, namely that of mutual gift-giving. This very Pauline theme of self-giving for others (expanded to include the whole creation) is a crucial element missing in a theology such as the evangelical response to environmentalism offered by E. Calvin Beisner (*Where Garden Meets Wilderness: Evangelical Entry into the Environmental Debate* [Grand Rapids: Eerdmans, 1997]), which stresses the ways in which creation—freed from the curse and transformed into a fruitful garden—allows human expansion and flourishing and meets human needs and aspirations.

Conclusion

The practical difficulties and challenging questions we rapidly encounter in any such attempts to begin to move towards ethical application clearly suggest that, to turn Lynn White's comment on its head, while inventing a new religion, or rethinking our old one, may well be crucial in confronting our "ecologic crisis," we shall certainly need more science and more technology too, as well as more hardheaded economics, ethics, and politics. And yet, to turn White's comment back upright once again, reconfiguring our religious and cultural traditions in light of the new challenges that face us is a crucial task, too. Paul may not perhaps offer "explosive power" when it comes to our response to the contemporary environmental crisis, but I do think that he offers important resources for an ecological theology and ethics. Given Paul's canonical importance and profound influence on the shape of Christian theology, it is crucial for any ecological reconfiguration of the Christian tradition to show how Pauline theology can inform and support that move. I propose that at the heart of Pauline theology, reread in the light of our ecological concerns, stands *the vision of God's incorporative transformation of the whole creation in Christ and the associated imperative to embody that transformation in human action shaped by the paradigm of Christ's self-giving for others.* These Pauline resources, creatively and constructively developed, offer the potential to reshape the Christian imagination, to reconfigure a sense of the value of the cosmos in whose ecosystems we are inextricably embedded, and to generate new ethical priorities. To date, however, readings of Paul have been largely shaped by anthropocentric concerns and priorities, whether those emerge from the crises of the sixteenth century or those of the twentieth. The challenge of our twenty-first-century crisis, one whose consequences we have only begun to experience, surely demands a(nother) new perspective on Paul.

Chapter 10

Ecojustice in the Bible?

Pauline Contributions to an Ecological Theology

Introduction

The question about whether, and in what way, the Bible supports the eco-justice agenda has been provoked both by the general rise in awareness of the extent of the environmental challenges facing us and by the specific criticism of the Christian tradition articulated by Lynn White Jr. and others. In broad terms, as with other ethical issues that stimulate investigations of the biblical material—issues concerning poverty, war, sex, and so on—it is the contemporary context that puts environmental questions onto the agenda of biblical studies. In recent years, environmental issues have moved from the fringes of political and ethical debate to the very center, rapidly and widely becoming acknowledged as among the most crucial and pressing issues faced by the whole global community at the beginning of the third millennium. More specifically, Christian theologians and biblical scholars have been forced to consider the ecological implications of the biblical tradition by the now famous Lynn White thesis.[1] White argued that the (Western) Christian worldview, rooted in the creation stories and the notion of humanity made in God's image, had swept aside other worldviews, with their sacred views of nature and cyclical notions of time, introducing instead a dualism between humanity and nature, and the notion that it was God's will that humanity exploit nature to serve human interests. Thus Christianity, according to White, bears "a huge burden of guilt" for introducing the anthropocentric Western worldview that has permitted and promoted

1. Lynn White Jr., "The Historical Roots of Our Ecologic Crisis," *Science* 155 (1967): 1203–7.

the active and aggressive conquest of nature to serve human ends.[2] White does not explicitly cite biblical texts, giving only an overview of the biblical creation story, and his arguments concentrate much more on the historical development of Christian thought and early science during his own period of specialism, the medieval era. Nonetheless, his forceful critique of the impact of the biblical tradition, especially the creation story of Gen 1, has raised a serious question about the Bible's green credentials, to which there has been a variety of responses.

Responses to the Lynn White Thesis: The Bible As an Ecofriendly Book?

One kind of Christian response has essentially taken the form of an affirmation of the kind of perspective White offers, albeit from an utterly contrary standpoint: Christianity's anthropocentric focus on personal salvation is accepted and affirmed. While White proposes that we need a religion that can reorient our relationship to nature and help us out of our ecologic crisis,[3] this approach, represented primarily by some American fundamentalists, sees the call to save the planet and discipline human activity in accord with this aim as a form of neo-pagan "New Age" pantheism, or as a distraction from the business of saving human souls through evangelism—as if a surgeon were to abandon an operation to go and unblock a toilet, as Todd Strandberg somewhat tastelessly puts it.[4] From this perspective, humanity, made in the image of God, is indeed supreme over nonhuman creation, which does indeed exist to serve human needs.[5] Furthermore, the construal of biblical eschatology among some such fundamentalist groups—with their expectation of an imminent parousia, or a rapture of Christians from the

2. White, "Ecologic Crisis," 1206.

3. White, "Ecologic Crisis," 1205–6.

4. See Todd Strandberg, "Bible Prophecy and Environmentalism" (n.d.), at http://www.raptureready.com/rr-environmental.html (accessed 15 Sept 2008). Examples of this kind of response to environmentalism are found in Constance E. Cumbey, *The Hidden Dangers of the Rainbow: The New Age Movement and Our Coming Age of Barbarism* (Shreveport: Huntington House, 1983); Constance E. Cumbey, *A Planned Deception: The Staging of a New Age "Messiah"* (East Detroit, MI: Pointe, 1985); and David Hunt, *Peace, Prosperity, and the Coming Holocaust: The New Age Movement in Prophecy* (Eugene, OR: Harvest House, 1983).

5. Cf. E. Calvin Beisner, *Where Garden Meets Wilderness: Evangelical Entry into the Environmental Debate* (Grand Rapids: Eerdmans, 1997), 48–49, 53, 117–23.

earth—adds further weight to a theology in which sustaining the earth is a pointless, even dangerous preoccupation.

Yet many evangelical (and other) responses to White's thesis specifically, or to the environmental crisis generally, have taken quite the opposite stance, arguing, contra White, that the Bible does not support aggressive human dominion over the earth in the interests of serving human needs and desires. Instead, it is argued, the Bible affirms the value of the whole created order and calls humanity to responsible stewardship of the earth.[6] Indeed, a focus on stewardship as a biblical image of humanity's role in the world is central to the realignment of major evangelical leaders and bodies behind a more environmentally conscious vision of Christian responsibility, as expressed, for example, in "An Evangelical Declaration on the Care of Creation" (1994)[7] and the "Evangelical Climate Initiative" (2006).[8] In many works of ecotheology, whether evangelical or not, the (often implicit) claim is that the Bible, rightly and constructively read, offers a positive vision of creation's value and a clear mandate for environmental concern.

In clear contrast to such an approach is the stance adopted by the Earth Bible Team, as presented in their five-volume Earth Bible series. Norman Habel, main editor of the series, is evidently concerned to confront and to challenge the naïve assumption "that the Bible is environmentally friendly."[9] The Earth Bible Team approach the biblical texts with a prior commitment to a clear and explicit set of "ecojustice principles," set out at the beginning of each volume in the series. These are as follows:

1. *The Principle of Intrinsic Worth*: The universe, Earth and all its components, have intrinsic worth/value.
2. *The Principle of Interconnectedness*: Earth is a community of interconnected living things that are mutually dependent on each other for life and survival.

6. See, e.g., Wesley Granberg-Michaelson, ed., *Tending the Garden* (Grand Rapids: Eerdmans, 1987); Loren Wilkinson, ed., *Earthkeeping: Christian Stewardship of Natural Resources* (Grand Rapids: Eerdmans, 1980), 203–38; and Douglas J. Hall, *The Steward: A Biblical Symbol Come of Age*, rev. ed. (Grand Rapids: Eerdmans, 1990).

7. Reprinted in R. J. Berry, ed., *The Care of Creation: Focusing Concern and Action* (Leicester: InterVarsity Press, 2000), 17–22.

8. Available at: http://www.christiansandclimate.org/statement/ (accessed 15 December 2017).

9. Norman C. Habel, "Introducing the Earth Bible," in *Readings from the Perspective of Earth*, ed. Norman C. Habel, Earth Bible 1 (Sheffield: Sheffield Academic Press, 2000), 30.

3. *The Principle of Voice*: Earth is a subject capable of raising its voice in celebration and against injustice.
4. *The Principle of Purpose*: The universe, Earth and all its components, are part of a dynamic cosmic design within which each piece has a place in the overall goal of that design.
5. *The Principle of Mutual Custodianship*: Earth is a balanced and diverse domain where responsible custodians can function as partners, rather than rulers, to sustain a balanced and diverse Earth community.
6. *The Principle of Resistance*: Earth and its components not only suffer from injustices at the hands of humans, but actively resist them in the struggle for justice.[10]

In effect, these principles form an ethical standard, an ecojustice canon, against which the biblical texts are measured: the key task is to discern whether "the text is consistent, or in conflict, with whichever of the six ecojustice principles may be considered relevant" in any particular case.[11] Where the texts cohere with the principles, they may be fruitfully and positively read; where they do not, exposing and resisting may be more appropriate interpretive strategies.

Critical Evaluation: Towards an Ecological Hermeneutic

Each of these approaches may be subjected to critical evaluation, in the interests of developing a more adequate basis for an ecojustice hermeneutic that is at the same time a form of Christian theological engagement with the Bible.[12] Fundamentalist and evangelical readings can often be criticized for obscuring the extent to which what they present as "biblical teaching" is not simply a repetition of "what the Bible says," despite claims to the contrary, but a particular construal of certain biblical texts, prioritized over other biblical texts, and read in the light of a particular understanding of the

10. Habel, "Introducing the Earth Bible," 24.

11. Earth Bible Team, "Ecojustice Hermeneutics: Reflections and Challenges," in *The Earth Story in the New Testament*, ed. Norman C. Habel and Vicky Balabanski, Earth Bible 5 (Sheffield: Sheffield Academic Press, 2002), 2.

12. For a fuller survey and critical evaluation of different approaches to using the Bible in ecotheology and environmental ethics, see David G. Horrell, Cherryl Hunt, and Christopher Southgate, "Appeals to the Bible in Ecotheology and Environmental Ethics: A Typology of Hermeneutical Stances," *Studies in Christian Ethics* 21 (2008): 219–38.

reader's contemporary context. The claim that stewardship, for example, constitutes the biblical view of humanity's responsibility towards creation fails to acknowledge the extent to which this is a doctrinal construction, prioritizing a certain reading of humanity's role in the creation stories (e.g., Gen 2:15), construing "dominion" to mean stewardly responsibility (Gen 1:26–28), and generally applying a model of divine and kingly oversight to the human-nature relationship. Furthermore, just as the model of divine/kingly dominion may be suspected of having its less benevolent side, so the model of stewardship may be more problematic for environmental theology than its proponents appreciate.[13] Of course, a particular (and high) view of biblical authority, when combined with a commitment to the need for environmental concern, *requires* a positive construal of the Bible's ecological message: without a cogent case that the Bible supports the environmental commitment, one or other of the convictions must give.[14]

By contrast, the Earth Bible Team's approach is ready both to recover and (crucially) to resist the range of biblical perspectives, depending on their coherence with the ecojustice principles. These principles, we are informed, were worked out "in dialogue with ecologists" and are deliberately not formulated using biblical or theological terms, so as "to facilitate dialogue with biologists, ecologists, other religious traditions . . . and scientists."[15] In other words, the Bible is granted no explicit authoritative status in this project—authority effectively lies with the ecojustice principles—nor are the ecojustice principles presented as emerging from the biblical or Christian tradition. The problem here is to see why, in the project as it is presented, what the biblical texts say should matter.[16] It may be interesting

13. See Clare Palmer, "Stewardship: A Case Study in Environmental Ethics," in *The Earth Beneath: A Critical Guide to Green Theology*, ed. I. Ball, M. Goodall, C. Palmer, and J. Reader (London: SPCK, 1992), 67–86; Richard J. Bauckham, "Stewardship and Relationship," in *The Care of Creation*, ed. Berry, 99–106; and Christopher Southgate, "Stewardship and Its Competitors: A Spectrum of Relationships between Humans and the Non-Human Creation," in *Environmental Stewardship: Critical Perspectives, Past and Present*, ed. R. J. Berry (London: T&T Clark, 2006), 185–95.

14. Cf. Horrell, Hunt, and Southgate, "Bible in Ecotheology," 231–32.

15. Earth Bible Team, "Guiding Ecojustice Principles," in *Readings from the Perspective of Earth*, ed. Norman C. Habel, Earth Bible 1 (Sheffield: Sheffield Academic Press, 2000), 38.

16. Francis Watson, interestingly, traces this type of modern approach back to Kant's attempt, in *Religion within the Limits of Reason Alone* (1793), to offer an account of how the truths embodied in biblical and Christian doctrine can be independently discerned by "reason." Watson comments: "Kant's work is the forerunner of all more recent attempts to interpret scripture on the basis of an ethical-political criterion that is already known

to see how some biblical texts, read in a certain way, seem to support some of the ecojustice principles, while other biblical texts do not. But it is the ecojustice principles that set out a set of ethical norms to inspire and instruct human belief and action. Those for whom such ecojustice principles are a compelling vision may find the principles useful, but it is unclear why they should be concerned about whether and where the biblical texts support or contradict the principles, unless they are Christians or Jews with some commitment to the value and status of these texts. On the other hand, for those for whom these texts do carry some authoritative force, it is unclear why the ecojustice principles should acquire the kind of status to stand as the arbiter of scripture. In other words, the Earth Bible Team's approach, which effectively makes a set of contemporary values the court of appeal, the canon, against which biblical texts are tested, fails sufficiently to show how these contemporary values might emerge (or indeed have emerged) from a (particular) reading of the tradition, and thus, crucially, severely limits its ability to be *persuasive* for those within that tradition. To be potentially persuasive as an attempt to reshape Christian ethics, an ecological reading of the Bible would need to demonstrate that it offers an authentic appropriation of the Christian tradition.

In sum, we might criticize both evangelical environmentalism and the Earth Bible Team—without, let it be stressed, meaning to deny the immensely valuable work that has been produced—with two corresponding points. The former, with its strong commitment to a particular understanding of the Bible's authority, tends to deny or veil the extent to which the work of interpretation is a constructive act, with doctrine and ethics made in the encounter between the (ancient) text and the (modern) reader, whose constructions are shaped by the contemporary reading context. The latter, with its strong and explicit commitment to the ecojustice principles, denies the Bible an explicit role in the construction of doctrine and ethics, and effectively measures the biblical texts against its adopted set of values.

What is needed, at least as a model for engaging the Bible in contemporary Christian theology and ethics, is an approach that falls somewhere

---

independently of the texts. Scripture can only say what the criterion allows it to say [or, we might add, is criticized and resisted where it does not say this], and what it is allowed to say is only what we can already say to ourselves even without scripture. The textual embodiment of the criterion is of only limited usefulness, for the particularity of biblical narrative is an imperfect and potentially misleading vehicle for the universal truths of reason or for the various contemporary projects of liberation" ("Hermeneutics and the Doctrine of Scripture: Why They Need Each Other," *International Journal of Systematic Theology* 12 [2010]: 139).

between these two alternatives. Just such an approach has been helpfully outlined, specifically in the context of an attempt to develop an ecological hermeneutic, by Ernst Conradie.[17] For Conradie, it is important to appreciate how appropriation of the Bible in Christian theology is shaped by heuristic or doctrinal keys—"justification by faith" in the Lutheran tradition, "liberation" in liberation theology, "stewardship" in some recent ecotheology, and so on.[18] The crucial point is that these doctrinal constructs "are not directly derived from either the biblical texts or the contemporary world but are precisely the product of previous attempts to construct a relationship between text, tradition and context." They are *made* in the ongoing encounter between reader and text, and in the attempt to fuse the distant horizons of both. As such, doctrinal keys have a "double function. . . . They provide a key to unlock the meaning of *both* the contemporary context *and* the biblical texts and simultaneously enable the interpreter to establish a *link* between text and contemporary context."[19] Just as any key offers a positive new way to construct relevant meaning from the Bible, so also, Conradie insists, it will inevitably "distort" both text and context, perhaps ideologically—that is, in legitimating and concealing the interests of dominant social groups. Doctrinal keys should therefore be subject to a hermeneutic of suspicion.[20] But precisely by identifying them as doctrinal or hermeneutical keys (or, perhaps better, lenses)[21]—rather than as simply what the text "says"—this critical suspicion is invited.

Such an approach invites an engagement with the biblical texts that is exegetically serious—otherwise it ceases to be a genuine attempt at reading—but that also acknowledges such an engagement to be, inevitably, a constructive and creative act, shaped by the perceived priorities of the contemporary context. To function as a form of constructive Christian theological engagement does not imply that such a reading must avoid any criticism of biblical texts. But it does mean that there will be some positive construction

17. See Ernst M. Conradie, "Towards an Ecological Biblical Hermeneutics: A Review Essay on the Earth Bible Project," *Scriptura* 85 (2004): 123–35; and Ernst M. Conradie, "The Road Towards an Ecological Biblical and Theological Hermeneutics," *Scriptura* 93 (2006): 305–14. This paragraph also draws on our more detailed articulation of this approach in Horrell, Hunt, and Southgate, "Bible in Ecotheology," 233–38.

18. Conradie, "Road Towards," 306–9.

19. Conradie, "Road Towards," 306 (italics original).

20. Conradie, "Road Towards," 308.

21. Cf. Horrell, Hunt, and Southgate, "Bible in Ecotheology," 235. Lenses shape the encounter between reader and text, bringing certain themes into clear and central focus, while blurring, distorting, or marginalizing others.

of (a) doctrinal lens(es), formed in the encounter between reader and text, which in turn may serve as a criterion for critical appropriation. Just as Luther found in Paul a message of justification by faith, through grace alone, which then became the hermeneutical and theological heart of the Lutheran tradition, shaping a whole tradition of (critical) biblical interpretation and theological doctrine, so our own context, with its ecological crises and environmental pressures, may inspire new kinds of engagement with the Bible, new readings with new doctrinal lenses at their heart.

In the remainder of this essay, I want to attempt to illustrate one way in which such work might possibly proceed, through an engagement with Pauline theology and ethics, focused on 2 Cor 5:14–21. Needless to say, the Pauline texts are only one among many possible sites for such interpretive endeavor; but they are an important site, given their central place in the Christian (especially Protestant) theological tradition. This will then lead, finally, to some broader conclusions, outlined in brief, concerning the ways in which a reconfigured Pauline theology might contribute to the development of an ecotheological ethic.

On Becoming the (Eco)justice of God? A Reading of 2 Cor 5:14–21

A glance at the abundant ecotheological literature will quickly reveal two favorite Pauline texts: Rom 8:19–23 and Col 1:15–20.[22] There is good reason for this selection: in their different ways, these texts provide a basis for the conviction that the whole of creation is bound up in God's redeeming and reconciling purposes; or, to express the point in terms of ecojustice principles (see above), that the whole cosmos has intrinsic worth and purpose. This is an important foundation for an ecotheology, which must confront and reorient a tradition that has largely focused on the salvation of human beings. These texts provide an important starting point, an initial orientation to certain potential doctrinal lenses. But an ecological hermeneutic must go beyond the citation of favorite prooftexts and begin to generate fruitful (re) readings of the wider Pauline (and biblical) tradition.

22. For a treatment of Rom 8:19–23, see Cherryl Hunt, David G. Horrell, and Christopher Southgate, "An Environmental Mantra? Ecological Interest in Romans 8:19–23 and a Modest Proposal for Its Narrative Interpretation," *JTS* 59 (2008): 546–79. Both Rom 8 and Col 1:15–20 are now dealt with in detail in David G. Horrell, Cherryl Hunt, and Christopher Southgate, *Greening Paul: Rereading the Apostle in a Time of Ecological Crisis* (Waco, TX: Baylor University Press, 2010).

At this point, we turn to 2 Cor 5:14–21, a passage that can reasonably be regarded as a rich statement of central themes in Pauline theology: the vicarious death and resurrection of Christ and the participation of believers in these saving events; new life in Christ; reconciliation and righteousness. (Such a claim, of course, already makes clear how lenses quickly come into play: placing this text as central inevitably displaces others from such a role, prioritizing certain Pauline motifs over others. Nonetheless, there are good grounds, both exegetically and theologically, for some such prioritizations, though they should always be subject to critical scrutiny.)

After describing himself and his co-missionaries as controlled (συνέχει) by the love of Christ, Paul reiterates a central early Christian creed. But instead of repeating the usual formula, that Christ died "for us," or "for our sins" (cf. Rom 5:8; 1 Cor 15:3; 1 Thess 5:10), Paul here chooses to make the point that Christ died "for all" (ὑπὲρ πάντων), and that therefore "all have died." Christ's death is not only, or even primarily, a sacrificial or representative death, but somehow a death in which all have participated (cf. Rom 6:3–8; 1 Cor 15:22). It is beyond question that Paul has humanity primarily in view here, and specifically the Corinthians to whom he is writing; his is an inescapably anthropocentric theology, though only in certain senses, as we shall see. Paul has little reason to pursue the question about the extent to which nonhuman creation might be affected by, or bound up in, the dying and rising of Christ. But there is scope enough in the Pauline texts (Rom 8:19–23; 1 Cor 8:6) to encourage the development of his thought in this direction, as is already evident in the cosmic Christology of Colossians.

The implication Paul proceeds to draw from Christ's death ὑπὲρ πάντων is that those who live should live for Christ. In other words, while Paul's theology, his message of justification and reconciliation, is in a sense anthropocentric, focused on human beings, it is more profoundly christocentric or theocentric (cf., e.g., 1 Cor 3:22–23; 15:28). Since all have died, any life they now live can only be life in Christ, oriented to Christ and not to the self (cf. Gal 2:20). The fundamental reorientation entailed in the death of the self is to Christ and, in Christ, to God. But this being in Christ—and conforming to the pattern of Christ's self-giving death (cf. Rom 15:1–3; 1 Cor 11:1; Phil 2:4–8)—also means a fundamental reorientation to the other, and to the needs and interests of the other above the self.[23] Once again it is beyond question that Paul's other-regarding ethic is focused on human relationships,

23. Cf. David G. Horrell, *Solidarity and Difference: A Contemporary Reading of Paul's Ethics* (London: T&T Clark, 2005), 204–45.

and specifically relationships ἐν ἐκκλησίᾳ—within the Christian community. And some might argue that the primary motivation for environmental action remains properly and inevitably anthropocentric, a matter, first and foremost, of *social* justice: to alleviate the impact of climate change on the most vulnerable poor, and so on.[24] But if our ethics are more radically shaped by the (theologically grounded) "ecojustice" principles of the intrinsic worth and ultimate purpose of all things,[25] then we may want to take the more constructive and creative step to broaden the scope of the community of others not only beyond the church community but also beyond the human community. If Christ's death encompasses "all things" in its reconciling, peacemaking act, then the "living for others" that is the ethical implication of dying to self may certainly be argued, logically if not in Paul's own expressions of the notion, to include all things, τὰ πάντα.

The new perspective on others that is the result (ὥστε) of the reorientation of the self that is now dead-but-alive-in-Christ includes everyone (presumably, though, only humans are explicitly in Paul's purview here), even Christ himself, who is no longer to be known κατὰ σάρκα, "according to the flesh" (v. 16). The corresponding, positive result (ὥστε, again) is new creation in Christ (v. 17). This is a famously elliptical phrase: εἴ τις ἐν Χριστῷ, καινὴ κτίσις, "if anyone in Christ, new creation." The translator clearly needs to supply verbs, and the choices made often give the individual person the identity of "new creation": "if anyone is in Christ, he is a new creation" (ESV, NIV).[26] But the ellipsis leaves room for a range of possible interpretations, discussed at length in the history of interpretation.[27] The only other occurrence of the phrase "new creation" (in Paul) is similarly terse: οὔτε γὰρ περιτομή τί ἐστιν οὔτε ἀκροβυστία, ἀλλὰ καινὴ κτίσις, "for neither circumcision nor uncircumcision is anything, but new creation" (Gal 6:15).

24. Cf. Paula Clifford, *"All Creation Groaning": A Theological Approach to Climate Change and Development* (London: Christian Aid, 2007).

25. These two principles can, for example, be grounded in the notion that all creation is called to praise God (e.g., Ps 148) and finds its telos in fulfillment of this calling; see David G. Horrell and Dominic Coad, "'The Stones Would Cry Out' (Luke 19:40): A Lukan Contribution to a Hermeneutics of Creation's Praise," *SJT* 64 (2011): 29–44.

26. Cf. also Margaret E. Thrall, *A Critical and Exegetical Commentary on the Second Epistle to the Corinthians,* 2 vols., ICC (Edinburgh: T&T Clark, 1994), 1:427–28.

27. On which see Ulrich Mell, *Neue Schöpfung: Eine traditionsgeschichtliche und exegetische Studie zu einem soteriologischen Grundsatz paulinischer Theologie,* BZNW 56 (Berlin: de Gruyter, 1989), 9–32; more briefly Moyer V. Hubbard, *New Creation in Paul's Letters and Thought,* SNTSMS 119 (Cambridge: Cambridge University Press, 2002), 1–5.

The phrase "new creation" occurs only twice in the entire Bible, both times in Paul's letters, though it is generally seen—as with the occurrences in intertestamental Jewish literature (e.g., Jubilees 4:26; 1 Enoch 72:1)—as originating as a motif in the eschatological hopes of the prophets, especially Deutero-Isaiah (see esp. Isa 43:18–19). This motif is developed in Trito-Isaiah into a depiction of the eschatological renewal of creation and specifically the idea of a "new heaven and new earth" (e.g., Isa 65:17–25; 66:22).

The contrasting interpretive proposals are well illustrated by the two most significant recent studies of this theme.[28] In a wide-ranging study of both the developments in Jewish literature and its use by Paul, Ulrich Mell sees apocalyptic Judaism, notably in Jubilees and also Qumran (11QTemple 29.9), as the tradition-historical precursors for Paul's use of the phrase καινὴ κτίσις, "new creation."[29] He argues against reading 2 Cor 5:17 (and Gal 6:15) as anthropological "conversion" texts and for understanding them as referring to a cosmic eschatological transformation that the Christ-event has wrought.

By contrast, Moyer Hubbard's 2002 monograph argues for a thoroughly anthropological reading of the two texts in Paul, proposing that in each case the focus of Paul's thought is on the Spirit-wrought transformation of the individual believer, their transition from death to life. In identifying relevant Jewish background material, unlike Mell, Hubbard focuses not on the appearance of the precise phrase "new creation" but on the ways the broader idea and imagery is expressed. For Hubbard, the crucial material to compare with Paul is not in apocalyptic texts such as Jubilees—which he sees as a response to the specific dilemma faced by such writers[30]—but in Joseph and Aseneth, where new creation imagery (though not the phrase itself) is used to depict the outcome of conversion.[31] Particularly important in Hubbard's argument is the attempt to set the two Pauline texts in their context in Paul's letters and thought. This, he maintains, "is the primary context for explicating Paul's new-creation motif."[32] Thus, after examining the death to life imagery in Rom 6 and 7, and Paul's focus on the Spirit as the bringer of new life, Hubbard concludes that in 2 Cor 5:17 "καινὴ κτίσις is an anthropological

28. In addition, see now T. Ryan Jackson, *New Creation in Paul's Letters: A Study of the Historical and Social Setting of a Pauline Concept*, WUNT 2/272 (Tübingen: Mohr Siebeck, 2010; repr. Eugene, OR: Wipf and Stock, 2016); see the brief comments in ch. 9, p. 200, above.

29. Mell, *Neue Schöpfung*, 172–73.

30. Hubbard, *New Creation*, 26–53.

31. Hubbard, *New Creation*, 54–76.

32. Hubbard, *New Creation*, 7.

motif relating to the new situation of the individual 'in Christ.'"[33] A similar conclusion goes for Gal 6:15.

A thorough comparison and critique of these works would require another lengthy work, and a few comments pertinent to the present task must suffice. It seems to me that Hubbard, with a method that looks at the broader exegetical and background material, makes some strong points in terms of seeing Paul's primary focus as anthropological, specifically on the experience of human beings like himself, who have found themselves taken from death to life. Yet there is a danger of misconstruing Paul when this focus is taken to imply that the transformation in view is that of the individual and that Paul's thought is anthropocentric. For a start, one must emphasize, as the "apocalyptic" readers of Paul since Käsemann have done, that the focus of Paul's thought is on the epoch-making action of God in Christ; it is more properly seen as theocentric or Christocentric than anthropocentric. As Mell rightly points out, what Paul sees as the achievement of the Christ-event is the inauguration of a new world, an eschatological transformation (*Umbruch*);[34] the ἀπὸ τοῦ νῦν, "from now on," of 2 Cor 5:16 is not "conversion terminology" (*Bekehrungsterminologie*) but "eschatological terminology."[35]

Moreover, while Paul's primary focus is undoubtedly on humanity, the background to the term "new creation" in the prophetic and apocalyptic depictions of the renewal of the whole creation strongly suggests that a notion of the Christ-event as having inaugurated a truly *cosmic* transformation may well be in view. Mell has shown this to be exegetically plausible in the two places where Paul uses this motif. It is notable that Paul does not say, in glossing what this new creation implies, that the old person has passed away, to be replaced by a new person. He does not speak here of the "outer person" (ὁ ἔξω ἡμῶν ἄνθρωπος) and the "inner person" (2 Cor 4:16), nor of the "new person" (ὁ καινὸς ἄνθρωπος; cf. Eph 4:24). Nor does he speak of the making of one new human, transcending the former division of humanity into Jew and gentile (Eph 2:15). Instead, Paul speaks of "the old things" (τὰ ἀρχαῖα) passing away, replaced by "new things" (καινά). And this is immediately followed by the assertion "and all things [come] from God" (τὰ δὲ πάντα ἐκ τοῦ θεοῦ), a phrase that recalls similar formulations elsewhere in Paul, where the work of God in creation is in view (1 Cor 8:6; 11:12). The Christ-event, in Paul's view, not only makes possible the transformation of

33. Hubbard, *New Creation*, 183.
34. Cf. Mell, *Neue Schöpfung*, 365.
35. Mell, *Neue Schöpfung*, 366.

individual believers but also, and more fundamentally, marks the decisive eschatological interruption that announces the end of the old age and the beginning of the new (cf. 1 Cor 10:11: τὰ τέλη τῶν αἰώνων).

In these new creation texts, then, Paul's thought is at least open to a construal focused less on the individual's new identity—a focus that may owe more to Western individualism than to Paul, as Krister Stendahl long ago argued[36]—and more on the sense that what God has achieved in Christ (or is in the process of bringing about) is a cosmic "new creation": anyone who is in Christ belongs to, participates in, this new creation, in which the former distinctions (between Jew and gentile, etc.) no longer count for anything.[37] The church is the locus where this new creation is (in Paul's view) acknowledged and made visible, but the whole cosmos is equally bound up in the Christ-event, and strains towards its eschatological consummation (Rom 8:19–23).

To be sure, Paul immediately stresses the implications of this divine creative activity for "us" (ἡμᾶς), whom God "reconciled to himself through Christ," and to whom God "gave the ministry of reconciliation" (v. 18). This is immediately expanded once again in the parallel reformulation in v. 19 to indicate that it was indeed the whole κόσμος that God was in Christ "reconciling to himself."[38] Yet once again, it is hard to deny that Paul's primary focus is anthropological—that the primary referent of κόσμος is, in Reimund Bieringer's words, *die Menschenwelt*, "the world of human beings"—given that this reconciliation of the κόσμος is immediately glossed with the phrase "not counting their trespasses against them."[39] There is some scope for developing a broader construal of the extent of sin and thus of God's gracious forgiveness of it, given the depiction in Gen 6–8 of the spread of corruption to "all flesh" (כל־בשר), clearly referring to living creatures beyond only the human (Gen 6:12, 13, 17; note esp. 7:21). Indeed, the covenant made after the flood is emphatically with the whole earth, and every living thing upon it

36. Krister Stendahl, "The Apostle Paul and the Introspective Conscience of the West," *HTR* 56 (1963): 199–215. Reprinted in Krister Stendahl, *Paul among Jews and Gentiles* (London: SCM, 1977), 78–96.

37. Cf. Ralph P. Martin, *Reconciliation: A Study of Paul's Theology* (Atlanta: John Knox, 1981), 104; Edward Adams, *Constructing the World: A Study in Paul's Cosmological Language*, SNTW (Edinburgh: T&T Clark, 2000), 227, 235.

38. Cf. Thrall, *Second Epistle*, 1:431. On the various possible construals of the crucial phrase in v. 19a, see Reimund Bieringer, "2 Kor 5,19a und die Versöhnung der Welt," *ETL* 63 (1987): 295–326.

39. Bieringer, "2 Kor 5,19a," 318. Cf. Adams, *Constructing the World*, 235.

(Gen 9:9–17). But there would be little indeed to indicate that Paul saw any such wider picture here, though it might find some support in, or at least plausibly cohere with, Rom 8:20–21, where Paul refers to creation's bondage to decay and subjection to futility.[40] The positive insistence that the whole creation is bound up in God's redeeming purposes would then have its correlate in a negative depiction of a corruption that afflicts not only humanity but τὰ πάντα, "all things"—even if it is hard to make theological sense of this in a scientifically cogent way.[41]

However, the key point in this text is to consider how we might construe the sense of "reconciliation" (καταλλαγή/καταλλάσσω), one of the few key expressions of this distinctively Pauline theme.[42] As Howard Marshall notes, there is a two-part structure to the act of reconciliation: the prior act of God in Christ and the appeal for a human response that it is the task of God's ambassadors to announce.[43] Typically for Paul, there is a tension here between the indicative of divine achievement and the imperative of human responsibility, just as there is, in the announcement of "new creation," an eschatological tension between the "already" and the "not yet."

Reconciliation language in the ancient world and the biblical tradition generally concerned the restoration of relationships and the ending of enmity and anger,[44] and is here depicted as specifically concerned with the

40. See Hunt, Horrell, and Southgate, "Environmental Mantra?"

41. In what way, for example, could one consider animals "fallen," not to mention inanimate things? Michael Lloyd's argument that evil in the natural world—which he takes to include the "evil" of predation—"is the result of the distortion of creation brought about by the angelic Fall" (160), illustrates the difficulties, since taking Darwin seriously (as Lloyd does; see 156) makes it impossible to accept that animals ever existed in some pre-Fall herbivorous paradise, even if a prehuman Fall can be conceptualized, albeit speculatively. See Michael Lloyd, "Are Animals Fallen?," *in Animals on the Agenda*, ed. Andrew Linzey and Dorothy Yamamoto (London: SCM, 1998), 147–60. On the wider issues involved here, see Christopher Southgate, *The Groaning of Creation: God, Evolution, and the Problem of Evil* (Louisville: Westminster John Knox, 2008).

42. Both noun and verb appear only in the Pauline letters in the NT, and are heavily concentrated here in 2 Cor 5: καταλλαγή (Rom 5:11; 11:15; 2 Cor 5:18–19), καταλλάσσω (Rom 5:10 [*bis*]; 1 Cor 7:11; 2 Cor 5:18, 19, 20).

43. I. Howard Marshall, "The Meaning of 'Reconciliation,'" in *Unity and Diversity in New Testament Theology: Essays in Honor of George E. Ladd*, ed. Robert A. Guelich (Grand Rapids: Eerdmans, 1978), 122.

44. So, e.g., Marshall, "Meaning of 'Reconciliation,'" 118–21; Stanley E. Porter, *Καταλλάσσω in Ancient Greek Literature, with Reference to the Pauline Writings* (Cordoba: El Almendro, 1994), 13; Cilliers Breytenbach, *Versöhnung: Eine Studie zur paulinischen Soteriologie*, WMANT 60 (Neukirchen-Vluyn: Neukirchener Verlag, 1989), 82.

relationship of people to God. What is most striking and unique in Paul, as both Marshall and Stanley Porter have stressed, is that the picture of reconciliation is one in which the offended party (here God) actively "reconciles" the offender to himself.[45] Again, Paul's perspective is theocentric more than anthropocentric. This does not mean, however, that this reconciliation has no other dimensions than the human-divine one. The most obvious of these, though unstated by Paul, ever the astute politician, is that underlying Paul's appeal is a desire to effect and cement the fragile reconciliation between himself and the Corinthian church, previously riven by hostility and suspicion. Being reconciled to God means, at the same time, being reconciled to Paul and his coworkers. While this may certainly be criticized as part of a strategic and concealed use of power on Paul's part,[46] it does at least indicate that reconciliation with God and with (certain) others is inseparable. But the ancient parallels also imply that reconciliation was only conceived as involving personal beings. In other words, there is no precedent for the idea that the reconciliation in view here includes the totality of the nonhuman creation. As elsewhere in our text, then, we have to acknowledge that Paul's primary focus is anthropological rather than cosmic, on *die Menschenwelt* rather than the whole creation. The question, though, is not only one concerning Paul's intentions or focus, but also one about the ways in which his text might plausibly and constructively be read.

It is clear enough that the overcoming of divisions and the creation of unity is, for Paul, one of the key achievements of what God has done in Christ; reconciliation is one important way to express the character of this achievement.[47] The ways in which Paul conceives and expresses this vision of unity or oneness reflect the particular contexts and arguments in which he is engaged. A prominent focus in Galatians and Romans, picked up as a leitmotif by the author of Ephesians, is the unity and equality of Jew and gentile. In 1 Corinthians it is the factional divisions in the church that evoke Paul's appeal that they be united (1:10).[48] For rather obvious reasons—he was hardly faced with the need to respond to a global ecological crisis caused

45. Marshall, "Meaning of 'Reconciliation,'" 127–28; Porter, *Καταλλάσσω*, 16, 143.

46. Cf. Elizabeth A. Castelli, *Imitating Paul: A Discourse of Power* (Louisville: Westminster John Knox, 1991).

47. Cf. Gal 3:26–28; 1 Cor 12:12–27; Daniel Boyarin, *A Radical Jew: Paul and the Politics of Identity* (Berkeley: University of California Press, 1994); Horrell, *Solidarity and Difference*, 99–132.

48. Cf. Margaret M. Mitchell, *Paul and the Rhetoric of Reconciliation* (Louisville: Westminster John Knox, 1991).

by humanity's exploitation of the planet—Paul did not reflect on this unity as a potentially *cosmic* achievement. But the author of Colossians does, of course, go some way towards developing the motif of reconciliation in a cosmic direction, perhaps in response to a philosophically influenced popular anxiety about the stability and duration of the cosmos.[49] While Paul's own notion of reconciliation is, then, focused on the relationships of humans with God and with one another, the Pauline trajectories already evident in the NT indicate the potential for constructive broader development, given new and pressing issues to address.

Finally we must consider v. 21, perhaps the most dense and disputed crux in our passage. Many issues regarding its interpretation must be left aside. Here we find another key Pauline theological phrase: δικαιοσύνη θεοῦ, "the righteousness of God." Much ink has been spilt on the topic of justification and righteousness in Paul, not least because of the central place this holds in Protestant theology. Paul's statements about the "justification" of the believer can reasonably be held to express an idea central to his gospel (especially in Romans and Galatians), though how central, and how the idea should be understood, is much more open to debate. The phrase δικαιοσύνη θεοῦ adds further complications, since in some places it seems to refer to the saving power of God (Rom 1:17; 3:21) and elsewhere to the righteousness bestowed by God (note both of these senses together in Rom 10:3). It is therefore unnecessary to assume or insist that it must always mean precisely the same thing, and here in 2 Cor 5:21 it seems most likely to mean essentially the state of being justified, or made righteous, with the genitive thus a genitive of origin: "(righteousness) deriving from God," "bestowed by God."[50] It remains striking, though, that Paul expresses the "interchange" of Christ and believers in such vivid terms, with Christ "becoming sin for us in order that we might become the righteousness of God in him."[51]

It also remains to be considered whether this "becoming the righteousness of God" might have more theological and ethical relevance than would

49. Eduard Schweizer, *Der Brief an die Kolosser*, EKKNT 12 (Zurich: Benziger; Neukirchen-Vluyn: Neukirchener Verlag, 1976), 217–20; cf. Gerhard Liedke, *Im Bauch des Fisches: Ökologische Theologie* (Stuttgart: Kreuz, 1979), 158–61.

50. So Thrall, *Second Epistle*, 1:442–43n1776; Porter, *Καταλλάσσω*, 143.

51. Cf. Morna D. Hooker, *From Adam to Christ: Essays on Paul* (Cambridge: Cambridge University Press, 1990), *pace* N. T. Wright, "On Becoming the Righteousness of God: 2 Corinthians 5:21," in *1 & 2 Corinthians*, ed. David M. Hay, vol. 2 of *Pauline Theology*, ed. Jouette M. Bassler, David M. Hay, and E. Elizabeth Johnson, 4 vols. (Minneapolis: Fortress, 1991–1997), 200–208.

seem to be conveyed in the rather bland interpretation of it as effectively a statement about being justified. We might first note the evident parallel with reconciliation in our passage: being reconciled to God is closely related to becoming the righteousness of God.[52] That Paul sees the two terms as closely parallel ways to express the relationship established between the Christian community and God is equally apparent from the other important reconciliation text in Paul: Rom 5:9–10. "Being justified/righteoused by his blood" (5:9) is equivalent to "being reconciled to God through the death of his son" (5:10), both phrases being immediately followed by statements about the promise of future salvation (σωθησόμεθα).[53]

Just as reconciliation implies more than the restoration of friendly relations with God, so too righteousness implies more than the removal of sin and guilt before God. It is also a moral category, describing both the character of God and the expected character of those who share God's righteousness/justice. As such, and typically for Paul, it constitutes both an *is* and an *ought*. Just as God's act of reconciliation—something somehow already achieved—undergirds an appeal to be reconciled, so being righteoused/justified carries with it the obligation to be righteous/just. Paul's ethics, and specifically the relationship between identity and action, have often been encapsulated in the catchphrase "be what you are," an attempt to express the intrinsic relationship between the indicative of God's achievement and the imperative of human responsibility.[54] So here, reconciliation and justice encapsulate both divine achievement and human calling.

It is clear enough, as I have stressed throughout, that Paul does not envisage cosmic or ecological dimensions to such moral imperatives, the "oughts" that follow from being reconciled and from becoming the righteousness of God. It would be anachronistic to expect them. Yet if we find sufficient grounds, in both the exegesis of Pauline texts and the demands of our contemporary context, for developing a truly cosmic understanding of

52. Cf. Marshall, "Meaning of 'Reconciliation,'" 124–25; Porter, *Καταλλάσσω*, 142–43.

53. Breytenbach argues strongly, and importantly, that reconciliation language (καταλλάσσω, etc.) does not stand in a close relationship to atonement language (ἱλάσκομαι, etc.). The two are not related in Paul, who does not use the two terminological groups in the same contexts (*Versöhnung*, 99, 220, etc.). Nonetheless, Paul clearly does, Breytenbach stresses, connect reconciliation with the death of Christ: "*Paulus interpretiert die Versöhnungsvorstellung so, daß Versöhnung durch den stellvertretenden Sühnetod Christi ermöglicht wird*" (221 [italics original]; see further 193–215, 222–24).

54. See further Victor P. Furnish, *Theology and Ethics in Paul* (Nashville: Abingdon: 1968); Horrell, *Solidarity and Difference*, 10–15. See also ch. 5 above.

the reconciliation and unity of τὰ πάντα in Christ, then the corresponding ethical imperatives become equally cosmic in their scope. In other words, if new creation in Christ is a cosmic and not merely personal or human transformation, then the responsibilities incumbent on those who respond to the vision are cosmic in scope and not merely interpersonal; they encompass, we might say, not merely social justice but also ecojustice. Needless to say, Paul gives us little indication of what, in concrete terms, such responsibilities might entail. Indeed, Paul's ethics are generally "underdeveloped" in terms of specific exhortations and duties.[55] The prophetic texts from which Paul's new creation language derives might fill out the vision a little further, with their depictions of an eschatological peace that brings an end to enmity among animals and people as well as social justice in the human realm.[56] Yet discerning what ethical responsibilities might follow from the conviction that the decisive inauguration of this eschatological vision has already taken place, and doing so in a way that is scientifically cogent, is a difficult task with few unambiguously clear answers. Suggestions as to appropriate actions range, for example, from a commitment to vegetarianism,[57] to attempts to end the extinction of species,[58] perhaps by physically relocating them in view of the impact of climate change.[59] But the fact that one finds no explicit answers, no prooftexts to detail ecoethical responsibilities, either in Paul or elsewhere in the Bible, does not make this topic any different from most other issues in contemporary Christian ethics, where the task is precisely to reflect on what commitments and actions, what form of Christian vocation, might appropriately reflect the narrative vision that the Christian is called to share.

55. Cf. Bernard C. Lategan, "Is Paul Developing a Specifically Christian Ethic in Galatians?," in *Greeks, Romans, and Christians: Essays in Honor of Abraham J. Malherbe*, ed. David L. Balch, Everett Ferguson, and Wayne A. Meeks (Minneapolis: Fortress, 1983), 320.

56. Isa 11:1–10; 61:1–11; 65:25; cf. Richard J. Bauckham, "Jesus and the Wild Animals (Mark 1:13): A Christological Image for an Ecological Age," in *Jesus of Nazareth: Lord and Christ. Essays on the Historical Jesus and New Testament Christology*, ed. Joel B. Green and Max Turner (Grand Rapids: Eerdmans, 1994), 3–21.

57. E.g., Andrew Linzey, *Animal Theology* (London: SCM, 1994); Stephen H. Webb, *Good Eating* (Grand Rapids: Brazos, 2001).

58. Christopher Southgate, *The Groaning of Creation: God, Evolution, and the Problem of Evil* (Louisville: Westminster John Knox, 2008).

59. See discussion in Christopher Southgate, Cherryl Hunt, and David G. Horrell, "Ascesis and Assisted Migration: Responses to the Effects of Climate Change on Animal Species," *European Journal of Science and Theology* 4.2 (2008): 99–111.

Conclusion: Towards an Ecological Reconfiguration of Pauline Theology

It should be clear that in this essay I have not intended to offer a proposal as to "what Paul really said." I am not arguing—crudely put, but in more subtle ways reflecting a stance that underpins a good deal of biblical interpretation—that Paul wanted to work for the reconciliation of the whole of creation, so we should too. Rather, I am attempting a constructive exercise in which a rereading of the Pauline tradition is explicitly shaped by the perceived priorities of the contemporary context, yet at the same time draws on and develops potential latent in the Pauline texts.

My main proposal is that God's act of cosmic reconciliation in Christ should stand as a doctrinal lens at the center of an ecologically reconfigured Pauline theology. Various Pauline texts, especially Rom 8:19–23 and Col 1:15–20, provide an exegetical foundation for the conviction that nonhuman creation is not merely the stage on which the drama of human redemption takes place, but is fully bound up in the process of reconciliation and salvation. Second Corinthians 5:19a—"God was in Christ reconciling the cosmos to himself"—can stand as a concise expression of the heart of this theology. Making such a lens central to an engagement with Paul may help to move the tradition away from a focus on the justification and salvation of human beings and towards a focus on God's reconciliation of the entire created order and the associated human responsibilities to enact—in relation to the whole cosmos—the imperatives of reconciliation and justice.

Other Pauline themes may also be reconfigured around this central notion of cosmic reconciliation. While placing reconciliation center stage inevitably displaces "justification" from that position, it does not imply that being righteoused is unimportant in an ecologically oriented Pauline theology. On the contrary, it remains significant both as a depiction of the kind of reconciliation that is in view—the restoration of (covenant) relationship to God—and as an indication of the moral responsibilities entailed for the people of God—embodying the justice of God in the world.

To this extent an ecojustice ethic finds roots in Paul, but requires substantial and constructive development beyond, even against, Paul. Paul's explicit contribution to an ecojustice ethic is severely limited by his focus on relationships ἐν ἐκκλησίᾳ and his generally anthropocentric sphere of concern. Nonetheless, if God's act of reconciliation in Christ is deemed to be cosmic in scope, then it seems reasonable to take the constructive step to develop the ethical motif of other-regard in relation not only to all people, but also to "all things." But what this might mean, in concrete ethical terms, in the context of current ecological issues and global climate change, remains unspecified and—crucially—requires contemporary theological and ethical work, in careful and attentive dialogue with science. In saying this I mean to reject the claim in some quarters that to have done exegesis is effectively to have done systematic theology and Christian ethics.[60] Paul may help to resource our efforts to reconfigure our vision of the world around us, and to ground a revised theology that (re)integrates humanity into solidarity with the whole community of creation—crucial tasks indeed—but neither he nor any of the biblical writers can give us substantive answers to the question as to what, in concrete terms, we then should do.

60. Cf., e.g., Wayne Grudem, *Systematic Theology: An Introduction to Biblical Doctrine* (Leicester: InterVarsity Press, 1994), 21, 26, 127–35.

Bibliography

Aasgaard, Reidar. "Brotherhood in Plutarch and Paul: Its Role and Character." Pages 166–82 in *Constructing Early Christian Families*. Edited by Halvor Moxnes. London: Routledge, 1997.

———. *"My Beloved Brothers and Sisters!": Christian Siblingship in Paul*. JSNTSup 265. London: T&T Clark, 2004.

Adams, Edward. *Constructing the World: A Study in Paul's Cosmological Language*. Edinburgh: T&T Clark, 2000.

———. *The Earliest Christian Meeting Places: Almost Exclusively Houses?* LNTS/Early Christianity in Context 450. London: Bloomsbury T&T Clark, 2013.

Adams, Edward, and David G. Horrell, eds. *Christianity at Corinth: The Quest for the Pauline Church*. Louisville: Westminster John Knox, 2004.

Albrecht, Gloria H. *The Character of Our Communities: Toward an Ethic of Liberation for the Church*. Nashville: Abingdon, 1995.

Alexander, Loveday C. "Ancient Book Production and the Circulation of the Gospels." Pages 71–105 in *The Gospels for All Christians: Rethinking the Gospel Audiences*. Edited by Richard J. Bauckham. Grand Rapids: Eerdmans, 1998.

Alexander, Philip S. Review of E. P. Sanders, *Jesus and Judaism*. *JJS* 37 (1986): 103–6.

Allison, Penelope M. "Using the Material and Written Sources: Turn of the Millennium Approaches to Roman Domestic Space." *AJA* 105 (2001): 181–208.

Allmen, Daniel von. *La Famille de Dieu: La Symbolique familiale dans le Paulinisme*. OBO 41. Fribourg: Éditions Universitaires; Göttingen: Vandenhoeck & Ruprecht, 1981.

Arnold, Bradley. *Christ as the* Telos *of Life: Moral Philosophy, Athletic Imagery, and the Aim of Philippians*. WUNT 2/371. Tübingen: Mohr Siebeck, 2014.

Arzt-Grabner, Peter. "How to Deal with Onesimus? Paul's Solution within the Frame of Ancient Legal and Documentary Sources." Pages 113–42 in *Philemon in Perspective: Interpreting a Pauline Letter*. Edited by D. Francois Tolmie. BZNW 169. Berlin: de Gruyter, 2010.

———. *Philemon*. PKNT 1. Göttingen: Vandenhoeck & Ruprecht, 2003.

Ascough, Richard S., Philip A. Harland, and John S. Kloppenborg. *Associations in the Greco-Roman World: A Sourcebook.* Berlin: de Gruyter, 2012.

Balabanski, Vicky S. "Critiquing Anthropocentric Cosmology: Retrieving a Stoic 'Permeation Cosmology' in Colossians 1:15–20." Pages 151–59 in *Exploring Ecological Hermeneutics.* Edited by Norman C. Habel and Peter Trudinger. SymS 46. Atlanta: Society of Biblical Literature, 2008.

———. "Hellenistic Cosmology and the Letter to the Colossians: Towards an Ecological Hermeneutic." Pages 94–107 in *Ecological Hermeneutics: Biblical, Historical, and Theological Perspectives.* Edited by David G. Horrell, Cherryl Hunt, Christopher Southgate, and Francesca Stavrakopoulou. London: T&T Clark, 2010.

Balch, David L. "The Church Sitting in a Garden (1 Cor 14:30; Rom 16:23; Mark 6:39–40; 8:6; John 6:3, 10; Acts 1:15; 2:1–2)." Pages 201–35 in *Contested Spaces: Houses and Temples in Roman Antiquity and the New Testament.* Edited by David L. Balch and Annette Weissenrieder. WUNT 285. Tübingen: Mohr Siebeck, 2012.

———. "Rich Pompeian Houses, Shops for Rent, and the Huge Apartment Building in Herculaneum as Typical Spaces for Pauline House Churches." *JSNT* 27 (2004): 27–46.

Balz, Horst R. *Heilsvertrauen und Welterfahrung: Strukturen der paulinischen Eschatologie nach Römer 8, 18–39.* BEvT 59. Munich: Kaiser, 1971.

Banks, Robert. *Paul's Idea of Community: The Early House Churches in Their Historical Setting.* Rev. ed. Peabody, MA: Hendrickson, 1994.

Barclay, John M. G. "'Do We Undermine the Law?' A Study of Romans 14:1–15:6." Pages 287–308 in *Paul and the Mosaic Law.* Edited by James D. G. Dunn. WUNT 89. Tübingen: Mohr Siebeck, 1996.

———. "Food, Christian Identity and Global Warming: A Pauline Call for a Christian Food Taboo." *ExpTim* 121 (2010): 585–93.

———. *Jews in the Mediterranean Diaspora: From Alexander to Trajan (323 BCE to 117 CE).* Edinburgh: T&T Clark, 1996.

———. "'Neither Jew Nor Greek': Multiculturalism and the New Perspective on Paul." Pages 197–214 in *Ethnicity and the Bible.* Edited by Mark G. Brett. Leiden: Brill, 1996.

———. "Paul among Diaspora Jews: Anomaly or Apostate?" *JSNT* 60 (1995): 89–120.

———. *Pauline Churches and Diaspora Jews.* WUNT 275. Tübingen: Mohr Siebeck, 2011.

———. "Poverty in Pauline Studies: A Response to Steven Friesen." *JSNT* 26 (2004): 363–66.

———. "Thessalonica and Corinth: Social Contrasts in Pauline Christianity." *JSNT* 47 (1992): 49–74.

Barrett, C. K. "Cephas and Corinth." Pages 1–12 in *Abraham unser Vater: Juden und Christen im Gespräch über die Bibel. Festschrift für Otto Michel zum 60. Geburtstag.* Edited by Otto Betz, Martin Hengel, and Peter Schmidt. Leiden: Brill, 1963. Reprinted in C. K. Barrett, *Essays on Paul,* 28–39. London: SPCK, 1982.

———. *The New Testament Background: Selected Documents.* Rev. ed. London: SPCK, 1987.

Barrett, Stanley R. *Anthropology: A Student's Guide to Theory and Method.* Toronto: University of Toronto Press, 1996.

Bartchy, S. Scott. "Undermining Ancient Patriarchy: The Apostle Paul's Vision of a Society of Siblings." *BTB* 29 (1999): 68–78.

Barth, Fredrik. "Introduction." Pages 9–38 in *Ethnic Groups and Boundaries.* Edited by Fredrik Barth. London: Allen & Unwin, 1969.

Barth, Markus, and Helmut Blanke. *The Letter to Philemon: A New Translation with Notes and Commentary.* Eerdmans Critical Commentary. Grand Rapids: Eerdmans, 2000.

Barton, Ian M., ed. *Roman Domestic Buildings.* Exeter: University of Exeter Press, 1996.

Barton, Stephen C. "Early Christianity and the Sociology of the Sect." Pages 140–62 in *The Open Text: New Directions for Biblical Studies?* Edited by Francis Watson. London: SCM, 1993.

Barton, Stephen C., and Greg H. R. Horsley. "A Hellenistic Cult Group and the New Testament Churches." *JAC* 24 (1981): 7–41.

Basore, John W., trans. *Seneca's Moral Essays.* Vol 1. LCL. Cambridge: Harvard University Press, 1970.

Bauckham, Richard J. "For Whom Were the Gospels Written?" Pages 9–48 in *The Gospels for All Christians: Rethinking the Gospel Audiences.* Edited by Richard J. Bauckham. Grand Rapids: Eerdmans; Edinburgh: T&T Clark, 1998.

———. "Introduction." Pages 1–7 in *The Gospels for All Christians: Rethinking the Gospel Audiences.* Edited by Richard J. Bauckham. Grand Rapids: Eerdmans; Edinburgh: T&T Clark, 1998.

———. "Jesus and the Wild Animals (Mark 1:13): A Christological Image for an Ecological Age." Pages 3–21 in *Jesus of Nazareth: Lord and Christ. Essays on the Historical Jesus and New Testament Christology.* Edited by Joel B. Green and Max Turner. Grand Rapids: Eerdmans; Carlisle: Paternoster, 1994.

———. "Response to Philip Esler." *SJT* 51 (1998): 249–54.

———. "Stewardship and Relationship." Pages 99–106 in *The Care of Creation: Focusing Concern and Action.* Edited by R. J. Berry. Leicester: InterVarsity Press, 2000.

Bauer, Walter. *Orthodoxy and Heresy in Earliest Christianity.* London: SCM, 1972.

Baur, Ferdinand Christian. "Die Christuspartei in der korinthische Gemeinde, der Gegensatz des petrinischen und paulinischen Christentums in der ältesten Kirche, der Apostel Petrus in Rom." *Tübinger Zeitschrift* 4 (1831): 61–206.

Beisner, Calvin E. *Where Garden Meets Wilderness: Evangelical Entry into the Environmental Debate.* Grand Rapids: Eerdmans, 1997.

Beker, J. Christiaan. *Paul the Apostle: The Triumph of God in Life and Thought.* Edinburgh: T&T Clark, 1980.

Bell, Daniel. *Communitarianism and Its Critics.* Oxford: Clarendon, 1993.

Benhabib, Seyla. *Situating the Self: Gender, Community and Postmodernism in Contemporary Ethics.* Cambridge: Polity, 1992.

Berger, Peter L., and Thomas Luckmann. *The Social Construction of Reality: A Treatise in the Sociology of Knowledge.* Garden City, NY: Doubleday, 1966.

Berry, R. J., ed. *The Care of Creation: Focusing Concern and Action.* Leicester: InterVarsity Press, 2000.

———. *Environmental Stewardship: Critical Perspectives, Past and Present.* London: T&T Clark, 2006.

Berry, Sam [R. J.], et al. *A Christian Approach to the Environment.* Gloucester: John Ray Initiative, 2005.

Best, Ernest. *The First and Second Epistles to the Thessalonians.* BNTC. London: Black, 1972.

———. "Paul's Apostolic Authority—?" *JSNT* 27 (1986): 3–25.

Betz, Hans Dieter. *Galatians.* Hermeneia. Philadelphia: Fortress, 1979.

Beyschlag, Karlmann. *Clemens Romanus und der Frühkatholizismus: Untersuchungen zu I Clemens 1–7.* BHT 35. Tübingen: Mohr Siebeck, 1966.

Bieringer, Reimund. "2 Kor 5,19a und die Versöhnung der Welt." *ETL* 63 (1987): 295–326.

Biggar, Nigel. "Is Stanley Hauerwas Sectarian?" Pages 141–60 in *Faithfulness and Fortitude: In Conversation with the Theological Ethics of Stanley Hauerwas.* Edited by Mark Nation and Samuel Wells. Edinburgh: T&T Clark, 2000.

Billings, Bradly S. "From House Church to Tenement Church: Domestic Space and the Development of Early Urban Christianity—The Example of Ephesus." *JTS* 62 (2011): 541–69.

Bindemann, Walther. *Die Hoffnung der Schöpfung: Römer 8,18–27 und die Frage einer Theologie der Befreiung von Mensch und Natur.* Neukirchen-Vluyn: Neukirchener Verlag, 1983.

Black, David A. "A Note on 'the Weak' in 1 Corinthians 9,22." *Bib* 64 (1983): 240–42.

———. *Paul, Apostle of Weakness.* New York: Lang, 1984.

Blasi, Anthony J., Jean Duhaime, and Paul-André Turcotte, eds. *Handbook of Early Christianity: Social Science Approaches.* Walnut Creek, CA: Alta Mira, 2002.

Bockmuehl, Markus. *The Epistle to the Philippians.* BNTC. London: Black, 1998.

———. *Jewish Law in Gentile Churches.* Edinburgh: T&T Clark, 2000.

Bookides, Nancy, and Ronald S. Stroud. *The Sanctuary of Demeter and Kore: Corinth 18.3.* Princeton: ASCSA, 1997.

Botermann, Helga. *Das Judenedikt des Kaisers Claudius: Römischer Staat und Christiani im 1 Jahrhundert.* Hermes Einzelschriften 71. Stuttgart: Steiner, 1996.

Bouma-Prediger, Steven, *For the Beauty of the Earth: A Christian Vision for Creation Care.* Grand Rapids: Baker Academic, 2001.

Boyarin, Daniel. *A Radical Jew: Paul and the Politics of Identity.* Berkeley: University of California Press, 1994.

Breytenbach, Cilliers. *Versöhnung: Eine Studie zur paulinischen Soteriologie.* WMANT 60. Neukirchen-Vluyn: Neukirchener Verlag, 1989.

Bronner, Stephen Eric. *Of Critical Theory and Its Theorists.* Oxford: Blackwell, 1994.

Brothers, A. J. "Urban Housing." Pages 33–63 in *Roman Domestic Buildings.* Edited by Ian M. Barton. Exeter: University of Exeter Press, 1996.

Brown, Colin. "Ernst Lohmeyer's *Kyrios Jesus.*" Pages 6–42 in *Where Christology Began: Essays on Philippians 2.* Edited by Ralph P. Martin and Brian J. Dodd. Louisville: Westminster John Knox, 1998.

Brown, Raymond E., and John P. Meier. *Antioch and Rome: New Testament Cradles of Catholic Christianity.* London: Chapman, 1983.

Brown, Rupert. "Tajfel's Contribution to the Reduction of Intergroup Conflict." Pages 169–89 in *Social Groups and Identities: Developing the Legacy of Henri Tajfel.* Edited by William Peter Robinson. International Series in Social Psychology. Oxford: Butterworth Heinemann, 1996.

Brox, Norbert. *Die Pastoralbriefe.* RNT 7. Regensburg: Pustet, 1969.

Bultmann, Rudolf. "Das Problem der Ethik bei Paulus." *ZNW* 23 (1924): 123–40.

———. *Jesus Christ and Mythology.* London: SCM, 1960.

———. *New Testament and Mythology and Other Basic Writings.* Edited and translated by Schubert Miles Ogden. London: SCM, 1985.

———. "The Problem of Ethics in Paul." Pages 195–216 in *Understanding Paul's Ethics: Twentieth Century Approaches.* Edited by Brian S. Rosner. Grand Rapids: Eerdmans, 1995.

Burridge, Richard A. *Imitating Jesus: An Inclusive Approach to New Testament Ethics.* Grand Rapids: Eerdmans, 2007.

———. Review of *The Moral Vision of the New Testament: A Contemporary Introduction to New Testament Ethics* by Richard Hays. *JTSA* 102 (1998): 71–73.

Byrne, Brendan. "Creation Groaning: An Earth Bible Reading of Romans 8:18–22." Pages 193–203 in *Readings from the Perspective of Earth.* Edited by Norman C. Habel. Earth Bible 1. Sheffield: Sheffield Academic Press; Cleveland: Pilgrim, 2000.

———. *Romans.* SP 6. Collegeville, MN: Liturgical Press, 1996.

Callahan, Allen Dwight. *Embassy of Onesimus: The Letter of Paul to Philemon.* New Testament in Context. Valley Forge, PA: Trinity Press International, 1997.

Campbell, Douglas A. *The Deliverance of God: An Apocalyptic Rereading of Justification in Paul.* Grand Rapids: Eerdmans, 2009.

———. *Framing Paul: An Epistolary Biography.* Grand Rapids: Eerdmans, 2014.

Campbell, R. Alastair. *The Elders: Seniority within Earliest Christianity.* SNTW. Edinburgh: T&T Clark, 1994.

———. Review of Roger W. Gehring, *House Church and Mission. JTS* 58 (2007): 666–71.

Carter, Timothy L. *Paul and the Power of Sin: Redefining "Beyond the Pale."* SNTSMS 115. Cambridge: Cambridge University Press, 2001.

Castelli, Elizabeth A. *Imitating Paul: A Discourse of Power.* Louisville: Westminster John Knox, 1991.

Cheung, Alex T. *Idol Food in Corinth: Jewish Background and Pauline Legacy.* JSNTSup 176. Sheffield: Sheffield Academic Press, 1999.

Chow, John K. *Patronage and Power: A Study of Social Networks in Corinth.* JSNTSup 75. Sheffield: JSOT Press, 1992.

Christoffersson, Olle. *The Earnest Expectation of the Creature: The Flood-Tradition as Matrix of Romans 8:18–27.* Stockholm: Almqvist & Wiksell, 1990.

Clarke, Andrew D. "Jew and Greek, Slave and Free, Male and Female: Paul's Theology of Ethnic, Social and Gender Inclusiveness in Romans 16." Pages 103–25 in *Rome in the Bible and the Early Church.* Edited by P. Oakes. Carlisle: Paternoster, 2002.

———. *Secular and Christian Leadership in Corinth: A Socio-Historical and Exegetical Study of 1 Corinthians 1–6.* AGJU 18. Leiden: Brill, 1993.

Clifford, Paula. *"All Creation Groaning": A Theological Approach to Climate Change and Development*. London: Christian Aid, 2007.

Coad, Dominic. "Creation's Praise of God: A Proposal for a Theology of the Non-Human Creation." *Theology* 112 (2009): 181–89.

Collins, Raymond F. *First Corinthians*. SP 7. Collegeville, MN: Liturgical Press, 1999.

Conradie, Ernst M. "The Road Towards an Ecological Biblical and Theological Hermeneutics." *Scriptura* 93 (2006): 305–14.

———. "Towards an Ecological Biblical Hermeneutics: A Review Essay on the Earth Bible Project." *Scriptura* 85 (2004): 123–35.

Conzelmann, Hans. *1 Corinthians: A Commentary on the First Epistle to the Corinthians*. Translated by James W. Leitch. Hermeneia. Philadelphia: Fortress, 1975.

———. *The Quest for Paul's Gospel: A Suggested Strategy*. JSNTSup 274. London: T&T Clark, 2005.

Corley, Kathleen. "1 Peter." Pages 349–60 in *A Feminist Commentary*. Vol. 2 of *Searching the Scriptures*. Edited by Elisabeth Schüssler Fiorenza. London: SCM, 1995.

Countryman, L. William. *Dirt, Greed, and Sex: Sexual Ethics in the New Testament and Their Implications for Today*. Philadelphia: Fortress, 1988.

Cumbey, Constance E. *The Hidden Dangers of the Rainbow: The New Age Movement and Our Coming Age of Barbarism*. Shreveport: Huntington House, 1983.

———. *A Planned Deception: The Staging of a New Age "Messiah."* East Detroit: Pointe, 1985.

Daux, G. "Chronique des fouilles et découvertes archéologiques en Grèce en 1961." *Bulletin de correspondance hellénique* 86 (1962): 629–974.

Dawes, Stephen B. "*ʿănāwâ* in Translation and Tradition." *VT* 41 (1991): 38–48.

———. "Humility: Whence This Strange Notion?" *ExpTim* 103 (1991): 72–75.

Deissmann, G. Adolf. *Light from the Ancient East*. London: Hodder & Stoughton, 1910.

———. *Paul: A Study in Social and Religious History*. 2nd ed. London: Hodder & Stoughton, 1926.

De Vos, Craig S. *Church and Community Conflicts: The Relationships of the Thessalonian, Corinthian, and Philippian Churches with Their Wider Civic Communities*. SBLDS 168. Atlanta: Scholars Press, 1999.

———. "The Significance of the Change from οἶκος to οἰκία in Luke's Account of the Philippian Gaoler (Acts 16:30–4)." *NTS* 41 (1995): 292–96.

Dickson, John P., and Brian S. Rosner. "Humility as a Social Virtue in the Hebrew Bible?" *VT* 54 (2004): 459–79.

Dixon, Suzanne. *The Roman Family*. Baltimore: Johns Hopkins University Press, 1992.

Doble, Peter. "'Vile Bodies' or Transformed Persons? Philippians 3:12 in Context." *JSNT* 86 (2002): 3–27.

Doohan, Helen. *Paul's Vision of Church*. GNS 32. Wilmington, DE: Glazier, 1989.

Douglas, Mary. *Purity and Danger: An Analysis of Concepts of Pollution and Taboo*. London: Routledge & Kegan Paul, 1966.

Dübbers, Michael. *Christologie und Existenz im Kolosserbrief: Exegetische und semantische Untersuchungen zur Intention des Kolosserbriefes*. WUNT 2/191. Tübingen: Mohr Siebeck, 2005.

Duling, Dennis C. "The Matthean Brotherhood and Marginal Scribal Leadership."

Pages 159–82 in *Modelling Early Christianity*. Edited by Philip. F. Esler. London: Routledge, 1995.

Dunbabin, Katherine M. D. "Convivial Space: Dining and Entertainment in the Roman Villa." *JRA* 9 (1996): 66–80.

———. *Mosaics of the Greek and Roman World*. Cambridge: Cambridge University Press, 1999.

———. "Triclinium and Stibadium." Pages 121–48 in *Dining in a Classical Context*. Edited by William J. Slater. Ann Arbor: University of Michigan Press, 1991.

Dunn, James D. G. *The Epistles to the Colossians and to Philemon*. NIGTC. Grand Rapids: Eerdmans; Carlisle: Paternoster, 1996.

———. *Jesus, Paul and the Law: Studies in Mark and Galatians*. London: SPCK, 1990.

———. "The New Perspective on Paul." *BJRL* 65 (1983): 95–122.

———. *The New Perspective on Paul: Collected Essays*. WUNT 185. Tübingen: Mohr Siebeck, 2005.

———. "Paul: Apostate or Apostle of Israel?" *ZNW* 89 (1998): 256–71.

———. Review of Gerd Theissen, *The Social Setting of Pauline Christianity*. *Theology* 86 (1983): 456–59.

———. *Romans*. 2 vols. WBC 38A, 38B. Dallas: Word, 1988.

———. "Who Did Paul Think He Was? A Study of Jewish-Christian Identity." *NTS* 45 (1999): 174–93.

Earth Bible Team. "Ecojustice Hermeneutics: Reflections and Challenges." Pages 1–14 in *The Earth Story in the New Testament*. Edited by Norman C. Habel and Vicky Balabanski. Earth Bible 5. Sheffield: Sheffield Academic Press, 2002.

———. "Guiding Ecojustice Principles." Pages 38–53 in *Readings from the Perspective of Earth*. Edited by Norman C. Habel. Earth Bible 1. Sheffield: Sheffield Academic Press, 2000.

Elliott, John H. *1 Peter: A New Translation with Introduction and Commentary*. AB 37B. New York: Doubleday, 2000.

———. *A Home for the Homeless: A Sociological Exegesis of 1 Peter, Its Situation and Strategy*. London: SCM, 1982.

———. "Peter, Silvanus and Mark in I Peter and Acts: Sociological-Exegetical Perspectives on a Petrine Group in Rome." Pages 250–67 in *Wort in der Zeit: Neutestamentliche Studien. Festgabe für Karl Heinrich Rengstorf zum 75. Geburtstag*. Edited by W. Haubeck and M. Bachmann. Leiden: Brill, 1980.

Ellis, Simon P. *Roman Housing*. London: Duckworth, 2000.

Engberg-Pedersen, Troels. *Paul and the Stoics*. Edinburgh: T&T Clark, 2000.

Eriksen, Thomas H. *Small Places, Large Issues: An Introduction to Social and Cultural Anthropology*. London: Pluto, 1995.

Esler, Philip F. "Community and Gospel in Early Christianity: A Response to Richard Bauckham's *Gospels for All Christians*." *SJT* 51 (1998): 235–48.

———. *Conflict and Identity in Romans*. Minneapolis: Fortress, 2003.

———. "Family Imagery and Christian Identity in Gal 5:13 to 6:10." Pages 121–49 in *Constructing Early Christian Families*. Edited by Halvor Moxnes. London: Routledge, 1997.

———. *Galatians*. New Testament Readings. London: Routledge, 1998.

Fee, Gordon D. "Εἰδωλόθυτα Once Again: An Interpretation of 1 Corinthians 8–10." *Bib* 61 (1980): 172–97.

———. *The First Epistle to the Corinthians*. NICNT. Grand Rapids: Eerdmans, 1987.

———. *Paul's Letter to the Philippians*. NICNT. Grand Rapids: Eerdmans, 1995.

Fergusson, David A. S. "Another Way of Reading Stanley Hauerwas?" *SJT* 50 (1997): 242–49.

———. *Community, Liberalism and Christian Ethics*. Cambridge: Cambridge University Press, 1998.

Fitzmyer, Joseph A. *The Letter to Philemon*. AB 34C. New York: Doubleday, 2000.

Forrester, Duncan B. "The Church and the Concentration Camp: Some Reflections on Moral Community." Pages 189–207 in *Faithfulness and Fortitude: In Conversation with the Theological Ethics of Stanley Hauerwas*. Edited by Mark Nation and Samuel Wells. Edinburgh: T&T Clark, 2000.

Fotopoulos, John. *Food Offered to Idols in Roman Corinth*. WUNT 2/151. Tübingen: Mohr Siebeck, 2003.

Fowl, Stephen E. "Christology and Ethics in Philippians 2:5–11." Pages 140–53 in *Where Christology Began: Essays on Philippians 2*. Edited by Ralph P. Martin and Brian J. Dodd. Louisville: Westminster John Knox, 1998.

———. *Engaging Scripture: A Model for Theological Interpretation*. Oxford: Blackwell, 1998.

———. *The Story of Christ in the Ethics of Paul: An Analysis of the Function of the Hymnic Material in the Pauline Corpus*. JSNTSup 36. Sheffield: Sheffield Academic Press, 1990.

Friberg, Timothy and Barbara. *Analytical Lexicon to the Greek New Testament*. Grand Rapids: Baker, 2000.

Friesen, Steven J. "Poverty in Pauline Studies: Beyond the So-Called New Consensus." *JSNT* 26 (2004): 323–61.

———. "The Wrong Erastus: Ideology, Archaeology, and Exegesis." Pages 231–56 in *Corinth in Context: Comparative Studies on Religion and Society*. Edited by Steven J. Friesen, Daniel N. Schowalter, and James C. Walters. NovTSup 134. Leiden: Brill, 2010.

Furnish, Victor Paul. *Theology and Ethics in Paul*. Nashville: Abingdon, 1968.

Gadbery, Laura M. "Roman Wall-Painting at Corinth: New Evidence from East of the Theater." Pages 47–64 in *The Corinthia in the Roman Period*. Edited by Timothy E. Gregory. JRASup 8. Ann Arbor: Journal of Roman Archaeology, 1993.

Gardner, Paul D. *The Gifts of God and the Authentication of a Christian*. Lanham, MD: University Press of America, 1994.

Geertz, Clifford. *The Interpretation of Cultures*. New York: Basic Books, 1973.

Gehring, Roger W. *House Church and Mission: The Importance of Household Structures in Early Christianity*. Peabody, MA: Hendrickson, 2004.

Gibbs, John G., *Creation and Redemption: A Study in Pauline Theology*. NovTSup 26. Leiden: Brill, 1971.

———. "Pauline Cosmic Christology and Ecological Crisis." *JBL* 90 (1971): 466–79.

Giddens, Anthony. *Central Problems in Social Theory*. London: Macmillan, 1979.

———. *The Constitution of Society: Outline of the Theory of Structuration*. Cambridge: Polity, 1984.

———. *New Rules of Sociological Method: A Positive Critique of Interpretative Sociologies*. London: Hutchinson, 1976.

———. *Profiles and Critiques in Social Theory*. London and Basingstoke: Macmillan, 1982.

Gill, David W. J. "In Search of the Social Elite in the Corinthian Church." *TynBul* 44 (1993): 323–37.

Gnilka, Joachim. *Der Philipperbrief*. HThKNT 10.3. Freiburg: Herder, 1968.

Gooch, Peter D. *Dangerous Food: 1 Corinthians 8–10 in Its Context*. Studies in Christianity and Judaism 5. Waterloo, Ont.: Wilfred Laurier University Press, 1993.

Goodrich, John K. "Erastus of Corinth (Romans 16:23): Responding to Recent Proposals on His Rank, Status, and Faith." *NTS* 57 (2011): 583–93.

———. "Erastus, *Quaestor* of Corinth: The Administrative Rank of ὁ οἰκονόμος τῆς πόλεως (Rom 16:23) in an Achaean Colony." *NTS* 56 (2010): 90–115.

Gordley, Matthew E. *The Colossian Hymn in Context: An Exegesis in Light of Jewish and Greco-Roman Hymnic and Epistolary Conventions*. WUNT 2/228. Tübingen: Mohr Siebeck, 2007.

Gordon, William M., and Olivia F. Robinson, trans. *The Institutes of Gaius*. London: Duckworth, 1988.

Gorman, Michael J. *Cruciformity: Paul's Narrative Spirituality of the Cross*. Grand Rapids: Eerdmans, 2001.

———. *Inhabiting the Cruciform God: Kenosis, Justification, and Theosis in Paul's Narrative Soteriology*. Grand Rapids: Eerdmans, 2009.

Goulder, Michael D. *Paul and the Competing Mission in Corinth*. Peabody, MA: Hendrickson, 2001.

———. "ΣΟΦΙΑ in 1 Corinthians." *NTS* 37 (1991): 516–34.

———. *A Tale of Two Missions*. London: SCM, 1994.

Granberg-Michaelson, Wesley, ed. *Tending the Garden*. Grand Rapids: Eerdmans, 1987.

Grudem, Wayne. *Systematic Theology: An Introduction to Biblical Doctrine*. Leicester: InterVarsity Press, 1994.

Gummere, Richard M., trans. *Seneca ad Lucilium Epistulae Morales*. Vol. 1. LCL. New York: Putnam; London: Heinemann, 1925.

Gundry Volf, Judith M. *Paul and Perseverance: Staying in and Falling Away*. WUNT 2/37. Tübingen: Mohr Siebeck, 1991.

Guttenberger Ortwein, Gudrun. *Status und Statusverzicht im Neuen Testament und seiner Umwelt*. NTOA 39. Göttingen: Vandenhoeck & Ruprecht, 1999.

Habel, Norman C. *An Inconvenient Text: Is a Green Reading of the Bible Possible?* Adelaide: ATF, 2009.

——— "Introducing Ecological Hermeneutics." Pages 1–8 in *Exploring Ecological Hermeneutics*. Edited by Norman C. Habel and Peter Trudinger. SymS 46. Atlanta: Society of Biblical Literature, 2008.

———. "Introducing the Earth Bible." Pages 25–37 in *Readings from the Perspective of Earth*. Edited by Norman C. Habel. Earth Bible 1. Sheffield: Sheffield Academic Press; Cleveland: Pilgrim, 2000.

———, ed. *The Earth Story in the Psalms and the Prophets*. Earth Bible 4. Sheffield: Sheffield Academic Press, 2001.

———, ed. *Readings from the Perspective of Earth*. Earth Bible 1. Sheffield: Sheffield Academic Press, 2000.

Habel, Norman C., and Shirley Wurst, eds. *The Earth Story in Genesis*. Earth Bible 2. Sheffield: Sheffield Academic Press, 2000.

———, eds. *The Earth Story in Wisdom Traditions*. Earth Bible 3. Sheffield: Sheffield Academic Press; Cleveland: Pilgrim, 2001.

Habel, Norman C., and Vicky Balabanski, eds. *The Earth Story in the New Testament*. Earth Bible 5. London: Sheffield Academic Press; Cleveland: Pilgrim, 2002.

Habel, Norman C., and Peter Trudinger, eds. *Exploring Ecological Hermeneutics*. SymS 46. Atlanta: Society of Biblical Literature, 2008.

Habermas, Jürgen. *Erläuterungen zur Diskursethik*. Frankfurt: Suhrkamp, 1991.

———. *Justification and Application: Remarks on Discourse Ethics*. Cambridge: Polity, 1993.

———. *Moral Consciousness and Communicative Action*. Cambridge: Polity, 1990.

———. *Religion and Rationality: Essays on Reason, God, and Modernity*. Cambridge: Polity, 2002.

———. "Transcendence from Within, Transcendence in This World." Pages 226–50 in *Habermas, Modernity, and Public Theology*. Edited by Don Browning and Francis Schüssler Fiorenza. New York: Crossroad, 1992.

Hahne, Harry Alan. *The Corruption and Redemption of Creation: Nature in Romans 8:19–22 and Jewish Apocalyptic Literature*. LNTS 336. London: T&T Clark, 2006.

Hall, Douglas J. *The Steward: A Biblical Symbol Come of Age*. Rev. ed. Grand Rapids: Eerdmans; New York: Friendship, 1990.

Hanson, K. C. "Kinship." Pages 62–79 in *The Social Sciences and New Testament Interpretation*. Edited by Richard L. Rohrbaugh. Peabody, MA: Hendrickson, 1996.

Harink, Douglas. *Paul among the Postliberals*. Grand Rapids: Brazos, 2003.

Harris, Gerald. "The Beginnings of Church Discipline: 1 Corinthians 5." Pages 129–51 in *Understanding Paul's Ethics: Twentieth Century Approaches*. Edited by Brian S. Rosner. Grand Rapids: Eerdmans, 1995.

Hauerwas, Stanley. *A Community of Character: Toward a Constructive Christian Social Ethic*. Notre Dame: University of Notre Dame Press, 1981.

———. *After Christendom? How the Church Is to Behave If Freedom, Justice, and a Christian Nation Are Bad Ideas*. Reissued with a new preface. Nashville: Abingdon, 1999.

———. *Character and the Christian Life*. Notre Dame: University of Notre Dame Press, 1975.

———. *Dispatches from the Front: Theological Engagements with the Secular*. Durham, NC: Duke University Press, 1994.

———. *The Peaceable Kingdom: A Primer in Christian Ethics*. Notre Dame: University of Notre Dame Press, 1983.

———. "The Testament of Friends." *ChrCent* 107 (1990): 212–16.

———. "Where Would I Be without Friends?" Pages 313–32 in *Faithfulness and Forti-*

tude: In Conversation with the Theological Ethics of Stanley Hauerwas. Edited by Mark Nation and Samuel Wells. Edinburgh: T&T Clark, 2000.

———. "Will the Real Sectarian Stand Up?" *ThTo* 44 (1987): 87–94.

———. *With the Grain of the Universe: The Church's Witness and Natural Theology*. Grand Rapids: Brazos, 2001.

Hays, Richard B. *First Corinthians*. IBC. Louisville: Westminster John Knox, 1997.

———. *The Moral Vision of the New Testament: A Contemporary Introduction to New Testament Ethics*. San Francisco: HarperCollins; Edinburgh: T&T Clark, 1996.

Hellenkemper Salies, Gisela. "Römische Mosaiken im Griechenland." *BJ* 186 (1986): 241–84.

Hellerman, Joseph H. *Reconstructing Honor in Roman Philippi*. SNTSMS 132. Cambridge: Cambridge University Press, 2005.

Héring, Jean. *The First Epistle of Saint Paul to the Corinthians*. Translated by A. W. Heathcote and P. J. Allcock. London: Epworth, 1962.

Hill, John M. *The Cultural World in Beowulf*. Anthropological Horizons. Toronto: University of Toronto Press, 1995.

Hillert, Sven. *Limited and Universal Salvation: A Text-Oriented and Hermeneutical Study of Two Perspectives in Paul*. ConBNT 31. Stockholm: Almqvist & Wiksell, 1999.

Hodge, H. Grose, trans. *Cicero: The Speeches*. LCL. Cambridge: Harvard University Press, 1943.

Hofius, Otfried. *Der Christushymnus Philipper 2,6–11: Untersuchungen zu Gestalt und Aussage eines urchristlichen Psalms*. 2nd ed. WUNT 17. Tübingen: Mohr Siebeck: 1991.

Holmberg, Bengt. "The Methods of Historical Reconstruction in the Scholarly 'Recovery' of Corinthian Christianity." Pages 255–71 in *Christianity at Corinth: The Quest for the Pauline Church*. Edited by Edward Adams and David G. Horrell. Louisville: Westminster John Knox, 2004.

———. *Sociology and the New Testament: An Appraisal*. Minneapolis: Fortress, 1990.

Hooker, Morna D. "1 Thessalonians 1:9–10: A Nutshell—But What Kind of Nut?" Pages 435–48 in *Frühes Christentum*. Edited by Hermann Lichtenberger. Vol. 3 of *Geschichte—Tradition—Reflexion: Festschrift für Martin Hengel zum 70. Geburtstag*. Edited by Hubert Cancik, Hermann Lichtenberger, and Peter Schäfer. Tübingen: Mohr Siebeck, 1996.

———. *From Adam to Christ: Essays on Paul*. Cambridge: Cambridge University Press, 1990.

———. "Philippians 2:6–11." Pages 151–64 in *Jesus und Paulus: Festschrift W. G. Kümmel*. Edited by E. Earle Ellis and Erich Gräßer. Göttingen: Vandenhoeck & Ruprecht, 1978.

Horrell, David G. *Becoming Christian: Essays on 1 Peter and the Making of Christian Identity*. LNTS/Early Christianity in Context 394. London: Bloomsbury T&T Clark, 2013.

———. "'Becoming Christian': Solidifying Christian Identity and Content." Pages 309–35 in *Handbook of Early Christianity: Social Science Approaches*. Edited by

Anthony J. Blasi, Jean Duhaime, and Paul-André Turcotte. Walnut Creek, CA: Alta Mira, 2002.

———. *The Bible and the Environment: Towards a Critical Ecological Biblical Theology*. Biblical Challenges in the Contemporary World. 2010. Reprint, London: Routledge, 2014.

———. "Biblical Vegetarianism? A Critical and Constructive Assessment." Pages 44–59 in *Eating and Believing: Interdisciplinary Perspectives on Vegetarianism and Theology*. Edited by Rachel Muers and David Grumett. London and New York: T&T Clark, 2008.

———. "The Development of Theological Ideology in Pauline Christianity: A Structuration Theory Perspective." Pages 224–36 in *Modelling Early Christianity*. Edited by Philip F. Esler. London: Routledge, 1995.

———. "The Ecological Challenge to Biblical Studies." *Theology* 112 (2009): 163–71.

——— "Ecological Hermeneutics: Reflections on Methods and Prospects for the Future." *Colloquium: The Australian and New Zealand Theological Review* 46 (2014): 139–65.

———. "*The Green Bible*: A Timely Idea Deeply Flawed." *ExpTim* 121 (2010): 180–86.

———. "Leadership Patterns and the Development of Ideology in Early Christianity." Pages 309–37 in *Social-Scientific Approaches to New Testament Interpretation*. Edited by David G. Horrell. Edinburgh: T&T Clark, 1999.

———. "'The Lord Commanded . . . But I Have Not Used . . .': Exegetical and Hermeneutical Reflections on 1 Cor 9:14–15." *NTS* 43 (1997): 587–603.

———. "'No Longer Jew or Greek': Paul's Corporate Christology and the Construction of Christian Community." Pages 321–44 in *Christology, Controversy and Community: New Testament Essays in Honour of David R. Catchpole*. Edited by David G. Horrell and Christopher M. Tuckett. NovTSup 99. Leiden: Brill, 2000.

———. "The Product of a Petrine Circle? A Reassessment of the Origin and Character of 1 Peter." *JSNT* 86 (2002): 29–60.

———. "Restructuring Human Relationships: Paul's Corinthian Letters and Habermas's Discourse Ethics." *ExpTim* 110 (1999): 321–25.

———. Review of *Paul among the Postliberals,* by Douglas Harink. *JTS* 55 (2004): 663–68.

———. *The Social Ethos of the Corinthian Correspondence: Interests and Ideology from 1 Corinthians to 1 Clement*. SNTW. Edinburgh: T&T Clark, 1996.

———. "Social Sciences Studying Formative Christian Phenomena: A Creative Movement." Pages 3–28 in *Handbook of Early Christianity: Social Science Approaches*. Edited by Anthony J. Blasi, Jean Duhaime, and Paul-André Turcotte. Walnut Creek, CA: Alta Mira, 2002.

———. *Solidarity and Difference: A Contemporary Reading of Paul's Ethics*. London: T&T Clark, 2005.

———. "Solidarity and Difference: Pauline Morality in Romans 14–15." *Studies in Christian Ethics* 15.2 (2002): 60–78.

———. "Theological Principle or Christological Praxis? Pauline Ethics in 1 Corinthians 8:1–11:1." *JSNT* 67 (1997): 83–114.

———. "Whither Social-Scientific Approaches to New Testament Interpretation? Reflections on Contested Methodologies and the Future." Pages 6–20 in *After the First Urban Christians: The Social-Scientific Study of Pauline Christianity Twenty-Five Years Later*. Edited by Todd D. Still and David G. Horrell. London: T&T Clark, 2009.

———, ed. *Social-Scientific Approaches to New Testament Interpretation*. Edinburgh: T&T Clark, 1999.

Horrell, David G., and Dominic Coad. "'The Stones Would Cry Out' (Luke 19:40): A Lukan Contribution to a Hermeneutics of Creation's Praise." *SJT* 64 (2011): 29–44.

Horrell, David G., Cherryl Hunt, and Christopher Southgate. "Appeals to the Bible in Ecotheology and Environmental Ethics: A Typology of Hermeneutical Stances." *Studies in Christian Ethics* 21 (2008): 219–38.

———. *Greening Paul: Rereading the Apostle in an Age of Ecological Crisis*. Waco, TX: Baylor University Press, 2010.

Horsley, G. H. R. *A Review of the Greek Inscriptions and Papyri Published in 1976*. *NewDocs* 1. Macquarie University, NSW: Ancient History Documentary Research Centre, 1981.

———. *A Review of the Greek Inscriptions and Papyri Published in 1977*. *NewDocs* 2. Macquarie University, NSW: Ancient History Documentary Research Centre, 1982.

Hoskins Walbank, Mary E. "The Foundation and Planning of Early Roman Corinth." *JRA* 10 (1997): 95–130.

———. "The Nature and Development of Roman Corinth from 44 BCE to the End of the Antonine Period." PhD diss., Open University, 1986.

Hubbard, Moyer V. *New Creation in Paul's Letters and Thought*. SNTSMS 119. Cambridge: Cambridge University Press, 2002.

Hunt, Cherryl. "Beyond Anthropocentrism: Towards a Re-reading of Pauline Ethics." *Theology* 112 (2009): 190–98.

Hunt, Cherryl, David G. Horrell, and Christopher Southgate. "An Environmental Mantra? Ecological Interest in Romans 8:19–23 and a Modest Proposal for Its Narrative Interpretation." *JTS* 59 (2008): 546–79.

Hunt, David. *Peace, Prosperity, and the Coming Holocaust: The New Age Movement in Prophecy*. Eugene, OR: Harvest House, 1983.

Hurd, John C. *The Origin of 1 Corinthians*. London: SPCK, 1965.

Hurtado, Larry. "Jesus as Lordly Example in Philippians 2:5–11." Pages 113–26 in *From Jesus to Paul: Studies in Honour of Francis Wright Beare*. Edited by John C. Hurd and Peter Richardson. Waterloo, Ont.: Wilfrid Laurier University Press, 1984.

Husson, Geneviève. *OIKIA: Le vocabulaire de la maison privée en Égypte d'après les papyrus grecs*. Papyrologie 2. Paris: Publications de la Sorbonne, 1983.

Jackson, T. Ryan. *New Creation in Paul's Letters: A Study of the Historical and Social Setting of a Pauline Concept*. WUNT 2/272. Tübingen: Mohr Siebeck, 2010; repr. Eugene, OR: Wipf and Stock, 2016.

Jewett, Robert. "The Corruption and Redemption of Creation: Reading Rom 8:18–23 within the Imperial Context." Pages 25–46 in *Paul and the Roman Imperial Order*. Edited by Richard A. Horsley. Harrisburg: Trinity Press International, 2004.

———. "The Redaction of 1 Corinthians and the Trajectory of the Pauline School." *JAAR* 44.4, Supplement B (1978): 396–404.

———. *Romans*. Hermeneia. Minneapolis: Fortress, 2007.

———. "Tenement Churches and Communal Meals in the Early Church: The Implications of a Form-Critical Analysis of 2 Thessalonians 3:10." *BR* 38 (1993): 23–43.

Jones, Gareth. *Bultmann: Towards a Critical Theology*. Cambridge: Polity, 1991.

Jongkind, Dirk. "Corinth in the First Century AD: The Search for Another Class." *TynBul* 52 (2001): 139–48.

Judge, Edwin A. *The Social Pattern of Early Christian Groups in the First Century: Some Prolegomena to the Study of the New Testament Ideas of Social Obligation*. London: Tyndale, 1960.

Käsemann, Ernst. "Kritische Analyse von Phil. 2,5–11." Pages 51–95 in *Exegetische Versuche und Besinnungen*. 2 vols. Göttingen: Vandenhoeck & Ruprecht, 1960–1964.

———. *New Testament Questions of Today*. Translated by W. J. Montague. London: SCM, 1969.

Keesing, Roger M. *Cultural Anthropology: A Contemporary Perspective*. 2nd ed. New York: Holt, Rinehart & Winston, 1981.

Kent, John H. *Corinth VIII.3, The Inscriptions 1926–1950*. Princeton: ASCSA, 1966.

Klauck, Hans-Josef. *Hausgemeinde und Hauskirche im frühen Christentum*. SBS 103. Stuttgart: Katholisches Bibelwerk, 1981.

Knox, John. *Philemon among the Letters of Paul*. London: Collins, 1960.

Koch, Dietrich-Alex. "'Alles, was ἐν μακέλλῳ verkauft wird, eßt . . .': Die *macella* von Pompeji, Gerasa und Korinth und ihre Bedeutung für die Auslegung von 1Kor 10,25." *ZNW* 90 (1999): 194–219.

Kooten, George H. van. *Cosmic Christology in Paul and the Pauline School: Colossians and Ephesians in the Context of Graeco-Roman Cosmology with a New Synopsis of the Greek Texts*. WUNT 2/171. Tübingen: Mohr Siebeck, 2003.

Kurz, William S. "Kenotic Imitation of Paul and of Christ in Philippians 2 and 3." Pages 103–26 in *Discipleship in the New Testament*. Edited by Fernando F. Segovia. Philadelphia: Fortress, 1985.

Lampe, Geoffrey W. H. "Church Discipline and the Interpretation of the Epistles to the Corinthians." Pages 337–61 in *Christian History and Interpretation: Studies Presented to John Knox*. Edited by William R. Farmer, Charles F. D. Moule, and Richard R. Niebuhr. Cambridge: Cambridge University Press, 1967.

Lampe, Peter. "Affects and Emotions in the Rhetoric of Paul's Letter to Philemon: A Rhetorical-Psychological Interpretation." Pages 61–77 in *Philemon in Perspective: Interpreting a Pauline Letter*. Edited by D. Francois Tolmie. BZNW 169. Berlin: de Gruyter, 2010.

———. *From Paul to Valentinus: Christians at Rome in the First Two Centuries*. London: T&T Clark, 2003.

———. "Keine 'Sklavenflucht' des Onesimus." *ZNW* 76 (1985): 135–37.

———. "Das korinthische Herrenmahl im Schnittpunkt hellenistisch-römischer Mahlpraxis und paulinischer Theologia Crucis (1 Kor 11, 17–34)." *ZNW* 82 (1991): 183–213.

———. "The Roman Christians of Romans 16." Pages 216–30 in *The Romans Debate*.

Revised and expanded edition. Edited by Karl P. Donfried. Edinburgh: T&T Clark, 1991.

Lanci, John R. *A New Temple for Corinth: Rhetorical and Archaeological Approaches to Pauline Imagery*. Studies in Biblical Literature 1. New York: Lang, 1997.

Langton, Daniel R. "Modern Jewish Identity and the Apostle Paul: Pauline Studies as an Intra-Jewish Ideological Battleground." *JSNT* 28 (2005): 217–58.

———. "The Myth of the 'Traditional View of Paul' and the Role of the Apostle in Modern Jewish-Christian Polemics." *JSNT* 28 (2005): 69–104.

Lategan, Bernard C. "Is Paul Developing a Specifically Christian Ethic in Galatians?" Pages 318–28 in *Greeks, Romans, and Christians: Essays in Honor of Abraham J. Malherbe*. Edited by David L. Balch, Everett Ferguson, and Wayne A. Meeks. Minneapolis: Fortress, 1983.

Laurence, Ray, and Andrew Wallace-Hadrill, eds. *Domestic Space in the Roman World: Pompeii and Beyond*. JRASup 22. Portsmouth, RI: Journal of Roman Archaeology, 1997.

Liedke, Gerhard. *Im Bauch des Fisches: Ökologische Theologie*. Stuttgart: Kreuz, 1979.

Lindemann, Andreas. *Der erste Korintherbrief*. HNT 9.1. Tübingen: Mohr Siebeck, 2000.

Linzey, Andrew. *Animal Theology*. London: SCM, 1994.

Lloyd, Michael. "Are Animals Fallen?" Pages 147–60 in *Animals on the Agenda*. Edited by Andrew Linzey and Dorothy Yamamoto. London: SCM, 1998.

Lohmeyer, Ernst. *Kyrios Jesus: Eine Untersuchung zu Phil. 2,5–11*. Darmstadt: Wissenschaftliche Buchgesellschaft, 1961.

Lohse, Eduard. *Die Briefe an die Kolosser und an Philemon*. 2nd ed. KEK 9.2. Göttingen: Vandenhoeck & Ruprecht, 1977.

Longenecker, Bruce W. "Exposing the Economic Middle: A Revised Economy Scale for the Study of Early Urban Christianity." *JSNT* 31 (2009): 243–78.

———. *Remember the Poor: Paul, Poverty, and the Greco-Roman World*. Grand Rapids: Eerdmans, 2010.

MacDonald, Margaret Y. *The Pauline Churches: A Socio-historical Study of Institutionalization in the Pauline and Deutero-Pauline Writings*. SNTSMS 60. Cambridge: Cambridge University Press, 1988.

MacIntyre, Alasdair. *After Virtue: A Study in Moral Theory*. Notre Dame: University of Notre Dame Press, 1981.

MacMullen, Ramsay. *Roman Social Relations 50 BC to AD 284*. New Haven: Yale University Press, 1974.

Maier, Harry O. "Green Millennialism: American Evangelicals, Environmentalism, and the Book of Revelation." Pages 246–65 in *Ecological Hermeneutics: Biblical, Historical, and Theological Perspectives*. Edited by David G. Horrell, Cherryl Hunt, Christopher Southgate, and Francesca Stavrakopoulou. London: T&T Clark, 2010.

Malherbe, Abraham J. "Hellenistic Moralists and the New Testament." *ANRW* 26.1:267–333. Part 2, *Principat*, 26.1. Edited by H. Temporini and W. Haase. New York: de Gruyter, 1992.

———. *Social Aspects of Early Christianity*. 2nd ed. Philadelphia: Fortress, 1983.

Marshall, I. Howard. *1 and 2 Thessalonians*. NCB. London: Marshall, Morgan & Scott, 1983.

———. "The Meaning of 'Reconciliation.'" Pages 117–32 in *Unity and Diversity in New Testament Theology: Essays in Honor of George E. Ladd*. Edited by Robert A. Guelich. Grand Rapids: Eerdmans, 1978.

———. *The Pastoral Epistles*. ICC. Edinburgh: T&TClark, 1999.

Martin, Dale B. "The Construction of the Ancient Family: Methodological Considerations." *JRS* 86 (1996): 40–60.

———. *The Corinthian Body*. New Haven: Yale University Press, 1995.

———. "Paul without Passion: On Paul's Rejection of Desire in Sex and Marriage." Pages 201–15 in *Constructing Early Christian Families*. Edited by Halvor Moxnes. London: Routledge, 1997.

———. "Review Essay: Justin J. Meggitt, *Paul, Poverty, and Survival*." *JSNT* 84 (2001): 51–64.

Martin, Ralph P. *Reconciliation: A Study of Paul's Theology*. Atlanta: John Knox, 1981.

Martin, Ralph P., and Brian J. Dodd, eds. *Where Christology Began: Essays on Philippians 2*. Louisville: Westminster John Knox, 1998.

Matera, Frank J. *New Testament Ethics: The Legacies of Jesus and Paul*. Louisville: Westminster John Knox, 1996.

Matlock, R. Barry. "Almost Cultural Studies? Reflections on the 'New Perspective' on Paul." Pages 433–59 in *Biblical Studies/Cultural Studies. The Third Sheffield Colloquium*. Edited by J. Cheryl Exum and Stephen D. Moore. JSOTSup 266. Gender, Culture, Theology 7. Sheffield: Sheffield Academic Press, 1998.

May, Alistair S. *"The Body for the Lord": Sex and Identity in 1 Corinthians 5–7*. JSNTSup 278. London: T&T Clark, 2004.

Meeks, Wayne A. *The First Urban Christians: The Social World of the Apostle Paul*. New Haven: Yale University Press, 1983.

———. "The Man from Heaven in Paul's Letter to the Philippians." Pages 329–36 in *The Future of Early Christianity: Essays in Honor of Helmut Koester*. Edited by Birger A. Pearson. Minneapolis: Fortress, 1991.

———. *The Origins of Christian Morality: The First Two Centuries*. New Haven: Yale University Press, 1993.

———. "The Polyphonic Ethics of the Apostle Paul." *Annual of the Society of Christian Ethics* (1988): 17–29.

Meggitt, Justin J. "Meat Consumption and Social Conflict in Corinth." *JTS* 45 (1994): 137–41.

———. *Paul, Poverty, and Survival*. SNTW. Edinburgh: T&T Clark, 1998.

———. "Response to Martin and Theissen." *JSNT* 24 (2001): 85–94.

———. "The Social Status of Erastus (Rom 16:23)." *NovT* 38 (1996): 218–23.

———. "Sources: Use, Abuse, Neglect. The Importance of Ancient Popular Culture." Pages 241–53 in *Christianity at Corinth: The Quest for the Pauline Church*. Edited by Edward Adams and David G. Horrell. Louisville: Westminster John Knox, 2004.

Mell, Ulrich. *Neue Schöpfung: Eine traditionsgeschichtliche und exegetische Studie zu einem soteriologischen Grundsatz paulinischer Theologie*. BZNW 56. Berlin: de Gruyter, 1989.

Merz, Annette. *Die fiktive Selbstauslegung des Paulus: Intertextuelle Studien zur Intention und Rezeption der Pastoralbriefe*. NTOA 52. Göttingen: Vandenhoeck & Ruprecht; Fribourg: Academic Press, 2004.

Milbank, John. *Theology and Social Theory: Beyond Secular Reason*. Oxford: Blackwell, 1990.

Miller, Stella G. "A Mosaic Floor from a Roman Villa at Anaploga." *Hesperia* 41 (1972): 332–54.

Mitchell, Margaret M. "Concerning περὶ δέ in 1 Corinthians." *NovT* 31 (1989): 229–56.

———. "Patristic Counter-Evidence to the Claim that 'The Gospels Were Written for All Christians.'" *NTS* 51 (2005): 36–79.

———. *Paul and the Rhetoric of Reconciliation*. Louisville: Westminster John Knox, 1991.

Mitton, C. Leslie. "New Wine in Old Wineskins: IV. Leaven." *ExpTim* 84 (1973): 339–43.

Moo, Douglas J. *The Letters to the Colossians and to Philemon*. PNTC. Grand Rapids: Eerdmans, 2008.

Morgan, Robert. "Incarnation, Myth, and Theology: Ernst Käsemann's 'Interpretation of Philippians 2:5–11.'" Pages 43–73 in *Where Christology Began: Essays on Philippians 2*. Edited by Ralph P. Martin and Brian J. Dodd. Louisville: Westminster John Knox, 1998.

Moulton, James H., and George Milligan. *The Vocabulary of the Greek Testament Illustrated from the Papyri and Other Non-Literary Sources*. 1930. Repr., Peabody, MA: Hendrickson, 2004.

Mulhall, Stephen, and Adam Swift. *Liberals and Communitarians*. 2nd ed. Oxford: Blackwell, 1996.

Müller, Peter. *Der Brief an Philemon*. KEK 9.3. Göttingen: Vandenhoeck & Ruprecht, 2012.

Murphy-O'Connor, Jerome. "Freedom or the Ghetto (1 Cor.,VIII,1–13; X,23–XI,1)." *RB* 85 (1978): 543–74.

———. *Keys to First Corinthians: Revisiting the Major Issues*. Oxford: Oxford University Press, 2009.

———. *St. Paul's Corinth: Texts and Archaeology*. 3rd rev. and exp. ed. Collegeville, MN: Liturgical Press, 2002.

Neusner, Jacob. "Mr Sanders' Pharisees and Mine: A Response to E. P. Sanders, *Jewish Law from Jesus to the Mishnah*." *SJT* 44 (1991): 73–95.

Newton, Derek. *Deity and Diet: The Dilemma of Sacrificial Food in Corinth*. JSNTSup 169. Sheffield: Sheffield Academic Press, 1998.

Oakes, Peter. "Methodological Issues in Using Economic Evidence in Interpretation of Early Christian Texts." Pages 9–34 in *Engaging Economics: New Testament Scenarios and Early Christian Reception*. Edited by Bruce Longenecker and Kelly Liebengood. Grand Rapids: Eerdmans, 2009.

———. *Philippians: From People to Letter*. SNTSMS 110. Cambridge: Cambridge University Press, 2001.

———. *Reading Romans in Pompeii: Paul's Letter at Ground Level*. Minneapolis: Fortress, 2009.

Ogletree, Thomas W. *The Use of the Bible in Christian Ethics*. Minneapolis: Fortress.

Osiek, Carolyn, and David L. Balch. *Families in the New Testament World: Households and House Churches*. Louisville: Westminster John Knox, 1997.

Palmer, Clare. "Stewardship: A Case Study in Environmental Ethics." Pages 67–86 in *The Earth Beneath: A Critical Guide to Green Theology*. Edited by I. Ball, M. Goodall, C. Palmer, and J. Reader. London: SPCK, 1992.

Parsons, Michael. "Being Precedes Act: Indicative and Imperative in Paul's Writing." Pages 217–47 in *Understanding Paul's Ethics: Twentieth Century Approaches*. Edited by Brian S. Rosner. Grand Rapids: Eerdmans, 1995.

Pascuzzi, Maria. *Ethics, Ecclesiology and Church Discipline*. Tesi Gregoriana, Serie Teologia 32. Rome: Gregorian University Press, 1997.

Peppard, Michael. "'Poetry,' 'Hymns' and 'Traditional Material' in New Testament Epistles or How to Do Things with Indentations." *JSNT* 30 (2008): 319–42.

Pervo, Richard I. "With Lucian: Who Needs Friends? Friendship in the *Toxaris*." Pages 163–80 in *Greco-Roman Perspectives on Friendship*. Edited by John T. Fitzgerald. RBS 34. Atlanta: Scholars Press, 1997.

Petersen, Norman R. *Rediscovering Paul: Philemon and the Sociology of Paul's Narrative World*. Philadelphia: Fortress, 1985.

Porter, Stanley E. *Καταλλάσσω in Ancient Greek Literature, with Reference to the Pauline Writings*. Cordoba: El Almendro, 1994.

Probst, Hermann, *Paulus und der Brief*. WUNT 2/45. Tübingen: Mohr Siebeck, 1991.

Rasmusson, Ame. *The Church as Polis: From Political Theology to Theological Politics as Exemplified by Jürgen Moltmann and Stanley Hauerwas*. Lund: Lund University Press, 1994.

Rawls, John. *Justice as Fairness: A Restatement*. Edited by Erin Kelly. Cambridge: Harvard University Press, 2001.

Rawson, Beryl. "'The Roman Family' in Recent Research: State of the Question." *BibInt* 11 (2003): 119–38.

Reasoner, Mark. *The Strong and the Weak: Romans 14:1–15:13 in Context*. SNTSMS 103. Cambridge: Cambridge University Press, 1999.

Rehrl, Stefan. *Das Problem der Demut in der profan-griechischen Literatur im Vergleich zu Septuaginta und Neuem Testament*. Aevum Christianum 4. Münster: Aschendorff, 1961.

Reumann, John. "Philippians, especially Chapter 4, as a 'Letter of Friendship': Observations on a Checkered History of Scholarship." Pages 83–106 in *Friendship, Flattery, and Frankness of Speech: Studies on Friendship in the New Testament World*. Edited by John T. Fitzgerald. NovTSup 82. Leiden: Brill, 1996.

Richardson, Peter. "Judaism and Christianity in Corinth after Paul: Texts and Material Evidence." Pages 42–66 in *Pauline Conversations in Context: Essays in Honor of Calvin J. Roetzel*. Edited by Janice C. Anderson, Philip Sellew, and Claudia Setzer. JSNTSup 221. Sheffield: Sheffield Academic Press, 2002.

Robinson, William Peter, ed. *Social Groups and Identities: Developing the Legacy of Henri Tajfel*. International Series in Social Psychology. Oxford: Butterworth Heinemann, 1996.

Romano, David Gillman. "Post-146 B.C. Land Use in Corinth, and Planning of the Roman Colony of 44 B.C." Pages 9–30 in *The Corinthia in the Roman Period*. Edited by Timothy E. Gregory. JRASup 8. Ann Arbor: Journal of Roman Archaeology, 1993.

Rosner, Brian S. *Paul, Scripture, and Ethics: A Study of 1 Corinthians 5–7*. AGJU 22. Leiden: Brill, 1994.

———, ed. *Understanding Paul's Ethics: Twentieth Century Approaches*. Grand Rapids: Eerdmans, 1995.

Ross, W. D. *The Works of Aristotle*. Vol. 9. Oxford: Oxford University Press, 1915.

Rothaus, Richard M. *Corinth: The First City of Greece*. RGRW 139. Leiden: Brill, 2000.

Rowland, Christopher, and Mark Corner. *Liberating Exegesis: The Challenge of Liberation Theology to Biblical Studies*. Biblical Foundations in Theology. London: SPCK, 1990.

Sanders, E. P. *Jesus and Judaism*. London: SCM, 1985.

———. *Paul*. Oxford: Oxford University Press, 1991.

———. *Paul and Palestinian Judaism: A Comparison of Patterns of Religion*. London: SCM, 1977.

———. *Paul, the Law and the Jewish People*. London: SCM, 1983.

Sandnes, Karl Olav. "Equality within Patriarchal Structures: Some New Testament Perspectives on the Christian Fellowship as a Brother- or Sisterhood and a Family." Pages 150–65 in *Constructing Early Christian Families*. Edited by Halvor Moxnes. London: Routledge, 1997.

Schäfer, Klaus. *Gemeinde als "Bruderschaft": Ein Beitrag zum Kirchenverständnis des Paulus*. Europäische Hochschulschriften 23/333. Frankfurt: Peter Lang, 1989.

Schapera, Isaac. *Kinship Terminology in Jane Austen's Novels*. Royal Anthropological Institute Occasional Paper 33. London: Royal Anthropological Institute of Great Britain and Ireland, 1977.

Scheidel, Walter. "The Roman Slave Supply." Pages 287–310 in *The Ancient Mediterranean World*. Edited by Keith Bradley and Paul Cartledge. Vol. 1 of *The Cambridge World History of Slavery*. Edited by Keith Bradley, Paul Cartledge, David Eltis, and Stanley L. Engerman. 4 vols. Cambridge: Cambridge University Press, 2011–.

Scheidel, Walter, and Steven J. Friesen. "The Size of the Economy and the Distribution of Income in the Roman Empire." *JRS* 99 (2009): 61–91.

Schelke, K. H. "Bruder." *RAC* 2 (1954): 631–40.

Schmithals, Walter, *Gnosticism in Corinth: An Investigation of the Letters to the Corinthians*. Translated by John E. Steely. Nashville: Abingdon, 1971.

Schnelle, Udo. "Das frühe Christentum und die Bildung." *NTS* 61 (2015): 113–43.

Schöllgen, Georg. "Hausgemeinden, οἶκος-Ekklesiologie und monarchischer Episkopat." *JAC* 31 (1988): 74–90.

———. "Was wissen wir über die Sozialstruktur der Paulinischen Gemeinden?" *NTS* 34 (1988): 71–82.

Schowalter, Daniel N. "Seeking Shelter in Roman Corinth: Archaeology and the Placement of Paul's Communities." Pages 327–41 in *Corinth in Context: Comparative Studies on Religion and Society*. Edited by Steven J. Friesen, Daniel N. Schowalter, and James C. Walters. NovTSup 134. Leiden: Brill, 2010.

Schrage, Wolfgang. *Der erste Brief an die Korinther (1 Kor 1,1–6,11)*. EKKNT 7.1. Zurich: Benziger; Neukirchen-Vluyn: Neukirchener Verlag, 1991.

———. *Der erste Brief an die Korinther (1 Kor 6,12–11,16)*. EKKNT 7.2. Zurich: Benziger; Neukirchen-Vluyn: Neukirchener Verlag, 1995.

———. *Der erste Brief an die Korinther (1 Kor 11,17–14,40)*. EKKNT 7.3. Zurich: Benziger; Neukirchen-Vluyn: Neukirchener Verlag, 1999.

———. *Die konkreten Einzelgebote in der paulinischen Paränese*. Gütersloh: Mohn, 1961.

Schweitzer, Albert. *The Quest of the Historical Jesus*. Edited by John Bowden. First complete ed. London: SCM, 2000.

Schweizer, Eduard. *Der Brief an die Kolosser*. EKKNT 12. Zurich: Benziger; Neukirchen-Vluyn: Neukirchener Verlag, 1976.

Scranton, Robert. L. *Corinth XVI: Mediaeval Architecture in the Central Area of Corinth*. Princeton: ASCSA, 1957.

———. "The Upper Town." Pages 6–12 in *Kenchreai: Eastern Port of Corinth*. Edited by Robert L. Scranton, J. W. Shaw, and Leila Ibrahim. Leiden: Brill, 1978.

Scroggs, Robin. "The Sociological Interpretation of the New Testament: The Present State of Research." *NTS* 26 (1980): 164–79.

Sellin, Gerhard. "Hauptprobleme des Ersten Korintherbriefes." *ANRW* 25.4:2964–82. Part 2, *Principat*, 25.4. Edited by H. Temporini and W. Haase. New York: de Gruyter, 1987.

Shear, T. L. *Corinth V: The Roman Villa*. Cambridge: Harvard University Press, 1930.

Sim, David C. "The Gospels for All Christians? A Response to Richard Bauckham." *JSNT* 84 (2001): 3–27.

Sittler, Joseph. "Called to Unity." Pages 38–50 in *Evocations of Grace: The Writings of Joseph Sittler on Ecology, Theology, and Ethics*. Edited by Steven Bouma-Prediger and Peter Bakken. Grand Rapids: Eerdmans, 2000.

Smit, Joop F. M. *"About the Idol Offerings": Rhetoric, Social Context and Theology of Paul's Discourse in First Corinthians 8:1–11:1*. Leuven: Peeters, 2000.

Smith, Ian K. *Heavenly Perspective: A Study of the Apostle Paul's Response to a Jewish Mystical Movement at Colossae*. LNTS 326. London: T&T Clark, 2006.

Smith, J. T. *Roman Villas: A Study in Social Structure*. London: Routledge, 1997.

Söding, Thomas. "Starke und Schwache: der Götzenopferstreit in 1Kor 8–10 als Paradigma paulinisher Ethik." *ZNW* 85 (1994): 69–92.

Sölle, Dorothee. *Political Theology*. Translated by John Shelley. Philadelphia: Fortress, 1974.

South, James T. "A Critique of the 'Curse/Death' Interpretation of 1 Corinthians 5:1–8." *NTS* 39 (1993): 539–61.

———. *Disciplinary Practices in Pauline Texts*. Lewiston, NY: Mellen, 1992.

Southgate, Christopher. *The Groaning of Creation: God, Evolution, and the Problem of Evil*. Louisville: Westminster John Knox, 2008.

———. "Protological and Eschatological Vegetarianism." Pages 247–65 in *Eating and Believing: Interdisciplinary Perspectives on Vegetarianism and Theology*. Edited by Rachel Muers and David Grumett. London: T&T Clark, 2008.

———. "Stewardship and Its Competitors: A Spectrum of Relationships between Humans and the Non-Human Creation." Pages 185–95 in *Environmental Stewardship: Critical Perspectives, Past and Present*. Edited by R. J. Berry. London: T&T Clark, 2006.

Southgate, Christopher, Cherryl Hunt, and David G. Horrell. "Ascesis and Assisted Migration: Responses to the Effects of Climate Change on Animal Species." *European Journal of Science and Theology* 4.2 (2008): 99–111.

Spicq, Ceslas. *Theological Lexicon of the New Testament*. Translated and edited by James D. Ernest. 3 vols. Peabody, MA: Hendrickson, 1994.

Sproston North, Wendy E. "John for Readers of Mark? A Response to Richard Bauckham's Proposal." *JSNT* 25 (2003): 449–68.

Stambaugh, John E. "The Functions of Roman Temples." *ANRW* 16.1:554–608. Part 2, *Principat*, 16.1. Edited by H. Temporini and W. Haase. New York: de Gruyter, 1978.

Standhartinger, Angela. *Studien zur Entstehungsgeschichte und Intention des Kolosserbriefs*. NovTSup 94. Leiden: Brill, 1999.

Stendahl, Krister. "The Apostle Paul and the Introspective Conscience of the West." *HTR* 56 (1963): 199–215. Reprinted as pp. 78–96 in Krister Stendahl, *Paul among Jews and Gentiles*. London: SCM, 1977.

Stettler, Christian. *Der Kolosserhymnus: Untersuchungen zu Form, traditionsgeschichtlichem Hintergrund und Aussage von Kol 1, 15–20*. WUNT 2/131. Tübingen: Mohr Siebeck, 2000.

Still, Todd D. "Eschatology in Colossians: How Realized Is It?" *NTS* 50 (2004): 125–38.

Still, Todd D., and David G. Horrell, eds. *After the First Urban Christians: The Social-Scientific Study of Pauline Christianity Twenty-Five Years Later*. London: T&T Clark, 2009.

Stout, Jeffrey, *Democracy and Tradition*. New Forum Books. Princeton: Princeton University Press, 2004.

Stowers, Stanley K. "Friends and Enemies in the Politics of Heaven." Pages 105–21 in *Thessalonians, Philippians, Galatians, Philemon*. Edited by Jouette M. Bassler. Vol. 1 of *Pauline Theology*. Edited by Jouette M. Bassler, David M. Hay, and E. Elizabeth Johnson. 4 vols. Minneapolis: Fortress, 1991–1997.

Stuhlmacher, Peter. *Der Brief an Philemon*. 2nd ed. EKKNT 18. Düsseldorf and Zurich: Benziger; Neukirchen-Vluyn: Neukirchener Verlag, 1981.

Swartley, Willard M. *Covenant of Peace: The Missing Peace in New Testament Theology and Ethics*. Grand Rapids: Eerdmans, 2006.

Tajfel, Henri. *Social Identity and Intergroup Relations*. Cambridge: Cambridge University Press, 1982.

Theissen, Gerd. "Social Conflicts in the Corinthian Community: Further Remarks on J. J. Meggitt, *Paul, Poverty, and Survival*." *JSNT* 25 (2003): 371–91.

———. *Social Reality and the Early Christians: Theology, Ethics, and the World of the New Testament*. Translated by Margaret Kohl. Edinburgh: T&T Clark, 1993.

———. *The Social Setting of Pauline Christianity: Essays on Corinth*. Edited and translated by John H. Schütz. Edinburgh: T&T Clark, 1982.

———. "The Social Structure of Pauline Communities: Some Critical Remarks on J. J. Meggitt, *Paul, Poverty, and Survival*." *JSNT* 84 (2001): 65–84.

———. "Soziale Integration und sakramentales Handeln: Eine Analyse von 1 Cor. XI 17–34." *NovT* 16 (1974): 179–206.

———. "Soziale Schichtung in der korinthischen Gemeinde: Ein Beitrag zur Soziologie des hellenistischen Urchristentums." *ZNW* 65 (1974): 232–72.

———. *Studien zur Soziologie des Urchristentums*. WUNT 19. 3rd ed. Tübingen: Mohr Siebeck, 1988.

———. *A Theory of Primitive Christian Religion*. Translated by John Bowden. London: SCM, 1999.

Thiselton, Anthony C. *First Corinthians: A Shorter Exegetical and Pastoral Commentary*. Grand Rapids: Eerdmans, 2006.

———. *The First Epistle to the Corinthians*. NIGTC. Grand Rapids: Eerdmans, 2000.

Thomas, R. S. *Later Poems: A Selection 1972–1982*. London: Macmillan, Papermac, 1984.

Thompson, Geoff. "'. . . As open to the world as any theologian could be'? Karl Barth's Account of Extra-Ecclesial Truth and Its Value to Christianity's Encounter with Other Religious Traditions." PhD diss., University of Cambridge, 1995.

Thompson, Michael B. "The Holy Internet." Pages 49–70 in *The Gospels for All Christians: Rethinking the Gospel Audiences*. Edited by Richard J. Bauckham. Grand Rapids: Eerdmans, 1998.

Thorsteinsson, Runar M. *Roman Christianity and Roman Stoicism: A Comparative Study of Ancient Morality*. Oxford: Oxford University Press, 2010.

Thrall, Margaret E. *A Critical and Exegetical Commentary on the Second Epistle to the Corinthians*. 2 vols. ICC. Edinburgh: T&T Clark, 1994.

Tolmie, D. Francois. "Tendencies in the Research on the Letter to Philemon since 1980." Pages 1–27 in *Philemon in Perspective: Interpreting a Pauline Letter*. Edited by D. Francois Tolmie. BZNW 169. Berlin: de Gruyter, 2010.

Tompkins, Daniel P. Review of D. Engels, *Roman Corinth*. *Bryn Mawr Classical Review* 1 (1990): 20–33.

Trebilco, Paul. "The Goodness and Holiness of the Earth and the Whole Creation (I Timothy 4:1–5)." Pages 204–20 in *Readings from the Perspective of Earth*. Edited by Norman C. Habel. Earth Bible 1. Sheffield: Sheffield Academic Press, 2000.

Troeltsch, Ernst. *The Social Teaching of the Christian Churches*. Translated by Olive Wyon. 2 vols. London: Allen & Unwin, 1931.

Turner, John C. "Henri Tajfel: An Introduction." Pages 1–23 in *Social Groups and Identities: Developing the Legacy of Henri Tajfel*. Edited by William Peter Robinson. Oxford: Butterworth Heinemann, 1996.

Verner, David C. *The Household of God: The Social World of the Pastoral Epistles*. SBLDS 71. Chico, CA: Scholars Press, 1983.

Wagener, Ulrike. *Die Ordnung des "Hauses Gottes": Der Ort von Frauen in der Ekklesiologie und Ethik der Pastoralbriefe*. WUNT 2/65. Tübingen: Mohr Siebeck, 1994.

Wallace-Hadrill, Andrew. *Houses and Society in Pompeii and Herculaneum*. Princeton: Princeton University Press, 1994.

Watson, Francis. *Agape, Eros, Gender: Towards a Pauline Sexual Ethic*. Cambridge: Cambridge University Press, 2000.

———. "Hermeneutics and the Doctrine of Scripture: Why They Need Each Other." *International Journal of Systematic Theology* 12 (2010): 118–43.

———. *Paul, Judaism and the Gentiles: Beyond the New Perspective*. Rev. and exp. ed. Grand Rapids: Eerdmans, 2007.

———. *Text, Church and World: Biblical Interpretation in Theological Perspective*. Edinburgh: T&T Clark, 1994.

Webb, Stephen H. *Good Eating*. Grand Rapids: Brazos, 2001.

Weiss, Alexander. "Keine Quästoren in Korinth: Zu Goodrichs (und Theißens) These über das Amt des Erastos (Röm 16:23)." *NTS* 56 (2010): 576–81.

Weiss, Johannes. *Der erste Korintherbrief*. KEK 5. Göttingen: Vandenhoeck & Ruprecht, 1910.

Weissenrieder, Annette. "Contested Spaces in 1 Corinthians 11:17–33 and 14:30: Sitting or Reclining in Ancient Houses, in Associations and in the Space of the *ekklēsia*." Pages 59–107 in *Contested Spaces: Houses and Temples in Roman Antiquity and the New Testament*. Edited by David L. Balch and Annette Weissenrieder. WUNT 285. Tübingen: Mohr Siebeck, 2012.

Wells, Samuel. *Transforming Fate into Destiny. The Theological Ethics of Stanley Hauerwas*. Carlisle: Paternoster, 1998.

Wengst, Klaus. *Der Brief an Philemon*. THKNT. Stuttgart: Kohlhammer, 2005.

———. *Humility: Solidarity of the Humiliated*. London: SCM, 1988.

West, A. B. *Corinth 8.2: Latin Inscriptions 1896–1926*. Cambridge: Harvard University Press, 1931.

Wheeler, M. *Roman Art and Architecture*. London: Thames & Hudson; New York and Washington, DC: Praeger, 1964.

White, Lynn, Jr. "The Historical Roots of Our Ecologic Crisis." *Science* 155 (1967): 1203–7.

White, L. Michael. "Morality between Two Worlds: A Paradigm of Friendship in Philippians." Pages 201–15 in *Greeks, Romans, and Christians: Essays in Honor of Abraham J. Malherbe*. Edited by David L. Balch, Everett Ferguson, and Wayne A. Meeks. Minneapolis: Fortress, 1990.

Wilkinson, Loren, ed. *Earthkeeping: Christian Stewardship of Natural Resources*. Grand Rapids: Eerdmans, 1980.

Williams, Charles K., II. "Roman Corinth as a Commercial Center." Pages 31–46 in *The Corinthia in the Roman Period*. Edited by Timothy E. Gregory. JRASup 8. Ann Arbor: Journal of Roman Archaeology, 1994.

Williams, Charles K., II, and O. H. Zervos. "Corinth 1985: East of the Theater." *Hesperia* 55 (1986): 129–75.

———. "Corinth, 1988: East of the Theater." *Hesperia* 58 (1989): 1–50.

———. "Corinth, 1987: South of Temple E and East of the Theater." *Hesperia* 57 (1988): 95–146.

Willis, Wendell L. *Idol Meat in Corinth*. SBLDS 68. Chico, CA: Scholars Press, 1985.

Wilson, Robert McL. *A Critical and Exegetical Commentary on Colossians and Philemon*. ICC. London: T&T Clark, 2005.

Winter, Bruce W. *After Paul Left Corinth: The Influence of Secular Ethics and Social Change*. Grand Rapids: Eerdmans, 2001.

Wiseman, James. "Corinth and Rome I: 228 B.C.–A.D. 267." *ANRW* 7.1:438–548. Part 2, *Principat*, 7.1. Edited by H. Temporini and W. Haase. New York: de Gruyter, 1979.

———. *The Land of the Ancient Corinthians*. Göteborg: Åströms, 1978.

Witherington, Ben, III. *Conflict and Community in Corinth: A Socio-Rhetorical Commentary on 1 and 2 Corinthians*. Grand Rapids: Eerdmans, 1995.

Wolff, Christian. *Der erste Brief des Paulus an die Korinther*. 2nd ed. THKNT 7. Leipzig: Evangelische Verlagsanstalt, 2000.

Wolter, Michael. *Der Brief an die Kolosser. Der Brief an Philemon*. ÖTK 12. Gütersloh: Gütersloher; Würzburg: Echter, 1993.

———. "The Letter to Philemon as Ethical Counterpart of Paul's Doctrine of Justification." Pages 169–79 in *Philemon in Perspective: Interpreting a Pauline Letter*. Edited by D. Francois Tolmie. BZNW 169. Berlin: de Gruyter, 2010.

Wright, N. T. *The Climax of the Covenant: Christ and the Law in Pauline Theology*. Edinburgh: T&T Clark, 1991.

———. "On Becoming the Righteousness of God: 2 Corinthians 5:21." Pages 200–208 in *1 & 2 Corinthians*. Edited by David M. Hay. Vol. 2 of *Pauline Theology*. Edited by Jouette M. Bassler, David M. Hay, and E. Elizabeth Johnson. 4 vols. Minneapolis: Fortress, 1991–1997.

———. *Paul and the Faithfulness of God*. Christian Origins and the Question of God. 2 vols. Minneapolis: Fortress, 2013.

———. *Paul: Fresh Perspectives*. London: SPCK, 2005.

———. *What Saint Paul Really Said*. Oxford: Lion, 1997.

Wynn, Mark. "Thomas Aquinas: Reading the Idea of Dominion in the Light of the Doctrine of Creation." Pages 154–65 in *Ecological Hermeneutics: Biblical, Historical and Theological Perspectives*. Edited by David G. Horrell, Cherryl Hunt, Christopher Southgate, and Francesca Stavrakopoulou. London: T&T Clark, 2010.

Yeo, Khiok-khng. "The Rhetorical Hermeneutic of 1 Corinthians 8 and Chinese Ancestor Worship." *BibInt* 2 (1994): 294–311.

———. *Rhetorical Interaction in 1 Corinthians 8 and 10*. Leiden: Brill, 1995.

Zaas, Peter S. "'Cast Out the Evil Man from Your Midst' (1 Cor 5:13b)." *JBL* 103 (1984): 259–61.

Zimmermann, Ruben. "Jenseits von Indikativ und Imperativ: Entwurf einer 'impliziten Ethik' des Paulus am Beispiel des 1. Korintherbriefes." *TLZ* 132 (2007): 259–84.

Index of Modern Authors

Index of Subjects

Index of Biblical References